FAITH

ON A STONE FOUNDATION

Free Will, Morality and the God of Abraham

Stephan Grozinger

Faith On a Stone Foundation

Free Will, Morality and the God of Abraham

Stephan Grozinger

Print ISBN: 978-1-48358-766-0

eBook ISBN: 978-1-48358-767-7

All Biblical citations in this book are taken or adapted from The World English Bible unless otherwise noted.

Cover and author photo © Claire Ingram.

Used with permission.

For my daughter, Zoë.

Table of Contents

Preface

In the 1980s the General Social Survey indicated that between five and eight percent of Americans were not affiliated with any particular religion.[1] In 2007, The Pew Forum on Religious and Public Life conducted a major survey of 35,000 adult Americans and discovered that the percentage of those who reported being unaffiliated in the intervening decades had grown to 16.1%. More than twice as many people who were unaffiliated as children were then in that group as adults. Pew conducted a second survey seven years later in 2014 and the results were nothing short of staggering. The number of unaffiliated adults in the United States had grown to 22.8% - an increase of nearly seven percent in just seven years. Those who identified as Christian decreased between 2007 and 2014 by almost 8% from 78.4% to 70.6%. While eight-five percent of American adults were raised as Christians, nearly a quarter of them no longer identify themselves as such. As a group, *former* Christians now represent almost a fifth of the total adult population of the United States. For the most part, those who left Christianity and other faith traditions did not become atheists. Atheism represents a mere three percent of the U.S. population today. Those who grew up Christian and left the faith still share the core belief in the existence of God, and still profess an interest in spirituality, but some part of what it means to be Christian leaves them cold. These are the 'spiritual but not religious' or the 'nones.'

Ask a dozen practicing Christians how to win the nones back and you will likely get a dozen answers. Some of us might say we have to be more hospitable, and personally invite these lapsed Christians back and ensure we warmly welcome them and make them feel like part of the community. We may say that we need better, more modern and attractive programing to lure the nones back into church. We may say that we need to curate an encounter with God or Jesus for them so that they can see what we see. We might suggest that we need to instruct them in a "truth" that we comprehend but they have somehow missed and if they could only be exposed to Sacred Scripture and tradition, it would inevitably speak to them on some deep level and they would return to the fold. Others may take the view that the nones are the victims of a culture of permissiveness and a general degradation of morals in society that discourages commitment to the moral demands of faith. What all these suggestions have in common is that they condescend to the nones and imply that the failing lies with them. They imply that the nones' objections to religion are trite at best or an indicator of moral weakness at worst. That it is we, who remain avowed Christians, who might be the ones missing something is a thought too close to what feels like a precipice to imagine.

Consciousness evolves. One of my father's earliest memories is being struck across the palms with a switch by his teacher for some small infraction. He knew that if he withdrew his hands to avoid the switch, the punishment would be doubled. Now that sort of discipline would be grounds for arrest. As a young child growing up in suburban Montreal and later in the suburbs of southern Connecticut, I was free - and expected - to spend entire summer days completely outside of adult supervision, sometimes riding my bicycle (without a helmet) for miles having told no-one where I was headed or when I would be back. Today, my young daughter, for better or for worse, lives in an entirely different world of constant adult supervision and structured, scheduled play. Perhaps religious consciousness has evolved in that timeframe too, for reasons we'll explore later. It has not diminished faith in God, but has diminished allegiance to our existing popular culture story of faith and the modern practices of faith. Perhaps rather than being somehow less sensitive to the urgings of faith, the nones are more sensitive. They are the canaries in the coal mine; unable to thrive in an environment that has become impoverished of that which speaks to our deepest intuitions of God as those intuitions have developed and emerged in the fullness of time.

Christianity's holiest season that culminates in Easter begins with Holy Thursday. The prior Sunday, Christians commemorated Jesus's triumphal entrance into Jerusalem. The congregation emulated the adulation of the crowd which threw palm fronds in front of the colt he was riding. But by the end of the service, the tone changed to hate, and Jesus is arrested, tried, and crucified. On Holy Thursday, we take a step back in the chronology. Jesus has entered Jerusalem, fully aware, according to the Gospels, that he will leave scourged and carrying the cross on which he is to die. Those who wish to execute him, however, must bide their time as Jerusalem celebrates Passover.

Passover is itself the commemoration of an extraordinary moment in the history of humanity's relationship to God. God had interacted with individuals for ages prior. He was known to Adam and Eve. God promised Abraham that he would be the father of a numberless people. Abraham's grandson, Jacob is renamed Israel after he wrestles with God and Israel's decedents are the fathers of all twelve tribes of the Israelites. Now God finds Abraham's descendants in brutal slavery in Egypt. With ever greater ferocity, God forces the Egyptians to succumb to the divine will and release His people. Before they even taste freedom, God tells the Israelites to commemorate this turning point in the human condition. As the Egyptians' first born die, the Israelites are having a last supper in captivity, making ready for a desperate flight into the desert. On the table of this divinely commanded Seder a bone in placed. This is a visceral, almost grisly symbol of God's strong arm wielded against the enemies of Israel to redeem and save them from slavery and servitude. From this point forward, God will not just interact with His creatures, but He will treat humanity as those He has chosen to be His beloved. And He does it with a show of extraordinary divine power. God unleashes evermore spectacular and evermore vicious plagues on Egypt culminating in the death of the first born of Pharaoh and every family and every animal in Egypt. He leads the Israelites out of Egypt as a pillar of fire by night and a pillar of cloud during the day. He splits the Red Sea to provide a passage for His newly adopted people and crushes the Egyptian charioteers who dare to follow with the thunderous weight of the returning water. Three months later, as a new moon enveloped in darkness and the shadow of the Earth rises, God descends onto the summit of Mount Sinai in fire, wreathed in cloud and accompanied by trumpet blasts, earthquakes, flashes of lightening and deafening thunder.

As his persecutors wait impatiently elsewhere in the city, waiting for the sun to go down and the holiday to end, Jesus commemorates and celebrates God's decision to adopt us as His own and this extraordinary show of power. No doubt, a dark cloud hangs close over the men gathered there and the tension and sadness at Jesus's imminent and hideously violent departure are soul-rending. To make it worse, Jesus knows that among those sharing the Passover Seder with him is Judas Iscariot who would slip away to betray him to the authorities that evening. The contrast between the Passover God at the pinnacle of His strength and the pathetic, humiliating circumstances of Jesus's approaching death is unmistakable. It is in this excruciating moment, rich with ancient significance that, according only to the Gospel of John, Jesus chooses to wash his apostles' feet. Although providing water in which a guest can wash his own feet was a common courtesy,[2] to actively wash another's feet was an act of total subservience.[3]

Christianity has overwhelmingly and reflexively decided that this is a story about Jesus providing an example of humility and service to others for us to imitate. *It is this reflex that has rendered*

Christianity so wholly irrelevant in our time. In the Gospel of John, with much greater clarity than in any of the other three Gospels, Jesus is not only the Son of God and messiah, but the incarnation of God. The opening lines of John identify Jesus as the Word, in existence from the beginning with God and through which all things were made.[4] In the closing lines of the John, Thomas, shamed by having doubted Jesus had been resurrected, declares him, "my Lord and my God."[5] We are supposed to experience Earth-shattering shock at the vision of the incarnation of God – the Alpha and the Omega, He Who set the world on its foundations, He who crushed the Egyptians to rescue His people from slavery and had every right to assume the role of master, as he strips, kneels and washes the feet of His creatures. Nothing robs Scripture of its existential power and reduces it to the insipid more rapidly than assuming that every word is part of a moral code and every act is a model to be imitated. But this is what Christianity has done.

When Jesus comes around to Peter, Peter insists he will not accept Jesus subordinating himself in this way:

Then he came to Simon Peter. He said to him, "Lord, do you wash my feet?"

Jesus answered him, "You don't know what I am doing now, but you will understand later."[6]

This is no mere message about the advantages of humility or setting of a good example. It would have been a simple matter for Jesus to explain that he was acting out, rather than simply exhorting them, to the important values of humility or service to make it more memorable. That would have been easy to understand. Instead, Jesus indicates that what he is doing will be incomprehensible to Peter. The apostles serve as foils throughout the Gospels. They strain at the edges of their seats to fathom what Jesus is telling them and almost inevitably misunderstand. Later in the same evening, Jesus appears to lapse into ordinary language for a moment and the apostles rejoice: "Ah! Now you are speaking plainly, not in any figure of speech!"[7] We should be on our guard that the example Jesus is providing by washing his apostles' feet may be far more meaningful than simply serving each other and avoiding arrogance and bragging.

Peter is justifiably appalled that His teacher, the Son of God and the Incarnation of God, would stoop to wash his feet.

> Peter said to him, "You will never wash my feet!"
>
> Jesus answered him, "If I don't wash you, you have no part with me."[8]

Jesus's retort indicates something of cosmic importance is occurring that is far beyond a call to service or humility. If Peter rejects what is being offered, he risks more than mere ignorance of some message or moral exhortation - he risks having no part of Jesus at all. This is no mere proverb delivered in the ordinary course of Jesus's ministry. This is Passover. This is the last meal Jesus will share with his apostles before he is tortured and killed, and they all know it. In the other three gospels, the highlight of the Last Supper is the consecration of bread and wine as Jesus's body and blood. The Gospel of John doesn't even mention it. Washing the apostles' feet is so important it essentially replaces the Eucharist for John. There is something so significant in this moment that God became incarnate to participate in it.

Peter, who most often leads the apostles in exuberant ignorance and misunderstanding, figures that whatever benefit is being conferred, he wants more of it:

> Simon Peter said to him, "Lord, not my feet only, but also my hands and my head!"
>
> Jesus said to him, "Someone who has bathed only needs to have his feet washed, but is completely clean."[9]

Here is the touchstone of the story. Jesus is not cleaning his apostles. They are already clean. He is not providing some real-world, practical benefit like cleanliness, purity, protection or good fortune. Whatever is occurring at this moment, it does not provide anything of worldly value nor does it include a moral message to be imitated for the benefit of the apostles or society. Jesus and God and the concerns of faith transcend purpose and morality. God is not the divine good luck charm Who will protect us from harm. Nor is God the cosmic moral enforcer Who will command us and reward and punish us according to our behavior. That is a very small, idolatrous god. Rather, there is something about God's relationship to us – something that began when the God redeemed the Israelites from slavery and was consummated by the birth, death and resurrection of Jesus that transcends any practical consideration. God's relationship to us is not defined by what He can do for us.

But Jesus is clearly providing us with an example of something:

> So when he had washed their feet, put his outer garment back on, and sat down again, he said to them, "Do you know what I have done to you? You call me, 'Teacher' and 'Lord.' You say so correctly, for so I am. If I then, the Lord and the Teacher, have washed your feet, you also ought to wash one another's feet. For I have given you an example, that you also should do as I have done to you. Most certainly I tell you, a servant is not greater than his lord, neither one who is sent greater than he who sent him." [10]

We might be justified to think that, regardless of any other consideration, this is incontrovertible evidence that Jesus is just saying we need to be of service to each other and humble. But the last line seems out of place and to contradict what has gone before. Why would Jesus close this statement on the importance of service and humility with an affirmation that a master is greater than a servant?

Fortunately, Jesus answers this definitively in the same farewell address but two chapters later:

> If the world hates you, you know that it has hated me before it hated you. Remember the word that I said to you: 'A servant is not greater than his lord.' If they persecuted me, they will also persecute you.[11]
>
> I have said these things to you so that you wouldn't be caused to stumble. They will put you out of the synagogues. Yes, the time comes that whoever kills you will think that he offers service to God. They will do these things because they have not known the Father, nor me.[12]

Jesus is not providing an example of how to live. *He is providing an example of how to die.* According to tradition, the apostles would go on to be hunted down and killed for their allegiance to Jesus. Each of them had cause to wonder what happened to the Passover God – the God who rescued His people from slavery with a strong arm and all His divine might. On the eve of his ignominious execution, Jesus pauses to celebrate the Passover God Who, by worldly standards, will abandon him.

Jesus is providing an example of faith in a God Who transcends purpose. God will not wash our head and our hands along with our feet, and will not provide worldly messages of service and humility to make Christians acceptable by secular standards. What God provides is not measurable by any worldly metric and will be rejected even by people of faith.

In the other three gospels, Jesus affirms the Golden Rule, which existed in every culture of the time; that we should act toward each other as we want others to act toward us. The Gospel of John rejects this practical advice and replaces it with something entirely different and new. Jesus tell his followers, "A new commandment I give to you, that you love one another as I have loved you."[13] He exhorts them to keep this commandment five more times before they leave the table that night.[14]

It is seductive to think that Jesus, the apostles and early Christians were persecuted because they preached an ethic of humility and service. But there is no reason a Pharisee or a Roman-installed governor or anyone else would hate someone committed to these values. Before Jesus and before Moses, parents loved their children, people had pity on the less fortunate and provided for the care of the old and the sick and the poor. Great pagan and secular empires were built on the capacity for human beings to cooperate and imitate the impulses of love with fair treatment, charity and doing your best in the service of the members of your community. They did this not because of divine commandments, the promise of divine reward or the threat of divine punishment, but because they were naturally inclined toward it.

The indisputable theme of John's Gospel is routinely held up on placards at sporting events. According to John 3:16, "For God so loved the world, that he gave his one and only Son, that whoever believes in him should not perish, but have eternal life." But Christianity has done precious little to explain how this manifests itself. How does belief - something entirely outside of our control - save us from our bad behavior? Contrary to the impression we may have, the Jesus of Scripture is not a particularly warm, approachable person, nor does he show other traits that we usually associate with being loving. If he manifested love, it was by dying for us. We say dogmatically that Jesus died for our sins, but what does it mean? Why did God need a horrific, grisly, bloody sacrifice to forgive bad behavior? Why couldn't He simply overlook it as we are encouraged to do?

Why should devout Christians ask themselves these potentially embarrassing questions? Why submit the image of Jesus as soft-hearted but demanding wonder-worker to such close scrutiny? Surely, and perhaps most importantly, as Christians we ought to strive to understand the God Who Is rather than the god we think we might need for social control. But also, although the popular culture Christian message has reigned over centuries of nothing but growth, now we are a Church in apparent sharp decline. Our message to be kind, humble, charitable and strive for self-improvement has been overtaken by secular commitment to the same values and renders our message insipid and lukewarm. Perhaps sensing an opening, a novel brand of atheism has arisen recently. The New Atheists are not content with holding a belief system that contradicts faith in God, but seek to undermine faith wherever they find it. They claim religion insults our intelligence and offends our moral sensibilities. Christianity's response has been strangely passive. The retort has largely been to abandon the God of Scripture to embrace a god that is just a metaphor, and to abandon the Jesus of the Gospels in favor of a vision of Jesus who is just a really good example. Nestled next to an ever-increasing number of atheistic books on library bookshelves are books that seek to make God and Jesus acceptable to the world that rejects transcendence and demands a return on every investment. These books exhort us to spend every hour productively and moralistically. Those who persist in belief in the God and Jesus of Scripture are pushed into ever more outlandish claims and ever more uncompromising moral positions.

On Holy Thursday, as the Passover God of power apparently becomes enfeebled and allows His son to be executed, His son exemplifies that his death is necessary to achieve some mysterious purpose. If this is an example of love that we are to imitate, we need to know what it means to love one another as Jesus loved us. If God's rescue of His people from slavery with a strong arm is not a promise of magical intervention in tough times but is somehow central to human dignity, we need to understand the nature of it.

Instead, Christianity has insisted that God washes our head and hands along with our feet and that we should do that too in imitation of Him. Something has happened in the last few decades that has given many people of faith the confidence to demand a better explanation. Perhaps the nones are seeking a bigger God, a transcendent God that is not exhorting us to humility, service, developing our talents, or any kind of behavior or belief, and is not going to save us from misfortune or bring us good luck, but stands in a far greater relationship with us that transcends purpose and morality. Perhaps we are all looking for that God. Perhaps this is the God of our deepest intuition, but that we have forgotten somehow.

There is vast asymmetry between God and humanity. We have very little to offer Him. This book will suggest we offer Him even less than we may have previously imagined. But He engages with us nonetheless. This is an example not of humility, but of transcendence. No physical, intellectual or moral achievement of ours can distinguish us from one another more than God is distinguished from us. Yet He washes our feet. Apparently, God did not free us from servitude to the Egyptians so that we can work for Him or even for each other. We are objects of divine unconditional love despite not having earned it, and we should be objects of each other's unconditional love too. If we see each other as God sees us, we will not need to forgive or demand the performance of good behavior, because we will recognize that moral behavior is not what makes us valuable. Just as a clean apostle can't be made more clean with water, a person who is beloved cannot be made more beloved by good or useful behavior.

From what slavery does God save us? How can so much of the language of faith and the words of Scripture seem to be so consumed with the concept of sin, command, reward and punishment if faith actually transcends them? What does it mean to have faith in a God Who transcends purpose and morality?

Does faith impose any obligations on us? Are religion's best years behind it? Those are the questions explored by this book.

I wrote this book with a single purpose: to strengthen the faith of those who read it in the God of Scripture. In it, I don't offer any new arguments for the existence of God. Rather, I seek to describe the nature of our relationship to God in a way that is consistent with what science and philosophy tell us about the universe and the bodies we inhabit. What emerges is an understanding of God free of some heavy baggage that has been loaded on it over the last two millennia, but in what I believe is better harmony with the God of Scripture and our sacred intuition of Him.

Holy Thursday 2016

Chapter One

Free Will and Faith

He does not deal with us according to our
iniquities.
For as the heavens are high above the earth,
So great is His steadfast love toward those
who revere Him;
As far as the east is from the west,
So far does He remove our transgressions
from us.
As a father pities his children,
So the Lord pities those who revere Him.
For He knows our frame;
He remembers we are dust.[15]

Free Will and Faith

In 1128, St. Bernard of Clairvaux famously wrote, "Take away
free will and there remaineth nothing to be saved."[16] From
the advent of Christianity, belief in God has been virtually

synonymous with belief in free will. Modern neuroscience's triumphal advances, and our ability to peer into the human brain with MRIs and watch emotions, thoughts and values light up physical structures and tissues, are demonstrating with ever greater certainty that, in fact, we are purely material beings and our consciousness is the product of electro-chemical reactions occurring in physical tissues rather than the product of the actions of an immaterial 'ghost in the machine'. Those physical structures are just as subject to the laws of physics as the rest of our world and how they respond to stimuli is determined by those laws. With virtual unanimity, scientists and philosophers are telling us that our behavior is the inevitable result of a mixture of our genetic inheritance and our lifetime of experiences – our nature and nurture. Our next 'moral' decision might have been 'chosen' by us, and may be the product of our deliberation of the pros and cons, but the reason we made the choice we did and the reasons why we found one set of pros and cons compelling was determined by forces ultimately outside of our control. Faith has responded to the growing consensus that free will is an illusion largely by seeking some tiny refuge for free will – some small suggestion that human beings can exert free will despite all the evidence to the contrary. Faith has sought some small place in human nature where free will can reside and give God something to judge, and some justification for loving us, and something to forgive us for.

There was great excitement among theologians and moral philosophers when the field of quantum mechanics revealed that there is genuinely random activity in the universe on the quantum level. Here was proof that not every action is an inevitable reaction to something that went before. The stuff that makes up our universe at the smallest level appears to be "free" of the normal, classic rules of physics. Quanta appear to wink out and back into existence, to occupy two places at once, and to move in a way that defies the laws of causality. But the excitement was brief. Acting in a random fashion may be "free" of the classic laws of physics, but it doesn't imply moral responsibility or autonomy. If the human mind can somehow exploit this randomness, it would not make us any more morally responsible for our actions. Random action is not morally responsible action. If I am compelled to act in a random way, I cannot be said to be responsible for it any more than if I was compelled to act in a way determined by classic physics.

Humanity's capacity to reason - to consider ideas and be motivated by them - might also seem to set us apart from the causal universe and give us some hint of freedom. Ideas are transmitted to us in words, arguments, and concepts – things that are not conveyed in a physical form but nonetheless influence us to act one way and not another. We seem to have some conscious control over our unconscious selves in a way that hints at freedom of will. But our ability to reason is clearly limited by our nature and our nurture. If I am by nature a rational person, if I have not suffered any disease or accident that might affect my ability to think and act reasonably, and if my upbringing and other influences were such that having good, compelling and justifiable reasons for what I do was valued, then I will tend to be reasonable. But I am not responsible for my nature or my nurture. I did not choose what brain I would be born with or the family, culture and educational system within which my capacity for reason would be nurtured. As such, although acting according to reason might be a great benefit to me and might cause me to act more morally than someone who cannot act according to reasons, I can't take credit for it. Nor can I blame someone who lacks these things.

Having failed to find a redoubt for free will, all we've been able to muster in the defense of faith is a weak insistence that paradox and mystery resolve the problem. It appears everything important to faith is at stake: our ability to be self-directing, moral, ensouled creatures capable of love and being deserving of love and being deemed to possess inherent dignity, and the perception, championed by faith, that the universe is not cold, impersonal and mechanistic, but a place of warmth, inhabited by a loving God. Faith is supposed to bring purpose and meaning to our lives. But if we are merely complex organic machines reacting to stimuli determined by outside forces, then freedom is an illusion and purpose and meaning, it seems to follow, are illusions too. Under the circumstances, it is tempting to simply close one's eyes to the issue, assert free will despite the evidence to the contrary, and declare it a paradox. Nobel Prize winning Yiddish author, Isaac Bashevis Singer, once said with deliberate irony, "we have to believe in free will, we have no choice"[17].

Certainly, there are those who say that our lack of free will demonstrates that God does not exist and leaves our faith a shamble. Atheism has existed for millennia. In recent years, however, a new movement has emerged that isn't satisfied with simply not believing in God, but actively seeks to stamp out belief in God. This movement asserts that faith "should not simply be tolerated but should be countered, criticized and exposed by rational argument wherever its influence arises." The New Atheism asserts that religion is stupid and dangerous[18] - the product of some kind of mental weakness and outright immoral. The New Atheism calls on its followers not to tolerate faith, or to distinguish between healthy faith and unhealthy faith, but to challenge all faith as a foolish, destructive cultural inclination that must be extinguished – the sooner the better.

The self-proclaimed 'Four Horsemen of the Non-Apocalypse' - Sam Harris, Richard Dawkins, Daniel C. Dennett, and the late Christopher Hitchens – are the veritable founders of the New Atheist movement. They aggressively challenge faith in the most mocking tone. Each of these men has written polemics hostile to faith: *God is Not Great: How Religion Poisons Everything* (Hitchens), *The God Delusion* (Dawkins), *Breaking the Spell – Religion as Natural Phenomenon* (Dennett) and *The End of Faith: Religion, Terror and the Future of Reason* (Harris). Embracing ridicule as a legitimate philosophical device perhaps reached its exuberant apex with Christopher Hitchens who referred to Mother Teresa, revered by millions as an extraordinary example of a lived faith, as a "lying, thieving Albanian dwarf."[19] The New Atheists are fond of wrapping themselves in the mantle of scientific objectivity and declaring faith as hate-filled and dangerous. However, they abandon science's most compelling feature - dispassionate objectivity - in favor of passionate harangue. In Sam Harris's book, *The End of Faith: Religion, Terror and the Future of Reason*, Harris argues that, literally to save humanity from self-annihilation, we must reject ideals of religious tolerance in favor of exterminating all religion.[20] Harris does not distinguish between religious extremists and moderates. In his view, faith that claims to be pluralistic misunderstands that faith is, at its core, irredeemably sectarian and divisive.[21] In an era of nuclear, chemical and biological weapons, according to Harris, faith can no longer be allowed to persist.[22]

It is no accident that all Four Horsemen (with the qualified exception of Hitchens) have written extensively on the subject of free will and concluded, in varying degrees of intensity, that it is an illusion. In addition to being the Horsemen of the New Atheism, they could well also be called the Horsemen of Determinism. Harris and Dennett dismiss the notion of free will as dependent on "soul-stuff" or "God-stuff" which, for them, is equating it with superstition[23]. In *Free Will*, Harris says, "few concepts have offered greater scope for human cruelty than the idea of an immortal soul that stands independent of material influences … Within a religious framework, a belief in free will supports the notion of sin – which seems to justify not only harsh punishment in this life but *eternal* punishment in the next." For these men, proving that we don't have free will deprives God of His function as moral judge and is therefore proof that He does not exist. Like someone pressing on a bruise, reminding us that it's there and how painful it is, the New Atheists seemingly aggravate something that, since at least St. Bernard's time, we've been careful not to touch.

But is a lack of free will really as inconsistent with belief in God as we assume? Is it really the existential threat to faith we have led ourselves to think it is? Or is it possible that the Scriptural God is entirely consistent with the idea that we lack free will? Can our conception of God as revealed by Scripture survive the conclusion that we have no free will, or must we redefine God to be just a principal, an energy, or a synonym for love or unity, or dismiss Him altogether? To affirm the existence of God as conceived by Judeo-Christianity must we make some logical leap or deliberately disregard some scientific and objective truth? Or can we be people of faith and firmly and unequivocally embrace science as well? This book will argue that Singer was wrong. We do not have to believe in free will in order to maintain our core belief in God, in human dignity and that our lives are saturated with meaning. We have a choice. By taking an unflinching look at the issue of free will and acknowledging that it is an illusion may reveal something unexpected. Rather than serving to prove God does not exist, it turns out there are tremendously valuable synergies between faith and the conclusion that human free will does not exist. It is ironic that the founders of the New Atheism, men whose stated goal is the diminishment, if not the destruction of faith, may help to suggest the means by which faith may well become richer and more compelling.

And while the question of free will nags at faith, there is a second issue as well – a seemingly insurmountable tension within

Christianity. Christianity tells us that God is unconditionally loving, but also says that God imposes commands and judges us according to how well we comply with those commands. We believe that Jesus was killed as a blood sacrifice by the design of a warm and loving divine Father. Christianity has, in short, two competing visions of God. On the one hand, we believe that God *invariably* loves and *invariably* forgives; on the other hand, we believe that God has expectations for our behavior. Those expectations are not hateful, sectarian or divisive, as Harris imagines, but are nonetheless imperatives followed by divine evaluation. In this view, God commands us to avoid sin and to feed the hungry and clothe the naked and that He will approve or disapprove, reward or punish us according to our compliance. What Christianity has largely failed to acknowledge is that these two visions of God are in irreconcilable conflict with one another. Either God is unconditionally loving and forgiving, or He is conditionally loving and forgiving. They cannot both be true at the same time, although much of Christian thought has been dedicated to showing how they can cohabitate or seeks to gloss over the conflict with the go-to doctrine of last resort: paradox. A libration point is a place in space between two bodies, such as the Earth and the Moon, where the gravitation attraction from each is equal and where a satellite can be "parked" and not get pulled into either body. Faith has sought the libration point between a conditionally and unconditionally loving God and has avoided facing the paradox head on.

As we've seen, religious observance is suffering a massive decline in the West. I suspect people of faith are leaving their churches because the internal conflict in Christianity between the loving God and the judging God seems to render the whole exercise nonsensical and archaic or, worse, morally offensive. We crave faith that does not insult our intelligence, is not mean-spirited, and affirms what we already know in our bones about the nature of God. We want religion to be something more than a scold. Can embracing a lack of free will actually resolve tensions within faith that have led to its deterioration? Can science not only co-exist with faith but have a hand in saving it? Can it finally resolve the inconsistencies in faith in favor of a loving God, discard the foundation built on sand, and rebuild faith on a stone foundation? The issue of free will is forcing the question and making the answer unavoidable and clear. The issue that looked like it would be responsible for the end of faith, may turn out to be its cornerstone. The most unlikely source of revelation may prove to be the most important.

Part of what makes us uncomfortable about the idea that we do not have free will is that it deprives us of all the ways we use to take stock of ourselves and measure ourselves against others. How well we are able to do what is good and avoid being bad is fundamental to our identities. There may be no more powerful a compliment than asserting that someone is basically well-intentioned and a 'good person'. And there is likely no greater condemnation than to say someone is fundamentally bad. Our capacity to do what is right of our own volition is what we assume gives us our human dignity. We hope to be seen by others as basically virtuous: companionable, industrious, talented, generous, intelligent, wise, disciplined, mature and, perhaps above all else, altruistic. We certainly don't want to be seen as the opposite of those terms. But if we do not have free will, then whether we are basically good or bad is not something for which we can be held responsible in any meaningful way. It might make sense to provide incentives for each other to behave well, with the promise of reward for socially useful behavior and punishment for anti-social behavior. But it would not make any sense to be angry with someone whose nature and nurture drive them to bad behavior, and it would not make sense to hate anyone. Secular writers have noted this for centuries. In his posthumously published book, *The Ethics*, Baruch Spinoza, a seventeenth century metaphysician, wrote:

> The mind is determined to wish for this or that by a cause, which has also been determined by another cause, and this again by another, and so on to infinity. This realization teaches us to hate no one, to despise no one, to mock no one, to be angry with no one, and to envy no one.

New Atheist, Sam Harris, makes the same point:

> Ordinary people want to feel philosophically justified in hating evildoers and viewing them

as the ultimate authors of their evil. This moral attitude has always been vulnerable to our learning more about the causes of human behavior—and in situations where the origins of a person's actions become absolutely clear, our feelings about his responsibility begin to change. What is more, they *should* change. We should admit that a person is unlucky to inherit the genes and life experience that will doom him to psychopathy. That doesn't mean we can't lock him up, or kill him in self-defense, but *hating* him is not rational, given a complete understanding of how he came to be who he is. Natural, yes; rational, no.[24]

This all sounds suspiciously like the Christian exhortation to forgive one another and love our enemies. It confirms the Christian conception of forgiveness as being far more than simply overlooking a wrong or being prepared to let something go once there has been an appropriate expression of remorse. If this is the Christian ethic, then we can be sure that when Jesus exhorted Peter to forgive not just seven times, but seventy times seven,[25] he did not mean that we should forgive 'a lot', and he did not mean we should forgive until the 491st infraction. Rather, it is call to recognize that it is fundamentally irrational to be angry and to hate. If this is the Christian ethic, then when Jesus tells us to love our enemies, it means more than simply choosing not to retaliate. The exhortation to love our enemies means to see them not as evil people who freely chose a bad path, but as the victims of their nature and nurture and the objects of pity rather than anger. In a bizarre twist, the determinism of the New Atheists helps illuminate a fundamental Christian message.

Certainly an entire book could be written on what our lack of free will means in terms of how we should treat one another. But acknowledging our lack of free will also should fundamentally change the way we see our relationship to God. If we do not have free will, then we are not, in the final analysis, morally responsible for our actions. *If God is aware that we do not have free will and is interested in being fair, then it is impossible – impossible – that God rewards or punishes us for our behavior.* If we are not free to choose one behavior over another and our choice is determined by our nature and nurture, then it is nonsensical that God would reward us for good behavior or proper belief and punish us for bad behavior or lack of belief or be favorably disposed to some of His creatures and not to all of them. *In fact, if a command is defined as being something that one is compelled to follow at risk of punishment for failure to comply with it, then it is impossible that God commands us to act in any particular way at all.* The question of whether God is unconditionally loving or conditional loving, has a definitive answer. God *must* be unconditionally loving and forgiving. There is no paradox and there can be no hedging. God *does not* require contrition, and He allows no distance to form between Himself and us when our nature and nurture drive us to bad behavior. God imposes no conditions whatsoever on His love. It would be irrational for Him to do otherwise.

I am not suggesting that we peevishly accept that free will doesn't exist and try to put the pieces of our faith back together. I am suggesting that this concept is fundamental to understanding our relationship to God and, finally, what the incarnation of God as Jesus Christ means. To believe that we do not have free will does not make us atheists. It would seem that rather than being at odds with faith, it is actually a central tenet of faith and Scripture that free will does not exist. I will call this *"theistic determinism"* – that a deterministic account of the universe and human behavior is consistent with the existence of a personal God and actually can provide indispensable information to us about the nature of our relationship to God.

This book does not propose any new proofs of God's existence. It does, however, seek to conceive of God in manner that is consistent with science; particularly behavioral science and the question of free will. In so doing, faith is revealed to be a transcendent concern – something more than a set of values or a moral position. It will not, I am sure, appease the New Atheists, but it exploits their challenge of faith to make faith stronger. The New Atheism is convinced that the issue of free will finally deal a fatal blow to faith and that faithfulness cannot survive if free will – the apparent focal point of all Scripture and Sacred Tradition – turns out to be illusory. What the New Atheists think is our Achilles heel is actually the fulcrum with which faith will raise itself to meet the challenge it faces today.

In his landmark book, *The Structure of Scientific Revolutions*, Thomas S. Kuhn asserted that science does not progress at a steady pace with the accumulation of new data, but rather in sudden bursts of insight. Scientific paradigms, according to Kuhn, most often contain some anomalies and inconsistencies that create a tension. As "normal science" - everyday experimentation - reveals more and more anomalies, the tension increases. Occasionally someone will "see" the problems with the paradigm in a whole new light and what Kuhn coined a "paradigm shift" occurs. Kuhn offers an example of this in the discovery of oxygen. Joseph Priestley, who will figure prominently in our discussion shortly, was an English clergyman and scientist active in the late 1700s. He was famous in part for discovering how to carbonate water; a process that Jacob Schweppe would refine and turn into a precursor of soda. He also was among the first to isolate oxygen from air. However, Priestley rarely gets credit for his discovery because he never understood what he had accomplished. Priestley was committed to the view that air supported combustion because it had a mysterious quality call phlogiston. Since the pure oxygen he had inadvertently isolated didn't support a flame, Priestley assumed that he had successfully "dephlogisticated" air. Instead, credit for 'discovering' oxygen goes to Antoine-Laurent Lavoisier who two years later concluded that a distinct element had been isolated from other constituent elements in air. Priestley simply couldn't comprehend the notion that air was a compound of several different and distinct elements. He could not "see" chemistry in a new way. The paradigm shift had occurred without him.[26] Faith has lived with the anomaly of a both conditionally and unconditionally loving God for centuries. Science and philosophy's concurrence that we don't have free will increases the tension inherent in that paradigm. To overcome that tension, we have to learn to "see" faith in another way. A paradigm shift is inevitable and overdue. This book seeks to give it a nudge.

I promise you, this book will strengthen your faith. Though you may disagree with some of what I will say in the coming pages, no matter where you are on the spectrum of faith now, by the turn the last page of this book, your belief and trust in the Judeo-Christian God of Scripture will be stronger. Any fear that your life lacks meaning or that the universe is a cold, uncaring, mechanical place will be lessened. Any anxiety that God cannot exist, has forgotten you, or has left you to your suffering, will be calmed. The divine exhortation to "be not afraid" will make more sense and be of true comfort. My goal is to describe our relationship to God in the most accurate, defensible way possible. I believe it is impossible to succeed there without strengthening faith. In fact, if you are willing, I would appreciate if you would consider participating in an informal survey. Please think about where you would rank the strength of your faith right now, however you define that term for yourself, on a scale of 1 to 100 and write the number on the last page of this book (or the electronic equivalent). When you are finished reading this book, I hope seeing that number will remind you to rank your faith again and to send both numbers to me at the email address you'll find there.

I expect this book will make many readers mad – at least initially. The idea that we do not have free will is disquieting for many reasons, not least of which is that it requires a dramatic change in our conception of God and the way we "see" that relationship. We say that God is just. A just God would not reward and punish what is not within our control. His forgiveness would not be retaliation deferred until an afterlife or a finger on the scale of judgment, but utter disregard of sin. For most of us, justice is another word for institutionalized revenge – we agree not to exact retribution as long as someone in authority does it for us. In this way of thinking, God is the final judge and last hope for justice, and we want that. But if there is no free will, God's justice must be total forgiveness. God's love of us must be truly unearned, unearnable and irrevocable – genuine grace. Sin is not forgiven; it is irrelevant as far as God is concerned. In the words of the Psalmist, "as far as the East is from the West, so far has he removed our transgressions from us"[27] We hate that. Scripture warned us that we'd hate it. This book will explore why we hate it, how we came to hate it and assert that we hate it so much that we'll change faith and Scripture to avoid it. This book will explore how judgment crept into Christian dogma so prominently and will finally explore what faith would look like without it. It will conclude that faith without free will is not cold and mechanistic but is rather beautiful, intelligent, warm and kind.

This perspective has virtually no natural friends. The great Schism between Catholicism and Protestantism was precipitated by an argument over whether St. James was right in saying that salvation could be achieved by good works, or if St. Paul's insistence that salvation comes from belief alone is more accurate. The answer, it appears, is that they were both wrong. If our works and our beliefs are the result of our nature and nurture, then salvation is something that has happened to us without our intervention and nothing we can do or believe can take it away. If God chooses one of us, He chooses all of us.

This perspective is also not naturally conservative or liberal. Both sides of the political spectrum agree that to understand what God commands is to understand God. They also agree that God requires us to develop our talents, give generously to charity, and strive for self-improvement. If we follow these commands, they reason, we can each claim to be a 'good person' and to have discharged our obligations as a person of faith. The only remaining question for many Christians is whether God commands a liberal-minded ethic of tolerance and equality, or a conservative-minded ethic of traditional values. As a result, few have made the argument that God commands nothing at all and stands in a relationship with us that transcends morality and purpose.

Abraham Joshua Heschel, who is perhaps the most revered Jewish thinker of the twentieth century, and who is most well-known for marching arm-in-arm with Martin Luther King in Selma, opens his extraordinary book, *God in Search of Man* with these lines:

It is customary to blame secular science and anti-religious philosophy for the eclipse of religion in modern society. It would be more honest to blame religion for its own defeats. Religion declined not because it was refuted, but because it became irrelevant, dull, oppressive, insipid.[28]

I believe Heschel is absolutely correct. Faith is perfectly defensible in the face of all science and philosophy. But in our anxiousness to make faith about following a moral model, self-improvement, modesty, sharing, humility and developing our talents, Christianity becomes pious and platitudinous. In a word, it becomes insipid. Science and philosophy are not our enemy. We have been our own worst enemy. We think faith has evolved when we abandon the angry puritanical god in favor of the god who demands service and self-improvement, but he is the same - the idolatrous god of good luck, nice behavior and pretty sunsets is the same as the idolatrous god of fire and brimstone, only nicer.

When we are complacent about the idea that God commands, rewards and punishes, it may cause us to be more socially useful, but it leads us to an insipid faith. If an atheist and person of faith volunteer at a soup kitchen and the local news crew stops by to interview them about their motivations, how will they answer? The atheist might answer that she is there because she identifies with the poor and feels an inborn sense of obligation toward them. If the person of faith responds that she feels commanded and hopes to receive reward or avoid punishment by providing this service, is this what we mean when we say we are Christian? Is this loving one another, or simply acting in ways that imitate love in order to receive reward and avoid punishment? Can true love or belief be commanded in the first place? At least part of the problem is that Christian morality and secular morality are virtually indistinguishable from one another. If faith is good conduct and is interchangeable with secular good conduct, then faith is irrelevant. Classically, almost every lapsed Christian will say that they don't need to affiliate with any religion because they are "a good person" and treat others well and fairly. In modern faith, such a high premium is placed on interacting with others and being kind to them that it becomes a surrogate for interacting with God.

I need God to command; Moses and the Burning Bush

We people of faith have managed to gloss the question of free will for centuries. It may feel far more comfortable to continue to gloss it and preserve the familiar and comfortable image of God as commander and judge. The idea that God is watching, and getting ready to pronounce judgment has had an undeniable wonderful social dividend and has kept generations of children and adults in line. Ultimately, as we'll see, faith is not amoral or even apolitical – it does impose moral and political obligations on us that are actually quite urgent and lie at the root of right and wrong - but it is not a command and is not enforced with reward and punishment. We might legitimately worry that without God reading hearts and minds and ensuring eventual punishment, people will generally behave worse. But as Christians, we are compelled to accept the reality of God as He is, not as is socially convenient.

The moment that God first introduces Himself to Moses and sets in motion the events that lead to the liberation of Israel from Egypt, may be one of the most important passages of Scripture. God appears in a burning bush and demands that Moses approach. Historians like to say that the novelty of the Judaism was monotheism; that this religion dispensed with a pantheon of gods and conceived of God as a single being. What's closer to the truth, or a more complete truth, is that Judaism did away with mythology. Although vestiges certainly remain, after Moses encounters God, faith becomes something more than using God to explain every gap in scientific knowledge or using God to meet every human need. In the encounter with Moses, God says that He will be gracious to whom He will be gracious, and will show mercy on whom He will show mercy,[29] evidently asserting that although human beings can strive to understand the will of God, after that encounter with Moses they can no longer simply make it up. God tells Moses from the burning bush, *"Ehyeh-'Asher-'Ehyeh"* "I will be Who I will be."[30] We cannot vote on God's nature. This book will challenge the assumption that God requires either repentance of, or punishment for sin. Many will respond by saying that they "need God" to impose rules and punish transgressions because either they need those rules to stay on the straight and narrow, or they believe that society would break down without divine command, reward and punishment. Scripture clearly does not allow us to mold God into what we need or think we need. That is idolatry. Our faith tells us that if the last person on Earth decides not to believe in the existence of God or to believe something about God's nature that is not true, it will not change the reality of who He is. It would be an unacceptable return to mythology to insist that a final, comprehensive and authoritative understanding of God is based on need or if a final, comprehensive and authoritative understanding of God is even really possible.

The Challenge to Know God's Ways

We should neither insist that God conform to what we think we 'need' Him to be, nor throw up our hands and give up on understanding the nature of God's relationship to us. We are all familiar with Islam's requirement that Muslims pray facing Mecca five times a day. Jews following an orthodox practice are required to say prayers three times a day in fulfillment of the passage in Deuteronomy in which God commands, that "you will love the Lord your God and worship Him with all your heart and with all your being." [31] This passage itself is part of the *Shema* – words that every Jew is supposed to say first thing in the morning, as the last thing at night, and with their dying breath. Catholicism has a similar practice called the Liturgy of the Hours which requires clergy to pray seven times a day, starting with Lauds in the pre-dawn darkness, and ending with

Compline in the evening, thus fulfilling St. Paul's advice to "pray without ceasing" [32] The Hours are primarily a collection of readings from the Bible for recitation, as well as psalms and prayers, with a different selection each day. Each day's prayers in the Hours begins with the Invitatory and so it is among only a few passages that are said daily without variation. It closes with the following remembrance of how the Israelites challenged Moses and God in the desert when they were hungry and thirsty:

Today, listen to the voice of the Lord:
Do not grow stubborn, as your fathers did
In the wilderness
When at Meriba and Massah
They challenged me and provoked me,
Although they had seen all my works
Forty years I endured that generation.
I said, "They are a people whose hearts go astray
And they do not know my ways."
So I swore in my anger,
"They shall not enter into my rest." [33]

This is a perplexing and disheartening way to start a daily devotion. It seems to be a threat and a remembrance of a time in the story of faith when God was distant and angry. But it actually functions as a challenge. As the person engaged in the Hours begins, he or she is encouraged not to give up on understanding God and His relationship to us, but rather to do his or her best to 'know His ways' through the spiritual exercise that is about to be undertaken.

If we are convinced that free will is an illusion, then if we are to be genuinely interested in understanding the true nature of God, we must accept that God is not in the business of commands and moral enforcement. This makes us uncomfortable, makes us angry, it challenges deeply felt instincts about God and even about our status as moral beings with dignity, but it is our obligation as Christians to seek God and know His ways to the best of our ability. The result may be that we are actually made more confident in our faith and more comfortable with the idea that we do not have free will.

Not a Compelling Illusion

We shouldn't be too anxious about recognizing free will as an illusion, because it never had our complete allegiance anyway. In our daily lives, we tacitly acknowledge that we and our children are the products of nature and nurture. As parents, we don't feel our children's personalities and moral sense will develop independently regardless of what we may do or not do. We actively try to form them and re-form them – we encourage behavior that will engender good habits, and discourage behavior that will lead to bad habits. Whenever someone does something extraordinarily good, we reflexively examine their background to understand how they came to be who they are. We don't assume their behavior came out of nowhere or is somehow self-made. Olympic coverage of a star athlete always includes a biography that traces the athlete's success back to the roots we know are going to be there. There is the inevitable study of the encouragement and guidance provided by parents, siblings, teachers, coaches, friends, and communities. In addition, maybe the athlete showed promise from the very beginning or has siblings that inexplicably show similar promise – hinting at a genetic predisposition for exceptional ability. We find this exercise as compelling as it is predictable. We recognize it tells us something indispensable about the individual when we know their nature and nurture. On the other side of the spectrum, when someone does something heinous and criminal, we initially react with outrage and anger. Eventually, though, we reflexively begin the process of examining their psychology and background to find the place where it all went wrong. Virtually inevitably, sometimes without much digging at all, evidence of a mental defect is discovered, or some catastrophic failing of the familial or community influence. As our understanding of the individual's nature and nurture develops, our outrage is tempered and our attention turns to something more strategic: we ask ourselves how we as a society can prevent this from happening again. Inevitably, we don't say that criminal behavior is the exercise of free will and can neither be controlled nor predicted. Rather, we seek to resolve the underlying problems that we know influenced and ultimately caused the behavior. We seek to re-form nature and nurture rather than chalking it up to free will beyond any influence.

Whether we think a particular action was the product of free will or not is always determined by the period of time before the action that we consider. Seen in isolation, every action appears to be free. Proponents of free will might say of a criminal that no one forced them to commit the crime and that when he or she got up that morning, committing a crime was not inevitable. Seen in that short timeframe, their crime was the product of something akin to free will – no outside force intervened. However, when we look at the full breadth of that individual's life, we see that what they did was the inevitable result of their nature and nurture. The reason free will is such a compelling illusion is that when we reflect on how we make a particular decision, it appears that the decision-making process has a distinct beginning point and occurs in a moment. In a manner of speaking this is true, but in the most important respects, nothing could be further from the truth. When we make a particular decision, innumerable influences have been at work in the background and the process of making the decision began many years before – a lifetime before. The moment of my conception determined a substantial amount of my future behavior. It established my place on innumerable behavioral spectrums; that I would be prone to be fairly anxious, for instance. It established my gender, which made it likely that I would be slightly more aggressive and have a more territorial impulse than otherwise (along with, I am sure, some positive traits that have not yet revealed themselves to me). In addition to their genes, my parents' own behavior was also an important determining factor to my future behavior. My parents did not leave my development to my free will, but rather, actively encouraged some traits and discouraged others. They rewarded good, constructive behavior in an attempt to form me as a reasonably good person capable of being part of society, and discouraged those impulses that were destructive or anti-social. Both my parents are research chemists and so they encouraged academics, with only limited success. They were both theists and maybe most relevantly to my effort to write this book, they never gave me the impression there was any conflict between faith and science. Several factors conspired to cause me to live across the street from St. Mary's Catholic Church in Ridgefield, Connecticut in my most formative years, which certainly did not hurt in encouraging faith. The economic circumstances, the community in which I grew up, and the peers with which I fell in, all continued to form me. Throughout, I was unconsciously synthesizing these influences and the innumerable other influences, experiences, and interactions that have made up my life from conception until this moment. When now, in adulthood, a decision is required of me, I don't draw significantly from the last five minutes of my life, or even the last five days, weeks or years. Instead, the full breadth of my forty-six years on the planet (and a few extra months in the womb) and the connections and synthesis and interpretation I have applied to them over time, representing a totally unique and almost unimaginably complex neural chemistry and neural mechanism, is brought to bear to *determine* how I will make the decision.

We are not causal wind socks blown in one direction or another based on what is going on in our vicinity at the moment a decision is required. When we make a particular decision, although we may experience it as occurring in one discrete moment, the decision-making process is the culmination of long biological inheritance and a lifetime of experiences. During the course of my lifetime I have developed fairly rigid and largely predictable and reliable behavioral patterns that are not nearly as susceptible to immediate change as I (or my wife) might like. When I make a decision it is made almost entirely with the materials within the confines of my skull – not as a result of the environment I find myself in at that moment. Unless someone is exerting some kind of control or influence on me – threatening me with violence if I don't 'decide' a certain way – I am, in manner of speaking, "freely" deciding on my own, as an individual. For all intents and purposes I am independent for that moment of other causal influences. This is free will in a manner of speaking. The illusion of free will is so powerful because it is not far from the truth. We don't experience the decision making process as occurring over a lifetime because most of it occurs subconsciously. When an opportunity arises to take something without paying for it, we don't have to weigh the pros and cons, we don't have to think back to the time our Nana told us not to steal, or the moment our parents punished us for stealing, and we certainly don't need to refer to a social contract or even a religious tenet. We either experience it as a broad value - "I don't steal" - or it simply doesn't tempt us at all. Someone with a different nature or nurture may well find the moment more challenging and may not be up to it. The value system or impulse I seemingly adopt anew and apply in a single moment, is actually adopted over my lifetime. We do not adopt values the instant they are needed and from nothing. How we came to be who we are at that moment is not the product of our free choice.

It makes perfect sense that, if an individual's nature and nurture have led them to a pattern of behavior that is predictably destructive or anti-social, society must take them in hand and restrain them - literally re-form them if possible - incarcerate them, and even, if there is no other way to control them and the harm they are causing is severe enough, to kill them. This is justifiable because they are the mechanism of destruction, no more morally condemnable than an out-of-control car. There need not be any confusion regarding the Christians' ability to resist otherwise uncontrollable violence with violence. What does not make sense, however, is to hate that individual or to seek to retaliate against them for their behavior. Here we must turn the other cheek without exception because it is the only rational response. We are called to be constantly vigilant against responding to even the most egregious crime with hate, even as we use everything in our power to restrain that crime. Because of the criminal's unique and highly complex nature and nurture, the choices he or she makes are independent of immediate causal influence but are nonetheless inevitable. The bad choice was fully determined by forces outside of his or her control. And if God is Who we say He is, when He considers our actions, He cannot possibly make the mistake of looking at them in isolation. He must see each one as the inevitable result of the nature and nurture we experience and was imposed on us until that point. God must take the long view. And with the long view comes mercy.

The Garden Reinterpreted

Scripture seems to be a catalogue of stories about God's commanding His people, promising reward and punishment, and His people responding either well or badly. Some of the most compelling and memorable passages seem to share this central theme. In the opening pages of the Old Testament, Adam and Eve disobey God's commands in The Garden and are exiled as punishment. Within a few chapters, God is exterminating all life on Earth with a flood, evidently because of a general failure to act correctly. Sodom and Gomorrah are utterly destroyed ostensibly for moral improprieties. What should we make of the seemingly clear theme of moral judgment that appears throughout Scripture and has been such a central concern of faith?

In Christian theology, the moment Adam and Eve disobey God's command and eat from the Tree of Knowledge of Good and Evil is of immense and central importance as it is the moment that "original sin" occurred. We are taught that everyone since Adam and Eve inherits this blameworthiness and that it is only expunged by the execution of Jesus Christ and our subsequent baptism. We have natural suspicions about this story. The concept of inherited sin is utterly alien to our understanding of justice. The idea that God was finally unable to forgive original sin until He somehow orchestrated the brutal torture and execution of His only Son doesn't seem loving or even remotely compassionate. Our new understanding of human behavior just seems to broaden the mystery. If free will is an illusion, and if not even Adam and Eve were finally responsible for their actions, how can they – never mind all the generations after them – be held accountable for their actions by a presumably intelligent and fair-minded God? How can God demand a blood sacrifice from His Son to expunge this guilt?

The answer is imbedded within the details of the story. Because it is so central to all that will come after, I have reprinted the important parts of the story below:

This is the history of the generations of the heavens and of the earth when they were created, in the day that God made the earth and the heavens. No plant of the field was yet in the earth, and no herb of the field had yet sprung up; for God had not caused it to rain on the earth. There was not a man to till the ground, but a mist went up from the earth, and watered the whole surface of the ground. God formed man from the dust of the ground, and breathed into his nostrils the breath of life; and man became a living soul. God planted a garden eastward, in Eden, and there he put the man whom he had formed. Out of the ground God made every tree to grow that is pleasant to the sight, and good for food, including the Tree of Life in the middle of the garden and the Tree of the Knowledge of Good and Evil. God took the man, and put him into the

Garden of Eden to cultivate and keep it. God commanded the man, saying, "You may freely eat of every tree of the garden; but you shall not eat of the Tree of the Knowledge of Good and Evil; for in the day that you eat of it, you will surely die." God said, "It is not good for the man to be alone. I will make him a helper comparable to him." Out of the ground God formed every animal of the field, and every bird of the sky, and brought them to the man to see what he would call them. Whatever the man called every living creature became its name. The man gave names to all livestock, and to the birds of the sky, and to every animal of the field; but for man there was not found a helper comparable to him. God caused the man to fall into a deep sleep. As the man slept, he took one of his ribs, and closed up the flesh in its place. God made a woman from the rib which he had taken from the man, and brought her to the man. The man said, "This is now bone of my bones, and flesh of my flesh. She will be called 'woman,' because she was taken out of Man." Therefore, a man will leave his father and his mother, and will join with his wife, and they will be one flesh. The man and his wife were both naked, and they were not ashamed.

Now the snake was subtler than any animal of the field which God had made. He said to the woman, "Has God really said, 'You shall not eat of any tree of the garden'?" The woman said to the snake, "We may eat fruit from the trees of the garden, but not the fruit of the tree which is in the middle of the garden. God has said, 'You shall not eat of it. You shall not touch it, lest you die.' "The snake said to the woman, "You won't really die, for God knows that in the day you eat it, your eyes will be opened, and you will be like God, knowing good and evil." When the woman saw that the tree was good for food, and that it was a delight to the eyes, and that the tree was to be desired to make one wise, she took some of its fruit, and ate. Then she gave some to her husband with her, and he ate it, too. Their eyes were opened, and they both knew that they were naked. They sewed fig leaves together, and made coverings for themselves. They heard God's voice walking in the garden in the cool of the day, and the man and his wife hid themselves from the presence of God among the trees of the garden. God called to the man, and said to him, "Where are you?" The man said, "I heard your voice in the garden, and I was afraid, because I was naked; so I hid myself." God said, "Who told you that you were naked? Have you eaten from the tree that I commanded you not to eat from?" The man said, "The woman whom you gave to be with me, she gave me fruit from the tree, and I ate it." God said to the woman, "What have you done?" The woman said, "The snake deceived me, and I ate." God said to the snake, "Because you have done this, you are cursed above all livestock, and above every animal of the field. You shall go on your belly and you shall eat dust all the days of your life. I will put hostility between you and the woman, and between your offspring and her offspring. He will bruise your head, and you will bruise his heel." To the woman he said, "I will greatly multiply your pain in childbirth. You will bear children in pain. Your desire will be for your husband, and he will rule over you." To Adam he said, "Because you have listened to your wife's voice, and ate from the tree, about which I commanded you, saying, 'You shall not eat of it,' the ground is cursed for your sake. You will eat from it with much labor all the days of your life. It will yield thorns and thistles to you; and you will eat the herb of the field. You will eat bread by the sweat of your face until you return to the ground, for you were taken out of it. For you are dust, and you shall return to dust." The man called his wife Eve because she would be the mother of all the living. God made garments of animal skins for Adam and for his wife, and clothed them. God said, "Behold, the man has become like one of us, knowing good and evil. Now, lest he reach out his hand, and also take of the Tree of Life, and eat, and live forever." Therefore, God sent him out from the garden of Eden, to till the ground from which he was taken. So he drove out the man; and he placed cherubim at the east of the garden of Eden, and a flaming sword which turned every way, to guard the way to the Tree of Life. [34]

It is no accident that the forbidden fruit is from the Tree of the Knowledge of Good and Evil. God did not choose a tree arbitrarily for the prohibition to test obedience. It is fairly clear that God wishes to prevent Adam and Eve from attaining the ability to distinguish between good and evil. What a strange goal! This is particularly strange if moral judgment is a central concern in our relationship to God. It seems He didn't even want us to have the ability to tell the difference! It is less strange, however, if this story represents God's advice to us not to assume that we have moral autonomy and adopt the illusion that we can freely choose between good and evil.

Notice that when Adam and Eve hide from God, they don't hide because they fear punishment for their disobedience. Rather, they say they are hiding because they now have the ability to distinguish between good and evil and have the capacity for shame – embarrassment by nakedness. If eating the fruit of the Tree causes the capacity for free will rather than the illusion of free will, and if this was a story about humanity being granted free will and then misusing it to disobey God, there is a major continuity error. It is clear that the act of eating the fruit – not anything that comes afterward – is what causes humanity to be exiled from the Garden.

The story is not about disobedience. Rather, it is an exhortation against adopting the illusion that we have free will and can exercise morally responsible judgment. In the Garden, Adam and Eve are blissfully unaware of good and evil and are unable to exercise moral judgment and we are invited to assume they do not have or think they have free will. The situation is described as paradisal! It is only when humanity adopts the presumption of believing they can choose between good and evil that things start to fall apart. Moments after Adam and Eve assumed that they had free will and that they were morally responsible agents, God asks Adam what happened. Adam's answer reverberates powerfully through the rest of human history. He says, "the woman who You gave to be with me, she gave me fruit of the Tree and I ate it"[35]. His answer is almost comic in that he instantly assesses blame against his companion for feeding him the fruit and even implies blame for God for ever bringing her into his life. Eve, not to be outdone, points the finger at the snake and says "the snake deceived me and I ate."[36]. God immediately recognizes what has happened – it is obvious from their answers and obvious from their newly fashioned fig leaf aprons. The language of Genesis reads that God imposes punishment for their disobedience, but we know that our ability and indeed our overwhelming instinct and propensity to judge is itself a road that leads directly out of paradise and into the world we inhabit now. Within a few chapters, the silliness of Adam, Eve and the snake assessing blame against one another gets far more serious as Cain, in a murderous rage generated by envy – an envy that would not be possible without the ability to distinguish good from bad - kills his own brother. Scripture is telling us that when we assume we have free will and exercise our ability to judge right from wrong, we risk filling our minds and tainting our society with hate, envy, jealousy and demands for retribution. We hate by attaching narratives to events. And the narratives we attached are almost always about free will. God was not lying when He said we would surely die if we ate from the Tree. It has been a rough road ever since, filled with moral judgment of each other, hatred and death. God does not react to Adam and Eve's disobedience as much as to the fact that they have developed a moral sense and are now engaged in moral judgment, blame and humiliation, as will all their descendants after them. Far from being a blessing, this ability is a curse. It is interesting that the scene of the Garden closes with the image of God fashioning clothing for Adam and Eve as if to say that now that humanity has falsely asserted that it can choose freely between good and evil, that the inevitable result is that we will each morally humiliate ourselves and each other by comparison and jealousy – and that God immediately set to work to relieve our shame. This theme – God mitigating our shame – will be a central theme throughout Scripture right up to the incarnation, death and resurrection of Jesus. The flaming sword set at the entryway to the Garden seems to be an allegory for the fact that we cannot get back into the Garden by the path we took to leave it. We will not be able mitigate the bad effects of exercising moral judgment and assuming free will by acting ever more morally, charitably, or by a commitment to social justice. We will only mitigate those bad effects by rejecting moral judgment itself and recognizing that our will is not free. We cannot re-enter paradise with moral perfection as both secular people and people of faith often assume. Rather, to inhabit a place without hate and jealousy we need to recognize that we are not morally autonomous and that we do not have free will. The Kingdom of God is not a possible future when everyone will act morally and charitably because of a desire to avoid divine punishment and receive divine reward. The aim of religion is not the creation of a moral utopia. Rather, the Kingdom of God is a possible future when judgment is replaced by forgiveness because it is right and just to do so. It is a possible future characterized by universal acceptance and love – not just forbearance or tolerance, but a genuine recognition that we are all in this together and there is no need or justification to place anyone anywhere on a moral spectrum. This is determinism nestled comfortably in one of the most important passages of Scripture, and actually seems to illuminate it.

Radical Forgiveness, Radical Grace and the Love of God

Our lack of free will has far greater consequences for faith than merely being a warning that judging each other is irrational and leads to strife. It also tells us some extraordinarily important facts about our relationship to God. As we've seen, it means God can command nothing because we are not free in any morally relevant way to choose to follow His commands. He would be rewarding or punishing creatures that could not have acted other than the way they did. This means that God will forgive everything. No individual is finally responsible for their own good and bad conduct and so a just God will always forgive any act and any omission, regardless of whether we are sorry. God's mercy is not merely looking the other way from time to time, giving us extra opportunities to recover, or giving us the benefit of the doubt. It is *radical forgiveness*. God's forgiveness requires no expression of remorse or some compensating goodness. It means our good and bad conduct is utterly irrelevant to God. It is forgiveness seven times seventy times.

The implications of our lack of free also include that we have no way of earning God's love. "Grace" means many different things among people of faith, but most would agree that it is the unearned love of God and that its unearned quality is central and indispensable to its meaning. We want to say that a prerequisite for grace is that we be open to it. We say grace is offered to all of us, but we can close ourselves off from it. But if we do not have the free will to choose to be open to it, or to avoid closing ourselves to it, then a just God will not withhold it. This is *radical grace* – fully and truly unearnable grace - grace that is unconditional and indelible.

If we don't have free will, then we have nothing to offer God in exchange for His love of us and His adoption of us as His children. What do you give the God who already has everything? For centuries, humanity's answer was good behavior, and using our free will to choose His will. If we don't have free will, we stand empty-handed before God with nothing to show for ourselves or recommend us to His love. This is, at first, disorienting and a little scary. Although we've always been fine with God stretching a little to love us, this suggests there is nothing inherently loveable about us at all unless and until God makes the seemingly unfounded decision to love us. We are utterly dependent on God's assurance, reflected innumerable times in Scripture, that He has made the irrational decision to love us for no reason. It is expressed most often in terms of ransom and redemption. Above all else, this should give us a sense of moral humility. We should recognize that however bad we might be, God is required to overlook a far more fundamental shortfall in order to love us – our inability to make free choices in the first place. Correspondingly, no matter how good we might be, it is merely the expression of nature and nurture and we are no better than our neighbor, and no more deserving of reward. It is a theology of universal salvation regardless of behavior, contrition or belief. It means that if God loves one of us, He loves all of us, equally and without qualification or condition. It means that if anyone is invited to a life after death, everyone and perhaps everything is invited to a life after death. It is statement about the fundamental unity and equality of all things and all persons regardless of where we might otherwise place them on a moral spectrum.

Our lack of free will finally means that *our relationship to God is not about what we can do for Him or what He can do for us*. If we have value in God's eyes it is because He chooses to value us, not because we earned it. The relationship between God and each of us is transcendent, and does not necessarily serve any function or purpose, although it may be infused with extraordinarily rich meaning beyond expression.

A lack of free will does not require us to reimagine faith. It requires us to see the full power and breadth of some concepts of faith that we may have lost sight of: radical forgiveness, radical grace, the truly unconditional, unearned quality of the love of God. It definitively resolves the conflict between an unconditionally loving God and conditionally loving One, in favor of the first. It understands God as transcending right and wrong.

God May Have Free Will – Don't Let Anthropomorphism Limit God

We might think that if humanity does not have free will, then there is no reason to think God is any freer than we are. If this is so, God might exist only as a metaphor for the inexorable mechanistic churning of the universe along the path that was pre-ordained from the moment of the Big Bang, perhaps with some variation as a result of quantum randomness. Such a god would be literally synonymous with Nature[37] - an ordering principal or a unity - rather than a living being with a personality distinct from His creation. The God of Scripture, Who sees, feels, loves, interacts and is even surprised from time to time, would be impossible. God could only be understood as a metaphor for natural forces of physics or, at best, serve as a figure of speech for what's noble and good about human beings.

Bookstore shelves groan under the weight of books that that seek to re-cast God in this way.

Scripture, certainly, does not suggest that God's mind works with the same limitations as ours. In fact, Scripture insists that on some level God is unimaginable to us. After Moses led the Israelites out of Egypt and before he ascended Mount Sinai a final time to receive the tablets containing the Ten Commandments to replace the ones destroyed in the episode of the Golden Calf, Moses demanded to see God's glory. God responded:

> "I will make all my goodness pass before you, and will proclaim before you my name, 'The Lord'; and I will be gracious to whom I will be gracious, and will show mercy on whom I will show mercy. But" He said, "you cannot see my face; for man shall not see me and live." And the Lord said, "Behold, there is a place by me where you shall stand upon the rock; and while my glory passes by I will put you in a cleft of the rock, and I will cover you with my hand until I have passed by; then I will take away my hand, and you shall see my back; but my face shall not be seen."[38]

We know this is not a statement about the deadly medical effect of looking at God because, only six verses prior, we are told that the Lord "used to speak to Moses face to face, as a man speaks to his friend."[39] A few chapters before, as she interacts directly with God, Sarah asks, "Have I really seen God and remained alive after seeing Him?"[40] Her grandson, Jacob, wrestled with a mysterious divine being who renames him "Israel" because he had "fought with God and with men, and prevailed"[41] Jacob renames the place in which this event took place as Peniel, a play on the Hebrew for 'face-to-face'[42] because, he says, "I have seen God face-to-face, and my life is preserved."[43] In Christianity, we believe that Jesus is the incarnation of God and innumerable people have therefore seen God face-to-face and not died. Instead, the message of God's prohibition to Moses is that the nature of God is finally indiscernible to us human beings and whatever we might think we know about God is only our best working theory based on what He has voluntarily revealed to us about Himself. That God is entirely unlike us – which may include a capacity for what we might call free will – is central to the story of faith from the very beginning.

And of course there are elements even of the known universe that don't comply with the laws of causation. Not only do quanta appear to move randomly, exist and not exist at once, and occupy two places at once, but neutrinos – the smallest sub-particles known to science – evidently change their type from one type to another without explanation. This classically impossible phenomenon may explain why the Big Bang was not a collision of equal parts of matter and anti-matter to result in a whole lot of nothing, but wound up creating the known universe – in other words, why there is something rather than nothing.[44] This turns classical physics on its head and is virtually unimaginable to us except in terms of allegory, but these processes occur all around us and within us all the time and are fundamental to the fabric of the universe. This is not a proof of God's existence or His capacity for free will. It simply asserts that it is not a stretch to allow for the existence of a God who is wholly different from ourselves and has capacities well beyond our comprehension – including the capacity for something like free will. Science was alerted to the possibility that classical physics was incomplete because light exhibited the qualities of both a particle and a wave, and touched off the investigation that led to quantum mechanics. Nothing in the physical universe is likely to alert us to the ways in which God might violate the classical laws of physics. Scripture indicates He stands outside of time and causality and while it may be difficult to imagine such a thing, it cannot be said to be impossible. Abraham Heschel says that we can only speak of God in allegorical terms.[45] To say that God is feeling anger may be a useful device for us to use to think about and talk about God's reaction to something, but we should not mistake it for the literal truth. We often think about God as hiding Himself from us, and we might imagine that He is testing our willingness to believe in Him without evidence. It seems to me more likely that He simply consists of stuff that is beyond comprehension and His hiddenness is not a test of belief without evidence, but rather a natural effect of being of a nature that is fundamentally incomprehensible and wholly outside human capacity to directly experience. In fact, it is probably an exercise in futility to philosophize about the nature of God beyond the nature of

His relationship to us. Understanding the nature of the God with the intellectual tools at our disposal is like holding smoke. But we can understand *our relationship to God* by examining Creation, and the revelation of Scripture.

Anthropomorphism; God as Wholly Other; Allegory; No One Can See God and Live

To attribute human limitations to God is to fall into the trap of anthropomorphism from which science has actually released us. Science and faith have regularly come into apparent conflict only to have faith emerge stronger than it was before, having been forced to abandon an anthropomorphic vision of God. The strengthening is a result of winnowing away of the supernaturalism and moralism of our reflexive and primordial faith, and leaving the fundamental and transcendent messages of faith purer. Primordial faith is anthropomorphic. God is seen as an essentially human figure subject to human impulses and human motivations. Like the Greek mythological gods, the anthropomorphic God is susceptible to rages and jealousies. We need only reflect on this for a moment to realize that it is highly unlikely that an entity that stands outside of time and causation and is capable of some fraction of the deeds we attribute to Him can lose His temper or peevishly demand worship and threaten punishment with more apparent impulsivity and less mercy than we tolerate in human judges. We assume with each scientific advance that faith has been dealt the final catastrophic blow and that science will march in triumph over faith's carcass. In practice, however, science challenges the anthropomorphic idea of God and faith, albeit slowly and gradually, accepts it, absorbs it and is stronger for it.

The vast majority of people of faith would agree that the Theory of Evolution does not challenge belief in God or the belief that God is responsible for Creation in some way. However, what it did do was to banish the anthropomorphic idea of God as grandfatherly Geppetto tapping away at His workbench at little models of animals and humans, breathing life into them, and releasing them complete and final into a static environment. It replaced this mythological vision with the enormous majesty and complexity of what science is continually revealing. We no longer believe that the Earth is the center of the universe (in fact, Scripture uses the lower-case "earth" instead of the capitalized word "Earth" because the idea that we inhabit a planet was completely foreign), nor do we believe the stars are applied to a dome above us. The immensity and generosity and abundance of the universe as we now know it does nothing to diminish God, but has the opposite effect.

The work is not nearly complete. In the religious mind, as well as many scientifically-oriented minds, the moment of Creation occurs at the Big Bang with the eruption of the Singularity into an ever expanding universe. My reflexive impression of this moment is, I have to admit, adapted from the scene of Michelangelo's Sistine Chapel as God's finger touches Adam's, but instead of Adam, my mind's eye places the Singularity. This represents a failure on my part to imagine the possibility that the universe is timeless and that it has no beginning and will have no end. God does not create the universe at His workbench, nor does He necessarily create it at a particular point in time. To be free of the remaining limitations of my imagination would undoubtedly bring me closer to a truer understanding the nature of God.

To assume that if humans do not have free will, that God cannot have something akin to free will is to retreat into anthropomorphism yet again. This is not the god of gaps, meant to resolve gaps in our understanding of the physical world. This is merely heeding the warning of Scripture that the nature of God may not be reducible to human terms and may not even be comprehensible to a human mind. Our eyes perceive yellow and green spectrum light best because our eyes evolved in a world lit by a star that emits yellow and green spectrum light most strongly.[46] Our minds conceive of time and causality as linear because our minds evolved in a world in which everything perceptible to us obeys the classic laws of physics. There well may be more things in heaven and earth than are dreamt of in our current philosophy and science or are even comprehensible to us.[47] Scripture tells us that, fundamentally, the nature of God is one such thing and science gives us no reason to doubt it.

Charles Townes – Science and Religion

Louis Pasteur, the father of microbiology and inventor of the process of pasteurization which bears his name, was a committed person of faith throughout his life. In his 1966 watershed *Think Magazine* article entitled, *"The Convergence of Science and Religion,"* Charles H. Townes noted that when Louis

Pasteur was asked how a scientist could be as religious as he was, Pasteur replied that his laboratory was entirely separate from his home and his faith. Townes, himself a devout Christian and Nobel Prize winning scientist for his work in the development of lasers and the discovery of the black hole in the center of our galaxy, was critical of Pasteur's insistence that science and faith are independent of one another. Townes called for a more robust relationship between science and faith. He asserted that faith in an orderly universe is a necessary starting point for any scientific endeavor. He also noted that scientific revelation when the most important hypotheses are realized, look very much like religious revelation. Of course science goes on to prove its hypotheses through the scientific method and the outcome is accepted but always subject to future discoveries proving them incorrect. Townes called for religious dogma and creed to be considered more a working theory than absolute truth, each subject to further advances. Townes asserted that Pasteur's separation of science and religion was an impoverished and finally incorrect view. He insisted that science and religion would converge and the relationship would strengthen both. In a 2005 interview with National Public Radio, Townes more clearly defined what he meant. "Consider what religion is," he said. "Religion is an attempt to understand the purpose and meaning of our universe. What is science? It's an attempt to understand how our universe works. Well, if there's a purpose and meaning, that must have something to do with how it works, so those two must be related."[48]

Townes died in 2015 at the age of 99. Little progress has been made in the half century since Townes called for a robust convergence of science and faith. If anything, science's triumphal successes in explaining the natural world have made the faithful, especially the literalist and dogmatist, ever more defensive. Determinism has, so far, only eroded faith and made it feel like it was built on the shifting sand of magic and moralism. But perhaps theistic determination is within the realm of what Townes had in mind. Certainly it is a challenge to religious dogma to the extent faith has become synonymous with command, reward and punishment and requires reform of that part of our dogma. However, instead of being simply an assertion that science does not contradict faith, theistic determinism exploits advances in science and philosophy to expand our understanding of the nature of our relationship to God in a fundamental manner. No, this will not create faith where there is none. But it definitively resolves the natural tension that always existed in faith between the god who has a temper and finally gives up on his creatures in favor of the unconditionally loving God. I will argue that it allows us a transcendent rather than magical or moral interpretation of Scripture. It finally makes faith more compelling and rebuilds faith on a stone foundation.

Carol The Night Nurse – The First Hiddenness Story

By the end of this book, I hope you will agree that the central theme of this book, theistic determinism, is not only true, but obviously true, and wonder how it could have been missed up until now. I recognize that I do need to account for this. But it is not hard. Failure to see the divine message and, in fact, the inevitability of the rejection of that message is a recurring theme throughout Scripture. I will argue that evolution itself predisposes us to miss what we are looking for, and even to make subconscious adjustments to adjust reality to meet our expectations – in this case, our expectation of a judging, commanding, conditionally loving God. Also, we will contend with the possibility that the authors of Scripture might have been unconsciously complicit in hiding the message so that it would be preserved until science caught up to faith and made its meaning clear - literally hiding the message from the messenger. Finally, everyone is familiar with missing something in plain sight, and this dynamic may well be at work in faith. My aunt-in-law, Carol, is an actress. Carol has many good roles under her belt but one of my favorites is her role as the night nurse in *The Godfather*. In the movie, the Godfather, played by Marlin Brando, has been shot by a rival mob family and is lying unconscious in a hospital bed. His middle child and the film's protagonist, Michael, arrives for a visit and is aghast to realize that the police protection assigned to his father has disappeared in an apparent conspiracy to allow assassins to finish the job. Michael asks the night nurse, Carol, to help him move the Godfather to another room to foil the plot. If you watch carefully, as Carol is wheeling Marlin Brando out of his hospital room and down the hall, she drives the gurney a little too close to the doorframe and Brando's hand, which is hanging off the gurney, is driven into the doorjamb. It looks painful.

The presumably unconscious Godfather jerks his hand up and shakes it in the air before letting it drop back down next to him. It is remarkable to me that this went unnoticed by the editors of the film, and it is even more remarkable that has gone unnoticed by the millions of fans of this exceptionally popular movie. Now that you are aware of it, I suspect you will never watch the scene without that little continuity error overwhelming your perception of it – it will be all you see. You will wonder how all those listmania sites of movie bloopers missed this, hiding in plain sight until now. For most of my life, I have been happy to read Scripture as a story about God commanding certain behavior and promising reward and punishment based on our response. It seems obvious now that the real message, hidden in plain sight, is that we do not have the moral autonomy to respond to moral commands and that if we allow ourselves the illusion of moral autonomy we play a blame game, and we wind up killing one another. We don't separate ourselves from God by doing this, but we make understanding the true nature of His relationship to us a virtual impossibility.

The Parable of the Sheep and the Goats

Scripture has many more stories aside from the Garden in which God initially appears to be depicted as commanding judge. The Parable of the Sheep and the Goats, in which God apparently separates the good from the bad to send some to reward and others to punishment is one of the most problematic:

But when the son of man comes in his glory, and all the holy angels with him, then he will sit on the throne of his glory. Before him all the nations will be gathered, and he will separate them one from another, as a shepherd separates the sheep from the goats. He will set the sheep on his right hand, but the goats on the left. Then the king will tell those on his right hand, 'Come, blessed of my father, inherit the kingdom prepared for you from the foundation of the world; for I was hungry, and you gave me food to eat. I was thirsty, and you gave me drink. I was a stranger, and you took me in. I was naked, and you clothed me. I was sick, and you visited me. I was in prison, and you came to me.'

"Then the righteous will answer him, saying, 'Lord, when did we see you hungry, and feed you; or thirsty, and give you a drink? When did we see you as a stranger, and take you in; or naked, and clothe you? When did we see you sick, or in prison, and come to you?'

"The king will answer them, 'Most certainly I tell you, because you did it to one of the least of these my brothers, you did it to me.' Then he will say also to those on the left hand, 'Depart from me, you cursed, into the eternal fire which is prepared for the devil and his angels; for I was hungry, and you didn't give me food to eat; I was thirsty, and you gave me no drink; I was a stranger, and you didn't take me in; naked, and you didn't clothe me; sick, and in prison, and you didn't visit me.'

"Then they will also answer, saying, 'Lord, when did we see you hungry, or thirsty, or a stranger, or naked, or sick, or in prison, and didn't help you?'

"Then he will answer them, saying, 'Most certainly I tell you, because you didn't do it to one of the least of these, you didn't do it to me.' These will go away into eternal punishment, but the righteous into eternal life. [49]

This parable is a double-edged sword. On the one hand, it visualizes God as identifying with and being concerned for the hungry, the thirsty, the lonely, the sick and even the imprisoned. This is the loving, compassionate God who feels empathy for us when we're at our lowest points – even, presumably, when we have fallen so short morally that we are in prison. On the other hand, it visualizes God as a harsh judge walking the Earth in disguise and, when any opportunity to change our behavior has ended, meting out the most frightening of punishments for behavior that is not even considered a crime in secular culture. One thing we know for sure is that we know we want to be sheep. Let's be honest, most of us read this passage with the calm assurance that we *are* sheep and that we can name a half a dozen goats that we wouldn't mind seeing punished. We know that even if we fall short, God will forgive us as long as we demonstrate the proper contrition – and of course we will. In short, we really like the story of the sheep and the goats – some Biblical commentators go so far as to call it a "much-loved" passage[50] - because it provides such a practical, accessible way of interacting with a God Who otherwise seems so inaccessible. Whatever God might be, we know it is important that His will be done. But how can we be sure what that will is? Whatever God might be, we know we should love Him. But how can love manifest itself at such a distance? We know we are to seek encounter with God, but what purpose does that encounter serve? Here are concrete, manageable guidelines against which we can measure ourselves and others. God's will is that we act charitably towards others. To love and serve God is to love and serve others. To encounter God is to encounter others with sensitivity and to confer real-world benefits to them and relieve real-world problems for them. The simple, straightforward, practical metric this provides seems reason enough to try to simply ignore the glaring problem of free will this passage exemplifies and to gloss over the image of an angry God that is included within it. Sure, it's a little insipid and requires very little more of us than is already required by secular morality. But it allows us to make sense of faith and the duties of faith. It allows us to define our faith in terms of purpose, responsibility, and consequences.

The parable of the sheep and the goats is utterly dependent on free will. It highlights the fundamental dichotomy in Christianity between the conditionally loving and unconditionally loving God. God commands that we act lovingly, or face the fires of hell. By this standard, God's commandment to love one another as He has loved us doesn't represent a challenge. It would mean that there is no duty to love unconditionally, but rather, only encouragement to love transactionally. How do we reconcile this theme that undeniably echoes throughout Scripture with what philosophy and science tell us about human free will? How can it be consistent with the story of the Garden? How can we wrest a loving God from this?

Much of the rest of this book will be dedicated to exploring and seeking to resolve this tension.

> Since Adam, being free to choose,
> Chose to imagine he was free
> To choose his own necessity,
> Lost in freedom, Man pursues
> The shadow of his images.[51]

Chapter Two

Ontology, Psychological Evolution and Intuition

All that matters is to be at one
with the living God
To be a creature in the house of the
God of Life
Like a cat asleep on a chair
at peace, in peace
and at home with the master of the house,
with the mistress,
at home, at home, in the house of the living
sleeping on the hearth, and yawning
before the fire
sleeping on the hearth of the living world
yawning at home before the fire of life
feeling the presence of the living God
like a great reassurance
a deep calm in the heart
a presence
as of the master sitting at the board

in his own and greater being,
in the house of life.[52]

PART ONE
THE PLATONIC GOD

The Greek God of Christianity

Christianity, a faith whose principal message is God's unconditional forgiveness of sins, has become overwhelmingly distracted by sin. The opening chapters of our Scripture include a warning against eating the fruit of moral judgment, and yet our faith has become so closely identified with moral judgment that sometimes faith and morality are treated as virtual synonyms. To be Christian, for many, means to behave well and charitably, to develop our talents for the good of others, to be humble, and to adopt certain political views - either on the liberal or on the conservative side. People who leave faith assure themselves that they are 'good people' and, since their secular lives don't violate the Christian ethic, the question of the nature of God's relationship to us has no further claim on their time or attention. How did this happen? The answer appears to be that we stopped worshipping the Judeo-Christian God of Scripture in favor of an ancient Greek god of philosophy. This came naturally to us because ancient Greek philosophy included attempts to prove the existence of that god, and, rather than being counter-cultural and challenging our natural impulses to seek command, reward and punishment, Greek philosophy satiated our desire for command, reward and punishment. It is the ultimate idolatry.

Readers of the New Testament can hardly miss the influence of Roman culture and the Roman occupation of Palestine on Christianity. Matthew's story of the nativity of Jesus includes the scheming of Herod the Great, the Roman-installed king of Judea, to murder all the male children in Bethlehem in an attempt to prevent the new Messiah from challenging him which causes Mary and Joseph to flee to Egypt.[53] Upon Herod's death, his kingdom was divided among his three sons: Archelaus, Herod Antipas, and Philip[54]. When Joseph, Mary and the infant Jesus return from Egypt after Herod's death, it was Archelaus's rule over Bethlehem that causes them to re-route to Nazareth in Galilee instead.[55] Archelaus's despotism was so offensive even to Rome that he was eventually removed from office and his kingdom was declared a province of Rome to be ruled by proconsuls. Jesus's ministry takes him to Jerusalem and it was Proconsul Pontius Pilate who tried to hand off the arrested Jesus to Herod Antipas (king of Galilee and visiting Jerusalem for Passover like Jesus), but who eventually succumbs to the mob and sentences Jesus to death. In Jesus's lifetime, corrupt tax collectors appointed by the Roman occupiers are the quintessential sinners. A Roman centurion's statement, "Lord, I am not worthy that you should enter under my roof, but only say the word and my soul shall be healed,"[56] is the responsorial recited by the congregation at the crescendo of the Catholic Mass. And a Roman centurion is given the honor of declaring Jesus as the Son of God at the foot of the Cross[57] while, it is implied, his apostles and disciples have lost faith and hid. The Greek occupation, which began 270 years before it fractured and was ultimately supplanted by the Romans sixty years before Jesus's birth, is not mentioned in the New Testament, but it had far greater and more persistent influence on Christianity.

Paul in Athens

Just over four hundred years before Jesus, there was an aligning of stars around a few men that would reverberate powerfully in culture, philosophy and faith to the present day. It is not clear whether Socrates actually existed or if he was an invention of the people who wrote about him. Nonetheless, he (or the men for whom he is a pseudonym) is widely considered to be the founder of Western philosophy. Everything that came before was pre-Socratic and everything that came after can be traced back to his thought, making Socrates, real or imagined, one of the most influential individuals in history. What we know of Socrates comes from several ancient writers, but none are more influential, and none wrote more detailed accounts of Socrates's life and thinking than Plato, who claimed to have been a student of Socrates. We know with greater certainly that Plato actually existed, that Aristotle was a student of Plato, and that Aristotle, in turn, was Alexander the Great's private tutor. Of course, Alexander the Great would go on to conquer and rule as a single empire a massive swath of the known world from Greece to India, and south through the Holy Land and Egypt. Greek colonization followed and Greek culture and

Greek language became preeminent throughout this part of the world. From the death of Alexander in 323 BC until the ascendance of the Roman Empire in 31 BC, is known to historians as the Hellenistic Period. Another student of Aristotle, Demetrius of Phaleron, is credited with beginning the Library of Alexandria in Egypt (Alexandria, having been founded by and, of course, named after Alexander the Great) during the rule of Ptolmey I and II, from a family of Greek ethnicity that ruled Egypt and the native Egyptian population following the collapse of Alexander's empire. According to legend, Demetrius wanted to add the Torah to the library's collection and petitioned Ptolemy II to have the Torah translated from the original Hebrew to Greek, the official language of the Egyptian empire at the time. Ptolemy agreed and asked the high priest in Jerusalem to send to Alexandria seventy-two elders - six from each of the tribes of Israel - to generate the translation for the library. In one version of the legend, the seventy-two elders were each placed in a separate cell and asked to translate the Torah independently. Miraculously, each produced precisely the same text. This translation (miraculous or not) is commonly known as the Septuagint, from the Latin word for seventy, reflecting the legend of the seventy-two translators with a little mathematical rounding. Over time, additional books in addition to the Torah were added to the Septuagint including some that were never written in Hebrew or Aramaic but were originally composed in Greek. The Septuagint was the principal version of the Old Testament that was circulating at the time of Jesus and was very clearly the translation used by the authors of the New Testament. Judaism, about a century after the birth of Jesus, would finally and definitively reject some of the books of the Septuagint and Protestantism followed suit, deeming them less genuine. Catholicism however, maintained its reliance on the Septuagint and to this day Catholic bibles include the books of Tobit, Judith, Wisdom of Solomon, and others, while Protestant bibles do not; or when they do, include them under the label "Apocrypha." The translation of the Torah into Greek is not a universally celebrated event in Judaism and in fact, it is mourned along with the siege of Jerusalem by Nebuchadnezzar II on the Tenth of Tevet of each year (about a week after Hanukah) by some sects of Judaism. It is a sad commemoration because the translation inevitably obscures some of the sacred meaning of the original text being trans-lated. And, in fact, we know this to be the case, as we'll see.

Christianity was born into a Hellenistic world. Christianity's early impulse to spread and evangelize made its contact with Greek philosophy, and Greek philosophy's influence on Christianity, virtually inevitable. Perhaps no discrete moment in history exemplifies the influence of Greek philosophy on the developing Christian faith and theology as the moment, recorded in Acts, when Paul, killing time in Athens while he waited for his traveling companions, told the Athenians that they were already familiar with the God of Scripture and they already worshiped Him at an altar erected in the name of the Unknown God:

Paul stood in the middle of the Areopagus, and said, "You men of Athens, I perceive that you are very religious in all things. For as I passed along, and observed the objects of your worship, I found also an altar with this inscription: 'TO AN UNKNOWN GOD.' What therefore you worship in ignorance, this I announce to you.[58]

If this event was historical (and there is some doubt), this may have been the first attempt to show that the Christian faith and Greek philosophy were compatible. For Greeks, philosophy encompassed physics, math and logic, and so Christianity's connection to it, allowed Christianity to graft an entire cross-disciplined world of ideas onto itself. I get a small sense of pleasure – maybe a satisfying sense of comradery – whenever I see an *ichthys* symbol on the bumper of a car. The early Christians must have had a very similar sense when they heard and read the teachings of the ancient Greek philosophers. Here were elements of Christianity seemingly arrived at independently and objectively, by individuals with no evangelical agenda and no skin in the Christian game. The effect would have been heightened as time went on and the line between what Greek philosophy had seemingly predicted about the Christian God and what Christianity adopted from Greek philosophy blurred. Greek culture and philosophy were deeply concerned with morality and the assumption that we have free will was central. The confluence of Greek concern for morality and the Christian rejection of judgment resulted in an unlikely and unhealthy relationship. The premise of this book is that science and philosophy can inform faith about the nature of our relationship to God and, specifically, that the fact that science and philosophy have debunked free will requires us to re-examine our assumption that moral judgment is central to our relationship with God. Ironically, the problem that science and philosophy are now solving for faith by eliminating free will, was created by the science and philosophy of Plato's day by integrating it so closely with free will. Paul's identification of the Hebrew God with the Athenian god was perhaps the most disastrous moment in the history of Christian theology. While science and philosophy abandoned ancient Greek theory long ago, faith has hung onto it, intoxicated with the elusive promise that it will definitively and affirmatively prove God's existence, prove the immortality of our souls, and teach us how to follow God's commands to receive reward and avoid punishment. It has become so integrated into our language of faith and concept of God that we no longer even recognize it for the theological interloper that it is. It has essentially made God and morality synonymous.

The Theory of Forms; Dualism

When we try to draw a straight line with a pencil, we know that while the line may look perfectly straight to the human eye, it will inevitably not be a perfectly and mathematically straight line. We seem to have an intuitive standard by which to judge straight lines that doesn't necessarily correspond to any line we have seen in our lifetimes or even necessarily to any line that exists in the world. Similarly, although we have an idea of perfectly honest conduct, "honesty" doesn't exist as a real thing in the world; it is merely a concept, but one that all of us mysteriously share and can express in a relatively uniform manner. The same treatment applies to objects: I easily recognize the leaf of a maple tree as being in the same class of object, namely "leaves" as the leaf of a thyme plant. The fact that one is radically different from the other, and from other plants' leaves, doesn't prevent me from recognizing it as part of a class of the same kind. Furthermore, if in the autumn, the maple leaf changes from being alive and green to being dead and bright red, and finally falls off the tree, curls and turns brown, I can still recognize as being in the class of "leaf" throughout the process. Its change from one thing to another doesn't prevent me from classifying it as the same thing. How is it that we are able to classify these things despite the fact that they either do not exist in reality, like a straight line, or a mathematical proof, or are different from one another, or change dramatically? Plato argued that this indicates that these things exist in an alternate, superior universe as perfect and eternal objects or concepts. While our bodies rely on our senses to see and apprehend objects in the world, these senses can be mistaken or tricked and are not really reliable. Our minds or our souls, according to Plato, have access to the alternate universe where the perfect forms of these objects and concepts exist and which allow us to recognize them in this world. In this world, we see these objects, but only as pale projections of their real selves in the alternate universe. Plato offered his Allegory of the Cave to illustrate. He said that most of us are like condemned prisoners chained from birth in a cave facing a blank wall. We are able to see the shadows of things projected on a wall as they pass in front of a fire behind us, but we can't make out any detail. To Plato, the philosopher alone is able to free him or herself from the cave and come to know the true nature of the objects. Plato felt that our minds or souls have an imperfect hold on the visible world and sense things here imperfectly, but are fully at home in the transcendent world of Forms where we sense things perfectly. This is quintessential *dualism* – the idea that there is transcendent and inherently moral and inherently superior world that is the essence of all things but which is largely invisible to us, and a material world fully accessible to us that is susceptible to corruption and as much as it strives to find perfection, will never achieve it.

Ontology – Proof of God

Plato's transcendent world included a form of everything, but the most important form was the Form of the Good. It, Plato said, was the form that allowed us to see and understand all the other forms. In *The Republic*, Plato offers that the Form of the Good – which he also called "The One" – is so extraordinarily transcendent that it is the source of all other being and is itself "beyond being in power and in dignity"[59] 'The One' was both the source of all knowledge and itself unknowable or ineffable.

Plato's 'The One' sounded a lot like the Judeo-Christian God. In fact, in time, Plato's intellectual successors would suggest that two additional entities emanated from the One and were distinguishable from it but were not entirely independent of it either. One of these entities was *Nous*, which corresponded to intellect or spirit, and the other a cosmic Soul from which all other souls emanated and some of which formed and inhabited material bodies.[60] It would be an avid follower of Neo-Platonism and recent convert to Christianity named

Theophilus of Antioch[61], who in the second century would first use the word "Trinity" to describe the Father, Son and Holy Spirit – a concept that had no precedent in Scripture and didn't exist in Christianity until then. All this cross-pollination led to an extraordinarily tempting implication: that perhaps the Judeo-Christian God's existence could be proven finally and decisively by Greek philosophy and logic.

Shortly after the turn of the first millennium, St. Anselm, then the prior of a Benedictine Abbey in Bec in Normandy but who would eventually become the archbishop of Canterbury, defined God much like Plato would have defined 'The One' – "something than which nothing greater can be conceived." St. Anselm reasoned that God, so defined, must exist because otherwise we'd be thinking about something that is greater than something than which nothing greater can be conceived, which doesn't make sense. René Descartes, most famous for his philosophical assertion, "I think therefore I am" picked up Anselm's argument six hundred years later and repackaged it. A triangle, Descartes's reasoning began, is defined as having three sides. You cannot conceive of a triangle that does not have three sides because that is part of a triangle's definition. Similarly, you can't conceive of a perfect being that does not exist, because such a being would not be perfect. This is the *ontological argument* for the existence of God. The argument's Platonic lineage is fairly clear: because we can conceive of perfection, there must be a Form of Perfection that actually exists, and this Perfection is the Judeo-Christian God.

Cosmology – Proof of God

Plato's 'The One' and its cohorts had another role in the cosmos besides being the source of all being; and that was to be the source of all celestial movement. Plato asserted that all movement must have been started by something that is not moved by anything else and is self-moved. Plato called this entity a 'Soul' and Plato reasoned the Soul must be a god. According to Plato, this god accounts for the movement of the Sun and the Moon and the stars and all orderly and regular movement. This god, according to Plato, must be perfectly good and all powerful. Plato also asserted that there must be at least one additional god responsible for wild, irregular movement and all that is evil and destructive. Plato's student, Aristotle, built on the notion of the Cosmic Soul responsible for celestial movement and proposed that all motion everywhere begins with an Unmoved Mover. But because this entity is immortal, unchanging, and immaterial – not part of the physical world at all - the Unmoved Mover does not physically push the universe into motion, but rather inspires the universe into motion by being the cosmic object of desire.

Sixteen hundred years later, St. Thomas Aquinas, who was so enamored of Aristotle that he would refer to him in his writing simply as "The Philosopher" made essentially the same argument in favor of the Judeo-Christian God, calling God the "First Mover." This is the *cosmological argument* for the existence of God.

The Theory of Forms Leads to Cosmology and Ontology – The Perfect God Leads to the Problem of Evil and Leads to Free Will

These theories have been largely discredited. The idea that our ability to conceive of objects and ideas being dependent on a perfect form of each in actual existence elsewhere, has been largely abandoned. A First Mover explanation of the universe is no more compelling than the idea that movement had no beginning and will have no end. Whatever philosophical certainty Christian thinkers like Descartes and Aquinas hoped to achieve has evaporated and left us with some fairly impoverished assertions. But what is much worse is that these arguments came with very heavy baggage from which we have not yet fully relieved ourselves.

In attempting to prove God's existence, the ontological and cosmological arguments changed the God of Scripture into something quite different, almost from the very birth of Christianity. Instead of being a God who is good, God became the very definition of good. Instead of being a God who is knowing, God became the very definition of knowledge. Instead of being a God who is loving, God became love itself. Instead of being a God who is moved by love and pity, moved to be merciful; a God who suffers with us - God became immovable - a cold and emotionless ordering principle. We confused God with an omniscient, omnipotent, omnibenevolent and ontological god of Greek philosophy with disastrous results for faith.

The Perfect God Leads to the Problem of Evil

The ontological god is an omnipotent god, projecting its will into the material world without any effort – its will and reality are one and the same thing always and forever. Although the Judeo-Christian God of Scripture is powerful, it is clear that there are limits to His power. God rarely simply changes things. Most often, He acts through human intermediaries. The individuals God chooses as His instruments are never perfect – in fact, they are characterized by imperfection. Abraham and Sarah, chosen to be the father of innumerable progeny, are too old to have even one child without the intervention of the miraculous. Jacob, later to be renamed Israel, being the younger of two twins, must steal his elder twin's birthright to achieve his destiny. Moses initially refuses to negotiate against Pharaoh on behalf of the Israelites because he is a stutterer. Peter, destined to be the leader of the nascent Christian church, is the inveterate goofball of the New Testament and, despite being warned in advance of the challenge to come, denies Jesus three times as Jesus is being processed for execution. If there is a most prominent theme in Scripture, it is that the stone rejected by the builder becomes the cornerstone. God's human intermediaries are not even necessarily willing to go along with what God wants. Throughout Scripture, God must cajole and negotiate with His chosen people. While the ontological god floats dispassionately outside of the realm of the material, throughout Scripture God walks among His people, is incarnate in the material world and, above all else, is passionate. He is not passionately angry – that would be impossible for a just God in the absence of human free will - but He is passionately loving and passionately concerned for us – one might even say He is loving beyond all reason. Rather than being an unmovable god, the God of Scripture is vulnerable and sympathetic.

Clearly, the Judeo-Christian God has to abide by certain ordering principles of the universe. The Judeo-Christian God cannot, for instance, make murder a moral act.[62] It appears He cannot make happiness in the absence of unhappiness. Unlike an ontological god, the Judeo-Christian God has to toe the line between suffering and happiness, knowing that to eliminate the first will make the second impossible. In the Judeo-Christian universe, good and evil are not separate Forms in conflict with one another; they are inextricably intertwined and interdependent. The Christian story is all about the imperfect choices God must make. If He squeezes the balloon in one place, it expands in another. Sometimes He seems utterly dismayed by the imperfect creatures and imperfect world with which He is confronted. Although we shouldn't slip into anthropomorphism, it is clear the Christian God can have a bad day. By some mechanism, the universe can unfold contrary to God's expectations.

In 1814, prominent French mathematician and scientist, Pierre-Simon, Marquis de Laplace proposed what has come to be known as LaPlace's Demon: that if someone could determine the position and velocity of every atom in the universe, then he or she could mathematically determine the future for the rest of time. Quantum physics has thrown a wrench into this idea. In particular, Heisenberg's Uncertainty Principle indicates that, on the quantum level, the more precisely the position of a particle can be determined, the less precisely the momentum of the particle can be known at that instant, and vice versa. There is, in fact, indeterminacy and genuine randomness in the universe. The next movement of a quantum particle is not necessarily pre-determined or predictable.

Everything I have proposed in this book so far is not new. As we've seen, Baruch Spinoza argued that we do not have free will but did not see this as inconsistent with the existence of God. However, he conceived of God as an ordering principal, nature itself, and as something akin to an Unmoved Mover – impersonal and, for lack of better or less anthropomorphic term, without personality. Joseph Priestley also argued that we do not have free will and also saw no inconsistency with the existence of God. In fact, Priestley felt that assuming that human beings have free will contradicts the idea that God is all-seeing, and all knowing because it would render some part of the universe unpredictable.[63] All this made him very unpopular in theological circles. If we don't have free will, some argued, then God alone must be responsible for suffering. While Priestley's concept of God was far closer to the God of Scripture than Spinoza's, he could not imagine God as having anything less than total control over how the universe unfolds. For Priestley, although God might exhibit something like the personality attributed to Him in Scripture, that He is the First Cause of everything and has predicted everything from the beginning of time, is the definitional attribute of God.[64] Just as scientific orthodoxy of his time blinded Priestley from recognizing that oxygen was a component part of air, his theological orthodoxy blinded him from seeing that maybe the universe contained some randomness not fully in God's control. Priestley of course, had no way of anticipating Heisenberg's Uncertainty Principle and quantum mechanics. By rejecting free will, Priestley thought that we must live in an entirely deterministic universe. He accepted that God must be responsible for suffering, and asserted that every instance of suffering must be part of the divine plan for some ultimate good – cold comfort for those of us who He decides must suffer. Only in the last few decades has science made an alternate view possible: that we do not have free will but that the universe is nonetheless unpredictable - even to God. As best as I can tell, the idea that we do not have free will but that the universe may unfold in ways that God does not plan for is entirely unexplored philosophical and theological ground. The implications may be profound.

Christianity has for centuries made Plato's Problem of Evil its own by adopting a vision of God as Unmoved Mover and as therefore responsible for everything that occurs in the universe, both good and bad, unless free will intervenes. It has meant that if bad things happen to good people, they are being taught a lesson in humility or being punished for some bad behavior. Christians are often fond of explaining bad events by saying they are "God's plan" or that "God doesn't close one door without opening another." This is a cold comfort that implies we have a heartless god. The Christian conception of God as reflected in Scripture, who is sometimes outright flummoxed by His Creation, implies a much better, more accurate understanding of the universe without Plato's philosophy than with it. The universe is not loving. It is capricious, cold and hard. God, however, is loving. Spirituality that treats God as another name for nature or the universe, or as the answer for physics riddles, cannot make sense of that.

In Homer's *Odyssey*, as Odysseus sails for home following the fall of Troy, his ship has to sail past a group of sirens. In Greek mythology, beautiful sirens would lure passing mariners with their enchanting song, causing them to steer their ships into the rocks in blind lust. Odysseus gets a tip from the goddess, Circe, that he will be able to hear sirens' song without being killed if he plugs his fellow sailors' ears with wax, and has himself tied to the mast. The plan works and although Odysseus demands to be untied when he hears the sirens singing, his shipmates row on, oblivious to the temptation.[65]

Maybe God arranged the universe in such a way that it unfolds independently and in a way that God Himself cannot foretell. Like Odysseus telling his shipmates to tie him to the mast and not to untie him no matter how much he begs, maybe God has tied His own hands to allow the universe to proceed naturally, in its own time and its own manner, and with some mystery. This would certainly get God off the hook for a friend developing cancer, or the existence of cancer itself. It is not God's plan that anyone develop cancer, but is rather something that God can mourn with us. Perhaps the kind of creature we are requires us to experience suffering in order to experience happiness, and to have the risk of the bad in order to appreciate the good. And perhaps God is not willing to mete out suffering but, like a parent allowing their child to ride a bike without training wheels, God allows us to make our way in the universe knowing that it will inevitably result in both suffering and happiness. I sometimes wonder if God seems distant because He can't bear to watch us as we set out on our way. God does not permit Himself to relieve our suffering because, in the long run, He would be relieving us of our ability to experience happiness – to become whole.

According to the legend of the Buddha, Siddhartha's parents sequestered him in their palace and did not allow him to be exposed to any suffering whatsoever. It was only when he escaped and saw sickness, poverty, and decrepitude that his journey to enlightenment could begin. Any faith that promises to remove the *external* causes of suffering is clearly lying. Faith can only sooth the *internal* causes of suffering – to help us to decide to react to the inevitable suffering we will experience without increasing our suffering with worry or regret, or what our faith tells us about God's response to our suffering. To see light, we have to suffer darkness, to learn we have to suffer ignorance, to achieve we have to suffer challenge and want, and to be happy we need to first know suffering.

God taking away the circumstances that cause suffering is far rarer in Scripture than we may be inclined to think. God did not free the Israelites - He instructed Moses on how to cajole Pharaoh to free the Israelites. Noah was not spared the Flood, but was instructed on how to survive it. Jesus rarely takes credit for miracles of healing. Rather, as we'll explore further in Chapter 6, Jesus says that it is the faith of the healed person that is responsible for the miracle. God's role is most often as fellow sufferer.

"Com-passion" means to "suffer with." God is the god of compassion, not the God of miraculous changes of circumstances or a cosmic good luck charm. Jesus is not the symbol of God's ability to relieve suffering. Jesus is the embodiment of God's compassion and willingness to walk with us. The Incarnation of God as Jesus demonstrates that He is unable to untie himself from the mast without denying us something more valuable, but He does not sit dispassionately on a heavenly throne out of the blood and muck. He chose to suffer with us and continues to suffer with us. The mystic, Julian of Norwich, who we will discuss in greater detail below, said that Jesus's suffering did not end on Good Friday because he is re-crucified every time one of us suffers.[66] If God is suffering with us then by calling us into being, God ensures His own suffering just as surely as the price of allowing us to find happiness. In the end, no amount of suffering can overcome the basic good of existence. The civil litigation system has enormous trouble with wrongful life cases – situations where a physician screws up a tubal ligation or vasectomy and a profoundly disabled child is born. The system usually seeks to compensate victims who have been injured by monetizing what they have lost. When someone who wasn't supposed to exist in the first place is born into suffering, it stands the usual goals of the system on its head. No one can say that they would have lost something by being born. No matter what may happen to God's creatures in the vagaries of the universe to which He consigns us at birth, calling them into being was not a cold act of an uncaring God but rather the ultimate act of selflessness.

This is no Unmoved Mover as imagined by Plato or Thomas Aquinas. This is no god as synonym for Nature as imagined by Spinoza – so perfect and immutable that He cannot desire anything but what already is. And this is no heartless god of Priestley, dispassionately dispensing suffering as a down payment on a better future. This is a living God capable of interaction with His creatures and capable of compassion and pity and love. Theistic determinism tells us that, while God is compassionate, He is not capable of rage or hatred for His unfree creatures. "For He Himself knows our frame; He is mindful that we are but dust." [67]

While the co-existence of suffering and a loving God was natural to the Judeo-Christian God who clearly had to operate within certain parameters, it was a major problem for Greek philosophy which defined the ontological god in terms of perfection and power, and this is where Christianity's allegiance to Greek philosophy became an albatross. By recasting God in the image of the ontological god, Christianity has adopted this problem - the *Problem of Evil* - as its own.

The only reasonable limitation on the ontological god's willingness and ability to make the world perfect is free will. Anything that results in suffering cannot be the result of any act or omission of the ontologically good god. And so suffering must be the result of someone or something else's free choice – a choice the good god is not at liberty to change. And so the free will of human beings was assumed to be responsible for evil caused by human hands, and the free will of a second god – an evil god with virtually all the power associated with the first god – was assumed to be responsible for earthquakes, cancer and other natural disasters. An attractive alternative, that sometimes co-exists with the first theory of suffering, was that it may be that the ontological god, as a function of its ontological goodness, must reward and punish us with natural disasters and illness according to our free choice to be good or bad or to believe or not to believe.

Because Greek philosophy offered the seductive promise of proving God's existence philosophically, Christianity was willing to reimagine God as Plato's god. So strong was the assumption that the two traditions were talking about the same god that Scripture was unconsciously re-interpreted to serve as further evidence. Instead of being a story about the illusory nature of free will and the absurdity and peril of moral judgment, The Garden of Eden became an improbable story about humanity obtaining free will and, apparently in the same instant, exercising it to incur the wrath of an otherwise loving God for generations. A free choice made by an ancient ancestor knocked the world off its axis and somehow forced the all-powerful ontological god to allow suffering to enter what otherwise necessarily would have been a perfect world, never to fully leave it again. One way or the other, because of our allegiance to ontology, free will became a central theme of the Christian message, even though the fit was terrible. Rather than diminishing over time as science and philosophy distanced itself from Plato,

Christianity's understanding of God has become more and more entangled with Platonism, even in modernity.

Most of the men who we recognize as the fathers of Christian doctrine: Philo, Plino, Origen, St. Augustine, St. Anselm, St. Thomas Aquinas, are all instantly recognizable as Platonists. In their desire to borrow from Platonism to prove God's existence, they have become ensnared in it instead. Platonism has been a distraction from the true nature of God's relationship to us virtually from the beginning. It was in the 1600s that Baruch Spinoza conceived of God as identical with everything in the universe; impersonal, immovable and the very Form of Perfection. In our era, writers such as Paul Tillich, A.T. Robinson, and the later writings of Dietrich Bonhoeffer, show a marked preference for the Platonic god over the Judeo-Christian God. To say that these thinkers support the idea that God is powerful is understatement – they tend to define God as the very ground of Being or the unity of all Reality, but in so doing they diminish or outright dismiss the one divine capacity Scripture emphasizes over all others – the capacity to encounter, empathize with, suffer with, and love individual human beings.

The growing evidence that free will is an illusion is not a challenge to faith, but is an opportunity to place faith on a more solid foundation. It allows us to take a fresh look at Scripture and our own intuition of God and discern if there is a more compelling image of God there that we haven't seen before – one that is free from Plato's influence. We find ourselves with a chance, not really available to past generations of Christians

– maybe not possible since Paul's arrival in Athens - to reconcile science and faith in a profound manner and to allow science to guide our understanding of our relationship to God.

PART TWO
THE SOUL

One reason why we so fervently want to believe that we have free will is that we believe whatever gives us the capacity for free will is the part of us that directs what our bodies do during life, survives death, is submitted to the judgment of God, and is finally directed to an appropriate afterlife. The argument against free will often goes hand-in-hand with the argument against dualism – it contradicts the idea that we are made up of two parts: fleshy bodies that respond to stimuli and immaterial souls that have free will.

Horseman of the New Atheism, Daniel C. Dennett, uses an almost mocking tone when speaking about the soul in relation to free will. Dr. Dennett opens his book, *Freedom Evolves*, closely identifying our desire for free will with belief in a soul:

> One widespread tradition has it that we human beings are responsible agents, captains of our fate, because what we really are are souls, immaterial and immortal clumps of Godstuff that inhabit and control our material bodies rather like spectral puppeteers.[68]

In my view, Dennett and others have legitimately disproven freedom of the will and the necessity of a soul to explain human behavior. The assumption, however, that this somehow disproves God's existence and that dualism is a critical component of Christianity or Christianity's hope in an afterlife, is a tremendous leap.

Greek Soul

Dualism was critical to Plato's thought – the idea that there is a realm of the physical and there is a realm of the transcendent. The Theory of Forms essentially distinguished between a perfect, eternal, transcendent world, and the imperfect, temporary, material and visible one. To Plato, our ability to access both worlds meant that we straddled the transcendent and the material. He reasoned that the soul's familiarity with the eternity of the transcendent world implied that the soul is immortal.

Plato adapted existing Greek thinking about the soul to illustrate his own philosophy. In *Gorgias* and again in the closing pages of *The Republic*, Plato vividly describes what we would call a near-death experience.

The Myth of Er

In Plato's Gorgias, Plato imagines a dialogue between Socrates and Callicles, who serves as a foil for Socrates's positions. As the dialogue closes, Socrates foretells his own execution for corrupting the youth of Athens and failing to recognize the deities of Athens. He asserts that he would never be defenseless in such a trial because he has done no wrong, but he might be incapable of convincing his philosophically challenged persecutors of his innocence. In that case, Socrates says, he would not fear execution and death:

> For no man who is not an utter fool and coward is afraid of death itself, but he is afraid of doing wrong. For to go to the world below having one's soul full of injustice is the last and worst of all evils. And in proof of what I say, if you have no objection, I should like to tell you a story.

Socrates then relates an account of the afterlife. He opens by exhorting his audience: "Listen, then, as story-tellers say, to a very pretty tale, which I dare say that you may be disposed to regard as a fable only, but which, as I believe, is a true tale, for I mean to speak the truth." Socrates tells us that the immutable laws of heaven require that when good people die, they go to the Islands of the Blessed to live in happiness, free from suffering. On the other hand, bad people go to Tartarus, "the house of vengeance and punishment."[69]

But there is an administrative problem, which is what draws Socrates's attention to the story. This judgment occurs on the day the individual to be judged is to die, but before his or her death actually has taken place. The judges also are living people and prone to error and prejudice. The authorities of the Islands of the Blessed complain to Zeus that souls are arriving at the wrong place. Zeus determines that the principal problem is that because the individual being judged is alive and clothed, the judges could be unduly influenced by clothing that indicates wealth or social status. To solve this problem, Zeus decrees that henceforth we will no longer know in advance when we will die, and we will be judged after death when we are naked – having left our "brave attire strewn upon the earth." Zeus names his three sons as the judges, and announces one of them to be the final court of appeal.

It is fairly clear from Socrates's analysis of the story that he believes being sentenced to Tartarus is, in most cases, a temporary circumstance. In addition to determining a soul's destination, the judges are also charged with stamping those sent to Tartarus as either curably or incurably evil and the latter are condemned to eternal torment. People in power are the most susceptible to being judged incurable and Socrates singles out as an example Archelaus, who had taken the throne of Macedonia by assassinating his uncle and half-brother, as someone who is certainly condemned to eternal damnation.[70]

With the use of this fable, Socrates asserts that good behavior in life will be rewarded in the afterlife while bad behavior inevitably results in punishment.

Plato ends his best-known work, *The Republic*, in a very similar fashion. Socrates, again the principal player, this time is in dialogue with a man names Glaucon. Socrates asserts the conclusion that he reached in *Gorgias*, that "the nature of both the just and unjust is truly known to the gods." Glaucon agrees, and Socrates continues that the just must receive from the gods only good things and if they suffer at all, it must be as a result of their former sins. Most behavior, Socrates asserts, is rewarded or punished during life, but it is in the afterlife that the accounts are finally settled; "All these are as nothing either in number or greatness in comparison with those other recompenses which await both the just and unjust after death."

Socrates relates to Glaucon the story of Er, who is killed in battle but a full twelve days after his death, wakes up to tell a remarkable tale of the afterlife. In classic Platonic dualistic form, Er says his soul left his body and went on a journey with a group of other souls. They finally arrived at a place with two openings next to each other in the earth and another pair of openings in the sky above. It turns out these are literally the entrance and exit to hell and heaven. Judges sit in the space between the holes and command the just to ascend to heaven and the unjust to descend to hell, the latter carrying symbols of their bad deeds fastened to their backs. At this point, Er is told that he is intended to serve as a messenger to bring back to the world of the living a description of the afterlife. As Er is standing there, souls emerge from the two exit holes. Those emerging from heaven are "clean and bright," they hug each other and walk to a nearby meadow and encamp as though they are at a festival. They describe to Er and the other souls a place of extraordinary happiness and beauty. By contrast, those who emerged from hell were dirty and tired and described their journey with weeping and sorrow. It is revealed that these souls were in their respective heaven or hell for a thousand years and each received reward or punishment ten times more than their behavior warranted. But, like in *Gorgias*, the term limit on suffering did not apply to everyone. In this case, a man named Ardiaeus the Great who lived a thousand years before Er's death and might have been expected to emerge from hell while Er was there, was nowhere to be seen. Like Archelaus, Ardiaeus was guilty of ascending to power by parricide – having killed his father and brother. When the souls asked about him they were told by another that, "He comes not hither and will never come." The souls in hell witnessed Ardiaeus attempt to re-ascend through the mouth of the cave only to have the cave roar. Demonic men, "wild men of fiery aspect," these soul related, seized Ardiaeus, bound him hand and foot, flayed him, and dragged him along the ground, "to be cast into hell."

Er and the other souls then were processed for re-entry into the world of the living. A prophet scattered sample lives among them from which the souls could choose their next life. Er reported that there were many more lives to choose from than there were souls to do the choosing and the lives ran the full gamut of possibilities. The souls could choose to be an animal in their next life, a tyrant, a celebrity, and could choose lives of either gender. They could choose of life of poverty or wealth, sickness or health. The first soul to choose did so unwisely. Having spent its previous life in comfort and having merited heaven for the last thousand years, it was complacent and chose a life of a tyrant. While it had led a good life previously, its goodness was from sheer force of habit and because its circumstances never challenged it morally. Now, it chose rashly, and was fated to consume its own children and almost certainly wind up in hell in the next go around. Some famous souls happened to be present as well. Odysseus, the quintessential hero of Greek literature, was slated to choose his next life last. He considered carefully and chose a humble life out of the limelight, without ambition or the corresponding stress. He was delighted to find this life lying around, passed over by all the other souls.

With the myth Er, Plato is asserting that our behavior is ultimately either rewarded or punished, so we had better behave ourselves. But he has another purpose as well. Plato ends both *Gorgias* and *The Republic* with these mythologies not only because he has the standard-issue dislike of immoral people and wants to see them punished, but also because it is an inevitable product of his theology. As the souls have the choice of new lives presented to them, they listen to a remarkable speech by a prophet:

> Mortal souls, behold a new cycle of life and mortality. Your genius will not be allotted to you, but you will choose your genius ... Virtue is free, and a man who honors or dishonors her will have more or less of her; the responsibility is with the chooser – God is justified.[71]

If God is conceived of as the Form of Good, then something else must be responsible for suffering and bad behavior. For Plato, the answer is free will. But clearly on some level Plato recognizes that the circumstances of our birth – our nature and our nurture – determine whether we will behave well or behave badly. To correct for this, Plato imagines that we have a soul separate from our body that freely chooses our nature and nurture and then promptly forgets having made the choice, and a god who judges and punishes the shortfalls. Having assumed that we have moral autonomy at least in our choice of life, Plato is then free to imagine eternal torment for the immoral person.

Judeo-Christian Soul

Dualism pervades Plato's understanding of the afterlife. The immaterial soul, of its own volition, tears itself away from the discarded material body and makes its way to a place where it is judged for how it conducted the activity of the material body during life. The soul is then treated to reward, or subjected to punishment, accordingly and is finally processed to inhabit a new material body. Plato's view is obviously susceptible to Dennett's critique. It is neurochemistry, rather than immaterial, immortal souls, that conducts the moral activity of our material bodies. This neurochemistry shows no capacity to survive the death of our bodies and, of its own volition, to carry on after the brain that produces it has stopped working. Fortunately, this Platonic view of the soul is not the Judeo-Christian view, although Dennett cannot be blamed for mischaracterizing our views. We have allowed Hellenistic influences to creep in our language and understanding of the soul.

The Jewish understanding of the afterlife was conceived much later than we might think, was envisioned in a radical different fashion from Plato's afterlife, and did not include punishment or eternal torment in a fiery hell. Judaism did not embrace a robust or meaningful concept of an afterlife until about two hundred years before Jesus's birth. This challenges the view of some atheists that belief in God arises from a desire for immortality, as Judaism arose, developed and thrived for centuries without providing for it. The ancient Jewish belief was that death was a final end of any kind of meaningful consciousness or ability to interact with God. The deaths of major Old Testament characters were noted in the Bible with no mention of any hope of afterlife. God ruminates over what to do about Adam and Eve after they have eaten from the Tree of the Knowledge of Good and Evil. God decides He must banish them from the Garden before they eat from the Tree of Life and achieve immortality. In a statement of total rejection of dualism, God reminds Adam that he fashioned him from the soil and announces that they will work for their livelihood until they return to the ground "for out of it you were taken; you are dust and to dust you shall return" – and, in fact, Adam's name means humus or dust. Whatever the reasoning, this early text clearly did not include any immaterial soul or afterlife for the characters. After the birth of Noah's sons but before the Flood, God suddenly and mysteriously shortens the span of human life. Where the descendants of Adam lived nine hundred years or more, now God, recalling the animating breath he breathed into the soil that he had formed into Adam, decrees that, "My spirit shall not abide in man forever, for he is flesh, but his days shall be one hundred and twenty years."[72] Noah, having been born before the decree lives to be nine hundred and fifty when he dies. His death is reported very simply as, "and he died"[73] There is no mention of a soul leaving a body. So too, the passing of Sarah, Abraham, Miriam and Moses all occur with a note of finality, describing details of burial but no expectation of survival. There are two exceptions to this rule. The first is the death of Enoch, a decedent of Adam and predecessor to Noah which includes some ambiguous language:

> And Enoch walked with God after he begot Methuselah three hundred years, and he begot sons and daughters. And all the days of Enoch were three hundred and sixty-five years. And Enoch walked with God and he was no more, for God took him.[74]

The meaning of this passage is unclear. The repetition of Enoch's walking with God may be instructive. Enoch walks with God and produces children and later walks with God after the end of his natural life – both seem like activities of a physical manifestation of Enoch rather than a soul. The other exception is the prophet Elijah who, we are told, does not die at all but is instead taken up into heaven by a fiery chariot pulled by horses in a whirlwind.[75] What is important to our purposes is that in both instances it appears that life after death is bodily – it is not an immaterial soul that enjoys continued existence, but rather the material body that, with God's intervention, continues to have life. In the Psalms and in Isaiah a concept vaguely like an immaterial soul is mentioned. The soul seems to descend into Sheol, but it does not appear to have any sort of consciousness, to enjoy (or suffer) an afterlife, or to be in the company of God:

Come back, Lord, deliver my life,
Rescue me for the sake of Your kindness.
For death holds no mention of You
In Sheol who can acclaim You?[76]

Psalm 6

The heavens are the Lord's heavens,
and the earth He has given to humankind.
The dead do not praise the Lord
Nor all who go down into silence.[77]

Psalm 115

Psalms and Isaiah also include the barest hints of
God's ability (or motivation) to rescue a person
from Sheol.
Lord you brought me up from Sheol,
Gave me life from those gone down to the Pit.[78]

Psalm 30

Will he yet live forever?
Will he not see the Pit?
For he sees the wise die,

both fool and the stupid man perish,
and they abandon to others their wealth
Their grave is their home forever,
their dwelling for all generations,
though their names had been called upon earth.

...

And they wear out their image in Sheol,
a habitation for them.
But God will ransom my life,
From the grip of Sheol He will take me. [79]

Psalm 49

Where can I go from Your spirit,
and where from before You flee?
If I soar to the heavens, You are there,
if I bed down in Sheol – there You are.[80]

Psalm 139

Behold, for peace I had great anguish,
but you have in love for my soul delivered it from
the pit of corruption;
for you have cast all my sins behind your back.
For Sheol can't praise you.
Death can't celebrate you.
Those who go down into the pit can't hope for
your truth.[81]

Isaiah 38

It is possible that it was the interpretation of these passages
that allowed Jewish thinkers in the last centuries before Jesus's

birth to assert that God resurrects the dead despite the pau-
city of Scriptural support. However it happened, by the time
of Jesus, resurrection was a commonly held belief among the
Jewish people. We know from Scripture and a Jewish-Roman
historian named Josephus who wrote about fifty years after
Jesus death, that the Pharisees believed in life after death.[82]
The Pharisees' theology allowed them to creatively re-interpret Scripture to fill in gaps and to clarify the legal requirements of Torah. This may well have been the reason why they
defended and possibly developed the idea that God resurrects
the dead. We also know, directly from the New Testament, that
the Sadducees distinguished themselves from the Pharisees by
opposing this view. The Sadducees were the Martin Luthers of
their time, insisting that only Scripture itself was authoritative
and no oral tradition had any binding authority. As such, they
disputed any concept of life after death preferring the guidance of the early Old Testament which indicated that death was
final. Jesus comes closest to a philosophical argument when he
contradicts the Sadducees, saying God's declaration that He is
the God of Abraham, Isaac and Jacob, means those men must
be alive:

And Sadducees came to him, who say that
there is no resurrection; and they asked him a
question ... [to which Jesus replied] And as for
the dead being raised, have you not read in
the book of Moses, in the passage about the
bush, how God said to him, 'I am the God of

Abraham, and the God of Isaac, and the God of Jacob'? He is not the God of the dead, but of the living; you are quite wrong." [83]

For all his grousing against the Pharisees it's pretty clear Jesus had some sympathy for their theology - particularly on the issue of life after death. Paul also was a Pharisee, as he reveals in a remarkable scene in Acts where he plays the sects against each other:

Paul, looking steadfastly at the council, said, "Brothers, I have lived before God in all good conscience until today."

The high priest, Ananias, commanded those who stood by him to strike him on the mouth.

Then Paul said to him, "God will strike you, you whitewashed wall! Do you sit to judge me according to the law, and command me to be struck contrary to the law?"

Those who stood by said, "Do you malign God's high priest?"

Paul said, "I didn't know, brothers, that he was high priest. For it is written, 'You shall not speak evil of a ruler of your people.' " But when Paul perceived that the one part were Sadducees and the other Pharisees, he cried out in the council, "Men and brothers, I am a Pharisee, a son of Pharisees. Concerning the hope and resurrection of the dead I am being judged!"

When he had said this, an argument arose between the Pharisees and Sadducees, and the crowd was divided. For the Sadducees say that there is no resurrection, nor angel, nor spirit; but the Pharisees confess all of these. A great clamor arose, and some of the scribes of the Pharisees' part stood up, and contended, saying, "We find no evil in this man. But if a spirit or angel has spoken to him, let's not fight against God!"

When a great argument arose, the commanding officer, fearing that Paul would be torn in pieces by them, commanded the soldiers to go down and take him by force from among them, and bring him into the barracks.[84]

It would be easy to assume that Pharisaic Judaism adopted the Platonic notion of an immortal soul because the notion of an afterlife seemed to gain prominence when Greek influence was at its highest in Palestine. However, while the Platonic afterlife was a dualist notion of the separation of an immaterial soul from its body, the Jewish afterlife was, almost without exception, non-dualistic – the resurrection of the body itself. Dennett's criticism has no foothold here.

Perhaps the best example of the corporeal nature of resurrection in the Jewish tradition of the time and the early Christian tradition is the resurrection of Jesus.[85] After all, in Christianity, Jesus's resurrection implies the promise of our own resurrection, and we have no Scriptural basis to expect ours to be a resurrection of an immaterial soul, while his was the resurrection of his material body.

Each of the Gospels and Acts includes details of Jesus's appearance after the Resurrection that can only be explained as a strong desire to affirm that Jesus was resurrected bodily, in the Jewish tradition, rather than as a Platonic immaterial soul.

In the Gospel of Matthew, as Mary Magdalene and another Mary run from the tomb to tell the disciples that Jesus had risen, they meet Jesus and Matthew records that "they came up and took hold of his feet." In Mark, a mysterious young man in a white robe invites the two Marys to look at the place where Jesus had lain and confirm for themselves that the body was gone. In Luke, several women see the empty tomb but the real proof of Jesus's bodily resurrection is Jesus's appearance among them. He invites them to confirm it: "See my hands and my feet that it is I myself; handle me, and see; for a spirit has not flesh and bones as you see that I have." They are still doubtful and, as if to provide incontrovertible evidence, he asks for food. "They gave him a piece of broiled fish, and he took it and ate it before them."[86] In John, Mary Magdalene sees the empty tomb and is distraught. Jesus appears to her but commands her not to touch him because he had not yet ascended to God. Thomas is absent from Jesus's first appearance to the disciples and expresses doubt. Jesus appears again, this time with Thomas present, and invites him to put his finger in the wounds on his hand and his hand into the wound on Jesus's side. Finally, in Acts, Jesus is bodily swept into heaven in front of the apostles in a scene reminiscent of Elijah's ascent.[87] However resurrection may take place, clearly the earliest tradition was not dualistic and did not depend on the existence of an immaterial soul thrown clear of the body at death.

This non-dualistic tradition does survive into modern Christianity. The Apostles' Creed, which is sometimes recited instead of the Nicene Creed, especially during the Easter season, specifically states this anti-Platonic principle. It concludes:

I believe in the Holy Spirit,
the holy catholic Church,
the communion of saints,
the forgiveness of sins,
the resurrection of the body,
and life everlasting. Amen.

Even as Jesus tells the story of the afterlife of Lazarus and the rich man in the Gospel of Luke,[88] which we will examine in much greater detail later on, Jesus avoids imagery of an immaterial soul leaving a material body. Although he adopts Greek imagery of ascension to heaven and descent in to hell (using the Greek word "Hades" instead of the Jewish "Sheol") it is the bodily Lazarus who enjoys heaven and the bodily rich man who suffers the fires of hell. As we'll see, this allegory is not intended to be Jesus's theology on the afterlife at all, but it is interesting that while he freely borrows from Greek mythology to construct his story, he does not adopt its dualism.

The Wisdom of Solomon

There is one prominent exception to this rule which deserves some scrutiny. The Wisdom of Solomon does present the soul and body as separate entities in an overtly dualistic manner. The author is silent with respect to resurrection of the body and clearly envisions the survival of an immaterial spirit. This is expressed in beautiful terms, comparing souls to mysterious sparks, probably referring to the appearance of St. Elmo's fire in harvested fields in the winter-dry air:

> In the time of their visitation they will shine and will run back and forth like sparks through the stubble.[89]

The author begins by mocking those who believe they can act immorally because they will escape punishment at death.

> Because we were born by mere chance, and hereafter we will be as though we had never been; because the breath in our nostrils is smoke, and reason is a spark kindled by the

> beating of our heart; which being extinguished,
> the body will be turned into ashes, and the
> spirit will be dispersed as thin air.[90]

But these individuals will be surprised, says the author, because God has created human souls for immortality and He will judge them at the end of their lives and reward the worthy with peace and punish the unworthy with torment. This is very similar to the Myth of Er, and the parallels to Platonism don't end there. It is paying attention to Wisdom that leads to immortality and Wisdom is described in perfectly ontological terms, being the source of motion, an emanation of 'The One', the Form of Goodness:

> For wisdom is more mobile than any motion.
> Yes, she pervades and penetrates all things
> by reason of her purity.
> For she is a breath of the power of God,
> and a pure emanation of the glory of the
> Almighty.
> Therefore nothing defiled can find entrance
> into her.
> For she is a reflection of everlasting light,
> an unspotted mirror of the working of God,
> and an image of his goodness.
> She, being one, has power to do all things.
> Remaining in herself, she renews all things.
> From generation to generation passing into

holy souls,
she makes friends of God and prophets.
For God loves nothing as much as one who
dwells with wisdom.
For she is fairer than the sun,
and above all the constellations of the stars.[91]

The concept introduced here is clearly a departure from the materiality of Judeo-Christian bodily resurrection and is instead a full embrace of Platonic dualism. And, in fact, The Wisdom of Solomon was likely written only about fifty years before the birth of Jesus, which would make it the most recently written book of the Old Testament.[92] Unlike the vast majority of the books of the Old Testament, it was not first written in Hebrew or Aramaic and translated into the Greek Septuagint, but was first written in Greek, probably after the Septuagint was already generated. The author is suspected to have been an educated resident of Alexandria and Jewish but heavily influenced by Greek culture and philosophy. For these reasons, The Wisdom of Solomon was one of the books that was removed from among the books considered genuine by Jewish and Protestant authorities and it remains only as one of the Apocryphal books included in Catholic bibles.

The dualistic concept of the soul and body that appears in The Wisdom of Solomon is virtually unique in the Bible, but it and Greek influence generally clearly had an impact, not just on the doctrine of the Church, but just as certainly on the popular conception of the soul and the body. Christianity, in some limited way, has adopted Plato's dualism problem as its own. But this, far from being a necessary component of Christian thought, in fact contradicts the vast majority of Scriptural authority on the subject.

In fact, it seems to me the existence of a soul separate and distinct from the body which can somehow, of its own volition, tear itself away from our physical bodies at death and live on independently like a ghost is not an essential part of belief in God's existence at all. It is perfectly consistent with belief in God that, without the intervention of God, death is final. [93] God is not a traffic cop directing souls that have been thrown clear of their bodies either up, down or to a middle ground. He is indispensable to anything that comes after, whatever it may be. In this respect, faith is perfectly suited to the idea that when we speak of a "soul" what we are saying is an allegory or a shorthand for the vital spark; that which distinguishes life from death - but is nonetheless the product of neurochemistry. When we suffer a brain injury or disease, the change in our mental function and our mind-body connection do not occur because the ghost in the machine's grip on the controls has slipped. It is our fundamental selves that have been injured and changed. Christianity does not see human beings as having little bits of 'God-stuff' in us – that is pure Plato. Christianity is consistent with the idea that human beings are material things and if anything survives the destruction of our bodies it will only be with the help of Something outside of ourselves. Upon death, it is the whole individual that dies, not just some part of us. If there is life again, it is because it has been recreated by a process or entity wholly separate and independent from ourselves and unlike anything with which we are familiar. Maybe it is a recreation of our neurochemistry in a new physical form. Maybe it is something entirely unimaginable. It is fairly clear it is not a process that is accomplished by our minds without divine help. It is evident that this is not just pretty imagery but is an allegorical fact of some importance. The Catholic assertion that the bread and wine when consecrated become God in a real sense in a process of transubstantiation seems like archaic nonsense, but in fact reflects a rejection of dualism and an assertion that the divine does not inhabit the material, but is identical to the material. The Catholic commitment to preserving kneeling and standing as integral parts of the Mass affirms the inseparability of body, mind and soul – that it is not only inaccurate, but virtually unhealthy to think of them as separate or distinct from one another. Our liturgies have greater immediacy when they acknowledge the pure materiality of the soul. As C.S. Lewis stated in *Letters to Malcolm*, "The body ought to pray as well as the soul."[94] Our material, non-magical nature, as it turns out, is central to faith and the practice of faith – immaterialism is not. The assumption made by modern atheistic materialists that faith relies on an immaterial, independent soul is what philosophy calls a "straw man": defining faith inaccurately in order to disprove it.

We can't blame Dennett and atheism for characterizing our understanding of the soul and our faith as dualistic. There is no question that some people of faith are absolutely committed to a dualistic view of body and soul and I don't pretend to know whether they represent a minority or majority.[95] It is also indisputable that the language of faith habitually uses immaterialism in several applications as a surrogate or shorthand. Just as we talk about the soul as if it were an entity separate and independent of our material bodies, similarly, we talk about love, morality and rights as though each of them had material form and are poured in and out of our bodies. Shorthand is useful, but when it comes too easily to our lips, it can serve to distract.

Even among Christian writers, it is very much in vogue to dismiss the possibility of an afterlife as simply too good to be true. We are invited to reject the idea of heaven being someplace out there and rather accepting the reality that it is a state of mind or a social goal. The promise of heaven too often gets re-interpreted as the good feeling we get when we behave well and kindly, or even the promise of an Earthly future political utopia where good conduct will be universal. I see no reason for such pessimism. If God is Who we think He is, nothing is impossible for Him and we have no reason to doubt His love and sympathy might extend to want to remove the cause for the anxiety arising from our ability, unique among His creatures, to contemplate and regret our mortal nature. We need not understand ourselves as a dualist combination of material body and immaterial soul for God to rescue us from death. It may be that God's exhortation to "be not afraid" means something more readily imaginable than life after death, but God does have a habit of defying expectations of the possible and the probable. Abraham was promised that his descendants would number as the stars and probably wondered how he and Sarah were going to manage this extraordinary sexual feat. In fact, God meant something far more profound than merely having a lot of genetic offspring. As the story progresses, we see that God intended Abraham to be the father of three great religions whose members would number over a billion in our day. Truly, "no eye has seen, nor ear heard, nor the heart of man conceived, what God has prepared for those who love Him."[96]

PART 3
C.S. LEWIS AND THE ARGUMENT FROM MORALITY

The Argument from Morality & Evolutionary Psychology

So far we've seen that the Platonic understanding of God, including the idea that God is an Unmoved Mover, or the Form of Good, and including the idea that we are partly material beings and partly ghost, straddling material and immaterial worlds, are not native concepts to Judeo-Christianity at all and are actually contradicted by it. To explain how evil can exist in a universe created by an all-powerful, immovable Form of Good Plato relied heavily on human free will, which makes his solution untenable if free will is an illusion. But that is not a problem for pre-Platonic Judeo-Christianity which conceived of God as being in less than full control of Creation - sometimes He is even flummoxed by it and mourns the directions it goes. One remaining feature of Platonic thought has been a greater distraction than any other and deserves separate treatment.

Archaeological Evidence for
Compassion and Empathy

Social morality emerged at the same time we first gathered together as primitive people in familial and tribal groups and, except for the ability to identify with and have empathy for others outside of our group, morality looks pretty much the same in us as it did in our Paleolithic ancestors. In 2007, archaeologists examining the skeleton of a young man excavated from a four-thousand-year-old burial site in North Vietnam wondered why this skeleton had been laid to rest in a fetal position, while all his companions in burial were laid straight. Close examination revealed that the skeleton had fused vertebrae and a very compromised bone structure. They concluded that the boy was extremely disabled: paralyzed from the waist down and barely able to use his arms. Nonetheless, it appeared the boy lived another ten years after the onset of his disease, clearly receiving constant care to help to feed himself and keep himself clean.[97] Life in this early culture was not brutish and short but clearly included empathy, compassion and morality. Nor is this an isolated case or even the earliest evidence of ancient humanoid compassion. The 500,000 year-old bones of a member of Homo Heidelbergensis were uncovered in Spain that showed evidence that the individual was elderly by that species' and that period's standard – over forty-five years old. The man's spine was deformed, forcing him to walk in a stooped fashion and potentially to use a cane. In this early and indeed pre-human environment, one might expect the individual to die or be killed almost immediately as he fails to keep us with his healthier, stronger, younger comrades. But instead it appeared he was cared for in his disability and aged state by his community.[98]

C.S. Lewis

In C. S. Lewis's classic work, *Mere Christianity*, Lewis takes notice of the fact that we all share a very similar moral code. We demand fairness of one another, we demand that we keep our promises, and we demand that we basically treat each other decently. There are differences in this moral code among individuals and cultures, but ultimately they are all very minor variations. We don't all necessarily comply with this universal moral code all the time, but we all clearly apply the same basic understanding of what it is in the first place. For Lewis, the only reasonable explanation of the fact that we all share a moral code is that it comes to us from outside the material universe. Like the form of a straight line, or the form of maple leaf, for Lewis it appeared there is a Form of Good. Lewis surmised that this Form of Good must be something conscious and alive. Lewis says of this source of morality, "I think we have to assume it is more like a mind than it is like anything else we know – because after all the only other thing we know is matter and you can hardly imagine a bit of matter giving instructions."[99] Lewis concludes that this proves that a god, which he eventually equates with the Judeo-Christian God, exists.

This is, of course, classic Platonism – the Form of Good projected into the material world to be clumsily handled by humanity.[100] I found this argument very compelling for many years. I set aside my discomfort with the ambiguities of free will, adopted Singer's view that, "we have to believe in free will, we have no choice"[101], and set out to find God in morality. It seemed like a pretty good place to look. The impulse to act morally was mysterious and, as Lewis asserted, it seems like God was the best explanation of its source. My Christian upbringing did nothing but support that conclusion with its overwhelming concern with sin avoidance, acting charitably and being the best person morally that I could be (whether or not I always hit the mark). So convinced was I that I could pull aside the curtain and reveal the divine wizard in morality that I took as many moral philosophy courses as I possibly could in my years as an undergraduate at the University of Toronto. But four years later I had a degree that prepared me for precious little except a glancing trajectory into the legal profession, and a nagging sense that I was on the wrong track. I had assumed that I would find that God had written some overarching moral principal on human hearts and would judge us on how closely we cleaved to it. The Golden Rule seemed like an excellent candidate. Expressed as some variation of "do to others what you would like them to do to you" in three Gospels[102] it seemed to express what most of us intuited about morality. Jesus claims to be summarizing all divine commandments this way. Only in the Gospel of John does Jesus express it slightly differently, and announces it as a brand new command: "love one another as I have loved you."[103] (This little difference may be of exceptional importance, as we'll see.) Immanuel Kant, a giant of moral philosophy, seemed to put a variation on the Golden Rule into philosophical language with what he called the *categorical imperative*: act only according to those princi-pals that you can want to become a universal law." Another candidate was *moral utilitarianism*. Championed by English philosopher, Jeremy Bentham, utilitarianism held that an act is moral if it creates the greatest amount of happiness for the greatest number of people. This seemed like a pretty good principal too, until we students were posed a difficult ques-tion. We were asked to imagine that we were the sheriff in a remote town and had taken into protective custody someone we knew was innocent. A violent mob forms and demands that we turn the innocent man over to them. If we turn him over, he would almost certainly be killed by the mob. It is just as cer-tain that if we don't turn him over, the mob will torch the town and many more people will be killed. If memory serves, we unanimously thought turning over the innocent man would be abhorrent, even though it would tend to maximize happiness. It was instantly clear that utilitarianism, without at least some adjustment, was wrong. Bentham's philosophical successor, John Stuart Mill, offered some of that adjustment, which we'll explore later on. But what was most interesting to me at the time, and seemed to confirm my strategy to find God, was that we students didn't use reason to judge whether utilitarianism was right or wrong. We intuited it. We evidently compared it to what we knew in our hearts was right and wrong and rejected it solely on that basis. The Golden Rule seemed to be winning the day, and C.S. Lewis's proof of God's existence seemed to be getting more credible.

But free will instantly reasserts itself as a problem both for the Golden Rule and for Lewis. If morality is proof of God's existence, it also implies that God is, in Lewis's words, "intensely interested in right conduct" and that He commands us to act morally. But it makes little sense to be commanded by God to engage in behavior that we do not have the free will to choose or reject. A god who is the source of morality cannot be unconditionally loving, nor can such a god exist unless there is free will. As Abraham asks God at the gates of Sodom as he pleads for mercy, "Will not the Judge of all the earth do justice?"[104] Lewis asserts that we have free will, as indeed he must, which puts him in direct conflict with modern science and philosophy. Science also has an alternate theory for the source of morality – a material source in the form of our evolved brains - which cuts to the heart of Lewis's argument that God is the only reasonable explanation for a shared moral code.

Natural Selection; Psychological Evolution

In 1859, Charles Darwin revolutionized biology and, in the process, sparked debate in every corner of the human imagination including theology and moral philosophy – a true paradigm shift. In essence, Darwin observed that populations of living organisms often exhibit variations in physical attributes – birth defects. Some of those variations represent advantages – they allow the individual to survive into reproduction at better rates than are experienced by the part of the population that doesn't share the variation. The individual passes along their advantageous variation to their offspring and, all else being equal, the bearers of that variation will tend to thrive and their population will tend to outstrip the others'. Over time and the aggregation of these variations, entirely new species arise. The vast majority of theists and atheists alike accept the theory of natural selection as correct and it hardly needs further description or defense here. However, when we reject dualism and accept that the mind is a product of our physical brains, we see the theory has broader implications than just the explanation of the physical attributes of living things. It becomes immediately evident that the theory of natural selection applies also to behavioral attributes. Any variation in the brains of an animal that allows it - or compels it - to engage in a behavior that makes it more likely that the animal will survive into reproduction, is likely to persist and allow that animal's genetic legacy to continue. Darwin mentioned this in passing in the first chapter of his book, but the idea did not take hold and flourish in any meaningful way for another century, until the 1970s.[105] The most basic behavioral impulses arose in this way. Whatever creature first developed the impulse to cover its eggs inadvertently made it more difficult for predators to find them and may have insulated them from heat loss and accelerated their development. The impulse to cover one's eggs, therefore, would tend to allow the organism to pass on that genetic legacy. It is the first rudimentary expression of love.

Love and Empathy

One of the most useful behavioral impulses (from an evolutionary standpoint) is the impulse to care for one's offspring.

This is probably as powerful and resolute an impulse as it is precisely because it is so useful to the perpetuation of a species. The impulse to care for offspring does not manifest itself as a decision to act in a certain way because the animal has made the mathematical calculation that it is the better way to ensure it passes along genes. Rather, it manifests itself as love. When a bird exhausts itself looking for food for its hatchlings, the bird probably experiences that impulse as some kind of rudimentary love or empathy for its hatchlings – the ability to recognize that the hatchlings experience hunger, and that hunger is unpleasant, and to have the desire to relieve them of that suffering – rather than just some mechanistic desire to find, obtain, and drop food in their mouths. Our brains, of course, are far more complex than a bird's, and our long post-gestational period makes the requirements of parenthood and the impulse of love far more complex too, but it appears that our love for our children is very much parallel to the love for offspring experienced by other animals. Far from making love a cold product of neurochemistry, it seems to me that this makes love far more reliable and lends far more cosmic meaning and purpose to love than an alternative rooted in the illusion of free will. If my love for my child is merely the product of my free will determined by an immaterial soul, my inability to account for any of that or to account for *why* I love my child would seem to me to make love capricious and unreliable. Capricious and unreliable love is not really what we want from love. On the other hand, if I love my child as a result of the relentless march of evolutionary processes that began when the first reptile covered its eggs with leaves and detritus and continued through virtually every higher species thereafter for millennia to the point where love is indelibly etched on the human mind, love is the furthest thing from capacious or unreliable and, although it may lose some of its mystery, it gains so much of what we crave in love.

Love of Community

For many mammals and birds, and a few others, the impulse to love and to care for offspring has to last through a lengthy developmental stage, while the offspring is unable to feed or maybe defend itself. Human beings have a particularly long developmental period before adulthood because if our complex brains had to develop fully within the womb we could never pass through the birth canal and pelvis. As it is, we are born with fontanels – soft channels through our skulls that allow our already large heads to flex and pass through our mother's birth canal, and the joints between the bones of our mother's pelvis relax as birth becomes imminent. But the ability of the circumference of our heads to continue to increase for five years after birth, initially at a rate of two centimeters per month, provides the greatest potential for cognitive development past gestation. This means we are born with under-developed brains and bodies and need to gestate, in manner of speaking, helpless and needy, outside of our mothers' wombs.

The impulse to love offspring during this period of relative helplessness is critical to survival even in an environment that has abundant food and water and no risk of attack. Humanity, however (and virtually all species) evolved in an environment characterized by scarcity. In such circumstances, the impulse to love and to empathize with a larger family group, hive, pack, herd or tribe - not just offspring - becomes an exceptionally important advantage. It allows certain species to hunt and forage in concert, to have look-outs that will alert the rest of the group to danger, and basically cooperate in such a way that makes the survival of their genetic code more likely than it would be if they could only act only selfishly. Even something as relatively simple as a honeybee has evolved countless communal behaviors.

From time to time, I keep honeybees, although it's gotten much harder since colony collapse disorder arrived. Honeybees are extraordinarily fascinating creatures, and the most fascinating thing about them is their capacity to act in concert to increase the likelihood of their survival as a hive. Honeybees assign distinct roles in the hive. Some honeybees serve as the guards, standing outside and evicting other insects, animals, and honeybees from other hives trying to poach honey. Most forage for nectar and pollen – the carbohydrates and protein the hive needs to breed and survive. These foragers can even signal to the rest of the hive where the individual forager has found a good source of nectar and direct the others to it. This makes honeybees virtually irreplaceable to agriculture since instead of visiting whatever individual flowers may be in close proximity opportunistically, a single honeybee can enlist an entire hive to visit a single type of flower and distribute that plant's pollen to plants of its same species - a process which is necessary to produce fruit. On a hot day, the honeybees do something even more remarkable. A number of them will go to a water source and bring droplets back to the hive. They put the droplets all over the comb and then stand in a line, head to stinger, from the center of the hive to the entrance, and beat their wings. This little bee conga line, the end of which you can see at the entrance to the hive, acts like an organic air conditioner – evaporating the water on the comb and directing the airflow out.

Most of us are, unfortunately, familiar with the honeybee's stinger. Unlike some wasps and other stinging inspects, a honeybee stinger has a barb on the end so that it can't be withdrawn. If you are stung and you slap the bee off of you, you might see the stinger with some entrails hanging off it and those entrails may still be pumping. This is the bee's venom delivery system and it is 'designed' to survive the death of the individual bee to maximize your pain. The honeybee's evolved impulse to sacrifice itself for the good of the hive means that it is valuing not just the survival of its genetic code as an individual, but is actually more 'interested' in perpetuating the genetic code that it shares with the rest of the hive. This ability to place one's own individual interests on par with or even below the interests of the family group is the basis of altruism and love. It is most pronounced where an organism's body (including its brain) compels it to self-sacrifice: as in the honeybee, with any animal that protects itself by being toxic to eat, or which will throw itself into an uneven fight to protect not just offspring, but the group. Human beings display the impulse to self-sacrifice for the family group from time to time, but display other less-intense forms of altruism all day long. This ability, and the complex brain from which it arises, has allowed our species to survive and thrive in a scarce environment. It is not our individual genes that we are most committed to passing on, it is our familial or even tribal genes. New Atheist Horseman, Richard Dawkins gloomily entitled his book on the subject, "*The Selfish Gene*," but it is more accurate to call it the altruism gene. We do want our genes to persist but our desire is not individualistic in goal nor in practice - it is a collective desire that the genes of our family group and those we identify as our tribe persist and we cooperate, sometimes to the detriment of our individual selves to accomplish this. This is not a mysterious ability imposed on our material brains as an immaterial Form of Good, but is the product of the evolution of our material brains in a material environment.

Empathy; Animal Rights; Celebrities and Ethiopia; Religion as Good at Tribal Identity

As mentioned earlier, our desire to care for our offspring isn't manifested in our minds as a mathematical calculation of what behavior will ensure our genetic survival, but is felt by us as empathy and love for our offspring. Similarly, the desire to care for our immediate family group and more extended family and tribe is not manifested as a calculation either, but is felt by us as empathy and love for those we recognize as our own. In an environment characterized by scarcity and sometime violent conflict, the inability to recognize family from stranger or friend from foe could be instantly fatal, and those family groups without that ability would tend to die out.

We see in our daily interactions and relationships that we feel most empathetically towards our children and immediate family. We also feel empathy towards people with whom we interact often, whether that's in a work environment, a church or otherwise. Evolution is guessing that that those we see often are the most likely to share some of our genetic code. This was a pretty good bet in a Paleolithic environment, where our ancestors were likely to be born, live and die within a radius of few miles. Engaging in some sort of work together, ritual or surviving some kind of scary situation heightens those feelings of empathy. That's why the premise of so many movies is the gorgeous woman who will have nothing to do with the dorky guy until they survive an alien attack or finish some dangerous quest together. Then, suddenly, her sense of empathy and love is awakened, she falls in love, and she and the dorky guy live happily ever after. Evolution is again betting that people we have intense experiences with are likely to be extended family, share enough of our genetic code to make it worthwhile to share scarce resources with them, or defend them in a fight.

Religion was probably among the first influences that was inadvertently and unconsciously used to exploit our natural allegiance to people we identify as our own and expand the tribe beyond our immediate vicinity. Religion, with its shared ritual and shared beliefs, and its altruistic impulses, had the ability to create tribes that shared little genetic similarities but nonetheless inspired the individual members to a feeling of mutual empathy and, as a result, cooperation. Contrary to what the New Atheists would like us to believe about religion, religion is actually an excellent way to create unity among massive numbers of individuals who otherwise would have no natural feeling of commonality or empathy and would be more inclined to violence as a result. In fact, the impulse to religiosity may be one of the principal evolved traits that allowed humanity to form large regional, national and even international affiliations rather than being limited to small clans. The fact that the lines *between* religions are often the fault lines of violence should not diminish the fact that *within* each of those religions countless potential fault lines of violence have been effectively erased by the natural tendency to feel empathy for our own.[106] Evolutionary psychology would suggest that we would not reduce violence by diminishing the influence of religion, but we'd actually accentuate it.

Our natural ability to feel empathy for those we see often has been inadvertently exploited by television too, sometimes for good and sometimes in a venal way. When I was growing up in the mid-1980s, Ethiopia was ravaged by a drought and hundreds of thousands died. There was certainly concern in the international community, but it was the television broadcast of images of individuals suffering horrible conditions that moved individuals in the West to action. When the afflicted become more than statistics or vague stories, but entered our living rooms to suffer in front of us, our natural empathy for our own was finally sparked. It was, to our evolved brain which doesn't do an efficient job of distinguishing digital images of human beings from natural ones, as though a human being was starving right there in front of us. The same impulse causes us to love celebrities, allow their political views to have a disproportionate influence on us, and to mourn when they die, far more than other people we have never actually met. When the image of someone is broadcast into our living rooms day after day in the context of stories and dramas such that we might feel we've experienced things together, our evolved brains don't fully distinguish between the broadcast image and a fellow villager, and we fall in love or at least feel empathy and a sense of comradery.

This impulse even leads us to identify with certain animals and feel empathy towards them – particularly ones that have human-like expressions and mannerisms and who we see and interact with every day. Sorry, spiders - not you. Sometimes an animal landing in a sympathetic circumstance is enough to switch their moral standing from farm animal destined for slaughter to beloved pet. The recognition of animal rights should be fairly mysterious to most dualists, such as C.S. Lewis. If we have rights as a result of the projection of a Form of Good onto our material bodies, then does our sympathy toward some animals, some of the time indicate they receive the same projection? Human and animal rights are not a material or immaterial substances poured in and out, but are rather a function of our evolved empathy for them.

A Moral Sense; Hatred of the Freeloader

Our ability to combine our efforts, lay aside our selfish desire for survival and act as a herd, pack or tribe is a powerful tool for genetic survival. But inevitably there will be those individuals whose nature or nurture motivates them to exploit the group's cooperation and pursue their own interests. A freeloader will draw away precious resources and diminish the group's ability to survive and compete in a scarce environment. There were probably clans in our evolutionary history which couldn't distinguish between members who were pulling their weight and members who did not. And there were probably clans who could identify freeloaders but who did not evolve the capacity to feel indignant about it and be motivated to eject them. The strength of those clans would be sapped away at critical moments – when food ran short or as the clan was facing a violent enemy – and they would not survive to pass on their genetic lineage. A freeloader who doesn't pull his weight in a time of scarcity is frustrating, but a freeloader who enjoyed the benefits of the community's commitment to moral conduct but doesn't himself exhibit moral conduct – a moral freeloader - is the most odious of freeloaders. This probably reflects that while a lazy person drains resources away, a dishonest or disloyal person rends at the heart of community. And so, naturally, clans that evolved the ability to identify freeloaders and moral-freeloaders and evolved the impulse to treat them as outsiders and to hate them would be more likely to survive. We don't think of this as hatred, of course. We prefer terms like "fairness" and "justice." But by whatever words we use, the assumption that each of exercises free will and that we must each exercise moral judgment is part of our evolutionary heritage. It is in our nature.

The impulse to feel empathy and the impulse to hate the free-loader, and the corresponding desire to be well regarded by our peers, are the basic building blocks of morality and develops into the notion of fairness. When we say something is not fair what we are really saying is that the accused is being a free-loader - somehow not respecting rules from which they themselves benefit. Fairness is probably the first moral principal of which we become aware. Our children will accuse us and others of not being fair incredibly early in life and will ferret out hypocrisy like the most tenacious attorney. And this impulse does not seem to be the exclusive purview of humans.

In 2003, researchers at the Yerkes National Primate Research Center at Emory University trained monkeys to hand them a small rock to receive a piece of food. At first, all the monkeys received a piece of cucumber as the reward and they performed consistently to get the reward. However, when some of the monkeys started getting grapes as their reward while the rest continued to get cucumber, the ones receiving the cucumber revolted. They would throw the cucumber away, throw the rock away and eventually just wouldn't participate anymore. A few years later, researchers at the University of Vienna, Austria did a similar experiment with dogs. Initially, they asked all the dogs to give the researcher their paw (to "shake") which the dogs did happily. But when some of the dogs started receiving treats, the dogs who were working for nothing allowed more time to pass before they would shake and, like the monkeys, eventually wouldn't participate any more.[107] This is undoubtedly a rudimentary moral sense. I know from my own experience that my daughter's dog, Millie, is a moral being. If I scold Millie, she will drop down to her belly, her ears will droop, her eyes will convey utter misery and she'll crawl out of the room. After a few seconds, she'll crawl back in and roll over on her back. Once I make soothing sounds and scratch her belly, she hops up and clearly feels she has been forgiven and the bad conduct is behind us. Millie obviously has a sense of having done wrong and even has a sense of being contrite, offering penance and being forgiven! On the other hand, if I scold Petunia, my daughter's cat, she will look at me with what is probably total, vapid incomprehension but I imagine as being annoyance that the fleshy, largely hairless thing that puts food in her bowl is making noise again. I think Petunia may not be very smart – even for cat – but I think the primary difference is that while Millie's evolutionary heritage - animals who live in packs - need a basic moral sense to successfully live together and leverage their community, Petunia's evolutionary heritage - solitary animals – have no need for morality and are so ornery that the phrase "herding cats" is a catchphrase for a total inability to cooperate. Here in my little stable of animals is evidence that morality is not imposed on us by God, but rather is the product of our evolutionary path as a social animal with a complex brain. C. S Lewis is correct in that there is global standard of right and wrong that has only minor differences between cultures. But this does not indicate that morality comes from an outside source. Rather, it indicates that we all come from common ancestors and have evolved in a fairly similar environment to develop a largely uniform sense of empathy and fairness.

The Freeloader and God; The Overarching Themes of Scripture

Although our evolution impels us to hate the freeloader, if free will is an illusion, hatred does not make sense. This does not mean that we should accept freeloading – we can still discourage it and punish it in order to reform the freeloader or provide incentive to stop. But it does foreclose any justification for hate and retribution. The futility and peril of engaging in moral judgment is the message of the Garden of Eden and recurrent theme throughout Scripture. In fact, by any reading of the story of the Garden of Eden, God did not want us to have the ability to make moral judgements or even to discern right from wrong – we simply took it against His express wishes! This is not a command to be forgiving but a description of how we should treat each other logically given our nature and a path to happiness if we can transcend our nature. Secular science and philosophy are only now seconding the motion that faith made millennia ago. Also within Scripture is the theme that God is fully aware of our unfree nature and, if He judges us at all, He judges us knowing full well that we are not free which means He must be merciful. Furthermore, He assures us that there is enough forgiveness and divine love to go around – the divine environment is wholly unlike the environment we evolved in – there is no scarcity. Finally, Scripture predicts that we will hate the idea of forgiveness and love that is not rationed. We won't hate this because we're bad or choose to be cynical, but rather because it is so unlike the world in which our brains evolved that we find it difficult to transcend our mentality of scarcity.

Manna

As the Israelites wandered the barren desert after being freed from Egypt on their way to the Promised Land, God made manna rain down from heaven in sufficient quantities that everyone had enough every day, and made water gush from stones. This is not a story about God providing everything we need wherever we need it. That would contradict reality as we all know and experience it. Rather, it is an illustration of the divine economy and how very different it is from the human condition. God is saying that the divine is characterized by abundance, where competition for scarce resources is totally unnecessary. No, this is not an endorsement of socialism or any particular political or economic position. Rather, God is saying we do not need to compete for God's love like it is a limited resource. God's love and concern do not need to be rationed among the deserving or the meritorious and kept from the freeloader. We'll see this theme repeated in the story of the multiplication of loaves and fishes, the parable of the vineyard workers, the stories of the lost coin and the lost sheep, and the parable of the prodigal son. It is possible that God's love truly is unconditional and irrevocable, and indeed, if we do not have free will and God is just, then He does not judge us according to our acts or beliefs. Forgiveness of sins is automatic regardless of the gravity of that sin and regardless of whether we are contrite. And that should be ok, because there is enough forgiveness to go around. In fact, as we'll see in the next chapter, there is finally little Scriptural support for the idea that God imposes morality on us at all. *Faith is not about how we should act morally* – it is about how God acts morally. Faith is not a prescription; it is a description. The divine economy is flummoxing to us, and we are inclined to reject it, sometimes viciously, and interpret Scripture in a way that ignores it, because it doesn't resemble the environment in which our minds evolved to exist. It is difficult to know the ways of God – it is much more than counter-cultural or counter-intuitive. It goes against our very nature. Religion has not been extremely good at inoculating us against moral judgment. Natural hatred of freeloader makes every Christian denomination dance around the idea of universal salvation but not accept it: Catholic dogma insists that baptism eliminates original sin but good works and the avoidance of evil are needed to maintain salvation, Lutheran dogma insists on the need for right belief to achieve salvation; Calvinist dogma asserts that some of us are predestined for salvation, which actually seems to eliminate free will from the equation, but it sneaks right back in as good works and belief are necessary to demonstrate one's predestined status and distinguish them from those predestined for something worse. Though none would freely admit it, they essentially eliminate unearned grace and rely on free will. Karma sneaks into otherwise non-judgmental Buddhism and asserts that the universe rewards and punishes behavior. Our natural impulse to punish the moral freeloader is powerful.

Williams Syndrome

There is a fascinating genetic condition called Williams Syndrome which causes the person afflicted with it to absolutely trust everyone. The evolutionary mechanism that allows us to distinguish between our tribe and the other has been turned off. Children afflicted with Williams Syndrome often announce to everyone they meet that they love him or her[108]. They will jump into the car of a stranger because they have no natural fear. In an environment of scarcity, competition and possible violence, this genetic predisposition would not survive into reproduction and even in our present environment, is not an advantage, and people with Williams Syndrome are susceptible to being exploited in every interaction with people willing to take advantage of them. There are other developmental problems that are associated with Williams Syndrome, but I wonder if those other issues didn't exist, if such a person would tend to be an excellent theologian – naturally predisposed to seeing the universe as a place of abundance and trustworthiness, and seeing humanity as a single tribe, and not having to contradict any evolutionary impulse to the contrary. Maybe sometime the sufferers of Williams Syndrome will have the evolutionary advantage and be the seed for a new, pretty wonderful, human species.

God as Night Watchman; Being Well Regarded

So, contrary to C.S. Lewis's assertion, the existence of a common moral code is not incontrovertible evidence of a god who imposes moral commands on His creatures and judges them according to their obedience. Evolution provides a perfectly good explanation of how a common moral code can arise within material creatures. C.S. Lewis's account of Christianity as a principally moral concern arising from a Platonic under-standing of God fails for another reason; namely, that it cannot account for the lack of human free will. Perhaps this is fortu-nate, because Lewis's philosophy commits him to an under-standing of God's love as conditional and ultimately not a true expression of the God of Abraham.

The moral responsibilities of a god conceived of in the Platonic tradition includes more than simply being the source of all our good and moral impulses. He is also called upon to be a moral night watchman capable of reading thoughts and motivations and who ensures that we will act according to that moral code and suffer the consequences if we don't. Plato closes two books with a warning to behave well, even when we can't be caught by any human authority, or suffer potentially eternal conse-quences at the hands of a divine judge and Christianity was more than happy to adopt the notion. What good is a natu-ral hatred for the freeloader, if the freeloader can evade detec-tion? Evolution suggests that we have an internal watchman in the form of our impulse for empathy and our natural desire to be well-regarded. Although empathy and a desire to be well-regarded is not a foolproof guaranty of good, socially con-structive behavior, the idea of a punishing God has not been foolproof either. God is not needed for this purpose. A per-fectly healthy, mature human being is not capable of behaving viciously or in an unduly selfish manner even when he or she could get away with it. To the extent that someone can engage in viscous conduct, we can be sure they are unhealthy, and to the extent someone can be unduly selfish, they are almost certainly operating from an unhealthy, fearful, immature place. The threat of divine punishment in these situations would be socially useful, but that does not make them reality.

In fact, it appears God really is not that concerned with preventing sin. Rather, His message time and again is exclusively about God's forgiveness of sin. He calls for repentance as if avoiding sin in the first place just doesn't concern Him. The original infraction is not nearly as important as expressing God's willingness to overlook it. Confronted with an adulterous woman, Jesus declines to impose sentence. His parting words as she leaves, "go and sin no more" seem calculated to be off-handed, and to have no bearing on whether he would be willing to forgive her again if she was hauled before him the next day. At the Last Supper, Jesus indicates that he knows that Judas has betrayed him, and although he predicts Judas will regret it, he doesn't overturn the table and throw Judas out, or even demand that he make it right. Within a few lines, Jesus predicts the apostles will abandon him on the Mount of Olives when he is arrested, and prophesies that Peter will betray him three times.[109] These are all stories, related in rapid succession in all four Gospels, to demonstrate a total lack of concern for sin and speaks only of his ability to eat, pray and interact lovingly with his betrayers, requiring nothing of them. After his resurrection, the Gospel of John describes Jesus's forgiveness of Peter's betrayal. It is extraordinary in that Jesus does not require repentance, or remorse. In fact, there is every appearance that Peter has no idea that he is being forgiven or what he is being forgiven for. As Peter betrayed Jesus three times,

Jesus asks Peter if Peter loves him three times. This is a question even Peter, the perennial screw-up of the bunch, can't get wrong and he answers "yes" three times.[110] According to the Gospel of John, at the Last Supper, when Jesus reveals that he is going to be betrayed, Peter enlists the beloved disciple who is lying close to Jesus to find out who his betrayer will be. Jesus indicates it is Judas by giving him a morsel of food.[111] In the closing lines of the Gospel, as Peter and the other disciples follow Jesus, Peter spies the beloved disciple following behind, presumably at a distance. Peter, perhaps angry that the disciple failed to tell him that Judas would be the betrayer in time to save Jesus, asks Jesus if he should be permitted to follow. Jesus's answer, "what is it to you?" indicates Jesus will not engage in human hatred of the freeloader."[112]. The Gospel ends three lines later. This is no divine night watchman searching hearts to exact punishment. Why this overwhelming concern with forgiveness instead of sin avoidance? Empathy and love come naturally as an evolved capacity and it is easy to imagine God being loving. It is unnatural for us, however, to think of the moral freeloader as our equal and it is virtually impossible for us to imagine that God does either. This is the challenge of faith. We naturally love those we see as good. To love those who are decidedly not good requires us to expand past our evolution. More importantly, to understand our relationship to God we have to abandon the idea that He commands, rewards and punishes although that is what we want of Him. Clearly He does not, and spends most of His energy cleaning up the shame we impose on ourselves by thinking that we can please or displease Him with our actions. That is what makes faith counter-cultural. That is why the Old Testament prophets were persecuted – not because they were nice in a mean world but because they spoke of abundance to we who evolved to assume, and even prefer scarcity. They refused to envision God as serving some purpose or imposing some morality. Instead, they saw God as transcending purpose and morality. This is mysticism. Instead of answering the question – how can we please God - mysticism changes the assumptions underlying the question itself and answers that we already do. But this does not make mysticism magical or necessarily incomprehensible. It is a paradigm shift. Like seeing oxygen as one of several elements in air rather than phlogiston, mysticism sees God as serving no purpose. Mysticism is less immediately accessible than the alternatives suggested by the minds we inherited from our ape ancestors. That is why Jesus is rejected in his time and homogenized to be the "nice guy" in our times, and why faith is so inclined to identify itself with commanding morality rather than striving to transcend morality. That is why faith became addicted to free will to the point where it thought it couldn't live without it anymore. When we acknowledge that free will has no place in faith any more than it has in science, we transcend morality and we come closer to understanding the nature of our relationship to God. The more we learn about the universe through science, the more it reveals how ultimately abundant it is. We have to transcend our evolved assumptions of scarcity if we are to understand the nature of God.

The apparent concern over morality in Scripture is not an illusion, but it is largely a description of God's morality and His chosen relationship to us, rather than a series of commands or divine promises of reward and punishment. There is also a moral component for us embedded in Scripture. That moral component is integral to the story of the Garden, the Exodus and the life, death and resurrection of Jesus, but it is not commanded by God nor is He the enforcer of it. It underlies much of what we recognize as secular morality, and secular morality relies on it, but this Judeo-Christian moral foundation is entirely distinct from secular edifices built on it. Before we get there, however, we need to prepare the ground.

PART FOUR
INTUITION

The God of Physics v The God of Scripture

In the preceding pages, I have been very dismissive of most of the classic proofs of God's existence. The fact that God exists does not mean that every argument in favor of His existence is a good argument, or one that ultimately nourishes faith. When we reject the classic proofs, we reject the god of Plato, which has been a distraction for faith. The Theory of Forms begins as a hypothesis about how our minds recognize things as being part of a class, or persist over time. It is also a hypothesis about how movement and the universe began and why it is mostly orderly but also includes disorder, and where our common standard of morality comes from. Plato's god is the god of gaps. Plato uses his conception of god to fill in where science and philosophy had not yet been able to offer a good, alternate explanation.

Christianity, almost from its outset, identified Plato's Form of Good as God and treated Plato's arguments as proofs of God's existence. Of course, the problem with a "god of gaps" theology is that it is in a constant state of retreat. As science inevitably explains what was previously unexplainable, the god of gaps occupies a smaller and smaller landscape. Science may well someday have a good explanation for the entirety of the universe and all its processes which will deprive Plato's god of gaps of its last redoubt.

Fortunately, the god of gaps is not the Judeo-Christian God. Unlike Plato's scripture, Sacred Scripture is not concerned with explaining the natural world or proving God's existence. We may reflexively assume that the first Creation story is a story about physics – how the universe can come from nothingness. But Scripture opens assuming that the basic building blocks of the universe exist already:

> When God began to create heaven and earth, and the earth then was welter and waste and darkness over the deep and God's breath hovering over the waters, God said, "Let there be light.[113]

God's role is not so much to call forth from nothing, but to separate, distinguish and name. God separates light from darkness and calls one "day" and the other "night." God separates the sky from the waters, and calls it "heaven." God separates dry land from water and calls it "earth." God places the stars, moon and sun in the sky to separate night from day and season from season. Finally, God makes humanity – this too is a separation as he makes us in His own image.[114] This was not an attempt to explain physics or an ancient intuition of the Singularity (although it is interesting to note as an aside that this process of gradual division into more and more complex systems and organisms parallels both the Big Bang and evolution). Scripture's concern was far more human and addressed God's power to bring order and distinction from chaos and hopelessness as we'll see again in the story of Noah.

Unlike the Platonic god which serves a function and serves as an explanation, The Judeo-Christian God doesn't claim to serve any particular purpose in the workings of the universe. As we saw, the story of the burning bush is a warning not to use God to explain physical phenomena. When Moses asks how he is to describe God to the Israelites, God answers:

And God said further to Moses, "Thus shall you say to the Israelites, "The Lord God of your fathers, the God of Abraham, the God of Isaac, and the God of Jacob, sent me to you. That is my name forever and thus am I invoked in all ages."[115]

God doesn't assign a purpose or function to Himself, although it would be natural for Him to awe Moses with the fact that He is the ontological god, the unmoved mover or the source of morality. Instead, God simply declares – not proves – His existence, and seems to actually go out of His way to disassociate Himself from the Platonic god or to serve as the explanation of physics. The entirety of Scripture seems unconcerned with proving God's existence. God is more interested in identifying Himself as the One who was encountered by Moses's ancestors – Abraham, Isaac and Jacob. He is not an explanation or a mythology; He is who He is. When we associate God with Plato's arguments, we are ignoring the demands of Scripture and engaging in a kind of idolatry. The New Atheists believe that by adequately explaining the natural world they have disproved God's existence. But the Judeo-Christian God is not an explanation for the natural world and the New Atheists have really only succeeded in disproving Plato's god. Ironically, the notion that we do not have free will is perfectly compatible with the Judeo-Christian God of unconditional love, it is directly opposed to the Platonic God.

This has not been a harmless dalliance into Greek philosophy. Plato's Theory of Forms inevitably requires free will to explain how suffering and disorder can exist in a universe dominated by the Form of Good. It compounded the mistake of Adam and Eve by lending credibility to the idea that we have free will and further encouraged us to see ourselves and God as locked in a moral contest. Science and philosophy are now abandoning free will and the last vestiges of the Platonic vision of the universe are falling away. In the meantime, however, Christianity has so completely adopted free will, morality and sin as central to our relationship with God, that it can hardly imagine another way. Powerful forces in our very DNA hide the transcendent alternative from us. We do not want to be freeloaders, and we are inclined by our evolution to cling to the idea that we have free will and that God commands, rewards and punishes us according to our freely chosen deeds and beliefs, regardless of the image of the truly unconditionally loving God we find in Scripture.

Intuition

At the time of Jesus, Judaism was expanding at a tremendous pace. It is estimated that Jews represented about seven percent of the population of the Roman Empire, numbering about 4,500,000 individuals, the majority of whom did not live in Palestine, but were concentrated in the major Hellenistic cities of Egypt and Syria.[116] This large population cannot be explained by a high birthrate, but is clearly the result of conversions from the pagan faiths of the day.[117] There was active Jewish evangelization, including evangelization by the Pharisees, as is evidenced by Jesus's statement in Matthew: "Woe to you, scribes and Pharisees, hypocrites! For you traverse sea and land to make a single proselyte; and when he becomes a proselyte, you make him twice as much a son of hell as yourselves."[118] The pervasive Christian belief is that it was Paul who asserted against Peter that circumcision wasn't necessary to become a Christian. But in fact, many Hellenistic Jews outside of Palestine, of which Paul was one, already did not see circumcision as a necessary step to becoming a Jew. Fairly rapidly after the emergence of Christianity, Christian evangelization and conversions eclipsed Jewish expansion. About six hundred years later, Islam emerged. Now, a mere two thousand years after the death of Jesus, adherents to the Abrahamic faiths together represent over half of the global population. The Abrahamic faiths went viral (without the benefit of social media!). What accounts for this extraordinary spread? It was almost certainly not because the Abrahamic God was consistent with then-current ideas about physics. Instead, the Jewish Scripture, followed by Christian and Muslim Scripture, confirmed a concept of God that was already known to humanity on an intuited level. The God of Abraham was not proven to exist. Rather, He was recognized as being the God we already know exists. Ironically, in the pagan religions that the Abrahamic faiths supplanted, gods typically had a function: they were the gods of fertility, lightening, war, beauty, or the underworld. Perhaps God first spoke to our intuition that the divine does not serve a purpose or provide an explanation for physics, but transcends all of those considerations, and that God will be Who He will be.

Abraham Heschel said that, "proofs for the existence of God may add strength to our belief; they do not generate it."[119] It is true, in my experience, that we use the classic proofs to justify our belief to others and sometimes to ourselves but it is really our intuition of God that forms the foundation of our belief. However, our compulsion to identify God with classic proofs has not actually strengthened our belief. Instead, it tied us to a Platonic image of God and, instead of seeing God as unconditionally loving and dispensing unearned grace, our idolatrous

Platonic god is always something just a little short of all that. The Platonic god is addicted to free will and is inevitably conditionally loving and dispenses grace when it is earned by good conduct or proper belief. Far from strengthening faith, the Platonic proofs have been a monkey on the back of Christian faith for two millennia, satisfying our evolutionary dislike of freeloaders, but holding us back from seeing the true nature of God as revealed by the better part of our intuition and by the prophetic intuition recorded in Scripture.

After the resurrection of Jesus, he appeared to the apostles, but one of them, Thomas, was absent. Thomas was suspicious of what the other apostles told him about their encounter with the risen Jesus and insisted that he would not believe until he could stick his fingers into Jesus's wounds. Jesus reappears, calls Thomas's bluff, and scolds him, saying, "blessed are those who have not seen, and have believed."[120] It is a wonder that despite having this story in our canon, so many devout and celebrated Christians have spent their lives developing proofs of God's existence. Jesus's exhortation does not mean that it is immoral to seek to prove God's existence, but something more serious - that those proofs can lead us further away from understanding the true nature of God, which is precisely what has happened. Thomas was not scolded because he didn't find the proofs of Jesus compelling – he wasn't offered any. He was scolded for not trusting his intuition of the divine. To believe based on intuition alone is "blessed" not because it is more moral, but because it avoids the pitfalls of turning God into a function-serving, purpose-driven idol.

Malcolm Gladwell explores our mysterious capacity for intuitive thinking in his book, *Blink: The Power of Thinking Without Thinking*. In it, he concludes that there is such thing as too much information. We have a natural capacity for subconsciously cutting through the informational clutter and discerning a correct conclusion. This capacity is known to psychology as "thin-slicing." It can be crippled, however, by flooding our perceptions with information. Gladwell uses the example of a Greek statue of a nude male youth that had been offered to the J. Paul Getty Museum as an authentic sixth century B.C. Greek kouros. The museum hired highly credentialed scientists and lawyers to run tests, examine documents and confirm the statue's pedigree. With the guidance of these experts the museum ultimately decided it was real. However, with just a glance, several experts having quite casual contact with the kouros recognized the truth intuitively – that is was a fake. Imagine two Christians: one thinks of faith as the parsing of the evidence for and against the existence of God and who considers himself a Christian because he believes the evidence weighs in favor of God. The second is satisfied that his intuition of God is compelling and believes faith is the exploration of the relationship. The first will pore over Scripture trying to determine if there is evidence within it for God – despite the fact that Scripture itself warns against this exercise. He will study the Platonic proofs and the scientific evidence knowing full well that God's existence can be neither proven nor disproven this way. The second Christian is satisfied that his intuition of God's existence is compelling. He is free to explore the relationship and abide in it. His faith is not an endless source of intellectual tension, but an infinite source of richness, meaning and consolation. It was the nature and nurture of Thomas to doubt and he was not disappointing God by doing so. But those whose nature and nurture allow them to move beyond evidence-seeking are richer for it.

The Music of Faith

Human beings are masters of seeing and hearing patterns and, especially, interruptions of patterns. When my shirt is sporting the smallest stain, all I can see is the stain. This is undoubtedly also an evolved trait that helped us survive. It probably allowed us to see the deliberate movement of predators and prey through a forest of leaves being blown by the wind, or to hear the crack of a twig underfoot through a cacophony of crickets. Our ability to hear music as something other than a bunch of noises is in all likelihood an accidental benefit of our ability to sense acoustical patterns. Music is a form of mathematics consisting of sometimes incredibly complex mathematical formulae. Our sense that some music is beautiful is a product of our attraction to patterns. The complex mathematics inherent in music might never have been evident to the composer, but the same composer is intuitively making use of mathematics to exploit our attraction to it. What is truly remarkable is that I, who have absolutely no mathematic skill, can nonetheless recognize music as beautiful. This is my intuition revealing something real – a mathematical pattern - despite my personal inability to quantify it.

Faith, on some level, is sensing a non-mathematical pattern or a resonance in the universe. Intuition, and therefore faith, are not supernatural abilities. Music is experienced through our eardrums and, if it is loud enough, in our chests. As a result of neurochemical and neuro-mechanical mechanisms, it lights up a part of our material brains and we experience it as music and as beautiful. Faith is experienced through all of our faculties, lights up our material brains too, and is manifested not as a vision or a heard sound, but as a sense of encounter with something not visible or audible. In an interview on the radio program, *On Being*, Vigen Guroian, the author of *The Fragrance of God*, suggested that the way we experience God and the divine is more like a smell than a vision or a sound. Our sense of smell is probably our most evocative sense. The smell of creosote instantly takes me back to my early childhood in Dollard des Ormeaux, Quebec. I am not sure I ever saw creosote being put to use there. I assume my neighbors used creosote-soaked lumber to edge their gardens or maybe their driveways. Wherever it may have been, when I smell it I can remember it and the experiences of my childhood associated with it, with utter clarity. Unlike sight or sound, smell preserves mystery at the same time it evokes certainty.

Faith and the Brain

Neuromechanically, we know that people who engage in intense centering prayer or meditation temporarily suppress the function of their parietal lobe. This part of the brain governs our ability to make sense of spatial relationships, including helping us sense the margins of our bodies - where 'we' end and the rest of the world begins.[121] Suppressing this function blurs the boundary line between 'self' and 'other' and gives the person engaged in prayer a sense of being part of a 'oneness' and the unity of all things. Notice that this is not achieved through the use of reason, but is rather a byproduct of closing down part of the brain. It is experienced not as a rational conclusion after carefully reasoned deliberation, but an intuition. One might say it is 'super-rational' or 'extra-rational' in that it is not arrived at by rational means. Ironically, Rene Descartes used the self as the unassailable starting point of all reason: "I think therefore I must exist." From this point, he sought to build a complete universe of rationally determined facts. Remarkably, when we engage in prayer or meditation, we have an intuition practically of the opposite. And it is an intuition so powerfully felt and compelling that many faith traditions would claim that the self - this thing that was supposed to be the very founda- tion of reason and the empirical ground floor of everything that gets built after it – is actually an illusion! For the person of faith, "wisdom" inevitably includes consideration of these extra-rational experiences rather than being just the linear stringing-together of demonstrable facts.

In addition to sensing a unity, many spiritual traditions claim that a benevolence and a Presence are revealed in prayer and meditation. That Presence is experienced as having a salvific quality and being an appropriate object of reverence. As we'll see in the next chapter, the nature of the relationship is both infinitely personal but also fearsomely asymmetric. It seems to be characterized by both intimate proximity and yawning abysmal distance at the same time. Taken as a whole, these intuitions are experienced as an awakening; when suddenly innumerable ineffable hypotheses are confirmed and the last critical piece of the puzzle falls into place. Suddenly, while a universe without God remains conceivable, it would be somehow hopelessly incoherent. It is this dynamic that gives the faithful their confidence and their willingness to tolerate apparent paradox, mystery and a lack of demonstrable proof.

The prophetic intuition recorded in Scripture, as well as our own intuition, reveals God's personality and the nature of His relationship to us and is finally a means of encountering God, rather than proving merely that He exists. There are discernable themes in those intuitions, all of which, in the absence of God's revelation, might otherwise be considered counter-intuitive; each is a totally unexpected message in a relationship that is so thoroughly asymmetrical. Perhaps the most surprising theme is the message that God is engaged with us in the first place – that He is not a dispassionate observer, and not just a benevolent one, but intimately identifies with us and with our suffering. Yet another theme is that we should not be afraid, and that somehow in the end, God will make everything work out. This book, of course, is focused on the theme that God loves and accepts us regardless of our conduct or belief and despite our inability to make free choices in the first place. The intuition that our relationship to God is not purpose-driven is consistent with an existentialist theme that pervades Scripture. That intuition in particular will be the subject of Chapter 4.

Many non-spiritual people are willing to ascribe to the idea that there is a Unity among all things even if they haven't had the experience directly, because it does not offend them morally or politically. That the universe is characterized by loving-kindness and a Presence, although it comes from the same place, has had far more moral and political baggage loaded on it and understandably requires greater faith in intuition.

Indeed, no person of faith would claim that the full and complete nature of God is revealed by their intuition of Him, but they might well claim that their intuition of the presence of God is as reliable as any other one of their senses. Music and mathematics are the discernment of relationships. They don't seek to prove the existence of the Form of Music or the Form of Mathematics, but for those who are lucky enough by the circumstances of their birth and upbringing to discern them, the proposition that the relationships don't exist is virtually unthinkable. The divine relationship is similar. Faith does not reveal the face of God but the fragrance of God, revealed in the divine relationship to the world. It is an inexpressible, inexhaustible source of wonder and comfort. Many Christian thinkers have come to accept doubt as an inexorable part of faith. I am not sure this needs to be the case. Our intuitions of the broad brushstrokes of faith – confidence that a personal God exists and has loving concern for us – can be felt so clearly so as to remove any real doubt. The fact that we cannot demonstrate His existence to others, or by any metric, or with Cartesian exactitude, does not make doubt in our own experience inevitable or desirable.

Faith, like music appreciation, can be accentuated in the right environment or any natural proclivity for it can, by neglect or design, wither and go dormant. To lack faith is not a moral failing any more than a lack of music appreciation is a moral failing. I am not responsible for how my neurochemistry reacts to beautiful music and neither am I responsible for how I tend to react to the divine. Like every other human capacity, the ability to sense the divine is on a spectrum and every individual lies somewhere else on the breadth of that spectrum. For some, depending on their nature and nurture, the resonance of faith is strong and insistent. For others, it is weaker. An atheist may simply be tone deaf to the divine. A New Atheist, on the other hand, is tone deaf to the divine and argues that everyone else is crazy or self-deceived. The claim of the New Atheist is that he or she has not sensed the presence of God and neither has anyone else. Far from being objective or scientific, it is blatant conjecture and is really a form of parochialism.

Some, looking at the illustration below, will realize that it can be seen as a duck facing left and a rabbit facing right. Some will only see one or the other (usually the duck). This latter group may angrily insist there is only a duck and that if others see another animal they must be self-deceived or weak-minded. Nothing they can say, however, can shake the confidence of those who see both. Once seen, it cannot be unseen. To see both is not an act of intellect or rationality, it is not a fact to be learned in a linear way and committed to memory, but something more visceral.

Duck head illusion[122]

I am not arguing that the existence of an intuition of God must come from God and therefore proves God's existence. An intuitive sense of the divine may be an evolved trait just like the ability to sense patterns, giving those of us with the trait a survival advantage. But the fact that our evolution has allowed us to hear patterns in music does not mean those patterns do not exist. In fact, hearing them is incontrovertible evidence of their existence for the hearer. In fact, our ability to hear patterns in music reveals the existence of mathematic truths that most certainly do exist. Similarly, our evolved sense of God, although it does not provide proof of God to anyone else, allows us to intuit the nature of God. The only difference is that one is mathematically verifiable and measurable – provable on some level even to the tone deaf - while the other, by virtue of its nature as 'wholly other', is not verifiable

Intuition is not proof nor is it error free. The history of faith is a history of competing intuitions of the nature of God. Most broadly, it is a competition between the intuition of God as unconditional loving and an intuition of God as imposing conditions on His love.

In 1373 in Norwich, England, a young widow named Julian[123] became desperately ill with a raging fever. During her illness she saw visions of Jesus Christ so powerful and compelling that, when she recovered, she committed herself to a life of solitude as an anchorite. Fairly common in Medieval Europe, anchorites agreed to be sealed in a small cell built against a church wall. Some anchorholds had no door whatsoever, as the occupant was expected to spend his or her entire life in the cell or face possible excommunication. Julian's cell was a nine and one half by eleven and one half foot stone structure with an earthen floor and a thatched or tile roof. It likely had three windows. One window opened into the adjacent church and allowed the anchorite to see the altar and tabernacle. A second window opened into a service room from which the anchorite would receive meals and books. Finally, a third window, always obscured with cloth or whorled glass, faced outward to allow the anchorite to speak with visitors.

Julian immediately set about committing her visions to writing, first as a short summary, and then, after many years of reflection in solitude, a longer version.[124] Julian famously asserted that she "saw no wrath in God"[125] and that God recognizes that we are not morally responsible agents, and forgives everything. Mourning humanity's proclivity for sinful behavior, Julian is answered by her vision of Jesus in what to her was a totally unexpected way:

> Sin is inevitable,
> but all shall be well,
> and all shall be well,
> and all manner of thing
> shall be well.[126]

Between the concept of God as unconditionally loving and the competing, contradictory concept of God as commanding, rewarding and punishing, Julian's mystical vision definitively asserts the first. This comes as a shock to Julian, who fully expects God to embody judgment, and is disturbed by this apparent violation of accepted dogma to which she is utterly committed. Her discomfort at contradicting her beloved Church is evident:

> I had two kinds of observations: the one was of endless continuing love, with a security of protection and blissful salvation (for the whole showing was about this); the other was the common teaching of Holy Church, in which teaching I was previously formed and grounded and was willingly keeping it in practice and in understanding.[127]

Clearly, for Julian, the strength of her intuition of the unconditionally loving God overwhelmed the Platonic-infused understanding of God she had been taught to seek out. We have a distinct advantage over Julian. Science can inform faith and help us to discern which of our intuitions and ideas of God make sense as a cohesive whole given what we know about the universe. The result will never be final or dispositive but simply our best working theory given the information available to us. What we now know about our capacity for free will is strong evidence that the concept of God as unconditionally loving is correct. It reveals that the alternative is a hybrid Platonic god. While the God of Abraham is characterized by abundance, forgiveness and unconditional love and grace, the Platonic god commands, rewards and punishes because free will is an inescapable element of Platonic scripture. The Platonic god chooses favorites from among who were lucky enough to be inclined, through nature and nurture, to act and believe according to the commanded model. The Platonic god protects and rescues those who are well connected enough to have many people praying for them and disregards the suffering of social outcasts. That the Platonic god teaches humility or punishes bad behavior with cancer, or consigns some of his creatures to eternal torment for their sins is perfectly rational and even necessary if you are a Platonist, but it grinds against intuition of the God of Abraham. The Platonic god is a small idolatrous god who commands us to worship him like a cosmic egomaniac, who loses his temper at bad behavior and flies into rages, and who needs blood sacrifice to satisfy the demands of retribution for sin. This is not the God of the Christian intuition informed by science or the God we encounter in prayer, Who is inevitably characterized by overwhelming love and immensity, eternity and grandeur.

Intuition of Morality and Politics

Intuition doesn't just inform faith. It is the unexpected driver of much of what we would like to think is the product of pure reason. In his book, *The Righteous Mind: Why Good People are Divided by Politics and Religion*,[128] Jonathan Haidt argues that much of what we think is the product of rational deliberation is actually largely a pre-cognitive, emotional reaction. Haidt conducted studies in which subjects were read a story designed to test whether the subjects would make a rational moral judgment or something more visceral. One story asked the subjects to judge whether a person has done anything wrong who, in private where no one can see her, cuts up an American flag and cleans the toilet with it. Many of the study's subjects insisted that the behavior was immoral even though no one was harmed by it. When asked why they felt the woman's actions were nonetheless wrong, many of them embellished the story to create a victim. Some ignored the fact that it was done in private and asserted that someone might have seen it and been offended. One even insisted that cleaning the toilet with a flag was wrong because it could clog the building's plumbing. When the researcher challenged the study participants, some would relent and agree that nothing wrong had occurred. Others would become what Haidt calls 'morally dumbfounded' – fully convinced that an immoral act had occurred, but unable to rationalize it. Clearly, the subjects were not making a decision based on reasons, but rather they were making a decision and then using reasons to defend it.

We often assume that our capacity for reason directs our decision making process about morality, politics and faith. In fact, pre-cognitive emotional response has far greater influence. Haidt offers the metaphor of the elephant and the rider. The rider is our capacity to employ conscious reasoning – to allow our mind to engage in an internal debate about the pros and cons of a particular decision and apply general principals to a specific situation. We expect the rider to be in charge. The elephant in the unconscious, emotional part of our mental process that actually accounts for a majority of how we make decisions. Haidt's research indicates that it is the elephant rather than the rider which decides the direction we are going to go. All the rider does is come up with reasons after the fact to justify why they went a particular way. We rely on the elephant to make the countless decisions we are faced with every day. In fact, it appears the rider just isn't capable of that much work. Haidt points out that people who suffer a trauma to that part of the brain that governs emotions (the elephant) remain capable of making rational and moral decisions if they are given enough time to reflect on each decision, but because their ability to intuit the right answer is gone, they often make bad decisions probably because their rider's ability to make rational choices hundreds or thousands of times a day is simply overwhelmed.

In another interview on the radio program, *On Being*, Haidt indicated there is overwhelming evidence that liberals and conservatives hold the views that they do on a visceral, pre-cognitive level. Their differences are not fundamentally political, moral or even intellectual. Rather, they exhibit a preference either in favor of establishment or a bias against it:

Psychologically, what we find empirically, is that people who identify as conservative tend to like order and predictability, whereas people who identify as liberal, they like variety and diversity. I have one study where we have dots moving around on a screen. Conservatives like the images where the dots are moving around more and lock step with each other. Liberals like it when it's all chaotic and random.[129]

The implications of this simply study are monumental. Our cherished notion that where we are on the political spectrum is a reflection of our intelligence or moral development is an illusion! We have an impulsive preference for order or disorder, establishment or critiquing the establishment, and all our elaborate and emotion-laden reasoning that we apply to our political allegiances is merely the rider justifying where the elephant has already gone. As it turns out, according to another study by Haidt, both liberals and conservatives are motivated by values of caring and fairness more than any other. But where liberals are more single minded about those values, conservatives tend to also value loyalty, authority, and sanctity[130] – values that promote order and establishment. This colors even how we hear the same words. While when a conservative might envision a fire chief directing efforts to put out a fire when he or she hears the word "authority," liberals are more likely to envision Hitler. Haidt would predict that very liberal-minded readers might find it preposterous that conservatives value caring above all other considerations (Haidt is an avowed liberal and an atheist). This too is explainable in terms of intuition and empirically testable. When Haidt asked members of each political group to fill out a questionnaire pretending to be on the opposite side of the spectrum, conservatives did quite well in predicting liberal responses while liberals foundered. Evidently, the staunchest liberals simply cannot even imagine preferring order or that it might serve some good.

Having the propensity toward both liberal and conservative impulses represented in a group might have given our evolutionary ancestors a survival advantage. The first debate between conservatives and liberals likely took place in our Paleolithic past, when we hunted and gathered our food and probably went a little like this:

Liberal Caveman: The clan should move to another valley. Any valley is better than this one. Change is good!

Conservative Caveman: This clan has always hunted and gathered in this valley. It is our traditional valley, it is the valley of our forbearers, destined to be our home forever!

The impulse to defend the status quo and the established way of doing things and to assume those things are the "right" or *a priori* or the God-given way is conservative. The impulse to critique and challenge the status quo and to assume that the way that has not yet been tried is better is the liberal impulse. On the one hand, the conservative impulse would allow the clan to become intimately familiar with their valley and all the places where game and forage was plentiful and the location of all the strategic high ground and defensive redoubts in times of conflict. However, remaining in a single valley would lead to an overhunted, picked-over environment incapable of sustaining a growing clan. Furthermore, it would leave that clan's gene pool susceptible to extinction if a local disaster struck their valley. To have the impulse to confidently expand beyond what is known and cherished as traditional would lead to greater likelihood that the clan's offspring would survive and thrive. So, while conservatives tend to leverage institutions to defend traditional values, liberals tend to leverage protest and grass-roots movements to challenge tradition.

In 2014, former New York City mayor, Michael Bloomberg gave the commencement speech at Harvard's graduation ceremony. He cited the remarkable statistic that in the 2012 presidential election campaign, ninety-six percent of all campaign contributions from Ivy League faculty and employees went to the liberal candidate, Barack Obama. Mayor Bloomberg went on to accuse liberal academia of systematically repressing conservative ideas, implying that the college level employment criteria favor liberals. There was a smattering of exultant, sarcastic applause and cheering when Mayor Bloomberg recited the statistic, indicating that at least some in the crowd felt it was evidence of the intellectual superiority of liberals. Much of the most toxic political grasping among liberals and conservatives arises from the idea, prevalent on both sides of the political spectrum, that one side is more intelligent or more morally developed than the other. Naturally, rarely does one side convince the other. In reality, each is operating from an assumed world view arrived at not by rational reflection, but largely by nature and nurture; one predisposed to social preservation and the other to social critique.

For every rule there is an exception, but academia at the college level will generally have a liberal bias because the higher levels of education must, if they are doing their job, be about questioning and challenging presumptions rather than mere indoctrination - and those who are naturally predisposed to it will recruit themselves. Comedy and journalism also are going to have liberal tendencies because social critique is a natural part of those endeavors as well. This does not make liberals more intelligent (or funny), or the perpetrators of an anti-conservative conspiracy, but rather simply affirms that they play the role of social critic that helped our Paleolithic ancestors survive. Religious and corporate hierarchy, law enforcement and the military on the other hand, will naturally lean towards conservativism because they tend to concern themselves with the preservation of the organizational order that allows for common endeavor. This does not make conservatives more morally developed, but affirms their role as social stewards also permitting our ancestors to survive and thrive in a Paleolithic environment.

In the same commencement address, Mayor Bloomberg declared that free will is "the core of every faith and philosophy known to human kind."[131] He presumed that this is a value that has the allegiance of both liberals and conservatives and could serve as some common ground from which to build consensus. But we will never find common ground in the assertion of moral autonomy. We have always only found divisiveness and hate there. This is the challenge that faces faith. While faith is the intuition of the existence of a God that transcends purpose and morality, we have opposing intuitions that demand that everyone complies with either establishment or anti-establishment ideals and be rewarded or punished according to their compliance.

Clearly the influence of intuition is powerful – affecting what seem to be our most fundamental values. What we might like to believe are conclusions we arrive at through pure reasoning are actually the product of something pre-cognitive. Faith allowed itself to be hijacked by Platonism in part to provide reasons to justify belief in God. But Platonism came with a lot of baggage and we may want to embrace our intuitive understanding of God instead. The New Atheists would like to believe that their view arises from pure reason. Probably not.

The Probability of God

According to New Atheist Horseman, Richard Dawkins, "We cannot, of course, disprove God, just as we can't disprove Thor, fairies, leprechauns and the Flying Spaghetti Monster. But, like those other fantasies that we can't disprove, we can say that God is very, very improbable."[132] Dawkins insists he has considered all the possible conceptions of God:

Of course, this all presupposes that the God we are talking about is a personal intelligence such as Yahweh, Allah, Baal, Wotan, Zeus or Lord Krishna. If by 'God' you mean love, nature, goodness, the universe, the laws of physics, the spirit of humanity, or Planck's constant none of the above applies. Well, if that's what you choose to mean by religion, fine, that makes me a religious man, But if your God is a being who designs universes, listens to prayers, forgives sins, wreaks miracles, reads your thoughts, cares about your welfare and raises you from the dead, you are unlikely to be satisfied. As the distinguished American physicist Steven Weinberg said, 'If you want to say 'God is energy,' then you can find God in a lump of coal.' But don't expect congregations to flock to your church.

Dawkins then goes on to debunk all the classic proofs of God's existence including the Unmoved Mover, the Ontological Argument and gives special attention to an argument I have virtually ignored, Intelligent Design. He concludes that the best estimate of the probability that God exists is "pretty low."

Dawkins has made compelling argument given his aim, but misses the mark entirely. He has persuasively (in my view) claimed the Platonic god does not exist - the god who is the solution for physics riddles. Ironically, the god which he argues so strenuously against is virtually identical to the god that he says makes him a religious man: the laws of physics. But neither Plato's god nor Dawkins' god is the God of Abraham.

I strongly suspect that Dawkins would insist that because there is no physical evidence of God, the probability of His existence is still "pretty low." What if we pressed Dawkins for a more exacting answer? What if we brought together a group of one hundred atheists and asked them, by secret ballot, to assign a specific percentage probability to the existence of God? Evidently, because they are atheists, we could assume they would all choose a number that is less than fifty percent but, if they agree with Dawkins that God cannot be disproven, the value would be greater than zero. Would they choose forty-nine percent? Twenty percent? Ten percent? One percent? A fraction of one percent? We can be certain there would be variation in their answers because they would not be selecting the number based on a scientific or mathematical analysis. Their answer would not be provable or repeatable by the scientific method. Their conclusion would be based on their intuition. I am sure their intuition is genuinely felt but it cannot claim to be any more objective or authoritative than someone with the opposite intuition. They can no more declare my genuinely felt intuitions objectively impossible or even improbable than I can theirs. The New Atheists wish to cultivate an image of refined reason - riders serenely guiding their elephants to objective truths with heroic detachment. But their vitriol alone indicates that their elephants are careening out of control and their riders are angrily excusing them.

No Mutuality

Our western culture values mutuality and we are inclined to presume that if science can inform faith then surely faith can inform science. However, this mutuality does not exist. Science is fundamentally an evidentiary standard and must include, if it is science, an element of skepticism. Science is, in that way, parallel to the criminal justice system with its evidentiary standards and presumption of innocence. The principal aim of a court case is not establishing the truth as it is establishing what can be proven according to a particular standard. It would be a bad idea to trust someone with your life savings just because they had recently been found not guilty of fraud. A not guilty verdict does not mean innocence so much as it means that the evidence presented did not definitively prove guilt. We accept, in our legal system, that guilty people will, from time to time, go free or unpunished because we set the standard of proof so high to try to avoid imprisoning or penalizing an innocent person at almost any cost. As a result, we decline to admit some evidence in a court case that in any other circumstance might help us discover the truth. We are sometimes appalled when a clearly guilty person goes free because critical evidence was obtained without a warrant or under duress, or was prejudicial. Science is very much the same way in that it is deliberately blind to what it cannot measure and test. Some might argue that what cannot be measured and tested necessarily does not exist, but that probably says more about them than it does about the nature of reality. Faith is intuitive. And while faith can be refined by what is testable and measurable, intuition is not itself testable or measurable, and science cannot put any stock in it. Science seeks to understand how the universe works and declines evidence that might lead to a mistake. Our confidence in science arises from this commitment to use only measurable, testable evidence and even then it (if it is true to itself) never treats any hypothesis as incontrovertible. But just as it would be foolish to trust your life savings to a defendant found not guilty and you might find yourself impoverished by disregarding the same evidence that the courts disregard, it would be unnecessarily impoverishing oneself to disregard intuition of the divine because it doesn't meet scientific evidentiary standards. One could argue that science could have concluded that human beings don't have free will millennia earlier than it did if it had just taken Scripture and the story of the Garden seriously. But although that may be true on some level, a person of faith wants science to limit itself to the testable, just as a person of faith wants the criminal justice system to apply a presumption of doubt. We don't want either system to come to final conclusions based on intuition.

To be a spiritual person finally means to be open - genuinely open - to all the promptings of the universe. This includes the products of scientific inquiry but also the whispering sounds of the intuition of the divine found in our hearts. To be a person of faith is to possess, receive or hear this intuition and to trust it. Trust it, not because it is infallible or has passed evidentiary muster, but because it is compelling to us. The faithful may also include those who do not intuit the presence of God directly, but trust the intuition of others, and everyone who falls somewhere on that spectrum. The Israelites at the base of Mount Sinai trusted Moses's encounter with God without encountering Him themselves. Each of us who belongs to a Scriptural faith, which certainly includes all three Abrahamic faiths, trusts the intuition of ancient prophets and mystics who wrote our sacred Scripture. The intuition of God is not an intuition of an idea or a belief in His existence. It is the sense of relationship and a call. It is not an exhortation, imperative or command. It is not "I exist" or "do this" or "don't do that." It is more akin to, "I Am here, I Am with you."   The person of faith never rejects science, but seeks greater understanding of God's relationship to us through science and is confident that he or she will experience ever greater wonder and awe with ever greater understanding. A person of faith must reject the idea that he or she may only consider what can be definitively proven by the scientific method. A person of faith does not pretend to be a computer that can only accept input that has been adequately measured and tested. The philosophy of Solipsism asserts that the existence of one's own mind is the only thing of which we can be absolutely certain. I cannot prove that I am not a brain in a vat someplace having my perceptions fed to me by a nest of wires. It is also philosophically possible according to Solipsism that I am the only real mind and the rest of you are just illusory projections of my mind. We don't hear much about this philosophy because it doesn't make a lot of sense for those who ascribe to this belief to hold meetings. But I have yet to hear the philosophical or scientific argument that disproves it. This imposes no obligation on me to believe it. The vast majority of us choose to live our lives trusting our intuition because to do otherwise would be live an impoverished life believing things that are most certainly wrong.

The New Atheist Horsemen gleefully heap ridicule on our evangelical brothers and sisters for reading Sacred Scripture literally and, despite the evident contradictions, cherishing it, preserving it against the politics of the day, and declaring it the inerrant Word of God. This is the evangelical charism in the service of what Paul called the Body of Christ – the membership of the greater church. But to the New Atheist, to the extent Scripture seeks to answer physics questions, it relies on magic and is clearly wrong. To the extent Scripture seeks to answer moral questions, it can be made to say anything, including the most morally abhorrent things. They assume that Scripture is intended to be a scientific dissertation and moral treatise, aiming to prove God's existence and be the means by which He imposes His moral commands. They find Scripture wholly wanting in serving these purposes and dismiss it as foolish, dangerous superstition. The New Atheist assumes the apparent inconsistencies in Scripture are evidence of fallacy, while evangelicals' confidence that all apparent inconsistencies will be resolved is just more fodder for mockery.

In fact, by recognizing the non-Judeo-Christian influences that have colored our interpretation of Scripture, many apparent inconsistences evaporate and we realize that Scripture does not serve the functions that the New Atheists assume. They are not reading it and coming up with the wrong answers; they are reading the wrong book for the answers they are looking for. It is not intended to be a catalogue of magical events written to describe the physical universe or a moral code to be followed. It is an extraordinary rich and nuanced description of our relationship to God. It describes the morality of God far more often than it exhorts us to behave one way or another. It reveals time and again, that the Platonic compulsion to find unmoved movers to explain the universe and dependence on free will for moral blame are not there. This view of Scripture is where we will turn next.

Chapter Three

Magic, Morality and Transcendence

For You formed my inmost being.
You knit me together in my mother's womb.
I will give thanks to You,
for I am fearfully and wonderfully made.
Your works are wonderful.
My soul knows that very well.
My frame wasn't hidden from You,
when I was made in secret,
woven together in the depths of the earth.
Your eyes saw my body.
In your book they were all written,
the days that were ordained for me,
when as yet there were none of them.[133]

Noah – Magic and Morality

The devastation is complete. In the global apocalypse all flesh;
human and animal, bird and reptile, is extinguished from the

face of the earth[134]. No living thing escapes the punishment of God except one family on a lifeboat carrying a representative pair of every species to someday repopulate the earth. The language is extraordinary in its breadth, grandeur and poetry. When the Flood occurs, "all the wellsprings of the great deep burst and the casements of heaven were opened. ... The waters surged and multiplied over the earth."[135] It is perhaps the most evocative and the most well-known story in the Bible.

We are inclined, by our adherence to the illusion of free will, to read this story in terms of the magical and the moral. We assume that the point of the revelation that authored it is that God was enraged by the sinfulness of humanity and executed punishment with all the divine power at His disposal. Furthermore, while most Christians would acknowledge that this story is not factual, we may assume that the author of the story hoped we would believe it as an accurate, historical account of a supernatural, miraculous event. However, the story itself contains clues that this is not a story about God's divine wrath and punishment, and that its author did not intend to make us believe in a supernatural global flood.

The story of the Flood famously closes with God promising never to destroy the earth again with floodwaters and sealing this new covenant with the appearance of a rainbow. If this story was intended to provide a warning to us to act morally or risk divine wrath, why would God promise not to do it again? The story set up is indeed God's disappointment with the state of morality of humankind, and it is Noah's apparent moral rectitude that sets him apart from those about to be slaughtered and drowned. But there is only passing reference to Noah's righteousness, and this righteousness abandons him in the very next chapter. After the Flood waters recede, Noah plants a vineyard and gets epically drunk, inadvertently exposing himself to his son, Ham, who apparently willingly looked on and was cursed for it.[136] But aside from these clues, we can be sure this story is not a threat of punishment because if we do not have free will then God would not punish humanity's bad behavior or reward Noah's righteousness - because God knows that we are not morally autonomous beings and therefore to exact punishment or bestow exclusive reward would be unfair and unjust. In fact, as God considers the new covenant He is about to announce to Noah, He says, "I will never again curse the ground because of man, for the imagination of man's heart is evil from his youth."[137] What a remarkable acknowledgement, millennia before science would find the language to express it, that humanity's behavior is not free but is governed by his nature. If this story is not about morality, then what is its purpose?

Jesus, the Canaanite Woman and Morality

Popular culture faith tells us Jesus was an extraordinarily moral man who acted first and foremost out of love and has come to exemplify kindness, even among secular people. Ask a Christian or non-Christian to describe Jesus, and you will inevitably hear about love, non-violence, service to the poor, sharing, and other laudable moral traits. The popular culture unchallenged assumption is that he was sent by God to provide a moral example and perhaps to be a cosmic wish-granter, doling out miraculous healing on behalf of the all-powerful, all loving, Form of Good. This vision of Jesus renders him so morally perfect that we dogmatically claim he is without sin, presuming that this means his behavior was invariably perfect. In scandalous contradiction of this, however, is the Jesus of Scripture.

The scene plays out in a virtually grotesque manner. While Jesus is travelling in Phoenicia (in an area that is within Lebanon today) a Canaanite mother begs Jesus to heal her epileptic daughter. The Canaanites were the people the Israelites conquered to occupy the Promised Land and traditionally considered the descendants of Ham, Noah's disgraced son. They were Gentiles (since Noah's story and Ham's curse occurs before God's choice of the Israelites as His people) and therefore considered unclean. Jesus ignores her. His disciples step in, presumably out of annoyance rather than sympathy, asking him to send her away. She goes so far as to kneel in front of him and pleads simply, "Lord, help me." He dismisses her in the harshest language, comparing her to a dog. It is only when she accepts her subordinate status and argues that even dogs can eat scraps from the master's table that Jesus relents and heals her daughter.

Jesus went out from there, and withdrew into the region of Tyre and Sidon. Behold, a Canaanite woman came out from those borders, and cried, saying, "Have mercy on

> me, Lord, you son of David! My daughter is severely possessed by a demon!" But he answered her not a word. His disciples came and begged him, saying, "Send her away; for she cries after us." But he answered, "I wasn't sent to anyone but the lost sheep of the house of Israel." But she came and worshiped him, saying, "Lord, help me." But he answered, "It is not appropriate to take the children's bread and throw it to the dogs." But she said, "Yes, Lord, but even the dogs eat the crumbs which fall from their masters' table." Then Jesus answered her, "Woman, great is your faith! Be it done to you even as you desire." And her daughter was healed from that hour.[138]

The dialogue within the story of the Canaanite woman contains something abhorrent to our modern values. Jesus appears to be indulging in foulmouthed bigotry, using his ministry to perpetuate and foment sectarian hatred in his region of the Middle East. We want to let Jesus off the hook. We might say that Jesus is testing this woman's faith or making this a teachable moment. But this exercise doesn't actually take Jesus off the hook at all. I can remember in my early childhood watching a homeless man ask for a dollar from someone seated in an outdoor café in the Old City of Montreal. The donor demanded that the homeless person dance to receive the dollar, which he did. My young self was horrified and the image is burned in my memory. If Jesus was using this woman's desperation to make a point, his exploitation of her circumstances is no less horrifying than if he was simply being a bigot. Another way we attempt to get Jesus off the hook is to say that this is a story about persistence. That the woman demonstrates how persistence in prayer will finally result in God's beneficence. But this too is not satisfying. After all, who is the God incarnate of the story? Why is a Canaanite woman the protagonist and moral example in the story while Jesus indulges in crass racism? Finally, we might say that this is a moment of Jesus's moral evolution, and we might praise Jesus for his ability to set aside his cultural bigotry in favor of the more generous world view exemplified by the Canaanite woman. But we don't expect that the incarnation of God sent to be a moral example would need further teaching and guidance here in the last three years of his life as he is fully embarked on his ministry. This is, of course, not the only instance of Jesus's failing to be a perfect moral example. Where are the women apostles? Popular culture faith tells us Jesus was a counter-cultural revolutionary, teaching kindness and equality in a society defined by brutality and injustice. But he somehow failed to outpace the values of his culture, and he appears to have simply accepted the misogyny of his day. To be a good moral example Jesus would have to be a consistent moral example. No one calls someone who is good some of the time an example of goodness.

Remarkably, by his treatment of the Canaanite woman, Jesus is actually violating one of the most repeated prescriptions in the Old Testament and one of the laws expressly imposed by

God at Mount Sinai: "If a stranger lives as a foreigner with you in your land, you shall not do him wrong. The stranger who lives as a foreigner with you shall be to you as the native-born among you, and you shall love him as yourself; for you lived as foreigners in the land of Egypt. I am the Lord your God."[139] This is the only time Jesus re-interprets or outright violates Torah to the disadvantage of the outsider and outcast. But, of course, the Old Testament itself is full of this kind of moral ambiguity:

> When the Lord your God gives them over to you, and you defeat them; then you must completely destroy them; you shall make no peace treaties with them, and show no mercy to them.[140]
>
> When the Lord your God has led you into the land you are entering to make your own, nations will fall before you. You must lay them under solemn ban and show them no pity. The Lord your God has given you this land as your own. All your fighting men must take up arms and march.[141]
>
> Devour the nations the Lord your God delivers over to you. Show them no pity. If you say in your heart, 'These nations are greater than I; how can I dispossess them?' you shall not be afraid of them ... until those who are left and hide themselves from you are destroyed.[142]
>
> In the cities of these peoples that the Lord

your God gives you for an inheritance, you shall save alive nothing that breathes, but you shall utterly destroy them.[143]

Annihilate the nations you are dispossessing and make your home in their country.[144]

Put the inhabitants to the slaughter without giving any quarter and burn their town down. [145]

Kill every woman who has had sexual intercourse but keep the virgins for yourself. Divide them up evenly.[146]

Destroy all that they have; do not spare them, but kill both man and woman, infant and suckling, ox and sheep, camel and ass.[147]

All this is, of course, offensive to Christian expectations *if we cast God as moral commander and Jesus as a divine moral example*. If we want to discern the divine in Jesus, we have to look elsewhere – somewhere besides his morality. It is critical to understanding our relationship to God and our understanding of the status we give Jesus when we declare him our Savior and Redeemer to wholly abandon the idea that Jesus is principally a moral example, or that Scripture is principally a set of moral commands and attendant promises of reward and punishment. The story of the Canaanite woman is not intended to warn us away from casting Jesus as a moral example, but it may be its highest and best use nonetheless. In a vast majority of cases, we interpret Scripture to include a command or an example to be imitated and we'll make whatever mental adjustments are necessary to confirm that result even when the text clearly doesn't support it at all. This phenomenon occurs with regularity at every level: from the most credentialed theologian through the most inveterate atheist seeking to root out hypocrisy among the faithful, and from the most officious papal encyclical through the most informal bible study group. We have rendered faith insipid by reflexively assuming that God and Jesus's every word and action is a moral exhortation or an example to be imitated. But the pearl of great price is not the message to be good. That God became incarnate to tell us to be good, use our talents, share and be humble has never really been believable and, worse, renders the Author of the Creation small and peevish. Now behavioral science makes that view a philosophical impossibility and we can confidently reexamine the life of Jesus and the Scripture in general to find other meaning.

Magic and Allegory

When it is not apparently commanding morality, the Bible often seems to showcase the miraculous and the magical. By now, that the Bible is not a scientifically accurate account of how the universe, life, or humanity came into existence is almost universally accepted. In fact, the occurrence of the magical and the miraculous in the Bible is rarely intended to showcase the magical powers themselves or to explain some mysterious natural process, but each is rather an allegorical statement to inform us about the nature of God.

As God prepares Moses and Aaron to demand that Pharaoh release the Israelites from slavery, God predicts that Pharaoh will require them to prove themselves by working a miracle.[148] God tells Moses to instruct Aaron to throw down his rod at that moment and turn it into a snake. Remarkably, when the time comes, Pharaoh is unimpressed and summons his sorcerers and magicians who successfully repeat the miracle themselves! Pharaoh's magicians later also repeat the miracle of changing the Nile to blood, and causing a swarm of frogs to descend on Egypt. It is finally the swarm of gnats that cannot be repeated by Pharaoh's sorcerers and convinces them that the plagues have divine origin.[149] Exodus does not suggest that God inexplicably granted Pharaoh's sorcerers the ability to turn rods into snakes and thereby embarrass God's own plan to impress Pharaoh. It is stated as a simple matter of fact that Pharaoh had sorcerers capable of magic. When we reflexively interpret Scripture through a lens of magic, we can miss the transcendent message and rob the narrative of any of its power. The snakes that Pharaoh's sorcerer conjure up are promptly eaten by Aaron's snake. Evidently, the point was not the performance of magic by both sides, but rather to increase the narrative tension – Pharaoh was not going to be a marshmallow pushover and concede at the first hint of divine power. It is hardly an impressive miracle comparatively that Aaron's one snake can beat several, but it is an effective allegory to indicate that God's team, even though outmatched in numbers, could overcome Pharaoh.

Magic would have been an assumed everyday occurrence in the ancient world and would not have been thought to be the exclusive purview of God. Among the laws God imposes on the Israelites on Mount Sinai in addition to the Ten Commandments is included a requirement that sorcerers be killed.[150] In The First Book of Samuel[151], having exiled all the mediums and wizards, Saul finds himself in need of a prophecy. Not hearing from God through dreams or prophets because he has fallen out of favor, Saul disguises himself to visit a medium in territory held by his enemy, the Philistines. The medium conjures the spirit of Samuel from the dead and *successfully* foretells the future for him – his death in battle the next day. It is interesting that Jesus's ability to perform miracles is depicted as being quite fragile. When he returns to his own city, each of the Gospels of Mark, Matthew and Luke records that he is unable to perform any miracles there because those who knew him as a child couldn't believe he was capable of them.[152] Jesus's ability to perform magic, it seems, was not a central part of his identity as far as the Gospel writers were concerned. For the modern reader of Scripture, proof of the ability of a prophet or Jesus to perform magic would be pretty good proof that God exists. But the Bible is not interested in proving that God exists because to the people the authors expected to hear the stories, atheism and agnosticism would have been virtually unheard of. So foreign an idea was atheism that of the 248 laws and 365 restrictions contained in the Torah, although several prohibit idolatry and worshipping gods other than God, none forbids atheism.

Biblical stories clearly used unexplained occurrences in the natural world as backdrops to their allegorical messages. No story seems to attempt to cover more ground than the story of the Garden of Eden. God's punishment of Adam and Eve's disobedience with the complicity of the snake is used to explain all snakes' lack of legs, our instinctual fear of snakes, the painfulness of childbirth, and the essentially hard nature of life.[153] Although more speculative, it may well be that the story of the Flood was written the way it was to include an ancient attempt to explain why fossils of fish and shells could be found on mountaintops before the study of tectonic plate movement provided a better explanation, or an explanation for the appearance of rainbows after rain. To connect an allegory to something visible and mysterious in the natural world made it more compelling, memorable, and provided triggers to tell the story again. To someone so inclined, spotting a snake or rainbow offers an opportunity to reflect on transcendent issues of unilateral covenant and maybe moral autonomy, and perhaps to begin the process of conveying them to the next generation. But to read these stories as scientific journals is to entirely miss the point. It is only when we look past the magical as well as the moral, that these transcendent messages about the nature of God and His relationship to us reveal themselves.

While most Christians accept that the two creation stories and the story of Noah are allegorical, we are not as ready to accept that what Jesus said might contain allegory as well. But allegory is one of Jesus's favorite tools. As Jesus leaves the Temple in the Gospel of John, he states that, if it was destroyed (an event that would actually occur a few years following Jesus's death but before the Gospels were written), he could rebuild it in three days. Although we don't hear this directly from Jesus's lips in the other gospels other than John, in Matthew and Mark, Jesus's accusers say at his trial that they heard him say it. Notice that it is the villains of the story that conclude Jesus's statements were literal rather than allegorical:

Now the chief priests, the elders, and the whole council sought false testimony against Jesus, that they might put him to death; and they found none. Even though many false witnesses came forward, they found none. But at last two false witnesses came forward, and said, "This man said, 'I am able to destroy the temple of God, and to build it in three days.' " [154]

In John, Jesus makes the statement much earlier in his ministry and his disciples, who often serve as foils, are aghast, taking him to be speaking literally.[155] In John, the author himself states that Jesus was speaking allegorically about the resurrection of his body. Again in John, Jesus declares that those who eat his flesh and drink his blood abide with him.[156] Many of the disciples recoil and leave his ministry and it is interesting that Jesus lets them depart rather than interpret it for them as allegory.

So Jesus's words were allegorical at least part of the time, but what about his ability to perform miracles? I will not take a definitive position as to whether Jesus performed all or any of the miracles attributed to him, which is to say, I acknowledge that he may have. I was not in attendance for any of them and although I have never seen anything like them in my lifetime, I cannot say with any certainty whatsoever that they did not happen. However, if it could be definitively proven that Jesus did not perform the miracles attributed to him in the New Testament, it would not change anything in this book. The context of miraculous events occurring in the New Testament indicates that extremely infrequently is a miracle principally intended to say "look, this individual can perform magic" or as an act of sympathy or morality. Instead, each was generally intended to fulfill a prophecy describing what the messiah would do or to make some other point. The intention of each is almost always the transcendent message behind it.

Cana – Not a Sorcerer's Coming Out Party

Jesus turning water into wine at the wedding feast of Cana, is traditionally thought of as Jesus's first miracle and the start of his public ministry. But was this a first magic trick to kick off a travelling magic show? Was this to demonstrate that Jesus had special powers? In all likelihood, there is far more importance to the source of the water that is transformed than simply a statement of where Jesus found it. John records that the water came from stone jars for the Jewish rites of purification.[157] Now in the era before indoor plumbing, let alone toilet paper, the last thing one would want to do is drink the water used to wash the hands of every attendee of a wedding. It may have been that the author of this story intended to show Jesus was a purifying force – so purifying that he could convert the filthiest water into not just into something drinkable, but sacramental wine. The beginning of Jesus's ministry is not so much sorcery as an allegory for cleansing, renewal and hope. As we discard the magical and moral from our image of Jesus, he reveals himself to be a savior rather than someone who teaches how to self-save. In this there is no contradiction to faith.

Saints; The Magical and the Moral

Nothing exemplifies the contemporary impulse to treat the magical and moral as synonymous with faith as the process of identifying new saints. To be declared a saint by the Catholic Church, an individual must have two miracles attributed to him or her and have demonstrated "heroic virtue." This assumed connection between the saintly and the magical and the moral contrasts with the more ancient practice of referring to everyone who follows Jesus as a saint. For instance, Paul opens his letters to members of the church in Ephesus and Corinth by referring to the entire congregations as the "saints."[158] In Judaism, the concept of sainthood is embodied in the ancient and virtually forgotten tradition of the Lamed-Vov, beautifully expounded in the opening pages of Andre Schwarz-Bart's 1959 novel, *The Last of the Just*:[159]

> According to it, the world reposes upon thirty-six Just Men, the Lamed-Vov, indistinguishable from simple mortals; often unaware of their

station. But if just one of them were lacking, the sufferings of mankind would poison even the souls of the newborn, and humanity would suffocate with a single cry. For the Lamed-Vov are the hearts of the world multiplied, and into them, as into one receptacle, pour all our griefs. Thousands of popular stories take note of them. Their presence is attested to everywhere. A very old text of Haggadah tells us that the most pitiable are the Lamed-Vov who remain unknown to themselves. For those the spectacle of the world is an unspeakable hell. In the seventh century, Andalusian Jews venerated a rock shaped like a teardrop, which they believed to be the soul, petrified by suffering, of an unknown Lamed-Vovnik. Other Lamed-Vov, like Hecuba shrieking at the death of her sons, are said to have been transformed into dogs. "When an unknown Just rises to Heaven," a Hasidic story goes, "he is so frozen that God must warm him for a thousand years between His fingers before his soul can open itself to Paradise. And it is known that some remain forever inconsolable at human woe, so that God Himself cannot warm them. So from time to time the Creator, blessed be His Name, sets forward the clock of the Last Judgment by one minute.

The Lamed-Vov are also known as the Nistarim, or "concealed ones." Islam has a parallel in the Abdals, or forty concealed individuals who serve as intermediaries between God and humanity; or the Qutb, a single individual whose heart resembles the heart of Archangel Raphael, who is known as Istrafil in that tradition. There are certainly magical and moral attributes associated with the Lamed Vov and the Muslim parallels, but the overwhelming and common characteristic is that they are unknown, and that sometimes their status is even unknown to themselves. Rather than principally being moral examples, they are simply "friends of god."[160] My intention is not to compare my native Catholicism unfavorably to Judaism and Islam in this respect, but rather to demonstrate that the connection between the saintly and the magical and moral is not a necessary, historic or universally recognized one. If we accept that we do not have free will, then we must also accept that God requires nothing of us and none of us is more favored than anyone else. As we peel away the magical and moral from our understanding of our relationship to God the inescapable conclusion is that God's beloved are not moral heroes and are not capable of feats of magic.

Mad Men

The television series, *Mad Men*, which ran until 2015, followed the various members of a Madison Avenue advertising firm from the 1950s until 1971. The show became a cultural phenomenon and was, in my estimation, brilliant. At first, it was worth watching for the impeccable attention to detail in the sets, costuming and storyline, especially as the story progressed from one spectacularly evocative decade to another. The culture in which the show was set was familiar to those in middle age and beyond but the differences to modern sensibilities were entertainingly jarring. The main character, Don Draper, and his cohort would drink copiously in the office all day long, and chain smoke at their desks, in airplanes - essentially everywhere. The series avoided moral parables. The characters were all deeply flawed and few ever found redemption. Don Draper was a serial adulterer throughout the show and was hypocritical about it – getting angry if his then current wife was flirtatious or scolding if a co-worker engaged in the same behavior. The characters did not necessarily get what they deserved. Don's philandering behavior most often never really caught up with him, and those characters on the show who worked hard were just as likely to fail as those who slept off hangovers on their office couches. What finally set the show apart from other dramas on television, however, is that as the series progressed, it became clear that there were underlying themes and perhaps an overarching theme in the show that were not obvious but only hinted at through tantalizing clues. Seemingly insignificant dialogue or props on the set in one episode would become the focal point of another episode and suggest a thread in the fabric of the story. As the series wound down, Don, having abandoned his job and apparently fled his life, is asked by a hotel clerk to repair a Coca-Cola dispensing machine. A desk attendant at an ashram, where Don experiences the series-ending final epiphany, is dressed exactly like one of the singers in the iconic Coca-Cola 'Hilltop' ad. It is a replaying of that ad that closes the series and, we are led to believe, Don creates that very ad after leaving the ashram and returning to his life. Don's creativity is restored in the ashram when the mantra he has followed and professed throughout the series is finally discredited. Don has an assumed identity, multiple failed marriages and relationships, is estranged from his children, and is essentially leaving one sinking ship after another throughout the show. Don is never more sympathetic to other characters than when they suffer a serious setback that threatens to destroy them. He always tells them that it is possible to put it behind them and move on; to pretend it never happened. This is Don's theory of life. It sounds so good – it evokes resilience, self-reliance and the ability to recreate oneself. The viewer is seduced into believing it. It is only when Don is dispensing the same advice to a young friend in the closing minutes of the show, and that friend's simple rejection of it, that we realize that Don's advice is not the moral of the show – it is actually the thing that weighed him down, crippled his ability to relate to others, and prevented him from unlocking the true nature of things and doing his best creative work. It is in all the inscrutable details that the true meaning of the story is hidden. And sometimes, what appears to be the moral of the story, is actually the antithesis.

This is how the Bible is written as well. We can read it as a historical account of the miraculous. We can also read it as a moral parable about divine command, reward and punishment. We can assume that sin is the moral of the story and miss the fact that it is our natural, evolved focus on sin - *not sin itself* - that weighs us down, cripples our ability to relate to one another, and prevents us from understanding the true nature of our relationship to God. Our single best clue to recognizing this theme is our new understanding that we do not have free will. The Bible is brilliantly written and compiled. Seemingly insignificant dialogue and seemingly insignificant detail can suddenly reveal a much deeper, transcendent thread. We do a disservice to ourselves when we assume that the Bible was written as a detailed moral guide or catalogue of magical events assembled to help us avoid divine punishment, obtain reward and believe in God's existence.

Combining Passages to Make Them More Moral: The Redactor

There is an old Irish joke that I love:

It was Paddy and Seamus giving the motorcycle a ride on a brisk autumn day. After a wee bit, Paddy who was sitt'n behind Seamus on the bike began to holler ...'Seamus ... Seamus ... the wind is cutt'n me chest out!'

'Well, Paddy my lad,' said Seamus, 'why don't you take your jacket off and turn it from front to back ... that'll block the wind for you.'

So Paddy took Seamus' advice and turned his jacket from front to back and got back on the bike and the two of them were off down the road again. After a bit, Seamus turned to talk to Paddy and was horrified to see that Paddy was not there. Seamus immediately turned the bike around and retraced their route. When after a short time he came to a turn and saw a bunch of farmers standing around Paddy who was lying motionless on the ground.

'T'anks be to heaven, is he alright?' Seamus hailed to the farmers.

'Well,' said one of the farmers, ' he was alright when we found him here, but since we turned his head back to front, he hasn't said a word since!'

Sometimes trying to help can really mess things up. Tradition says that Moses himself was the author of the first five books of the Bible, sometimes referred to as the Pentateuch. However, there are clues that this is not the case – particularly the fact that the Pentateuch records Moses's death and refers to events that occur afterward. Modern scripture scholarship noted that the name used in the Pentateuch for God alternated between Yahweh and Elohim, which suggested that there were at least two authors or schools of thought that contributed text to the Pentateuch which were eventually merged into a single work. In fact, by looking at the various styles in which the Pentateuch is written, it is now theorized that there were at least two more authors or schools of thought that contributed to the final written Pentateuch. The four are respectively called the Yahwist, Elohist, Deuteronomist, and Priestly traditions. The author who finally combined these traditions into a single work inevitably had to make some pretty important editorial decisions to make it all fit even as well as it does. This person or school is known as the "redactor."[161] Returning to the story of Noah reveals some of the fault lines left by the redactor. The story begins with a bizarre mythological story about divine beings having sexual relationships with humans and bearing demigod-like offspring that sounds like it should have no place in a monotheistic religion:

And it happened as humankind began to multiply over the earth and daughters were born to them, that the sons of God saw that the daughters of man were comely, and they took themselves wives howsoever they chose. And the Lord said, "My breath shall not abide in the human forever, for he is but flesh. Let his days be a hundred and twenty years." The Nephilim were then on the earth, and afterward as well, the sons of God having come to bed with the daughters of man who bore them children: they are the heroes of yore, the men of renown.[162]

The story then moves on to the set up for the Flood. God decides that humanity is evil and that he will therefore destroy humanity and, if all living things on the earth are destroyed too, it is as collateral damage. The story is interrupted by a genealogy of Noah and statement that he alone was righteous. Then the story picks up again, but now God says that all the earth is corrupt and filled with violence and all flesh – not just humanity – had corrupted itself and deserved to be destroyed[163] God initially tells Noah to bring two of every animal on the ark; male and female.[164] Just a few lines later, however, God's instructions are different. Now Noah is to bring seven pairs of clean animals and just one pair of unclean animals.[165] This may have been a corrective by one of the competing traditions of this story to make sense of the fact that Noah sacrifices one pair of every clean animal as soon as he disembarks[166] and he would be extinguishing some of the species he just saved if he had only one matched set of each. This story bears the scars of being at least two separate but roughly similar stories combined as one. It would appear that whoever did the combining was respectful of the originals and more interested in preserving as much of the text as possible, than in avoiding and hiding continuity errors. The redactor of the Old Testament clearly felt the text he was working on was sacred and, like an archaeologist who makes no effort to hide the cracks and voids when he or she reconstructs a pottery jar, the redactor too, seemed satisfied with an imperfect story that nonetheless preserved and respected the original text.

The New Testament authorship has a similar dynamic. It is widely accepted that the authors of the Gospels of Matthew, Mark, Luke and John were in all likelihood not the apostles of Jesus, but were rather unnamed authors writing in the name of the apostles. This was not an attempt to deceive, but was rather the accepted literary custom of the day to lend more credibility to the text - akin to what we would call "ghost writing." This custom is reflected in the Second Letter to the Thessalonians where Paul seems to be assuring his readers that this letter is authentic: "I, Paul, write this greeting with my own hand. This is the mark in every letter of mine; it is the way I write."[167] We now know that this desire to authenticate Paul's writings was a valid concern, as scholars now doubt that six of his letters were written by Paul, including, ironically, the Second Letter to the Thessalonians.[168] The author of Revelations was so concerned about this that he actually takes the time at the closing to curse anyone who edits his work:

I warn everyone who hears the words of the prophecy of this book: if anyone adds to them, God will add to him the plagues described in this book, and if anyone takes away from the words of the book of this prophecy, God will take away his share in the tree of life and in the holy city, which are described in this book.[169]

The letters of Paul were likely the first to be written of what we now think of as the New Testament, and the earliest preserved Christian writing is thought to be First Letter to the Thessalonians, probably less than twenty years after the death of Jesus.[170] It is believed that the Gospel of Mark was the first of the gospels to be written; probably around 68 to 73 A.D.[171], which would be more than thirty years after the death of Jesus.

The Gospels of Matthew, Mark and Luke are called the Synoptic Gospels because they appear to be so similar to each other, while the Gospel of John represents a radical departure from the first three. It was also written the latest; maybe as many as seventy years after the death of Jesus; beyond the lifespan of almost everyone who could have known Jesus in the flesh.

There is a tremendous amount of overlap between the Gospel of Mark and the two other Synoptic Gospels with Mark being the clear common denominator. This has led Scripture scholars to believe that the authors of Matthew and Luke had the Gospel of Mark, or some earlier version of it, available to them. Matthew and Luke do contain material common to each other but which is not found in the Gospel of Mark. Scripture scholars believe this material came from a source that is now lost to us. They call the author of this source "Q" which is short for the German word "Quelle" which translates as "source." Mark and Q likely collected fragmentary texts and remembrances about Jesus that were available to them and combined them in a manner that made the most sense. Like the Old Testament writers, they did make editorial decisions. Luke left out the miracle of Jesus feeding the four thousand probably because he thought it was a duplication of the story of Jesus feeding the five thousand, which he included. The Sermon on the Plain in the Gospel of Luke[172] bears a striking resemblance to the Sermon on the Mount in Matthew.[173]

There is strong evidence that both the Old Testament and New Testament writers combined texts to tell a chronological story but also to assert a divine program of command, reward and punishment. The redactors seemed to work to make the text fit a Platonic notion of God. Maybe the best example of this is Jesus's parable of the wedding feast. The first part of the parable seems to be, in its general thrust, consistent with theistic determinism. God initially invites a few to a feast, and when they refuse, He invites everyone. How remarkable that the bad are invited along with the good! It seems moral conduct is not a prerequisite for the love of God:

> Jesus answered and spoke again in parables to them, saying, "The Kingdom of Heaven is like a certain king, who made a marriage feast for his son, and sent out his servants to call those who were invited to the marriage feast, but they would not come. Again he sent out other servants, saying, 'Tell those who are invited, "Behold, I have prepared my dinner. My cattle and my fatlings are killed, and all things are ready. Come to the marriage feast!"' But they made light of it, and went their ways, one to his own farm, another to his merchandise, and the rest grabbed his servants, and treated them shamefully, and killed them. When the king heard that, he was angry, and sent his armies, destroyed those murderers, and burned their city. Then he said to his servants, 'The wedding is ready, but those who were invited weren't worthy. Go therefore to the intersections of the highways, and as many as you may find, invite to the marriage feast.' Those servants

went out into the highways, and gathered
together as many as they found, both bad and
good. The wedding was filled with guests.

But then the story takes a strange twist. While God is enjoying
the feast with this universal guest list, He apparently notices
that someone isn't dressed appropriately:

But when the king came in to see the guests, he
saw there a man who didn't have on wedding
clothing, and he said to him, 'Friend, how
did you come in here not wearing wedding
clothing?' He was speechless. Then the king
said to the servants, 'Bind him hand and foot,
take him away, and throw him into the outer
darkness; there is where the weeping and
grinding of teeth will be.' For many are called,
but few chosen.[174]

Scripture scholars agree that these were originally two separate remembrances combined into a single parable.[175] In fact,
the first part appears in Luke but the second part is entirely
absent, indicating that Luke treated these as independent, and
disregarded the wedding garment portion altogether.[176] In putting together material, probably from Q (as the parable does
not appear in Mark), the author has converted a message of
unconditional love into the transactional: while God's love is

unconditional, you must act appropriately to keep God's love.[177] Without changing a word, but simply combining some text, he has made the story comport with a Platonic view of God. With his natural human impulse to equate the divine with the moral, this author has twisted poor Paddy's head and added a distraction to the text that wasn't in the revealed Word. Of course, if this second part of the parable was a genuine remembrance of something Jesus said, then even it is not a part of the wedding feast parable, it appears God does command, impose punishment and mete out reward. How can we make sense of that? Let us put that question in our back pockets for now and deal with it shortly.

Not Just Combining Existing Text but Adding Text to Explain and Make Moral: The Sower, Weeds and Wheat

Careful study of Scripture reveals that the redactor did not just combine text, but sometime he added explanation or editorial to it as well. It is widely accepted that the Gospels include a very large amount of dialogue attributed to Jesus that probably was the work of the gospel author or a subsequent redactor. In the 1980s and 90s, a group of Scriptural scholars calling themselves *The Jesus Seminar* examined each passage of the New Testament and simply voted on whether it was likely to have been a direct quote from Jesus or a historically accurate account of what happened. There is much to dispute in their process and their conclusions, but that the Gospels contain editorializing is clear just from a careful reading of them.

Almost invariably, where the scars of this process are visible, the editor has made the text more pious and more moral and has taken a passage that seems to acknowledge or even state outright that we do not have moral autonomy, and changed it with the assumption that we do.

In the Gospel of Mark, Jesus says that "The kingdom of God is as if a man should scatter seed upon the ground, and should sleep and rise night and day, and the seed should sprout and grow, he knows not how. The earth produces of itself, first the blade, then the ear, then the full grain in the ear."[178] In beautiful allegory, Jesus indicates that the kingdom arises not from the efforts of the sower or the seed, but naturally and organically from the earth itself. Jesus seems to be saying that he knows that what good or bad arises in us is not the product of our independent decision-making or moral autonomy, but arises in us as the inevitable result of our nature and nurture. We need only be still. Mark continues with a parable of a tiny mustard seed growing into a massive shrub that birds nest in.[179]

The author or redactor of Matthew clearly read the story of the sower in Mark and decided it did not do a good job of demanding moral conduct from the reader, and, in fact, seemed to let us off the hook. In his Gospel, the story of the sower is expanded and then explained.[180] It is then followed by the parable of the mustard seed written almost word for word from Mark.[181] In Matthew's Gospel, however, the sower is no longer a recipient of inevitably abundant harvests. While the sower is asleep, an enemy sows weed seeds in the sower's garden. The sower's servants ask the sower if they should uproot the weeds, but the sower tells them to leave the weeds in place so that they don't inadvertently pull up wheat with the weeds. At first, it seems Matthew is saying that we should not judge one another and should not place each other on a moral spectrum in acknowledgement of the fact that the wheat and weeds are what they are, not as a result of anything they decided, but rather because of their nature. If true, this parable was first written as a statement about radical grace; we are exhorted not to hate and not to spend our time rooting out weeds. However, after a brief interruption with the story of the mustard seed and the story of the woman leavening bread, suddenly in this Gospel, the disciples demand an explanation of the wheat and the weeds. Matthew has Jesus explain in the harshest terms. Jesus, he says, "will send his angels and they will gather out of his kingdom all causes of sin and all evildoers, and throw them into the furnace of fire; there men will weep and nash their teeth."[182] Apparently for the author, this is not a parable about living together in peace or radical grace, but rather, it is a story of God withholding judgment until he can get a clear shot with minimal collateral damage. Evidently, for Matthew or the redactor, the earlier Gospel of Mark required expansion and explanation to fit the story into moral framework.

The Gospel of Mark does not consistently avoid the idea of a judgmental, harsh God. Both Mark and Matthew include another parable of a sower that immediately proceeds the one we just explored. In both Mark and Matthew, this sower sows on the path, where birds eat the seed, and on rocky ground, where it sprouts but later dies, among thorns, where it is choked, and finally, some lands in good soil where it bears fruit.[183] By itself, this parable could be read to be an acknowledgement that it is where the sower throws the seed that determines whether the seed will bear fruit and it is not by the efforts of the seed that it grows or fails to grow. But in both gospels, after a statement about the difficulty of understanding parables, the author offers his interpretation.[184] In each case, moral responsibility for where they are thrown is attributed to the seeds. Some seeds delight in riches while some initially do the hard work of discipleship but are not persistent enough. Interestingly though, both authors assume not only human free will, but the intervention of Satan. The seeds on the path that are eaten by birds, Mark tells us, are doomed because, "Satan immediately comes and takes away the word which is sown in them."[185]

Noah Reinterpreted; Chaos

We have already seen how the seemingly moral and magical messages of the Garden of Eden in the second story of Creation obscured a statement that our natural human assumption of moral autonomy inevitably leads us to hate and away from the paradisal. The story of the Flood has largely become a children's story because it is assumed to be about magic and morality; too heavy-handed and obvious to be of interest to adults. Looking at the story more carefully, we can discern deliberate echoes from the first lines of the first story of Creation in which God creates the universe in six days.

> In the beginning, God created the heavens and the earth. The earth was formless and empty. Darkness was on the surface of the

Deep and God's spirit was hovering over the surface of the waters.[186]

The Flood is a clear reference to The Deep that exists before God calls a vault into being which separates the water beneath the vault from the water above the vault. It is from both of these sources of water that the Flood later erupts. As we've seen, God gradually creates the world not from nothing but by dividing one thing from another: heaven from earth, earth from water, and from earth come living things, gradually creating order and pattern from chaos. This division and ordering is mirrored in the second creation story as well, as God creates man from dust, and woman from man. God has called each of us and all of creation out of chaos. When The Deep returns in the story of the Flood, it is an allegory for the return of chaos. What might this suggest about the nature of God and our relationship to Him?

First, contrary to the expectations of Plato and Priestley, the universe does not proceed in an orderly fashion from a first cause, unmoved mover or even according to a divine plan. If there is a plan, it is to have no plan at all. Chaos is an integral part of the universe and our lives and when it arises it may, in a manner of speaking, take God by surprise as much as it takes us by surprise. The terrible diagnosis, the meaningless loss, the gratuitous suffering that inevitably will enter our lives from time to time is not the execution of a plan to teach us something, or punish us for bad behavior or as a down payment for a better distant future. God does not promise to prevent those things from happening, but promises something more. As the Book of Genesis closes, Abraham's grandson, Jacob, and his descendants are safely ensconced in Egypt on the best lands of Pharaoh, having escaped a famine in Canaan and earned royal treatment. The Israelites are a well-respected and prosperous part of Egyptian culture; so much so that when Jacob and his son Joseph die, they are each accorded the Egyptian honor of being embalmed.[187] But as Exodus opens, a new Pharaoh has the throne and is worried about the ever growing Israelite population. He enslaves them and orders that all male children be drowned in the waters of the Nile. Chaos has returned, as it will so often in the Israelites' future.[188] He who will eventually lead his people to freedom is born to an unnamed father and mother during this pogrom. To save their son, they place the infant Moses in a basket made of bulrushes and place him in the reeds of the very river in which his contemporaries are being drowned. He, like Noah and his family, floats over the Chaos. When Pharaoh's daughter finds him and adopts him, she names him Moses because she drew him out of that water.[189] Moses will eventually part the Red Sea and drown the pursuing Egyptians.[190] The theme of ordering chaos in the form of bodies of water resounds through the entire Scriptural story. Elijah will part the Jordan River as he ascends into heaven and his successor prophet, Elisha, parts it again to cross back.[191] Jesus will perform the twin miracles of calming rough seas and walking on water to make the same point.

But it's critical to note that God does not magically intervene to take away the source of the chaos. Nor does God magically provide strength to overcome the chaos. The second lesson of the story of Noah is that God's help is not physical intervention. What God gives Noah is spiritual information – that chaos is inevitable, but it does not need to sink us – and that God is with us. Time and again, it is the revelation of God's loving concern and decision to love us that ultimately saves us. *God is not what He can do for us, but what He is to us.*

Reinterpretation of the Escape from Egypt – God is Not What He Can Do for Us

A similar dynamic occurs in Exodus as the Israelites escape from slavery. The details of the story make clear to anyone willing to see it that the point does not include a moral imperative or a magical intervention.

Pharaoh is the most villainous character in the Old Testament and is juxtaposed against Moses; a man of whom it is later said no greater prophet has been seen since. A book about theistic determinism could hardly mention this story without noticing that before Moses even meets Pharaoh, God tells Moses that God will harden Pharaoh's heart and that Pharaoh, as a result, will not listen.[192] And, in fact, God does harden Pharaoh's heart multiple times as the story unfolds.[193] The author would have had every reason to make this encounter morally unambiguous if morality was the point. Instead, it is made absolutely clear that Pharaoh is not acting with free will in a morally autonomous fashion and that he actually is not ultimately responsible for his actions. Here again, a theistic determinist message seems to be hidden in plain sight. This is the Pharaoh who orders the drowning of the Israelites' children, but although it would have made the story more heroic, we are denied the ability to hate Pharaoh because it was God would harden his heart to do what he did. Ultimately, Moses and God must exercise what Buddhism calls fierce compassion; restraining and finally even destroying Pharaoh's army to avoid re-enslavement. But as if to ensure we don't miss the point, God later expressly commands that the Israelites not hate the Egyptians and even provides a path to citizenship, saying that the children of the third generation of Egyptians can enter the assembly of the Lord.[194]

It is not God's moral teaching or His magic that frees the Israelites. It is His Presence. What is remarkable about the rescue of God's people and their escape to the Promised Land that follows is how limited God's physical intervention in events really is. God reveals Himself and identifies Himself to Moses at the burning bush.[195] God gives him a transcript of what he is to tell the Israelites about God and their inheritance as the decedents of Abraham.[196] He teaches Moses some magic tricks to convince the Israelites of Moses's divine authority.[197] He appoints Moses's brother, Aaron, first as his sidekick, but later for an important priestly role entirely distinct from Moses.[198] Finally, he sends Moses to Pharaoh to negotiate the release of the Israelites. By hardening his heart, God is as instrumental in preventing Pharaoh from submitting than He is instrumental in causing Pharaoh to submit by sending the plagues that devastate Egypt. When the Israelites finally make their escape,

God functions as guide – moving ahead of them as towering cloud. At night, He lights their way as a pillar of fire, and by His mere presence and clear allegiance to the Israelites, intimidates the Egyptian charioteers following them.[199] God does not save by doing, He saves by being there. In the divine economy, spiritual information is power - if we know our status as the beloved of God we will not necessarily act better or have better results, but there is nothing we can't endure. This is a theme that echoes throughout the Bible. When an angel appears to Zechariah to announce the conception of John the Baptist, and again when Gabriel appears to Mary to announce that Jesus will be conceived, he says "be not afraid."[200] When Jesus appears to the disciples after his death and resurrection, his first statement is "Peace be with you."[201] God's presence diminishes fear. Whatever the nature of this salvation, God is no passive observer or unmoved mover simply inspiring us to one emotion over another. God dutifully closes the door of the ark and locks the passengers inside until chaos subsides again. The story of the Flood is not a magical children's story to encourage good behavior and avoid enraging God, but a beautiful statement of God's promise that He is with us always.

At the crescendo of the escape story, when Pharaoh's forces are closing in and the Israelites are trapped at the Red Sea, God takes a more active role. Moses tells them "Fear not, stand firm, and see the salvation of the Lord, which He will work for you today; for the Egyptians whom you see today you will never see again. The Lord will fight for you, and you only have to be still."[202] At God's direction, Moses stretches out his arm and parts the Red Sea to allow the Israelites to escape and to lure the Egyptians to their watery deaths. This is another theme we'll see throughout Scripture. Unexpectedly, to be the beloved of God we only have to be still. If we are endowed with free will and moral autonomy, then God would justifiably command us to be good and reward and punish us on the basis of what we choose. We know we don't have free will, and so a just God would not reward or punish us according to our behavior, and would not even bother to command us. Although He may celebrate our successes and mourn our failures, He cannot possibly choose one of us over another or select some of us for reward and others for punishment. We have nothing to offer God. *We are not what we can do for God.* And so we can be still, accomplish no purpose, and be assured of God's presence and loving concern.

The Man Blind from Birth – God Doesn't Reward and Punish

But despite all the evidence in the Old Testament that God does not judge our moral behavior and mete out reward or punishment accordingly, the idea persisted into Jesus's time and persists today. In fact, I will argue *that the principal message of Jesus is a full-throated rejection of the idea that God commands, rewards and punishes morality and it was that rejection that got him executed.*

We have direct evidence in the Gospel of John that the overwhelmingly accepted theology of the Jesus's day was that if something bad happened to you, it was as a result of God's disfavor. John's Gospel describes an episode in which Jesus passes by a man who we are told was blind from birth.[203] The disciples casually ask Jesus who sinned to cause his blindness, and they can conceive of only two alternatives – the man himself or his parents. The idea that misfortune is just a matter of bad luck is alien even to Jesus's disciples. Jesus says that neither are responsible and heals the man by making a salve of clay and spittle and having him wash in the pool at Siloam. The Pharisees, who wholeheartedly believed that blindness was a curse from God for bad behavior, haul the man in to question him. In an extended discourse, the Pharisees interview the man and then his parents and finally the man again to determine how his healing was possible. The man is uncompromising that Jesus is clearly from God. In frustration, they reject the man's testimony as unreliable - because he "was born in utter sin," as demonstrated by his blindness. This view, in addition to being uncharitable, is wholly dependent on the assertion that we have free will to choose the behavior that will ultimately lead to our punishment or the punishment of our children. It is a Platonic hangover; seeing God as the unalterable Form of Good and explaining all evil with free will.

The Book of Job – God Doesn't Reward and Punish

No Biblical story begins with a more distracting set-up or initially appears to more support a testing, rewarding and punishing God than the Book of Job. Job is introduced to us as someone who is blameless and upright, and on whom fortune has smiled. We're given an inventory of his oxen, sheep, and camels, and told how happily and well his children interact with one another. We are told bluntly that Job is the greatest of the people of the east.[204]

But Job becomes the unwitting subject of a bet between God and Satan. Satan insinuates that Job's moral conduct and reverence for God is as a result of all the good fortune he enjoys and if it were to be taken from him, Job would curse God to His face. God accepts the bet and puts Job in Satan's power. Immediately, all of Job's cattle are stolen and the servants in charge of guarding them killed. While this is being reported to Job, another messenger tells him all his sheep have been burned up by the fire of God and the servants tending those animals killed as well. Scarcely does Job receive this report than he receives another, learning that all his camels have been stolen too. Finally, he is told that all of his children have been killed when a wind collapsed their house. Job is devastated, but does not blame God.

God and Satan assess how their bet is going, and Satan insists that taking away Job's possessions and children is not enough and that Job will surely break if his health is destroyed. Job is again put in Satan's power and Job is immediately afflicted with sores all over his body. Job tries to find relief by scraping the sores with a piece of broken pottery. Job's wife encourages him to "curse God and die," but Job steadfastly refuses. [205] Three of Job's friends show up and are shocked and appalled by the look of him. They sit silently with him, touchingly suffering with their friend. Job curses his own existence and insists he would have been better if had he not been born at all. Each of Job's friends, Eliphaz, Bildad, and Zophar, in succession offers an explanation of his radically changed circumstances. Each suggests, with increasing stridency, that he must have sinned to be punished in this way and now must seek God's forgiveness. Echoing the theology that the Pharisees would adopt in the story of the man blind from birth, they assert that bad things only happen to bad people, and therefore Job has clearly offended God. They are Platonists. Job insists to each of them that he hasn't done anything to deserve divine punishment and we know, from the opening of the Book, that this is true. Job says that good things do, in fact, happen to bad people.[206] This interchange goes on, back and forth for twenty-eight of the Book's forty-two chapters. Finally, God answers Job. His answer is not one that we are likely to find satisfactory. He does not mention the wager with Satan. Nor does God attempt to explain why bad things happen to good people. Rather, His answer, delivered in beautiful poetry laced with mythological creatures and majestic imagery, is best summarized as, "who are you to question Me about how I ordered the universe?"

Where were you when I laid the foundations of the earth? Tell me if you have understanding. Who determined its measurements – surely you know! Or who stretched the line upon it? On what were its bases sunk, or who laid its cornerstone, when the morning stars sang together and all the sons of God shouted for joy?[207]

What's remarkable about God's answer to Job is not what He says, but what He doesn't say. At no time does God suggest that evil is permitted in the world to preserve our free will. If ever there was a time to assert that our ability to choose to do good or bad and to be rewarded and punished accordingly were at the foundation of our relationship to God or underpins the way the universe operates, this would have been it. The divine silence speaks volumes.

In fact, what God does expressly declare is that Job's three friends' theology of command, reward and punishment is dead wrong. He goes so far as to impose a punishment on the three, requiring them to make a sacrifice to God and declaring that if Job prays for them, God will forgive them. God does not offer His own explanation of why bad things happen to good people, but he does utterly reject the friends' idea of divine reward and punishment for the sins. I have suggested that within the universe's capacity for randomness as revealed by quantum mechanics may lie the answer to the question of how suffering can exist in the presence of a good God. God did not set the universe on course that was inevitable from the moment of Creation as Plato would insist or have a plan that includes specific disproportionate suffering for some of us for some greater good as Priestley would assert. Rather, He included an element of randomness and pledged not to intervene because we, God's creatures, cannot realize wholeness and finally experience happiness in an environment free from suffering. The authors of the Book of Job would have no language or ability to conceive of a random universe and how bad things can happen to good people, and they characterize God's motivations as mysterious. But of one thing they were certain – the Problem of Evil is not answered by free will.

Job and Elihu

The Book of Job includes five chapters which most scholars agree were added to the original text.[208] After the three friends and Job end their argument, a fourth character is suddenly introduced and offers his own opinion.[209] The dialogue of Elihu is suspected to be a later addition because he uses words suited to Aramaic, while the rest of the book clearly started as Hebraic. Additionally, although the three friends of Job were named in the introduction and are called out by God by name in the conclusion, Elihu is never mentioned before or after his dialogue.[210] To the three friends' assertion that bad things always happen to bad people, Elihu adds that God is just, and so whatever bad things are happening to Job must be deserved. Elihu appears to want to make the three friends' argument more sophisticated and more compelling. It is almost as though the redactor thought the three friends' arguments were made too weakly and, perhaps feeling his own theology was getting maligned, the redactor included Elihu to make a stronger case. Because the original text did not include it, God does not expressly reject Elihu's argument at the end of the story when He discredits the other three, and appears to simply ignore it. This is a fascinating example of a redactor wanting to insert a moralistic element, but not wishing to change the original text except by adding to it in a very thinly veiled manner.

Job and *The Shack*

Another way in which we hedge suffering is to claim it isn't really happening, or that it will pale to insignificance when the grandeur of God's plan is revealed. In his 2007 book, *The Shack*, William P. Young imagines a figure representing the Holy Spirit tearing out a corner of a beautiful garden in order to make room for something even more beautiful. In the parlance of contemporary Christianity, God never closes one door without opening another, or God sends suffering to us to teach humility or in just that amount that He knows we can handle. Like Priestley, we often uncritically believe that everything happens according to God's divine plan and that everything will work out as a net benefit in the final accounting between happiness and suffering.

This concept is foreign to the Book of Job. Nowhere does God say that Job's suffering will reveal itself to be a blessing or result in a net good, to Job or future generations. In the Book of Job, the form and intensity of suffering is not in the hands of God. It is possible to get more than your fair share, and the clear implication of the wager itself is that, as we all know, suffering can be more than we can handle. Suffering is not another test from which we emerge to receive reward or punishment. It is the capricious nature of the universe that we inhabit and, if faith provides relief, it is that we do not travel alone.

Job and Satan

Of course this story, like Noah, Jonah, and, as we'll see, Sodom, has an intensely vivid set-up and it is very tempting to point at this story as proof of the existence of Satan. How better to satisfy our desire to see the moralistic than to focus on a character that is the very personification of the immoral? But as soon as Satan serves as literary device to set the scene, he disappears and is never mentioned again. Through many pages of dialogue addressing the very issue of evil, neither God nor any of the other characters of the story ever mention again that Job has been placed in Satan's power, or that Job is being tested as a result of a cosmic wager between God and Satan. Satan's role in the narrative is utterly ignored. The three friends are wholly committed to the view, ultimately forcefully rejected by God, that Job's sinfulness has attracted God's punishment, and that the misfortune will continue until he repents. In fact, this is Satan's only appearance as a personification in the Old Testament. Despite the wide assumption that the snake in the Garden of Eden is the devil, this is not the case.[211] God punishes the snake for its duplicity by making it slither on the ground.[212] In the opening of Job, God almost amicably asks Satan where he's been. Satan replies, "Going to and fro on the earth and walking up and down on it."[213] This is a clever trick given God's curse in the Garden. Satan is mentioned many times in the New Testament and was clearly a more prominent part of the theology of Jesus's time. But he actually appears as a personification only once outside of Revelations. No apostle claims to see him. Instead, we are told in the Gospels of

Mark, Matthew and Luke that he appears to Jesus and tempts him three times when Jesus is alone in the desert right after he is baptized by his cousin John and at the very beginning of his ministry. So whatever remembrance is recorded in those three Gospels, it is, at best, a story told by Jesus. And Jesus, as we've seen, is a notorious user of allegory stated as fact. The story itself is shockingly similar to the story of the Buddha who is threatened and tempted by a devil-figure named Mara three times as he sits under the Bodhi Tree moments before he achieves Enlightenment and begins his ministry. Alexander the Great's military conquests extended through Mesopotamia and deep into territory in which Buddhism had been practiced for centuries prior to Jesus's birth. There is no question that nascent Christianity was aware of the legend of Mara's temptation of the Buddha and could have sought to adapt it to its own purpose. The Mara-like figure already existed in the Old Testament story of Job, and the New Testament authors would have found it easy to put this literary device to a new purpose.

Although he was not particularly significant in Scripture as a whole, Satan certainly became a far more important figure as time went on. Satan occupies a position out of proportion to his presence in the Bible in all modern Christian theology and this rises to a near fever pitch among some Christians to the point where one wonders which deity is being worshiped. How did this allegorical and relatively minor figure come to have such prominence in Christianity?

The Greek ontological god, whose very identity is synonymous with perfection, has a philosophical problem. How can a perfect, unmoved mover create a world that contains suffering? The almost inevitable solution is one of three formulations dependent on free will: We bring on God's justifiable wrath when we misuse our free will, God allows us to use our free will to hurt others because He must respect our free will, and finally, the free will of a personification of evil, Satan, somehow outside of the control of God, is responsible for the capricious suffering that is caused by earthquakes, tsunamis, and cancer. We have borrowed the Form of Evil from Platonism and installed it as a demi-god alongside God. The idea that there is a real Satan figure with the power to read minds, to tempt, and to bring calamity - in other words, a god-like figure - should always have been offensive to a monotheistic faith. The God of Abraham is the master of His own house and is not challenged by a corresponding evil figure. One wonders what would happen to the world if Satan was responsible for evil, has a capacity for free will, and has a change of heart. Science and philosophy have come to the conclusion that human free will does not exist which, I have argued, is not contradictory to Scripture but is actually the message of the Garden of Eden, the Book of Job and countless other passages. When the Book of Job settles in our memory as the book that that confirms Satan's existence and his power over us, we have drawn a conclusion that is the precise opposite of the actual message.

Let's look at Jesus's encounter with Satan more closely. In the Gospel of Mark, it is simply noted that Jesus is tempted by Satan without any detail and the exchange is missing entirely in the Gospel of John. The story is more fleshed out in the Gospels of Matthew and Luke. Jesus goes into the desert and fasts for forty days and nights. The Gospels tell us that, naturally, he is hungry. At this moment, Satan appears and tempts Jesus three times:

Then Jesus was led up by the Spirit into the wilderness to be tempted by the devil. When he had fasted forty days and forty nights, he was hungry afterward. The tempter came and said to him, "If you are the Son of God, command that these stones become bread." But he answered, "It is written, 'Man shall not live by bread alone, but by every word that proceeds out of the mouth of God.' "[214]

Then the devil took him into the holy city. He set him on the pinnacle of the temple, and said to him, "If you are the Son of God, throw yourself down, for it is written, 'He will command his angels concerning you.' and, 'On their hands they will bear you up, so that you don't dash your foot against a stone.' "[215] Jesus said to him, "Again, it is written, 'You shall not test the Lord, your God.' "[216]

Again, the devil took him to an exceedingly high mountain, and showed him all the kingdoms of the world, and their glory. He said to him, "I will give you all of these things, if you will fall down and worship me." Then

> Jesus said to him, "Get behind me, Satan! For it is written, 'You shall worship the Lord your God, and you shall serve him only.'"[217]
>
> Then the devil left him, and behold, angels came and served him.[218]

These are strange temptations. The first two are particularly interesting. Both gospels specifically indicate this exchange happened when Jesus had completed his fast.[219] There would have been no failure of discipline or other sin in now eating bread, whether obtained in the usual way or by miraculous conversion from stone. Similarly, Jesus is about to embark on a ministry characterized by miraculous healings. Why is Jesus unwilling to work one now if only to get rid of Satan? Furthermore, isn't Satan in fact correct that the Psalms predict that the Son of God (or perhaps all of us) will be protected by angels? In fact, Jesus accepts this help at the close of the passage as angels appear and minister to him.[220] So why won't Jesus call on God to feed him or save him from injury? His refusal echoes the mocking crowd at the foot of the cross that asks why Jesus, who healed so many, can't save himself.[221] Is Jesus refusing to show off in a show of divine humility and as a moral example? Is this a warning that a Satan figure walks the earth in disguise testing us? If we do not have free will, and God is just, then those are impossible. In fact, Jesus is refusing to characterize his relationship to God by what God can do for him. The Platonic hybrid god, the god that has the Problem of Evil, is the god that blesses his favorites with good fortune, takes away their hunger, and prevents their injury. Jesus does not expect God to change his circumstances. Jesus does not look to God to miraculously resolve practical things like hunger, sickness and injury, or to improve his social standing. Our relationship to God transcends purpose. It is Satan, the most reviled supernatural character in the Bible, that tempts us to see God as the divine good luck charm. When Satan asks Jesus to prove he is the Son of the God of miraculous intervention for the favored, Jesus won't – he is not the son of that god.

Finally, Satan offers Jesus authority over all the world and Jesus refuses. Again, if we don't have free will, this cannot be a warning against craving power. But clearly ascending to power is a diabolical contradiction of Jesus's role. That theme reverberates toward the end of Jesus's life and we'll explore that more fully in Chapter 5.

The Tower of Siloam – God Doesn't Reward and Punish

The Problem of Evil appears again in the New Testament story of the Tower of Siloam.[222] Pontius Pilate had just executed a group of Galilean Jews who were in the very act of offering sacrifices to God. How people engaged in good behavior could nonetheless suffer such a terrible fate of course confused those who thought God intervenes to reward and punish. Evidently, Jesus had just fielded the usual question about how bad things can happen to good people. Jesus compares this event to a tragic accident that had just occurred in which a tower in the town of Siloam, in southern Jerusalem, apparently fell without warning and killed eighteen individuals. Jesus asks rhetorically whether the crowd believes that the victims of Pilate's executions and the collapse of the Tower of Siloam were worse sinners than themselves and were punished as a result. He asserts that they were not. So far, Jesus has expressed a theology fully consistent with the theology that he expresses in John, and a theology consistent with theistic determinism. God cannot possibly punish the sins of those who are not morally autonomous. But then Jesus contradicts himself. He says that if we don't repent, we'll all likewise perish.

> Now there were some present at the same time who told him about the Galileans, whose blood Pilate had mixed with their sacrifices. Jesus answered them, "Do you think that these Galileans were worse sinners than all the other Galileans, because they suffered such things? I tell you, no, but unless you repent, you will all perish in the same way. Or those eighteen, on whom the tower in Siloam fell and killed them; do you think that they were worse offenders than all the men who dwell in Jerusalem? I tell you, no, but, unless you repent, you will all perish in the same way. [223]

To make sense of this, we might say that Jesus rejects the idea that God punishes sin, but embraces the idea that God punishes for failure to repent. But his doesn't make a lot of sense either. This bears all the hallmarks of having been an editorial addition by the author. The author of Luke (the story is only recounted in Luke) seems at first ready to reject the idea that God punishes sin, but then pulls back and insists there must be some moral obligations, if only to repent of sins. This last statement that Luke attributes to Jesus hedges the idea that God loves unconditionally and makes God's role Platonic: we must freely make the decision to repent or suffer the consequences. Perhaps it is evidence that centuries before anyone would question that we have free will, Jesus was preaching truly unconditional love and was being undercut by a well-meaning, respectful redactor who, in trying to make sense of Jesus, contradicted him.

Feeding the Multitude – God's Love is Abundant; There is No Need to Ration

The one miracle that occurs in all four Gospels is Jesus's multiplication of the loaves and fishes. Having heard of the execution of his cousin, John the Baptist, by Herod, Jesus seems to want to be alone. His efforts are stymied and a crowd of five thousand men, in addition to an indeterminate number of women and children, follow him into seclusion. As night draws near, the disciples suggest that Jesus send the crowds out of the wilderness and into the villages to buy food. Jesus says that they don't need to go away because the disciples can feed them. But they insist, saying they only have five loaves and two fish. Jesus blesses this small amount of bread, breaks it and it is distributed to the crowd. Miraculously, the crowd is fed and twelve baskets of broken pieces are left over.[224] It has become in vogue, even among evangelical Christians, to assume that this was not a magical event, but rather a moral one.[225] Jesus's good example, it is said, caused the crowd to share what they brought with them. This is the worst possible demythologizing of Scripture; rejecting the miraculous only to emphasize the moralistic. Of the four gospel accounts of this story, John's gospel alone records that the bread is barley and this reveals what is likely the true message of the passage. In the Second Book of Kings, the prophet Elisha feeds a crowd of one hundred with twenty loaves of barley bread.[226] Jesus feeds five thousand with two loaves, and has demonstrated that he occupies some status even higher than the prophet Elisha. Jesus's repetition of the miracle, for John anyway, is a connection to that message of abundance of God's love. It echoes the fact that God's loving concern for us is not payment for our moral conduct. Our total inability to be morally responsible for our good and bad acts requires that if God is to love us, He must love abundantly notwithstanding the absolute lack of anything of value with which we approach Him. This story is not about the magic, nor is it about the moral. It is a transcendent message about grace and the nature of God's non-transactional relationship to us. Even more importantly, the point of the Elisha story and the Jesus story is that God's economy is an economy of abundance rather than scarcity and rationing. We don't need to cling to exceptionalism or presume only the best behaved among us will be loved because there is enough love of God for all with plenty left over. As human beings designed by evolution to value productivity and hate the freeloader, we naturally assume everything of value is scarce and only those at the head of the line will get some. Our human moral economy insists that the first shall be first – those who deserve the most will get the most. Scandalously, God doesn't think that way.

The Beatitudes – God Doesn't Reward and Punish – The First Shall Be Last

We don't need to blame a redactor for giving us the impression that God commands, rewards and punishes. We often read that into text where it doesn't exist at all. As Christians, we are often encouraged to "live the Beatitudes." One of the most respected Biblical commentators of the twentieth century, Raymond Brown, states that "for Christians, next to the Ten Commandments as an expression of God's will, the eight beatitudes have been revered for expressing succinctly the values on which Jesus placed priority."[227] But are these commands and means to avoid punishment and deserve reward, or are they statements about the nature of God's relationship to us, regardless of our ability or moral freedom to respond to them?

The Beatitudes appear in Matthew and Luke. They are probably originally from Q, because there is no comparative story in Mark. In Matthew and the Sermon on the Mount, the Beatitudes are expressed as follows:

Blessed are the poor in spirit,
for theirs is the Kingdom of Heaven.

Blessed are those who mourn,
for they shall be comforted.

Blessed are the gentle,
for they shall inherit the earth.

Blessed are those who hunger and thirst after
righteousness, for they shall be filled.

Blessed are the merciful,
for they shall obtain mercy.

Blessed are the pure in heart,
for they shall see God.

Blessed are the peacemakers,
for they shall be called children of God.

Blessed are those who have been persecuted
for righteousness' sake,
for theirs is the Kingdom of Heaven.

Blessed are you when people reproach
you, persecute you, and say all kinds of evil
against you falsely, for my sake. Rejoice, and
be exceedingly glad, for great is your reward
in heaven. For that is how they persecuted
the prophets who were before you. [228]

In Luke, the Beatitudes are slightly different, starting with the fact that they are delivered not on a mountain but are known here as the Sermon on the Plains as follows:

Blessed are you who are poor,
God's Kingdom is yours.

Blessed are you who hunger now,
for you will be filled.

Blessed are you who weep now,
for you will laugh.

Blessed are you when men shall hate you, and
when they shall exclude and mock you, and
throw out your name as evil, for the Son of
Man's sake. Rejoice in that day, and leap for
joy, for behold, your reward is great in heaven,
for their fathers did the same thing to the
prophets. [229]

Although we reflexively presume the Beatitudes are principally a command to serve the poor, they are not even stated as an imperative. Jesus does not say "serve the poor so that they will be blessed by your generosity" but, rather, he seems to say that the poor are already somehow blessed. Rather than describing a moral code for us to put into effect, Jesus seems to be describing the moral code that God follows. Further, if we focus only on the blessing of the poor, we might assume God wants us to be poor, or at least avoid excess wealth. But we can be fairly sure Jesus and God do not want us to be poor in spirit, to mourn, to weep, or to be hated. It makes no sense without a great deal of re-interpretation to think that these are commands or even goals in our spiritual lives. Rather, these are circumstances in which we may find ourselves and where God will feel for us the greatest compassion. When we are suffering, God suffers with us. When we are at our worst: economically, socially, emotionally - even morally - that is when God loves us most intensely. We can imagine that if a child of ours was convicted of a crime serious enough that the community expressed nothing but hatred for her, we would not withdraw our love and, in fact, it might intensify because we would suffer with our child in her moment of rejection. This is how the poor in spirit and even the unrepentant criminal can be blessed. While the theology of the day said that to be poor, poor in spirit, hungry or weeping was punishment meted out by God for sin, Jesus was saying was that when bad things happen to you, it is not God's fault and it is not God's doing. For Jesus, experiencing poverty, sickness and social rejection was not a matter of being cursed - it was bad luck. And experiencing wealth, health and social acceptance was not a sign of God's favor, but simply good luck. Of course, a faith that has integrated Plato's concept of God as Unmoved Mover and Form of Good doesn't have any room for luck. There cannot be any randomness in the operation of the universe if God is defined as that which moves and motivates everything. Everything must be the will of God or the will of another just as powerful Form of Bad. Jesus was offering a message of extraordinary comfort to those doubly burdened – first by their poverty, illness or outcast status, and then by the assumption that they were being punished by God. One can imagine the outrage of any of the religious upper class intermingled with the crowd. All their lives there were told their wealth, social position and health were rewards from God and proof of their good behavior. Now, an itinerant preacher tells them that their fortunes are a matter of luck. Worse, he says that the lion's share of God's sympathy and attention is directed to those in need because, well, to the extent we are not in need, we naturally don't receive sympathy or attention. Meanwhile, those in the crowd who are suffering from blindness, illness, poverty or are social outcasts, who have been told that they are clearly being punished for something they have done, now hear from Jesus that God is not angry with them, God has not forgotten them, but rather, God is with them more intensely than when their fortunes were better.

In Luke, Jesus closes the Beatitudes with a warning to the rich: "But woe to you who are rich! For you have received your consolation."[230] Note that Jesus does not suggest the rich are somehow sinful and will be punished because they hoarded wealth to the detriment of the poor, or failed to use their wealth to serve the poor. Rather, he is mocking the Pharisees with their own theology: if God has blessed them for good behavior with wealth, then they have already been rewarded and they shouldn't expect any more of God's attention. Jesus will repeat this in slightly different formulations again and again, as we'll see. This is the transcendent message of the Beatitudes; the recognition that God's relationship to us is not one of command, reward and punishment but practically the opposite. God does not reward good behavior, intense prayer, or unquestioning belief. God does not remove suffering at all, but rather, He suffers with us. Fortunately, none of us is left out because none of us is perfect; each of us suffers from some sort of brokenness, even if that brokenness is the impression that we are perfect. The Beatitudes are a full-throated rejection of the Platonic idea that God is the omnipotent Form of Good and we are morally autonomous and therefore anything bad that happens must be punishment and anything good must be reward. The Pharisees' and Sadducees' murderous hatred of Jesus didn't arise because Jesus preached love – to believe that makes them caricatures of evil. Rather, they hated Jesus because he insisted that God does not reward and punish and is not that concerned with morality at all. Finally, their hatred reflects their and our hatred of the idea that we do not have free will and that we can neither earn nor un-earn grace.

This is not a theological problem of the past. The concept of luck is still not acceptable in the religious imagination. We are still inclined to think about God as the great intercessor that, for reasons unknown to us, will occasionally reach into human lives and take away the cause of our suffering – whether it's the disease we've been diagnosed with, or the loss of a job, or the bully at school, or that He might punish bad behavior with karma. This is the rewarding and punishing god in sheep's clothing. We don't challenge the reflexive idea that if we get enough people to pray for a particular cause, God is more likely to listen. But, of course, everything we know about God is that He prefers the underdog; He is not more likely to intercede for the person with dozens of friends to pray for her. If anything, He is more likely to intercede for the person who has no friends to pray for her. If God interceded in a pragmatic way, this intercession ought to be measurable and Christians or people of faith generally should avoid suffering much more than non-believers. But we see no evidence of this. This false theology has a built-in defense mechanism, however, and claims that God's intercession will evaporate if it is tested. This re-introduces in the back door what we threw out the front door. God is again watching for lack of belief in order to decide who gets the help. Because our prayer often appears to go unanswered, we tell ourselves that, in the tradition of Joseph Priestley, this particular suffering is God's plan, or God teaching us something, which of course, finally leads us back to God imposing suffering on us, or at least failing to remove it, based on our behavior. But if we are not morally autonomous and God is just, this cannot be. Finally, we hedge our bets. Instead of praying for the return of health, we pray that the sufferer will get the strength she needs to persevere. This is nothing more than lowering the bar and making the outcome unverifiable. It makes God into a little good luck charm that sometimes works and sometimes doesn't, and is the worst kind of idolatry. Many popular culture Christian sayings in the face of suffering ignore the Beatitudes in favor of the god of the Pharisees and the god of Plato. In the last chapter, I asserted that statements like, "it's all part of God's plan" and "God doesn't close one door without opening another" are hangovers from Christianity's Platonic influences and ignore the Judeo-Christian image of God as sometimes being surprised and dismayed at the way Creation unfolds. Another set of these platitudes violates the Beatitudes. "God doesn't give us more than we can handle" and, "everything happens for a reason" assume that God is in the business of meting out good and bad fortune. The affirmation of the Beatitudes is that God did not, in fact, send prosperity to the good and suffering to the bad, but rather exults with you in your prosperity but, most especially, mourns with you in your losses. Christianity's message was never supposed to include that God is the author of everything that happens to us, that He has a plan and that He'll change our circumstances to thwart suffering. In fact, the message is nearly the opposite. The real message is that the good and bad that happens to us is sometimes undeserved, serves no purpose, and has no meaning – it is simply bad luck. But God is with us.[231] That is the comfort afforded by faith. The Problem of Evil for Christianity is the classic Gordian Knot or a Chinese finger puzzle: it seems intractable until we step back and re-consider the underlying assumption. Then, we can cleave through it with ease.

Directly after the Beatitudes, in both Matthew and Luke, Jesus restates some well-known commands and seems to intensify them. While we have been taught that killing is sinful, now, Jesus says, simply being angry or calling your brother a fool is sinful. He says that looking at a woman with lust is as sinful as committing adultery. Is Jesus making moral commands even harder to follow? If we are not morally autonomous beings, then it is unfair to hate us for our sins, so why would Jesus up the ante? It makes more sense to interpret the message as being that if we avoid sin or engage in charitable conduct, we should be motivated by something else besides the avoidance of punishment or the seeking of reward. If we volunteer at the proverbial soup kitchen of Chapter One, let it be because of love, not because we expect to be repaid later.

Lazarus – God Doesn't Reward and Punish – The First Shall Be Last

That God is not in the business of reward and punishment is put in even more stark terms by Luke in the story of Lazarus.[232] I examined this parable briefly in the previous chapter and concluded it was not a statement about the mechanics of the afterlife. In fact, Jesus's story just reemphasizes the same theme as the Beatitudes: good fortune is not divine reward, and bad fortune is not divine punishment.

In the parable, a rich man, who remains unnamed throughout the story, is clothed in purple – an immensely expensive dye - and feasts every day. A poor man named Lazarus lies at his gate and wishes he could eat the scraps from the rich man's table. To underline his dire circumstance and perhaps link him with Job, Jesus tells us the local stray dogs lick his sores. When the two die, Lazarus is carried by angels to the bosom of Abraham, while the rich man is consigned to the Greek Hades.

If we insist on finding overtly sinful behavior in the rich man's conduct, it is hard to discern. The story does not record whether or not the rich man and Lazarus ever interacted with one another in life except by implication. As far as we know, the wealthy man was unaware of Lazarus's condition and never had the opportunity to help him. Is wealth itself sinful? More likely, this is another story addressed to the Pharisees who believed wealth was a blessing from God and poverty and ill-ness were a curse.[233] Notice how Jesus mocks the idea that good fortune comes from God. From fiery Hades, the wealthy man begs:

> He cried and said, 'Father Abraham, have mercy on me, and send Lazarus, that he may dip the tip of his finger in water, and cool my tongue! For I am in anguish in this flame.' "But Abraham said, 'Son, remember that you, in your lifetime, received your good things, and Lazarus, in the same way, bad things. But here he is now comforted, and you are in anguish.[234]

That the rich man has already received his 'good things' is a clear reformulation of Jesus's statement in the Beatitudes that the rich have already received their consolation. In this parable, Jesus does not say the rich man is being punished for any act or omission. Jesus does not criticize him for hoarding wealth or being inattentive to Lazarus's suffering – he has merely used up all of the divine good fortune he presumed was responsible for his wealth. This turns the Pharisees' theology on its head, but is far from making wealth a ticket to hell. It means that wealth is not a sign of one's reward for the satisfactory execution of divine commands, and poverty is not a sign of sinfulness. God's relationship to us is not transactional, or economic, but transcends both.

Money, Poverty and Prosperity

One of the most common misconceptions about the Beatitudes and the parable of Lazarus and the rich man is that they include an exhortation to give away everything until you are poor. In his *The Genealogy of Morals*, Friedrich Nietzsche blasted his understanding of the Judeo-Christian ethic as exhorting us all to adopt a "slave morality" – a desire among the weak to recast their weakness as a virtue and aggrandize poverty, illness and weakness while demonizing prosperity, health and power. But faith does none of these things. It rejects that poverty is from God. In fact, neither Luke's nor Matthew's version of the Beatitudes treats poverty as something that ought to be achieved. They don't romanticize the pain of poverty. It is simply a statement about the nature of God's relationship to us, and His closeness to us when we are suffering. It is interesting to note that while, in Luke's version of events, Jesus blesses the poor, Matthew has Jesus blessing the *poor in spirit*. Raymond Brown theorizes that, unlike Luke's readership, Matthew's expected audience was a solidly middleclass community and he wanted to ensure they understood Jesus's message of God's loving concern when they suffer applied to them as well.[235] While many Christians believe this is a clear and urgent imperative to give away all of our worldly possessions, Matthew, evidently, felt free to reword it to make it wholly uneconomic.

Mark and Money; The Eye of the Needle

In the Gospel of Mark, Jesus is approached by a man who wants to know what command he needs to follow in order to receive reward. "Good Teacher, what must I do to inherent eternal life?" Jesus begins his answer with what we are tempted to see as a throw-away line – a statement of modesty: "Why do you call me good? No one is good but God alone." But far from being a throw-away line, this is the key to all that follows. Jesus is about to express the economy of grace. As unfree creatures, we cannot merit reward or punishment. We can only rely on God choosing to love us despite our lack of freedom and despite our inability to make truly moral choices at all. Jesus plays along with his questioner. He lists some of the Ten Commandments and the man enthusiastically answers that he has followed them all from his youth. The Gospel records that, "Jesus, looking upon him, loved him." Was this a look of admiring love? Or was it loving exasperation accompanied by a slow shaking of the head? Jesus tells the man he is "lacking one thing," according to Mark. In Matthews's version of this story, Jesus says the man can achieve "perfection" by doing one more thing. He must sell everything, give the proceeds to the poor, and follow him. The man cannot do it and departs in sadness. Jesus makes the divine command even harsher and even more difficult to his remaining audience. He states that it is easier for a camel to go through an eye of a needle than a rich man to enter the kingdom of God.

Again I tell you, it is easier for a camel to go through a needle's eye, than for a rich man to enter into God's Kingdom.[236]

The disciples are astounded. They are not foolish enough to assume that Jesus is talking about one tax bracket above their own. They know he has laid out an impossible task and that none of them will make it.

We think of the apostles as poor, simple fishermen, but their ownership of boats and nets[237] made them outright wealthy compared to the widows, beggars and lepers they passed along their way. We might also think of the apostles as having left all material wealth behind to follow Jesus, but at least the author of John felt no need to paint that picture. In John's Gospel, after Jesus is crucified and appears to the apostles after the resurrection, Peter and six other disciples are together. In an evocative moment, Peter evidently needs to clear his head and take it all in. He announces simply "I am going fishing" and the others say just as simply, "We will go with you." Evidently, the means of their livelihood were waiting for them when they came back from their time with Jesus. This is no small detail, but sets up the scene for the apostles' last encounter with Jesus. After an unsuccessful night of fishing, Jesus appears at the bank and directs them to try one more time and they haul up extraordinary abundance.

Nor does Scripture indicate that Jesus himself was poor. Jesus himself was in the bloodline of David and the nephew of Zechariah who clearly was a man of immense stature. Zechariah was among the priestly class that was exclusively permitted to enter the Holy of Holies – the dark cube in the center of the Temple where the Ark, some manna and Aaron's miraculous rod were kept. It is there, when he by the luck of the draw is chosen to be the one to enter, where he was told by the angel that his aged wife would bear John the Baptist. John clearly adopted a lifestyle of asceticism. We are told John wore a leather belt, a camel's hair coat and ate wild honey and locusts.[238] Although John appears in all four Gospels and is of particular interest to Luke, his clothing and this peculiar diet are only mentioned in Mark and Matthew. In Luke, it is prophesied at his birth only that he will not drink "strong drink." But Jesus pointedly does not adopt John's lifestyle. In fact, he contrasts his own lifestyle to that of John's by self-reporting in Matthew and Luke that he knew he was considered a glutton and drunkard.[239] As we'll see in Chapter Five, this is not just a different lifestyle choice. Jesus is making an extraordinarily important point by deliberately rejecting asceticism.[240]

We know that in his itineracy, Jesus did not suffer deprivation. He ate at the homes of high-ranking Pharisees and tax collectors.[241] Additionally, little indicates Jesus's family was poor. [242] I like to tell people that, when I immigrated to the United States I didn't have a penny in my pocket and only owned the clothes on my back. It sounds impressive but, in fact, I was ten years old and was immigrating with my parents who were solidly middle-class so I had access to everything I needed. Jesus also seemed to be in constant contact with his extended family throughout his ministry from Cana to the Cross. Furthermore, his family appears to be have been fairly well off. Luke tells us that Jesus's family made the sixty-mile trip from Nazareth to Jerusalem and back for Passover every year.[243] This would have been an extraordinarily expensive undertaking and probably not within the means of the poor. Also according to Luke, when Jesus is born, he is laid in a manger because there isn't room in the inn.[244] Contrary to the popular view, Luke's infancy narrative is not intended to show Mary and Joseph are poor. Jesus is not born in a stable (or cave according to some traditions) because they couldn't afford a room at the inn, but rather because they are traveling for an empire-wide census and the usual lodgings were full. Matthew doesn't even bother to include the physical circumstances of Jesus's birth and he states simply that Jesus is born in Bethlehem. Jesus is not wrapped in strips of cloth because they could not afford a onesie, but because swaddling infants was the custom of the day, and likely Luke was demonstrating that Jesus was loved and accepted by his mother and family. Jesus being placed in a manger is clearly important to Luke, but not because it is such a shabby start. Rather, this is the fulfillment of Isaiah's prophecy that "The ox knows its owner; and the donkey know the manger of its lord; but Israel has not known me; my people has not understood me."[245] Luke reminds us of this in the same chapter, when the angels appears to shepherds and tells them they will find the Christ in a manger wrapped in swaddling.[246]

Perhaps the best evidence that the disciples were far from poor is their reaction to Jesus's statement that the rich must negotiate an eye of a needle to enter heaven. Seeing that even they will not receive reward, the disciples protest, "Then who can be saved?" Jesus answers that no one will be saved, at least by their own merits. "With men it is impossible, but not with God; for all things are possible with God." Christianity has largely assumed that if we really embraced poverty, we would merit reward, but since few of us will actually do this, we have to rely on God's forgiveness. We imagine Jesus as the deliverer of divine economic policy. But our situation is even more dependent than that. If we do not have free will *then indeed no one is good.*[247] Rich or poor, moral or immoral – all are equally incapable of achieving anything of value because we don't have the moral autonomy to choose in the first place. We'll see in Chapter Five that this concept of sin as being shared by all human beings equally is the surprising key to understanding the nature of Jesus as the Incarnation of God.

What should we make of the reference to the eye of the needle through which a rich person has to pass to enter heaven? In The Song of Songs, God speaks to us as a heart-sick lover: "I sleep but my heart waketh, it is the voice of my beloved that knocketh: Open to me, my sister, my love, my dove."[248] This was interpreted and expanded upon in Jewish commentaries that may well have been oral tradition at the time of Jesus: "The voice of my beloved, the Holy One, Blessed be He, is calling: Open to Me an opening no bigger than *the eye of a needle*, and I will open to thee the supernal gates."[249] Jesus was not setting out an impossible goal only to mitigate it later, but was rather making a statement of radical grace from the onset - no one is good, but all God needs is the tiniest opening and He will exploit it to our benefit. The whole story may be even more stark: being unfree, we cannot of our own volition open even a small opening, but God opens the gates to us nonetheless.

We belittle Christianity when we assume we are all supposed to reduce ourselves to utter and dependent poverty and when we don't we are dependent on God's mercy not to punish us for the failure. Certainly, it is good to give generously to charity, but if we do so because we wish to receive reward and avoid punishment, we miss the point. God does not want us to be poor. Among other considerations, as the great twelfth-century Jewish philosopher, Maimonides, pointed out - to struggle to avoid hunger, thirst or discomfort distracts from seeking God and should be avoided if we can.[250] As we will explore later, as Christians we clearly have a duty, albeit not a commanded one, to ensure as few people as possible are the objects of God's sympathy for the poor. We should make reasonable, thoughtful decisions about charity based on our familial obligations, not to bemoan the fact that we don't willingly court grinding poverty. God suffers with us when we are poor, but it does not mean He wants us to suffer.

Dollard des Ormeaux - The Second Hiddenness Story

These clues to the true meaning of the Beatitudes and, indeed, all Scripture, abound. How have we missed them? The first ten years of my life were spent in a suburb of Montreal called Dollard des Ormeaux. Dollard was a fantastic place to be a kid, especially in the seventies. Mostly farmland in 1961, the town was rapidly developed as a residential community over the next decade by a single construction company. In a ten-year period, the population expanded from 1,800 to 25,000.[251]

As a result, in my childhood, there were always vacant fields to explore on the outskirts of the development with gravel dumped in preparation for roadbuilding rich with pyrite and mica to be collected until the weight in our pockets nearly pulled our pants right off. Ruts formed by the movement of construction equipment around the area were filled with algae-tinged rainwater and alive with tadpoles to catch and raise to frogdom. The company that developed Dollard seemed to have worked from a very small number of house designs, and every fourth or fifth house was identical to one down the street. Most of the trees had been planted in that decade, although there were a few mature ash trees that dropped seed pods each year, which spiraled down to the road in tight circles to be picked up and thrown back into the air by us kids. Because the houses were virtually identical in size and amenity, and had come on the market at the same time, the demographic of the residents was uniform. Every house had kids in roughly the same age group which made for unparalleled street hockey and hide and seek. One day, walking home from school by myself, I must have taken a wrong turn and, unbeknownst to me, headed down the wrong street toward what I thought was my home. Now there were innumerably small clues that I was not where I was supposed to be that would have been discernable to a more critical eye. I walked past dozens of houses that were different colors from the houses on my street and had different landscaping. Somehow, my mind corrected for all of these. I remember assuming that several of my neighbors had repainted their homes while I was at school that day. I recall marveling at a tree that had apparently grown considerably since the last time I looked at it carefully. This continued until I walked up to what I thought was my repainted front door. I don't know exactly what finally alerted me to the fact that I was on the wrong street, but the realization came as rush that wasn't pleasant. Because I was totally disoriented it took me a long time to retrace my steps and figure out where my house actually stood.

And it's not just me. In 1949, a group of social scientists performed an experiment using students from Harvard and Radcliffe as their subjects.[252] The subjects were shown a series of playing cards flashed briefly on a screen. The time they were given to look at them went from thirty milliseconds up to a full second. What the subjects were not told was that some of the playing cards had been modified so that they no longer looked exactly like the playing cards they would be used to seeing. Some of the suits that are normally red, such as hearts and diamonds, had been changed to black, while some of the customarily black suits, such as spades and clubs, were changed to red. As the cards were flashed on the screen, the subjects were asked to identify them. It generally took longer for the subjects to identify cards that had been modified. So, subjects could not identify the three of hearts as quickly when the hearts were black than when they were their customary red. Even more interestingly, the subjects appeared to unconsciously adjust their perception of the anomalous cards to better fit with their expectation. Some exhibited what the researchers called a "dominance reaction." They simply ignored the anomaly and declared that the red six of spades was either the six of spades or the six of hearts. Some exhibited the "compromise reaction." Instead of choosing one suit over another, they called the red six of spades a purple six of hearts and a black four of hearts was called a grayish four of spades. Finally, while some subjects began to recognize that something was wrong with the cards as the time they were given to view them increased, other subjects experienced "disruption." These students couldn't make any sense of what they thought they were seeing and threw up their hands in virtual despair. One subject, trying to make sense of a red spade flashed for about a third of a second, simply lost it:

I can't make the suit out, whatever it is. It didn't even look like a card that time. I don't know what color it is now or whether it's a spade or a heart. I'm not even sure now what a spade looks like! My God!

We naturally resist recognizing things that don't make sense to us or seem incongruous. As I walked down the wrong street in Dollard, I compromised my expectation that I was approaching my house with the many clues that I was on the wrong street. Faced with competing concepts of God as both unconditionally and conditionally loving, we naturally choose one as the dominant view, compromise and live with the paradox, give up entirely and become a 'none,' agnostic or atheist, or we come to realize that something is wrong with the paradigm.

Similarly, we naturally read Scripture with a moral bias. When we read, "blessed are the poor" it is natural for us to assume that God is requiring that we be poor or at the very least that helping the poor is a principle exhortation of Scripture and that He will impose punishment if we are not compliant. The clues that this may not be the case elude us because we are not naturally inclined to see them. We are willing to believe that God is unconditionally loving and forgiving, but we might be more naturally inclined to assume the opposite and adjust accordingly. We assume that God forgives, but does not forget. Or we might assume that God forgives when we are sufficiently apologetic. We ignore that, with Jesus's dying breath, he asks God to forgive us not because we are sufficiently remorseful, but because we know not what we do. What science and philosophy have done for us in this regard is to point out the impossibility that a fair God would command, reward and punish at all – at all.

The Prodigal Son – Rejection of Abundance – The First Shall Be Last

That we have a strong natural bias toward seeing Scripture as moral and will actually resist seeing anything else is an idea that is itself a recurring theme in Scripture. In Luke, three parables are offered in rapid succession, each of which is designed to elicit a negative response from us. We are supposed to find the message distasteful or discordant and, above all, to realize that our natural impulse and our natural value system is not necessarily shared by God. In the parable of the lost sheep, we are supposed to be scandalized by the fact that the shepherd abandons the ninety-nine sheep in the wilderness to find the one that wandered off, or that the woman overturns her entire house to find one small coin. This is not a value system we are used to. Luke's parable of the prodigal son makes the point even more directly. The younger son demands his inheritance early, leaves his father's house, and squanders the wealth he's received with prostitutes. When famine strikes, the son is in desperate circumstances, takes job as a swineherd and longs to eat the pig feed. Remembering the comfort he lived in with his father, he decides to go back. Pointedly, he rehearses the apology he will offer to his father. He goes back and is spotted by his father as he comes down the road. Abandoning all decorum, the father runs to meet his returning son, embracing and kissing him. *The son is able only to get out part of the speech he rehearsed before his father interrupts to start planning the homecoming party.* We might be inclined to think of this parable and the two parables that go before it to be stories about the importance of repentance. And, in fact, the author or redactor of these stories punctuates each parable with an explanatory note, equating the lost sheep and the lost coin to those who repent as compared to those who have no need of repentance. But the meaning of the prodigal son is unmistakable. The son fails, and *is not even permitted* to repent before the father accepts him back. Jesus offers a foil in this story in the form of the elder son. The elder son expresses our discomfort bluntly: I have never disobeyed your command; yet you never give me a kid that I may make merry with my friends."[253] Here it is in stark relief: God does not command, reward or punish, God does not require repentance. The father's response indicates that of course his concern is for the suffering – the non-suffering do not need any help. This is not about fairness of opportunity or fairness of outcome. It is about sympathy. In apparent recognition that we are not morally autonomous creatures, God does not require us to perform for Him. His message, to quote Paul Tillich, is simple:

> You are accepted! You are accepted, accepted by that which is greater than you, and the name of which you do not know. Do not ask for the name now; perhaps you will find it later. Do not try to do anything now; perhaps later you will do much. Do not seek for anything; do not perform anything; do not intend anything. Simply accept the fact that you are accepted![254]

And, perhaps more importantly than accepting the fact that we are accepted, we should acknowledge that God's acceptance is universal and irrevocable and that all human beings receive it as well. There is no need to ration God's love because it is abundant enough for all with plenty left over. The Pharisees and the rich man in the parable of Lazarus are sure God's grace will run out and want to see their good fortune as evidence that they got some. The elder son is insistent that his good behavior entitled him to a share of the scarce resource of God's grace and doesn't want it used up by his flighty brother. *In his mind, he was first in good behavior so why should he be last in reward?*

Note that while in the Beatitudes and the parable of Lazarus and the rich man it is poverty that puts you in first place, in the parable of the prodigal son it is immoral behavior that puts you in first place! Our relationship to God does not require us to live in poverty and scandalously doesn't even require us to be moral. Our relationship to God is not transactional at all, but is rather radically forgiving and accepting as it must be if we are not morally autonomous beings and if God is just.

The Vineyard Parable – Rejection of Abundance – the First Shall Be Last

Although the parable of the prodigal son exists only in Luke, a direct parallel appears in Matthew. In the story of the vineyard workers, a householder hires laborers to work in his vineyard early in the morning for a denarius. He hires additional laborers three hours later, and still more throughout the day until the last group starts work in the eleventh hour. When the time comes to be paid, he pays everyone a denarius. Those who began work first are annoyed to see those who worked only one hour receive the same wage. The householder responds to their grumbling: "Friend, I am doing you no wrong; did you not agree with me for a denarius? Take what belongs to you and go; I choose to give this last as I give to you. Am I not allowed to do what I choose with what belongs to me? Or do you begrudge my generosity."[255] So often this story is interpreted to mean that we can repent at the very last minute of our lives and still receive the God's forgiveness. We believe this is about beating the referee's whistle and being contrite before it's too late. Even this is hard for us to swallow because we, like the older brother in the story of the Prodigal son, don't like people getting something for nothing. But if we are not morally autonomous, then none of us has anything to give – not at the beginning of the day or the end. It rings more true that God is entirely rejecting a transactional approach where He commands, we obey, and we receive reward. Instead, in acknowledgement of the fact that we are not finally and fully responsible for our choices, God will not punish or reward anyone for anything they do or fail to do, believe or fail to believe.

This, then, is what is meant by a just God. God is not a god who ensures that no one escapes punishment. Rather, a just God recognizes that the genetics and circumstances of our birth and the experiences we have thereafter are responsible for our behavior and, although it makes sense to restrain bad behavior and encourage good behavior, it makes no sense from God's perspective to reward and punish unfree behavior or to issue commands to do something His creatures cannot freely and independently choose. And Scripture acknowledges we don't like this. We are evolved not to like freeloaders and those who get something for nothing. We insist we have moral autonomy, free will, and that this is a necessary component of faith even as Scripture tells us the opposite.

The owner of the vineyard ends his defense of his generosity with a fascinating statement: *"So the last shall be first and the first shall be last."*[256] This again is a reverberation of Jesus's rejection of the idea that the rich, healthy, and socially accepted are particularly blessed and his affirmation that those who look forgotten by God actually have His attention in abundance.

Jesus in His Hometown - The Chosen Shall Be Last and the Unchosen Shall Be First

Of course the people of Jesus's time did not expect moral behavior was the only factor in placing them first in line for salvation. They also thought they were entitled to a first position to receive a portion of a limited supply of salvation simply by being born as members of a chosen people.

In the Gospel of Luke, Jesus returns to his native Nazareth to teach in the synagogue.[257] We are told he read a specific passage from Isaiah:

> The Spirit of the Lord is on me,
> because he has anointed me to preach good
> news to the poor.
> He has sent me to heal the broken hearted,
> to proclaim release to the captives,
> recovering of sight to the blind,
> to deliver those who are crushed,
> and to proclaim the acceptable
> year of the Lord.[258]

Dramatically, Jesus stops there, hands the scroll back to the attendant and sits down. The tension rises and Luke tells us all eyes remained fixed on him. When he speaks, he all but declares himself the messiah and says, "Today, this Scripture has been fulfilled in your hearing." We would expect that this would instantly trigger a murderous furor. The members of the synagogue ask one another if this is indeed the Jesus who grew up in their midst. But, considering what he just claimed, their response is fairly muted. In fact, they appear to approve. Luke tells us, "All testified about him, and wondered at the gracious words which proceeded out of his mouth." So far, this is a pretty good session for Jesus. But then he blows it all up. Jesus references a story in the First Book of Kings in which the prophet Elijah is wandering through Phoenicia – an area part of modern-day Lebanon and the area in which Jesus encountered the Canaanite woman.[259] A massive regional drought is impoverishing Israel and Phoenicia alike. Jesus notes that Elijah miraculously multiplies flour and oil to feed a starving Phoenician widow and her son – while widows in Israel starve. He also notes that Elijah's protégé, Elisha, cured the leprosy of a Syrian while leprosy was undoubtedly rampant in Israel.[260] The synagogue goes crazy. They grab him and manhandle him to the edge of a cliff where they are going to throw him off. Jesus either takes advantage of the confusion or by some miracle simply loses himself in the crowd and escapes. Jesus had the audacity to challenge Israelite exceptionalism and suggest that the chosen might be last and the unchosen might be first - that God's love is universal. The members of the synagogue were perfectly willing to have him, who they remembered as a snot-nosed kid, declare himself the Messiah; but to suggest that God loves everyone regardless of the circumstances of their birth was beyond comprehension.

That the messiah would be accepted by, and represent salvation for non-Jews is a theme that repeats itself through Scripture. Zechariah, prophesying to the Israelites as they returned to Jerusalem from exile, promised that one day those returning would lead all the nations to God:

> Thus says the Lord of hosts: In those days ten men from the nations of every tongue shall take hold of the robe of a Jew, saying, 'Let us go with you, for we have heard that God is with you."[261]

Isaiah's prediction, one chapter prior to what Jesus read in the synagogue, is even more beautiful:

> Lift up your eyes all around, and see:
> they all gather themselves together.
> They come to you.
> Your sons will come from far away,
> and your daughters will be carried in arms.
> Then you shall see and be radiant,
> and your heart will thrill and be enlarged;
> because the abundance of the sea will be
> turned to you.
> The wealth of the nations will come to you.
> A multitude of camels will cover you,
> the dromedaries of Midian and Ephah.

All from Sheba will come.
They will bring gold and frankincense,
and will proclaim the praises of God.[262]

The gospel of Matthew would echo this and other passages in his story of Jesus's birth to make the point that Jesus is the Son of God, prophesied to be recognized as such by all the nations – Jew and non-Jew - including non-Jewish magi from the East bearing gifts. Jesus marvels throughout his ministry at foreigners with faith. In the story of the ten lepers, Jesus cleanses all ten and sends them off to have their cleansed status confirmed by the priests. [263] Only one returns to show his gratitude to Jesus's chagrin and, if one is inclined to seek moral messages in Scripture, the story is easily seen as a commandment to be grateful. But this ignores what is clearly the most important detail of the story. The one who returns, Luke notes, is a Samaritan. Jesus marvels not at the ingratitude of those who are healed and failed to return but the fact that it is a foreigner who returns: "Were there none found to return and give praise to God except this foreigner?"[264]

Jerusalem Suburbanites – Rejection of Abundance – The Chosen Shall Be Last and the Unchosen Shall Be First

---

Jesus passed through towns and villages,
teaching as he went and making his way to
Jerusalem.

Someone asked him,
"Lord, will only a few people be saved?"
He answered them,
"Strive to enter through the narrow gate,
for many, I tell you, will attempt to enter
but will not be strong enough.
After the master of the house has arisen and
locked the door,
then will you stand outside knocking and saying,
'Lord, open the door for us.'
He will say to you in reply,
'I do not know where you are from.
And you will say,
'We ate and drank in your company and you
taught in our streets.'
Then he will say to you,
'I do not know where you are from.
Depart from me, all you evildoers!'
And there will be wailing and grinding of teeth
when you see Abraham, Isaac, and Jacob
and all the prophets in the kingdom of God
and you yourselves cast out.
And people will come from the east
and the west
and from the north and the south
and will recline at table in the kingdom of God.
For behold, some are last who will be first,
and some are first who will be last."[265]

The people around Jesus were always pestering him to confirm that they were the favored, the saved, the blessed, the chosen, those who would be permitted to sit at his right and at his left. They never like his answer.

In the passage above, the inhabitants of Jerusalem's suburbs expect Jesus to confirm that they, not the nasty Gentiles, will be saved. But he defies their expectations again. Here he declares that the Gentiles who they expected to be last may well be first – the same message that had nearly gotten him killed in Nazareth.[266] This theme is not only a reverberation of the theme of the parable of the vineyard workers but is a variation of Jesus's message in the Beatitudes and in the parable of Lazarus – the economically last shall be first in the loving gaze of God. The parable of the prodigal son is even more shocking: the immoral have God's attention more than the moral placing the sinner over the righteous. God loves the outsider, the arrogant, the greedy, the lazy, the mean spirited and the unrepentant and that should be ok with us. As the vineyard owner says to the unhappy vineyard workers, "Friend, I am doing you no wrong." [267]

The Canaanite Woman Revisited

This, then, is what is going on with the Canaanite woman. It is not a story about her persistence in getting the recalcitrant (and somewhat nasty) Jesus to perform a miracle, and it is not a story about Jesus's ability to morally evolve from hating Canaanites to accepting them. Rather, it is a story demonstrating that Jesus is the fulfillment of a prophecy. Perhaps that he fulfills the prophecy is really less important than the prophecy itself: that salvation is not reserved for the chosen few – the first – but is available in such abundance that we don't have to worry about rationing it.

Notice that nothing that Jesus says to the Canaanite woman would indicate he deliberately wanted to convey a message of universal salvation - quite the opposite. It is the Canaanite woman's reaction to Jesus that alerts us that Jesus has a status - not a moral teaching - that is special. The Canaanite woman assumes that he represents her daughter's salvation. She does not assume he has something to teach her – only that he is something to her. I am not going to give Jesus credit for consistently teaching a message of universal salvation because he did the opposite with the Canaanite woman. But he clearly consistently represented a complete rejection of the idea that God favors some over others. But while the Canaanite woman with the ill daughter who insisted she was among the saved was portrayed as a heroine, those synagogue members in Nazareth who insisted she and people like her were not were portrayed as villains. In his book, The End of Faith: Religion, Terror and the Future of Reason, Sam Harris dismisses religious tolerance as fake:

> Many religious moderates have taken the apparent high road of pluralism, asserting the equal validity of all faiths, but in doing so they neglect to notice the irredeemable sectarian truth claims of each. As long as a Christian

believes that only his baptized brethren will be saved on the Day of Judgment, he cannot possibly respect the beliefs of others, for he knows that the flames of hell have been stoked by these very ideas and await their adherents even now.[268]

Indeed, many people of faith throughout history have engaged in a sort of exceptionalism and it persists today. But Sam Harris is wrong. Exceptionalism is discouraged in sacred texts. It is not fundamental to faith. To the extent Jesus seems to take an exceptionalist viewpoint, it is as a foil for the persistent confidence among people of faith that God transcends and challenges what our evolved sensibilities might want to maintain. When faith adopts a mythology of free will, its role inevitably changes. From that point forward, it seeks to distinguish between pure and impure, well behaved and poorly behaved, acceptable and unacceptable, native and foreign. And this just as inevitably eats faith from the inside out and destroys it, making it a host for a blandly human value system. It makes us believe that God's love is a scarce resource that can run out and must be rationed - it cannot be distributed to all and has to be doled out only to some. If we do not have free will then nothing we can do or fail to do, and nothing we can believe or fail to believe, can make us more favored and less favored in the eyes of God. This book seeks to demonstrate that this theme is entirely consistent with Scripture. Abandoning free will makes all the difference in our ability to see it.

Rejection of Abundance

In the Gospel of Luke, Jesus sounds like he is demanding religious zealotry of the worst kind – a call by God to His people to mercilessly impose His will:

I came to throw fire on the earth. I wish it were already kindled. But I have a baptism to be baptized with, and how distressed I am until it is accomplished! Do you think that I have come to give peace in the earth? I tell you, no, but rather division. For from now on, there will be five in one house divided, three against two, and two against three. They will be divided, father against son, and son against father; mother against daughter, and daughter against her mother; mother-in-law against her daughter-in-law, and daughter-in-law against her mother-in-law.[269]

But the passage should remind us of the parable of the prodigal son. It was the father's abundant mercy and his willingness to forgive everything and accept his wayward son back without even an apology that angered the elder son. There, the father's willingness to dispense love without rationing it pitted "son against father" and the father's message of universal salvation did not bring peace.

An often-repeated theme of Scripture is that God forgives all and loves all. Just as often repeated is the theme that universal salvation is unacceptable to us. The elder brother is piqued that the prodigal son's return is celebrated. The vineyard workers who started at sunrise are upset when those who started at sunset get equal pay. We marvel that a woman would sweep all day to recover a dime and a shepherd would leave his whole flock to find one lost sheep. But there is enough of God's love to go around with extra to spare. It does not have to be rationed, as Jesus and Elisha demonstrate in the stories of multiplication of bread to create abundance from apparent scarcity.

Jesus's insistence that the poor will have priority over the rich, the sick will have priority over the healthy, and the spiritless will have priority over the spiritual, at a time when poverty and sickness were thought to be divine retaliation for sin, and wealth and health were a divine blessing to reward good behavior, was apostasy. Universal salvation is really good news, unless you insist salvation must be earned and rationed; in which case it can make you angry enough to crucify the messenger.

Jonah – Rejection of Abundance – The Chosen Shall Be Last and the Unchosen Shall Be First

Most fictional stories include conflict, climax and resolution. Scripture often uses fictional stories to flesh out the non-fictional character study of God in which it is actually engaged. One of the strengths of using these stories is that they are vivid, memorable, and compelling. However, one weakness is that, if the stories themselves are taken as a historical account, or if the set up for the conflict is given too much importance, then the set up can be mistaken for the message and the overarching point is lost. In the story of Noah, the set-up is that God is angry at the evil in the world and decides to destroy it. We naturally like this. It contains command and punishment. Additionally, it contains compelling imagery: a global flood, a massive ark, and the animals boarding two by two. The story of Jonah is similar. Jonah is ordered by God to go to Nineveh – an Assyrian city in modern-day Iraq – to demand that the inhabitants repent. We are not told why Jonah refuses, but it is implied he wants nothing to do with helping the Ninevites, Israel's traditional enemy, avoid God's wrath. Jonah heads in the opposite direction. Instead of going inland, he heads for a ship in Joppa to sail to Tarshish, somewhere in the Mediterranean. As we all know, God is angry at Jonah's disobedience and nearly sinks the ship he's hired to take him away. In an effort to save themselves, the crew members throw Jonah overboard. Jonah is finally brought to heel by being swallowed by a fish. We intuitively like this – God has judged and commands repentance and will punish if He is not satisfied. At first, the book of Jonah appears to be a story of the inevitable punishment that follows disobedience. But the story has only begun. All of what had happened so far is merely set-up for a much richer message about our nature and our reaction to a God who commands nothing. When Jonah arrives at Nineveh and demands repentance, they embrace the message without argument. The ease of Jonah's mission is evident. We're told Nineveh is so enormous that it takes three days simply to walk the breadth of the city.

Jonah is only one day into the process when the inhabitants do precisely as God requires:

> Jonah began to go into the city, going a day's journey. And he cried "Yet forty days, and Nineveh shall be overthrown!" And the people of Nineveh believed God; they proclaimed a fast, and put on sackcloth, from the greatest of them to the least of them.[270]

God immediately accepts their contrition.

Jonah is not satisfied that is mission is accomplished. Rather, he is horrified and angry. He wants the Ninevites to be destroyed. Incongruently he prays to God and says, "I pray thee, Lord, is this not what I said when I was yet in my county?[271] That is why I made haste to flee to Tarshish; for I knew that thou art a gracious God and merciful, slow to anger, and abounding in steadfast love, and repentest of evil. Therefore, now, O Lord, take my life from me, I beseech thee for it is better for me to die than to live." [272] All God can manage in reply, His confusion evident, is "do you do well to be angry?" [273] God's question is an obvious parallel to the vineyard owner's assertion: "Friend, I am doing you no wrong." In a snit, Jonah leaves the city and sits down outside of the walls to see what happens to it. Evidently he believes he has laid down an ultimatum to God and expects God to destroy the city even though its inhabitants have turned themselves around.

God causes a plant to grow over Jonah to shade him from the sun and, we're told, Jonah is exceeding glad because of it.[274] But by dawn of the next day, God sends a worm to kill the plant and a hot dry wind to underline the point. Jonah again asserts that it is better for him to die than to live. In the closing words of the Book of Jonah, God delivers His message:

God said to Jonah, "Do you do well to be angry for the plant?" And [Jonah] said, "I do well to be angry, angry enough to die." And the Lord said, "You pity the plant for which you did not labor, nor did you make it grow, which came into being in a night and perished in a night. And should not I pity Nineveh that great city in which there are more than a hundred and twenty thousand persons who do not know their right hand from their left, and also much cattle?"[275]

God knows why the cattle are relevant here, but very clearly the Book of Jonah is not about the Ninevites' failure to obey divine command, nor is it about Jonah's refusal to obey God's command to preach to them. Rather, this is about Jonah as a representation of all of us who insist that God commands moral behavior and who are disappointed when good things don't happen to good people or bad things don't happen to bad people. Like the owner of the vineyard and the prodigal son's father, we think God ought to distribute His love and His grace on the basis of merit, and to withhold His forgiveness until satisfactory contrition is shown. In a world where humanity is not morally autonomous and God is just, this cannot be the program. Scripture predicts our natural distaste for God's economy of grace. There will be a large number of people who find the central premises of this book unacceptable if not wholly incomprehensible. Their feeling will be that a God who does not command, reward and punish is not worth having, as Scripture foretells.

The Centrality of the Theme of Rejection

This theme of rejection is not just important, but central, and occupies this central position throughout the Old Testament and New. The prophets' message is almost invariably rejected and the prophets themselves persecuted. As we'll see, Moses's authority and motivations are questioned continually by the Israelites as he leads them out of slavery in Egypt and even as they stand at the threshold of the Promised Land. In one of the most abused passages of the New Testament, Jesus whips the moneychangers and drives them out of the temple quoting Jeremiah's curse of the Ba'alists.[276] "Is it not written, 'my house shall be called a house of prayer for all the nations?' But you have made it a den of robbers."[277] Is this Jesus losing his temper and exacting corporeal punishment right there on the spot? Is this the wrathful God who despises the choices we make and reacts with anger? This is almost certainly not a moral statement about God's reaction to sinfulness or Jesus's ability to lose his cool. Again, we are alerted in the text itself that there is a deeper meaning here. In the Gospel of John, the apostles recall at this moment that it was written in Psalm 69 that, "zeal for thy house will consume me." Psalm 69 is a call for help by a devout man being persecuted by unnamed assailants. The psalmist complains his assailants give him vinegar for his thirst, just as Jesus is given vinegar on the cross. [278] Rather than being an incident of divine wrath, it is a very thinly obscured prophecy that Jesus's message will be rejected and he will be persecuted.

It would be easy to assume that the New Testament's focus on the rejection of the Christian message is the sour grapes of an emerging religion persecuted by its native Judaic roots and the Roman occupiers, or a form of Nietzsche's slave morality making persecution seem victorious. Even more tempting is the idea that Jesus's premonition of doom is a magical prediction of the future, meant to show again his ability to perform the miraculous and thereby prove his supernatural lineage. And finally, it would also be easy to assume that this rejection was a thing of the past. If we believe that Jesus's purpose was to encourage us to share, develop our talents and be humble, we might reflexively assume that the Pharisees found these goals objectionable and were inspired to violence to stop him. But no one finds these goals objectionable, and it is unlikely the Pharisees would have disagreed with these values at all. We've made Christianity toothless by assuming it is someone else besides ourselves that rejects Jesus. Rejection of the message of Scripture persists today and is perhaps more intense among people of faith then in secular society. Because of our evolutionarily programed distaste for the freeloader, we insist, against all the evidence, that we must have free will and God must command, reward and punish.

Fortunately, as Scripture demonstrates, this comes as no surprise to God. The Garden of Eden is the story of the notional moment humanity adopted the illusion that we are morally autonomous. The fate of the prophets and Jesus, and many of the narratives in the Old and New Testaments, are the story of the innumerable moments when we defend that illusion at all costs. Scripture invites us to realize that we do not have autonomy and, in God's justice, He does not hold our lack of moral autonomy against us. It is remarkable that the theme of unconditional love and acceptance has survived given our natural proclivity to reject it. It persisted in plain sight but virtually unapprehended for centuries, only to be finally revealed by religion's assumed opponent - science. How did this happen?

Tarquin – The Third Hiddenness Story

Lucius Tarquinius Superbus, or 'Tarquin the Proud' was the last king of Rome, finally deposed about five hundred years before the birth of Jesus. During his reign, Tarquin engaged in several wars with the towns and cities surrounding Rome. Unable to conquer the town of Gabii, he sent his son, Sextus, roughed up to create the appearance that he had fallen out of favor with his father, to ingratiate himself to the local population. Sextus encouraged the Gabians to raid Roman lands, and either because of the complicity of his father or because of Sextus's familiarity with Roman strengths and weakness, the

Gabians often won. When Sextus's influence over the Gabians was complete, he sent one of his friends to Rome to ask his father how he should exploit his new situation to deliver Gabii into his father's hands. Tarquin met the messenger in his garden, but because he did not trust the messenger, he did not verbally reply to his son's question. Instead, as he walked with the messenger through the garden, he silently swept a stick back and forth over the garden, chopping off the blooms of the tallest poppies. Perplexed and finally out of patience, the messenger returned to Sextus and described what happened. Sextus correctly understood his father to mean that Sextus should have the leading political figures of Gabii executed to clear the way for a surrender of Gabbii to Rome. Sextus followed the advice his father conveyed to him this way, and Gabbii became a Roman possession.[279]

God is in a similar situation when He reveals the nature of our relationship to His prophets. The message is almost always unacceptable to the messenger himself and would be scandalous to most listeners. We are committed to the illusion that we have moral autonomy and our desire to judge, to dislike the freeloader and to seek retribution and revenge is deeply ingrained in our genes. If revelation had consisted of a blunt statement that we are not morally autonomous and God treats us with mercy and love nonetheless, it would have been utterly incomprehensible to the individuals to whom He revealed it, and to the culture in which they conveyed it. Revelation would not have survived as an oral tradition, would never have been committed to writing, and finally, would never have ignited the world the way it has. It is more likely it would have died with the prophets. Instead, God has enfolded the message of His unconditional love and mercy in a narrative that includes elements that we readily and hungrily accept: judgment, reward, punishment. God has hidden the pearl of great price in the field of our moral expectations. God is like the old woman of the parable who hides leaven in some bread and only slowly and imperceptibly, but inexorably, the leaven spreads through the entire loaf. Our natural instincts and our cultural influences have left us blind to seeing the true message. Now, in the fullness of time, through science and philosophy, the subterfuge falls away and the true message – the good news – is revealed.

It bears mentioning that the best messenger for a narrative whose meaning is not obvious is a messenger who treats every word as sacred and is committed to preserving it whole and entire generation after generation without changing a word to 'clean it up' or make it more politically palatable. This is the charism of evangelical Christianity.

The Parable of the Talents

"For it is like a man, going into another country, who called his own servants, and entrusted his goods to them. To one he gave five talents, to another two, to another one; to each according to his own ability. Then he went on his journey. Immediately he who received the five talents went and traded with them, and made another five talents. In the same way, he also who got the two gained another two. But he who received the one talent went away and dug in the earth, and hid his lord's money.

"Now after a long time the lord of those servants came, and reconciled accounts with them. He who received the five talents came and brought another five talents, saying, 'Lord, you delivered to me five talents. Behold, I have gained another five talents in addition to them.'

"His lord said to him, 'Well done, good and faithful servant. You have been faithful over a few things, I will set you over many things. Enter into the joy of your lord.'

"He also who got the two talents came and said, 'Lord, you delivered to me two talents. Behold, I have gained another two talents in addition to them.'

"His lord said to him, 'Well done, good and faithful servant. You have been faithful over a few things, I will set you over many things. Enter into the joy of your lord.'

"He also who had received the one talent came and said, 'Lord, I knew you that you are a hard man, reaping where you didn't sow, and gathering where you didn't scatter. I was afraid, and went away and hid your talent in the earth. Behold, you have what is yours.'

"But his lord answered him, 'You wicked and slothful servant. You knew that I reap where I didn't sow, and gather where I didn't scatter. You ought therefore to have deposited my money with the bankers, and at my coming I should have received back my own with interest. Take away therefore the talent from him, and give it to him who has the ten talents. For to everyone who has will be given, and he will have abundance, but from him who doesn't have, even that which he has will be taken away. Throw out the unprofitable servant into the outer darkness, where there will be weeping and gnashing of teeth.'[280]

A version of this story, with some changes, also appears in Luke, but not in Mark, so we can assume the original text began with Q.[281]

A talent, or *talanton* in the form of Greek in which the New Testament was written, meant a particular weight or sum of money. Naturally, we assume that Jesus is speaking allegorically and that the servants' lord is God and that a "talent" is an allegory for our skills and mental endowments. So universal has been the assumption that this is a parable about self-improvement, exhorting each of us to develop our God-given skills to the best social utility, that this passage of Matthew's gospel is credited with giving the word "talent" its present meaning as a skill or aptitude.[282]

No story presents more of a challenge to the idea that God is aware that we are not morally autonomous and therefore, in fairness and justice, cannot reward the good and punish the bad. The story also directly challenges the idea of an unconditionally loving God. This parable appears to depict God as a fairly harsh judge. In fact, the harshness of God's judgment is expressed directly and is an integral part of the story. God, by this interpretation, demands that everyone put their shoulder to the wheel and deliver some profit on His investment in them. The fact that fear of God seems to have paralyzed the unprofitable servant and caused him to make a poor choice seems not to excuse or even mitigate his failure to be productive.

For that part of us that naturally does not like the freeloader or the person who gets something for nothing, this parable is very appealing. On the other hand, another part of us is discomforted by this harsh vision of God. These are passages that simply seem to contradict everything we thought we knew about God. As recently as the parable of the vineyard workers, Jesus closes with the statement that "the last will be first, and first last."[283] God's declaration at the end of the parable of the talents, that the rich will get richer and the poor will get poorer, seems discordant. Although much of the rest of the parable is changed in Luke's version, this passage is shared almost word for word, indicating that the two authors clearly felt it was an indispensable component.[284] What is going on here?

This passage occurs in both Matthew and Luke after Jesus arrives Jerusalem where he is to be crucified. The crescendo grows and the tone becomes more ominous as he clashes with religious authorities and his arrest becomes more imminent. In Matthew, Jesus spent the entirety of proceeding chapter speaking about the apocalypse.[285] He predicts the destruction of the Temple. In graphic terms, he warns his apostles of antichrist figures and total destruction of the world:

> Immediately after the tribulations of those days, the sun will be darkened and the moon will not give its light, and the stars shall fall from heaven, and the power of the heaven will be shaken.[286]

The chapter immediately following the parable of the talents,[287] opens with Jesus's prediction that he will be crucified. Within a few lines, Judas Iscariot is plotting to turn him over to the chief priests and the story turns to Jesus's last supper, arrest and crucifixion.

Luke also is building the crescendo toward Jesus's passion. In Chapter 17, we're told Jesus is passing between Galilee and Samaria on his way to Jerusalem when he prophesies that antichrist figures will follow him, and that the world will be destroyed without warning.[288] Jesus predicts his death as he approaches Jericho.[289] As he passes through, he stops to tell the parable of the talents. In the very next line, Jesus arrives in Bethany and Bethpage, outside the walls of Jerusalem, and sends his disciplines in to bring him a colt to ride into the city. The next day he arrives to the exultation of the populace who lay their garments and palms at the feet of the colt. Those of us familiar with Holy Thursday know the liturgy moves from a retelling of this moment, and transitions abruptly and directly into the Passion. From that point forward Jesus goads and is goaded by the Pharisees, and he predicts disaster for Jerusalem[290] and his execution[291] throughout the text until his arrest and death.

What is a parable about self-improvement doing in the middle of this inexorable march to the catastrophic climax of the Gospels?

Clearly, the parable of the talents is not an exhortation to be profitable servants. The harsh master of the servants *is not God*, and the servants are not us. Rather, the harsh master represents the world that demands profit and grinds the poor deeper into poverty. Jesus is the profitless servant, destined to be rejected, humiliated and killed. Jesus is the stone that is to be rejected by the builder and will be thrown out into the outer darkness, where there will be weeping and gnashing of teeth.[292]

Throughout Scripture, God demonstrates His solidarity with the poor and rejected. Almost every hero in the Bible has humble beginnings. Jacob overcomes his older brother to receive Isaac's blessing and inheritance and finally to be renamed Israel, Jacob favors his second youngest son, Joseph, who narrowly avoids murder at the hands of his brothers to become the ruler of Egypt. Moses, we're told, is a stutterer, and yet God appoints him chief negotiator with Pharaoh. Samuel names Saul Israel's first king notwithstanding that Saul came from the smallest clan of the smallest tribe.[293] When Samuel seeks to replace Saul, he interviews each of Jesse's sons, but finally anoints David, the youngest, who was out in the field during the interviews, not even considered a candidate. [294]

The God of compassion, of suffering with his creatures, always identifies with the downtrodden, the poor and the social outcast. The parable of the talents is meant to assure us that although the rich may get richer and the poor may get poorer, God is always with those who suffer and that, in Jesus, He shares in that suffering.

The parable of the wedding feast also interrupts Matthew's narrative of Jesus's approaching execution. This then, explains the second, discordant portion of the parable in which the harsh master throws the poorly dressed guest "into the outer darkness; there men will weep and gnash their teeth." The fate of the poorly dressed weeping guest is almost perfectly synchronous with the fate of the profitless servant[295] The redactor has clearly connected two parables; one in which the generous master who invites everyone to the banquet is God, and the other in which the harsh master condemns those who come inappropriately dressed is someone else – perhaps our human impulse to hate the freeloader. In these parables, the victim of the harsh master is Jesus, rejected and thrown out by social expectation and human nature.

The Sheep and the Goats

Now we can re-examine the parable of the sheep and the goats from the first chapter of this book. Is the king God, or is the king an allegory for a world that demands that we be its profitable servants, submissive to the social expectations of our day? Will our God separate us from one another and consign some of us to oblivion or torture for our unfree choices? Does God command his creatures, incapable of moral autonomy, to nonetheless choose correctly or face divine wrath?

There are some clues that the king in the story is not God. The story appears only in Matthew, which may indicate it was not in the Q materials from which he and Luke worked, or it was there and Luke dismissed it. It is directly appended to the parable of the profitless servant, with its master of questionable origins. The incidences of the imagery of fiery furnaces and gnashing of teeth included in the story are rare elsewhere. They all occur in Matthew and Luke, and most often within material that appears to be added by the redactor. In Luke, Jesus utters it as he is telling the Jews that men from the east and west and from north and south will enter the kingdom more surely than the chosen people.[296] In Matthew, it is used in the explanation of the wheat and weeds parable, and a similar parable right after it about dividing good fish from bad fish. [297] It is used one more time in a short parable about servants being attentive for the arrival of their masters.[298] Only in two places is the phrase accompanied by being thrown into the outer darkness - in the second part of the wedding feast parable, and in Matthew 8:12 when Jesus marvels at the centurion's faith and declares that the Gentiles will be welcomed into the kingdom while many of the chosen people will not be given entry.

A careful examination of the language also reveals some discrepancies. It opens with the statement that "when the son of man comes in his glory, and all the angels with him, then he will sit on his glorious throne."[299] As we'll see in more detail in Chapter 5, to be a "son of man" is to be a prophet or even a simple human being. It is distinct from being the Son of God. It appears most often in the Book of Ezekiel as the name that prophet uses for himself and twice in Daniel: first to say that a messianic figure will be "like a son of man," and second, as the way the angel Gabriel refers to Daniel himself.[300] In the parable of the sheep and the goats, there is a sudden shift and this personage on the throne previously called the son of man is referred to as "the King." If this is Jesus announcing himself to be incarnation of God, it is the only time he does so in all the Synoptic Gospels. It stands in sharp contrast to the Jesus who will wash the feet of his apostles and declare them friends at the Last Supper.

What the original purpose of this parable might have been and the identity of the king, may be lost forever and unrecoverable, at least with certainty. We can be reasonably sure, however, given what we know about human nature and the assumption that God is aware of our inability to make choices freely and is fair-minded enough not to reward and punish us on that basis, that it is not a commandment to love or risk losing divine love, or a warning that Jesus is in disguise and testing us. We can be sure that which divides us is not God.

To interpret the parable of the talents as an exhortation to self-improvement, or the parable of the wedding feast as a need to perform some task for God, or the sheep and the goats as a command and threat, is to belittle Jesus and the Messianic tradition that he fulfills. It seems to me highly unlikely that God would become incarnate in order to encourage His creatures, whether they are morally autonomous or not, to develop their talents, comport themselves correctly, and be good to receive reward and avoid punishment. This again would be interpreting Scripture to meet our moral expectations rather than seeking a transcendent message about God's relationship to us. Like the parable of the profitless servant, it is entirely possible that in the parable of the sheep and the goats, it is Jesus that is the goat to be rejected, persecuted and killed by a world that doesn't want to hear the Beatitudes and requires God to command, reward and punish.

Chapter Four

Existentialism

The mole had been working hard all the morning, spring-cleaning his little home. First with brooms, then with dusters; then on ladders and steps and chairs, with a brush and a pail of whitewash; till he had dust in his throat and eyes, and splashes of whitewash all over his black fur, and an aching back and weary arms. Spring was moving in the air above and in the earth below and around him, penetrating even his dark and lowly little house with its spirit of divine discontent and longing. It was small wonder then, that he suddenly flung down his brush on the floor, said 'Bother!' and 'O blow!' and also 'Hang spring-cleaning!' and bolted out of the house without even waiting to put on his coat. Something up above was calling him imperiously, and he made for the steep little tunnel which answered in his case to the graveled carriage-drive owned by animals

whose residences are nearer to the sun and air.
So he scraped and scratched and scrabbled
and scrooged and then he scrooged again and
scrabbled and scratched and scraped, working
busily with his little paws and muttering to
himself, 'Up we go! Up we go!' till at last, pop!
His snout came out into the sunlight, and he
found himself rolling in the warm grass of a
great meadow.[301]

In *No Exit*, Jean-Paul Sartre describes hell.

Garcin, who, over the course of the story reveals himself to
have been a war deserter, is led into a drawing room by a valet.
He has just died and finds himself in this place. Garcin expects
to be tortured and is surprised to learn that hell does not have
instruments of torture, but rather is appointed with sofas,
albeit somewhat tasteless ones. The room is warm and has no
mirrors in it. Garcin has no eyelids in this place which deprives
him of the thousands of little breaks from self-awareness and
self-critique that blinking afforded him in life.

The valet leaves and returns in a short time with Inez. Gradually
we learn that Inez lived with her cousin and his wife. When
her cousin died in a tram accident, Inez seduced his widow.
She describes herself as a bit of a sadist; finding herself without energy when she's alone, and taking pleasure in cruelly
exploiting others. Her lover, her spirit broken by Inez's cruelty,

eventually killed them both by turning on the gas in their apartment one night.

Finally, Estelle enters. Estelle is attractive and extremely appearance conscious. The lack of a mirror is intensely disturbing to her. Estelle, as it turns out, had an affair with someone she felt was beneath her social station, and which resulted in an unwanted pregnancy. Estelle drowned her newborn baby and her lover took his own life.

They all appear capable of seeing and hearing the world of the living. Garcin sees his co-workers revile him, while Inez watches her landlord re-let the apartment in which she died. But the ability fades as memory of them fades on Earth. The rest of the play is a dialogue between the three characters. It becomes clear that each one of them needs something from the others. Garcin needs redemption and affirmation that he is a good person. Inez identifies herself as beyond redemption and wants only to draw Estelle to her to be her next quarry. As in life, Estelle wants love and doesn't care whether it is of any depth or meaning. While Inez pursues Estelle, Estelle seeks Garcin's love. The three each tantalize each other with the acceptance they all seek but, because of their own weaknesses, wind up cruelly withholding it. They each exploit one to offend and hurt the other. No negotiation, no dialogue, no amount of intimacy or shared experience will allow them to give each other what they know they need. They are all fundamentally incomplete human beings seeking others to complete them, a project that for Sartre can never be satisfied. For Sartre, humanity is not individuals in community but, no matter how close the quarters, as indelibly separate and howlingly alone. For the three characters, the presence of the others is not a comfort, but a source of anguish. Love, acceptance, completeness seems within reach but is never attainable. Whatever has condemned them to hell is exploiting this profound aloneness in the human condition and our natural desire for redemption and torturing them with it. Garcin summarizes the situation:

> So this is hell. I'd never have believed it. You remember all we were told about the torture chambers, the fire and brimstone, the "burning marl." Old wives' tales! There is no need for red-hot pokers. Hell is other people![302]

The central assumption in Sartre's thinking is that God does not exist. Sartre conceived of God as the classic purpose-driven god; the god of morality and social control. God provided a moral code to follow and corresponding reward and punishment, He had a plan, He establishes a purpose for everyone's life, if not a specific mission. God gave humanity a sense of meaning. Sartre's project - really the project of every atheistic existentialist - was to discern some way for human beings to find purpose and meaning in the absence of this god. Sartre doesn't offer any argument to support the idea that God does not exist. Rather for Sartre, belief in God is immoral – it is a cowardly act to look to a divine being to establish your purpose and meaning rather than finding it for yourself and within yourself.

Existentialism is well aware that to establish human purpose, meaning and value without reference to God is a difficult project. We like the idea that someone has a plan. Christianity was happy, perhaps even anxious, to adopt the Platonic notion that God has a plan that is merely being executed, and that there is a divine reason and purpose behind every good and bad thing that happens, even though it is not really comforting. We like the idea that God has a quest or a mission for us – that our lives are purpose-driven. We especially like the idea that there is a set of specific moral guidelines that we are obligated to follow and that a definitive, cosmically determined answer for every moral question floats in some philosophical realm ready to be discerned. This is, in part, because our minds evolved in an environment of scarcity and those of us with the mental ability to plan in times of plenty for the scarcity of the future, and the ability to identify and reject the freeloader, were more likely to thrive. The world seems absurd when existentialists tell us God does not exist and there is no plan, things happen for no reason, our moral code is not handed down from above, and we have no God-given purpose. This absurdity naturally makes our evolved brains anxious. We are naturally inclined to reject it, to dismiss it as too mysterious or impractical. Our sense of the absurdity of that message and the anxiety it produces is incredibly powerful. It is not the denial of God's existence that seems absurd and makes us anxious; it is the idea that there is no divine plan and no assurance that, at the end of the day, we'll all get what's coming to us. Even if someone with unquestionable authority to do so and working miracles to prove it, told us that God does exist, but that He doesn't have a plan, He doesn't ensure everything happens for a reason, He doesn't command moral behavior, but loves us, could get himself crucified. Although his message may survive him and grow to a global faith, unless we can overcome our natural, cultural tendencies we would marginalized it - maybe even re-interpret it to mean the opposite – it will ultimately be lost unless we embrace the idea that God transcends purpose and morality. The counter-culturalism of existentialism and the counter-culturalism we are called to as Christians are closely related. It is not counter-cultural to be kind and charitable, to develop our talents for the common good, and to be humble. Those are all values people of faith share with secular culture. There is a story that I have seen attributed to any number of people of any number of faith traditions, but usually someone considered a "mystic":

A woman saw an angel rushing past her, carrying a torch and a bucket of water. "Where are you going with that torch and bucket?" she asked. "What will you do with them?" "With the water," the angel answered, "I will put out the fires of hell, and with the fire I will burn down the mansions of heaven; then we will see who really loves God."

The counter-culturalism of faith is to love the purposeless God. This is existentialism, but instead of denying God's existence, it challenges the believer to a new understanding of God's relationship to us. It starts with the premise that behavioral science has revealed – that we are not morally autonomous. If God is fair-minded and just, He cannot be angry with us for failing to do what wasn't in our power to change or do differently. God is not into rewarding and punishing. God does not serve a particular purpose. God is Who is. This is the *wu wei* of faith. Our evolutionary allegiance to the illusion of free will has burdened our intuition of God from the beginning. Now that science and philosophy have broken that spell and we can see the nature of God more clearly, we may be at the cusp of a revelatory era that rivals the era of the Biblical prophets. Faith's best years are almost certainly not behind it. Leaving Plato's cave and the God of physics behind, we'll walk into brilliant sunshine and a crisp breeze. This is theistic existentialism.

Existence Precedes Essence And You Are Not Your Biography

Existentialism has a reputation for being obtuse, inaccessible and strange. In fact, it is really quite simple and I suspect by the end of this chapter most readers will identify their own morality as existentialist. John O'Donohue, a former priest turned poet, once said that, "your identity is not equivalent to your biography." [303] This statement very much capturers the essential idea of existentialism.

If someone asks you to introduce yourself at a party or a social setting, you might describe yourself by starting with your name, what job you have, what school you attend, your interests, hobbies, and maybe your political views. Existentialism would say that's fine - that's how we tend to introduce ourselves for expedience sake and because greater intimacy is not really called for in that sort of setting. But that's not really who we are. You are not really reducible to those things. Whatever you may say identifies you with a certain group or a certain manner of living. You are telling people your biography. You are not really drilling down to who you are as a person - *the fact of your existence*. When I first joined Facebook, I made connections with people from high school which, for me, was about thirty years ago. Some of these people had faded into the margins of my memory. I hardly remembered who they were. I received a message from an acquaintance from high school who said, "Well, I knew you in high school, who are you now?" It seemed like simple enough question to answer, but I found myself flummoxed. I could tell my friend my history, about my career or my family life. I suppose I could tell him about my political persuasion or my religious views, but I could never really drill down to who I am – to give him a sense of how I am unique, as opposed to where I fit in on a spectrum. How do I describe who I am now? Ultimately, I gave up.

That's fundamentally the existentialist's point. Jean-Paul Sartre described this as, "Existence precedes essence." Frankly, I have never found this language particularly illuminating. The word "essence" has very positive connotations in the English language and implies something "essential" not, as Sartre intends, something disposable. It might be better to say "The fact of your existence is more important than your personal characteristics." Juxtaposing this with the O'Donohue quote reveals the similarities. Your existence, your identity, the very fact of your being, is not your biography and cannot be conveyed like a résumé. Really, these two quotes are synonymous with one another.

Existentialism invites us to reject the idea that we are defined by our jobs, our credentials, our place on the political spectrum or the religious spectrum, or our interests. Existentialism on this level says that we when we define ourselves in these ways we are engaged in the same exercise as Garcin, Inez and Estelle – seeking to define ourselves through others' eyes. It is an exercise in futility and you must define yourself, find meaning for yourself, and find dignity for yourself, by reference to yourself.

There is a moral component as well. Existentialism invites you to reject the idea that you or anyone else is identified by morality; whether you or anyone else is a good or bad person, and where you or anyone else is situated on the moral spectrum. For Sartre, discerning our place on the moral spectrum is just another way of applying a cultural metric rather than embracing our individuality and uniqueness. When you start thinking about it, you realize just how much human interaction is moral judgment and how much energy we put into putting people onto a moral spectrum, and how reflexive and compulsive that is. It is an evolved sense and one that we are loathe to part with.

As soon as we meet someone, we decide if we like them on the basis of whether they seem like a good person, or an honest person. If we watch a political pundit on television, we instantly measure our value system against theirs and decide whether we agree or disagree; whether they are part of our group, of someone else's. Of course, if we are not morally autonomous, then there is no reason to place too much stock on where someone is situated on a moral spectrum. We certainly can make practical decisions about whether someone can be trusted with our money, or whether someone needs to be incarcerated because of in inadequate sense of empathy expressed as violence or an inadequate allegiance to laws, but one cannot logically find meaning there. We cannot logically love them or hate them or claim that it is central to their identity. We should not crave redemption and to be well regarded by our peers because that is ephemeral. For Sartre, seeking meaning or dignity through the moral praise of others or avoidance of disgrace is a pathetic surrender of our existential independence. For the person of faith, it is a miscalculation based on the erroneous idea that we are free and that we ultimately self-direct our moral status and deserve either reward or punishment. It is to ignore the central Scriptural message of radical grace.

God Is Not What He Can Do For You, And You Are Not What You Can Do For God

I have suggested that, "existence precedes essence" and, "your identity is not equivalent to your biography" are synonymous. From the perspective of our relationship to God, we might express it in this way: "God is not what He can do for you, and you are not what you can do for God." That is the basic *theistic* existentialist perspective. We should not define our relationship with God in terms of utility - in terms of what we can accomplish for Him and what He can accomplish for us. We often define God in terms of His roles; especially moral roles like our judge, the forgiver of sins, the guy who's going to get us into heaven. We often define our relationship to God in terms of our roles. We're supposed to be good, we're supposed to give to charity, we're supposed to go and worship God every Sunday. Existentialism says those roles don't define the relationship. Scripture invites us to think about God as our father or our parent. If someone asks us what are parents are to us, would we respond by telling them what we do for them or what they do for us? Are our parents the people who fed us, and clothed us, and educated us and who commanded us to obey certain rules? Are we identified as those who obeyed our parents? Is it so central to the idea of the parent/child relationship that the relationship evaporates if the child disobeys? Presumably it is a much deeper relationship. That is what theistic existentialism says about our relationship to God. Are we always going to talk about and define God in terms of what we're supposed to be doing and what God is supposed to be doing for us? When we pray, are we asking God for something, or expecting God to command us, or send us on some purpose? Or is it a more direct relationship? A less purpose-driven relationship? If we are not morally autonomous and if God is just, then our relationship cannot be based on our usefulness to God because we are not free to respond freely – to act in a way different from what our nature and nurture determine. In fact, we must recognize that if we are not morally autonomous then God's acceptance and loving concern for us must be unconditional, unearned, and irrevocable.

What Guides You?

Both atheistic and theistic existentialists reject the idea that God commands moral behavior. Obviously, atheistic existentialism rejects that idea because they start from the assumption that there is no God in the first place, so how could He possibly be commanding anyone to do anything? Theistic existentialism rejects the idea of a commanding God because a person's usefulness does not define them in the eyes of God. But how, then, are we to be guided? What properly determines how we are to act?

Atheistic existentialism goes further and finally finds itself in fundamental opposition to the conclusions of behavioral science. Sartre insisted that human beings are radically free. Not only are they free of a commanding God, they are also capable of shaking off the influences of culture, of moral expectation, of peer pressure, and of their nature and nurture. Human beings, Sartre would insist, can be wholly self-directed. In fact, Sartre would say that this is our ultimate responsibility – to become free of any influence except our own. Sartre holds Garcin, Inez and Estelle in contempt because they cling to one another for redemption and meaning and, knowing full well it will result in eternal torture, cannot seem to accomplish the existential goal of freeing themselves – self-extricating from their nature and nurture. This is not a side issue for Sartre that can be abandoned or made less central now that science has essentially proven it impossible. This is the basis of human dignity for Sartre. To Sartre, a being which does not have God to give its life meaning and purpose and dignity, and cannot measure its dignity by how socially useful or celebrated it is, must have moral freedom to give it meaning and purpose and dignity. Atheism and determinism interact badly. As we'll see, together they inevitably result in a dark, grim, hollow view of human dignity.

Absurdity, Anxiety and a Search for Meaning

Each variety of existentialism acknowledges that acceptance of its central premise may seem utterly absurd and create a feeling of profound anxiety in us. For atheists, they face the challenge of existence unanchored from the usual source of meaning and purpose; namely God. How do you find meaning as a finite creature, somebody who's going to die fundamentally alone and quickly forgotten, not loved by God, and incapable of any kind of authentic intimacy from which to derive meaning and dignity? In the absence of a commanding God and without social expectations, how is one to live a purposeful, meaningful life? Sartre's answer - free will - seems to have collapsed, and so the atheistic existentialist absurdity and anxiety persist.

For theistic existentialists, the absurdity comes from being unanchored to the most commonly accepted concepts of God - that God expects you to be good and is commanding you and has a plan for your life. There is no question that this is anxiety producing. Our evolved desire to ensure the criminal does not profit from his anti-social behavior, along with the freeloader and the last vineyard worker, cannot be banished easily. We say we "need" God to punish bad people, and we "need" God to keep us on the straight and narrow, and we "need" God to promise reward and punishment to keep charity flowing, criminal behavior in check, and keep society from falling apart – to exert social control. But God is not what He can do for us, no matter how much we need it. God will be Who He will be, and the era of mythology where we started from a need and filled it with a divine provider or explanation is rejected in Scripture and in our faith as pure idolatry. For theistic existentialism, we can emerge from this anxiety when we realize the true nature of our relationship to God, internalize it and become comfortable with it. God is not commanding us to do anything. He has no goals for us. He is not particularly concerned with whether we are good or bad. He forgives every transgression before it happens - whether we are sorry for it or not. God is not going to use us as a means to an end. That's really a gospel of unconditional love and universal salvation. It is the message of Scripture finally affirmed now in our era by behavioral science. Scripture expects it to anger us initially and for us to reject it - violently. The challenge of faith is to transcend our visceral response and to answer in faith.

Theistic existentialism, like faith itself, is entirely consistent with the idea that we lack of moral autonomy. It does not claim that we have free will despite all the evidence to the contrary. Rather, it stands for the proposition that because we don't have free will it is impossible that we are here to fulfill some purpose, or to be put to a moral test so that we can be judged and separated from one another for reward or punishment. Theistic existentialism asserts that our relationship to God is like a healthy parental relationship. Neither as children nor as parents are we defined by the purposes we serve or the tests we pass or fail. Rather, we are fundamentally the objects of love. That is the heart of our relationship to God and it is unearned and irrevocable. We each are here simply to be an object of divine love.

Mysticism, Martha & Mary, The Transfiguration & Rudolf Otto

Virtually every ancient religious tradition has a mystical tradition that is thought of as a more highly developed form of the faith from which it springs. Christianity has asceticism and the monastic tradition, Judaism has Kabbalah, Islam has Sufism. Buddhism alone appears to treat mystic enlightenment as the goal of all its adherents. Mysticism is often thought of as mysterious, unattainable, maybe a little bizarre and over-zealous. When we imagine what a mystic looks like, we often think of the slightly crazy, unkempt hermit who rejects and eagerly flouts all social expectations. We think of them as exhibiting total control over their emotions and doling out obtuse advice; posing and answering questions with riddles. But it seems to me that at the heart of virtually all mysticism is the idea that our relationship to God or the divine is characterized by purposelessness rather than judgment. Like Julian of Norwich, mystics see no wrath in God. In perfect parallel to Julian of Norwich, Abraham Heschel would later write, "there is no conflict between God and man."[304] Perhaps at the heart of mysticism is the abandonment of the idea of free will. Mysticism seems mysterious and counter-cultural because it offends our evolved needs for purpose and judgment, but is vaguely attractive because it answers to a deeper intuition of God.

We often say that faith gives us "purpose and meaning" as though those terms are synonymous. But contrary to that assumption, faith's first priority is to express that we are *not* here to serve a purpose or fulfill a function and that our lives nonetheless have meaning. The lives of those of us that ended too young to have served any social goal or complete any task nonetheless have as much meaning as those of us who survive a normal lifespan. And because we are not purpose-driven, the process of dying can truly be a part of life – an opportunity to continue to develop and learn new things even if they never serve a social function. Rather than being a time only to look back, or a time to complete tasks, it may be the richest, most profound opportunity for development we can ever experience – if we can overcome the instinct that all development must produce a change and serve a purpose. If life has meaning but not purpose, the process of dying is an opportunity to develop, not regretful reminiscence.

The authors of Scripture, of course, were aware of our human inclination to prefer tasks to transcendence. When Jesus takes Peter and James[305] up a mountain and is transfigured, his face shining as Moses and Elijah appear, Peter instantly wants to perform a task – he wants to build booths for Jesus, Moses and Elijah. With timing that verges on comedic, Matthew records that God actually interrupts Peter's yammering to declare Jesus His beloved Son.[306] Mark and Luke admit that Peter is offering to perform this work because he is overawed by the moment and doesn't know what else to say or do.[307] In a more domestic scene, when Jesus visits his friends, Mary and her sister Martha, Martha is incensed that Mary is listening to Jesus instead of helping her with the household tasks.

"Lord, don't you care that my sister left me to serve alone? Ask her therefore to help me."

Jesus answered her, "Martha, Martha, you are anxious and troubled about many things, but one thing is needed. Mary has chosen the good part, which will not be taken away from her."[308]

Mary will appear again in the Gospel of John to anoint Jesus with expensive oil that the apostles note could have been used to feed the poor (although a different character performs this act in the other Gospels).[309] It is yet another failure to be task-oriented and will so disgust Judas Iscariot that he will betray Jesus as a result.[310]

The personage of Rudolf Otto, the author of the 1923 book, *The Idea of the Holy*, does not fit any common conception of a mystic. Photos of Otto reveal a white haired, impeccably dressed

German Lutheran theologian with an invariably severe look. Never to marry, Otto lived with his widowed sister and her daughter, teaching in some of the most respected German universities. His translator described his appearance as "tall and erect and suggested a soldier rather than a scholar, with his Kaiser mustaches and his tight, light, military looking jacket fastened high at the neck."[311] But Otto clearly shaded into the mystical by the definition I have proposed. Perhaps it was not a complete transformation. Otto was a product of his times and his first major work, *Naturalism and Religion*, was a fairly unremarkable attack on Darwinism and a defense (really more of a simple assertion) of free will. He states, "that we 'will'; and what it is to will, cannot really be demonstrated at all, or defended against attack. It simply is so. It is a fundamental psychical fact which can only be proved by being experienced."[312] Nothing better proves freedom of the will for Otto than our ability to make moral decisions.[313] But in *The Idea of the Holy*, Otto is willing to separate the moral from the divine. In fact, he quickly abandons the use of the word "holy" as being too closely associated with the good and the moral. Instead, he coins the term, the "numinous" as being holiness without the moral component.[314] In this study Otto concerns himself only with the person of faith's response to God. In this application, Otto is not trying to prove God's existence, but rather flesh out for us what a mystical experience consists of. He baldly invites the reader who has not had a "deeply-felt" religious experience to stop reading. To describe an experience of the divine to someone who has not shared in one, is like describing the experience of art to someone who has never seen it or music to the utterly tone deaf. He says that the numinous reveals itself to us as an emotional response. We don't see God, we only see the reaction He inspires in us. Those reactions include an overwhelming feeling of being a creature standing before its Creator; the sense that we are so small as to be virtually nothing in the presence of overwhelming absolute power.[315] It is mysterious insofar as it appears hidden to us and is not obvious.[316] It includes a feeling of dread and fear, not the kind of fear that arises with a threat, but a kind of vertigo in the presence of something that evokes awe. Martin Buber, of whom I will speak in greater detail shortly, spoke of this overwhelming fear of God in a similar way, setting aside moral threat in favor of impossible majesty:

O you safe and secure ones. You who hide yourselves behind the ramparts of law so that you will not have to look into God's abyss! Yes you have secure ground under your feet, while we hang suspended looking out over the endless deeps. But we would not exchange our dizzy insecurity and poverty for your security and abundance ... Of God's will we know only the eternal; the temporal we must command for ourselves...

It has been theorized that human beings are naturally predisposed to find "refuge and prospect" attractive. We like porches and landscapes that allow us to see great distances while we remain hidden because it gives us a natural sense of security that harkens back to our hunter-gatherer days. This is the impulse that sent Moses to the cleft in the rock at God's approach. The fear of God in Scripture is not fear of the threat of punishment or fear of a capricious god, but rather the natural and entirely creaturely human response we get when we sense that we are teetering on the edge of an abyss in pitch darkness. God is fearsome, He is awe-ful, He is even abysmal. This is the source of the impulse that sends us scrambling back to the cleft in the rock – the recognition of the pathetic asymmetry between ourselves and the divine. Otto notes that it is evident from the Old Testament that the wrath of God is not God's emotional response to moral iniquity, it is rather our projection on this awesome figure.

It is Otto who also coined the term "the Wholly Other"[317] to place God outside of the "usual, intelligible and familiar." Although finally inapproachable by us, Otto said that God is nonetheless fascinating to us. We are drawn to His presence even as we do so with fear and trembling.[318] Religion, according to Otto, is our attempt to deal with the Wholly Other and to package Him in a manageable way. The easiest way, of course, is anthropomorphism – seeing God as a person motivated as we are motivated and emotional as we are emotional, hating the freeloader as we hate the freeloader – essentially denying that the Wholly Other is other at all. This is the form of religion, according to Otto, that manifests itself as appeasing God, petitioning Him for good luck, and essentially treating the relationship as transactional.[319] On the other hand, says Otto, there are those who seek to encounter God, to understand His ways and perhaps even to identify with Him. Otto says we naturally pursue God through "magical" or "shamanistic" ways – using formula and ritual to capture God and compel Him to work His immense power in our favor. But ultimately, Otto assures, these practices stop being about compelling God – they stop being purpose-driven - and evolve into the desire to rest in God.[320] God then, ceases to be about the relief of suffering or even the relief of the burden of sin, and becomes a comfort without changing circumstances of suffering.

Trust Your Own Experience of God

Otto's examination of intuition to discern the nature of our relationship to God, and his confidence that it is valid, is a hallmark of existentialism. Mysticism and theistic existentialism would agree that there can be no second hand experiences of faith. In these traditions, every individual is capable of having a direct experience of God without any intermediaries; no priests, no ministers, no rabbis, no church authorities. They would insist that we trust our own experience of God over anyone else's. Faith is not knowledge of dogma or familiarity with papal encyclicals, it is to seek encounter with God.

Paul was a rabid persecutor of the early Christian Church. In Acts,[321] he relates how he approved of Stephen's murder and held the outer garments of the people who stoned him to death so they could get a good arc in their throw. On the road to Damascus to root out more Christians for persecution, Paul sees a vision of the risen Jesus. Jesus says simply "Saul, Saul, why do you persecute me?" and disappears. Paul leaves for Arabia for a time to process what he has experienced. When he reappears, Paul is a changed man. Instead of persecuting the new church, he becomes its most important and celebrated booster. He hits the road, visiting Jewish and non-Jewish communities around the Roman Empire and setting up small Christian churches in each one. Those communities send him letters, asking his advice and he responds to them, encouraging them and offering them guidance. Those letters become part of the New Testament and excerpts are now the second reading almost every Sunday in the Catholic Church. For Paul and for all the early Christians, Christianity or, "the Way," as it was then called, was a culmination of Judaism and not independent of it. Almost immediately the question arose whether converts to this new kind of Judaism needed to first convert to Judaism and be circumcised. Paul insisted they did not, which put him in conflict with Peter and the church hierarchy back in Jerusalem. On the strength of Paul's vision of the risen Jesus, Paul refused to comply with the dogma of the early church and insisted his way was right. The outcome of the very first Synod held by Paul and Peter is interesting in that it is the precise opposite of the traditional Christian practice. They agreed that Christians need not be circumcised as long as they kept Kosher![322] In any event, Paul is among the first Christians to champion the existentialist supremacy of personal encounter over dogmatic regulation.

Kierkegaard, Abraham and Isaac

After the story of Noah, the biblical narrative is interrupted by the account of Babel, which culminates in humanity being scattered across the face of all the earth and the confusion and multiplicity of language. From here, Genesis gives us a genealogy of Noah's decedents, ending in Abram, who is later re-named Abraham, by God. There is nothing remarkable, moral or otherwise, about Abraham to indicate why God would choose him to become the father of the Abrahamic religions of Judaism, Islam and Christianity. He appears to be picked at random.[323] In fact, twice in the story, Abraham engages in the morally ambiguous practice of passing off his wife, Sarah, as his sister. In the first instance, Abraham engages in this deception as he approaches Egypt and tells Pharaoh that Sarah is his sister in order to ensure Pharaoh does not feel the need to kill him in order to obtain the beguiling Sarah. But Abraham also hopes that, as a result of the sexual relationship between Sarah and Pharaoh, things will "go well" for him. Indeed, in a precursor to God's rescue of the entire Jewish people from Egypt in the next book of the Bible, God afflicts Pharaoh's household with plagues, and Pharaoh not only releases Sarah, but makes Abraham extremely rich. The plagues hardly seem necessary in this instance because Pharaoh is aghast at the compromised moral position Abraham's deception has placed him in.[324] Abraham pulls the same trick again later. This time Abraham does not justify the deception as a means of self-preservation. He and Sarah simply hatch the plot, this time against Abimelech, the king of Gerar. We are not told why they think this is a good idea. God once again intervenes and Abimelech is left to plead his innocence to God in the face of Abraham's trickery. Abraham once again leaves the scene with even greater riches.[325] Abraham is clearly not chosen by God for his moral character.

When Abraham is chosen by God, God immediately promises Abraham that he will be made a great nation.[326] After the incident with Pharaoh, God repeats his promise, saying that "I will make your offspring as the dust of the earth, so that if a man can count the dust of the earth, then your offspring may also be counted."[327] A little while passes, and Abraham starts to wonder when God will fulfill his promise. God brings him outside and assures him, "Look now toward the sky, and count the stars, if you are able to count them." He tells Abraham, "So will your offspring be." [328] Sarah becomes impatient and suggests that she and Abraham can conceive a son through Sarah's Egyptian maid, Hagar. Hagar conceives a son, and Sarah's jealousy is so enflamed that she abuses Hagar until she flees into the desert only to be ordered back by an angel of God, but not before she too receives the promise that her son, to be named Ishmael, will have innumerable descendants. Eventually, Sarah's jealousy will overwhelm her and with God's consent, Abraham banishes Hagar and Ishmael into the wilderness where they enjoy the continued protection of God and, tradition holds, become the founders of Islam. This is the last we hear of Hagar and Ishmael. The promise that Abraham will have innumerable descendants is repeated several more times until finally, long after Abraham and Sarah would be naturally expected to be able to have children, Sarah gives birth to Isaac.

Finally, the principle obstacle to seeing God's promise fulfilled has been overcome and Abraham has a son. The path to nationhood seems clear. But suddenly God puts Abraham to the test.

> After these things, God tested Abraham, and said to him, "Abraham!"
>
> He said, "Here I am."
>
> He said, "Now take your son, your only son, Isaac, whom you love, and go into the land of Moriah. Offer him there as a burnt offering on one of the mountains which I will tell you of."
>
> Abraham rose early in the morning, and saddled his donkey; and took two of his young men with him, and Isaac his son. He split the wood for the burnt offering, and rose up, and went to the place of which God had told him.[329]

One remarkable element of God's command is that it is delivered by God and received by Abraham so unremarkably and dispassionately. The concept of a test is very reminiscent of the test of Job, which turned out to be a literary device to set up the conflict rather than a moral judgment. Abraham's reaction is muted to say the least. This is the son God promised him without condition. It was in reliance on God's promise that this son would assure him descendants that Abraham banished Ishmael. Abraham, who would so eloquently argue for the preservation of Sodom, is venally complacent and obedient in this instance.

Abraham says nothing to Sarah or Isaac and takes Isaac on the three-day journey to Moriah. The narrative does not say anything about Abraham being grieved by what he has to do or that he hesitates for a moment. When Isaac notes the suspicious absence of a sacrificial animal, Abraham lies and says that God will provide a lamb. When they arrive, Abraham binds Isaac and prepares to kill him and burn his body. Whether he does so dispassionately or with regret is not noted. If the author intended to emphasize the moral dilemma Abraham is facing, he did a lousy job and missed every opportunity. At the very last moment, an angel stops Abraham. Abrahams's lie turns out to be mostly true after all, and God provides a ram to serve as the sacrificial animal in Isaac's place.

Soren Kierkegaard is considered the father of all of existentialism, both atheistic and theistic. Kierkegaard's critique of the Christianity of his native Denmark in the early 1800s would be entirely applicable to modern Christianity. In Kierkegaard's time, Christianity had come to mean behaving well, living a respectable life, and generally following all the social norms and values of the day. Kierkegaard was convinced that Christianity requires more of us. He felt Christianity had become wholly domesticated. It had abandoned any claim of being counter-cultural and has simply been absorbed into the culture. Dutch Christianity agreed with Dutch secular culture that we should share, develop our talents, and be humble.

Kierkegaard believed that true faith meant being prepared to violate what the rest of society says is good, in response to one's own encounter with God. To illustrate that, Kierkegaard spent nearly the entirety of his groundbreaking book, *Fear and Trembling*, studying Genesis 22 and the story of Abraham and Isaac.

Kierkegaard points out that Abraham's decision to do what God told him to do is absurd. It's not based on any recognizable moral code. It's murder. If he told his wife, Sarah, or the local authorities, or his son, what he was going to do, obviously, there would have been trouble for Abraham. Abraham does it because he trusts his experience of God over those social norms and over institutional expectation. Read literally, the story is disturbing; a father sacrificing his son at God's command. The point is not what God asks Abraham to do. The task was designed to be outrageous and to offend our moral expectations. The author of this revelation could have chosen any other morally outrageous task. The point is Abraham trusted his personal experience of God and followed through on it, right or wrong.

Kierkegaard believes that each one of us is called to this transformative relationship to God. We're called to be what Kierkegaard calls, a 'single one' or 'authentic self.' This can only be accomplished by relating to God as individuals, not as Christians, Jews or Muslims, but as our own individual selves.

At the end of the story, God once again promises Abraham innumerable decedents:

> The Lord's angel called to Abraham a second time out of the sky, and said, "I have sworn by myself, says the Lord, because you have done this thing, and have not withheld your son, your only son, that I will bless you greatly, and I will multiply your offspring greatly like the stars of the heavens, and like the sand which is on the seashore. Your offspring will possess the gate of his enemies. All the nations of the earth will be blessed by your offspring, because you have obeyed my voice.[330]

This is the first mention that God's multiplicity of promises to Abraham over the course of their relationship was conditional and that He demanded obedience in order to feel bound by them. God commanded Abraham, Abraham complied and was rewarded. But if we are not morally autonomous, then what is it Abraham accomplished here? Kierkegaard concluded that Abraham is a faith hero – he used his free will to do the will of God in complete derogation of social expectations. If this is not a story about God's favored son obeying a command, then what is it?

Kierkegaard has placed too much emphasis on the set up and too little emphasis on the outcome. As a result, he has portrayed Abraham as a moral hero, an 'authentic one,' when Scripture seemed to go out of its way to make Abraham seem morally ambiguous at best. The reason Abraham does not try to negotiate for his son's survival and the reason his emotional state is not explored, although each would have been natural to the narrative, is because Abraham's choices are not the story. Abraham's moral dilemma seems ancillary because it *is* ancillary. This is a story about God's choices, and the nature of our relationship to Him.

The pre-Abrahamic gods were something to be feared – really feared. Being mythological, they reflected nature – capricious, harsh and violent. The god with whom God is always competing in the Old Testament is Ba'al. Ba'al was sometimes referred to as a single god but often represented a whole family of gods including a Zeus-like leader called Ba'al Molech, and others including one whose name is familiar to many Christians as a synonym for the devil: Ba'al Zebub. People who worshiped Ba'al were in constant interaction with worshipers of the Hebrew God and they co-habitated in cities such as Jerusalem. God is constantly warning the Israelites not to worship false gods and to stay true to Him. There is recognition throughout Scripture of the fact that many Israelites strayed. Even at the moment God makes the defining covenant with the Jewish people at Sinai, the Jews have built a golden calf thought to represent Ba'al-Hamon or Ba'al Karnaim, a North African iteration of the Ba'al gods usually depicted as a bull or horned human, but rendered by the author of Exodus as a god native to Egypt from which the Jews had just escaped. In the First Book of Kings, Elijah challenges the priests of Ba'al to a showdown.[331] Each lays wood in a pile and calls for their god to ignite it. Elijah ups the ante by soaking his pyre with water but God nonetheless ignites his pyre and shames the Ba'al priesthood. The Ba'al gods were essentially fertility gods, who would ensure good crops provided that they received adequate sacrifice from their human subjects. The Ba'al gods were cruel, demanding gods. It is widely believed that the worshipers of Ba'al would sacrifice their first born children on pyres, sometimes in the valley outside the walls of Jerusalem known as Gehenna. If true, one could imagine the hellishness of a valley filled with the acrid smoke from pyres fueled with child sacrifice.

The set-up of the story of Abraham and Isaac may be a reflection of this practice. Rather than receiving a commandment from God to kill his son and burn his body on a pyre like the Ba'alists, perhaps Abraham adopted this practice of his own accord. Abraham had an experience of the divine and, like virtually every human being before him and since, he assumed he knew how to respond – transactionally. The ancient audience of this story would have instantly recognized it as the standard theology and practice of the day among the local non-Jews.[332] God intervenes and stops the sacrifice because He is the covenantal God rather than a transactional one. This is the God who does not demand sacrifice, but only seeks to reveal His own moral nature and encourage knowledge of His ways. Abraham is meant to represent the turning point between a transactional mythological god and worship of the monotheistic, covenantal God. The story appears to be a turning away from mythological capricious and violent gods reflecting the violence and scarcity of the natural world to a covenantal God who requires nothing of His people. Perhaps God requires nothing of His people because He knows they are not morally autonomous, are not free, and therefore they have nothing to offer.

This then *is* an existentialist story. But it does not stand for the somewhat pedestrian proposition that we should trust our own experience of God over social expectations. Rather, it says that we are not what we can do for God. God is perfectly happy not to receive sacrifice from us or command us to be obedient or morally heroic, because our place on the moral spectrum is decided not freely by us, but by our nature and nurture. Our relationship to God transcends purpose and morality.

Martin Buber and the Ten Commandments

If we are not what we can do for God and God is not what He can do for us, then what is faith for? The answer is that faith serves no practical purpose. Faith is the relationship between God and humanity. It is not a relationship of mutual advantage or reward and punishment, but is a relationship of love. The challenge of faith for our evolved minds is to rest in that status and to savor the existential power of what it means to be loved unconditionally by the divine without re-interpreting love to be about performing tasks for one another, even if those tasks are socially useful and laudable. Because our minds are constructed in an environment of scarcity and naturally crave purpose and measurable results, this is not an easy task and we have relegated it to mystics. What behavioral science has done for faith is to give it a solid footing from which to leave the image of God as 'He who rewards and punishes' and embrace the image of God as 'He who simply loves.' This is what faith must become if it is to be true to itself and to make sense of what is revealed in Creation and in Scripture. It may indeed be what faith must become in order to survive.

How does love manifest itself between God and creature if not through command, reward and punishment? Contrasted to Jean-Paul Sartre's conclusion that "hell is other people," the theistic existentialist, Martin Buber, asserts that "real life is communion." In Buber's 1923 book, *I and Thou*, Buber makes a distinction between two basic types of relationships or communion that people are capable of: the I/It relationship and the I/Thou relationship.

In the "I/It" relationship, the "I" is the thinking feeling, sentient, person, and the "It" is an object, either an actual object, like a chair, or a person you are treating as an object. Buber isn't saying that we shouldn't treat people as objects, because it is inevitable that sometimes we will. If I am taking a cab across town, the person driving the cab is an object to me – a means of crossing town. It's a purely business relationship.

The "I/Thou" relationship however, is mystical and purposeless. The participants are drawn into a relationship with each other. They don't experience the other in terms of purpose or characteristic or association with a group and so they cannot describe the other in words. One can only, according to Buber, "actualize" the other. Both participants are made radiant in the splendor of the confrontation. The I/Thou encounter can occur between you and another person, like a friend or a family member or a stranger, a thing like a tree or a flower or a stone, but Buber says it's best actualized between an individual and God.

Abraham Heschel, a contemporary of Buber's, described our reaction to God in the I/Thou encounter as one of radical amazement or wonder. But this is more than just inspirational beauty. Heschel distinguishes it from the awe we might feel at seeing pretty sunsets: "Wonder is not a sense of esthetic enjoyment. Endless wonder is endless tension, a situation in which we are shocked at the inadequacy of our awe, at the weakness of our shock, as well as the state of being asked the ultimate question." For Heschel and for Buber, encountering God is like drinking out of a fire hose.

The following description of an anemone flower by Abraham Heschel's student and theological successor, Rabbi Neil Gillman, illustrates the "I/Thou" encounter quite well. It begins by regarding the anemone in terms of its utility and usefulness and its characteristics. This is what Sartre would have called its essence and O'Donohue would have called its biography. But then, suddenly, the tone changes, and the anemone ceases to serve a function and becomes an end unto itself. Its existence rather than any particular characteristic becomes the focus:

> I look at an anemone. The artist in me sees the play of line and color, shape and form. The botanist in me sees a field of research, an

opportunity to acquire knowledge of how this flower came to be what it is. The merchant in me sees a way of marketing it. The aesthete in me sees it as matching the color scheme of my living room. But the believer in me sees an infinitely more primitive dimension of the anemone. What cried for recognition here is the simple anemone itself, the fact that it is there in the first place, the inherent mystery of its very being, and my intrinsic inability to account for the fact that there are facts in the first place. I am then thrown back to a much more primitive level of awareness, a level that is pre-conceptual, that precedes my ability to think or say anything else about the flower or any aspect of my experience. What I see is the anemone, but I "see" it as transfigured, as calling attention to a dimension of reality beyond itself. That transcendent dimension of the world as infused with God's presence, one manifestation of the divine pathos. It is the world as embodying God's cry for attention.[333]

For Buber, this is relationship – we are not tortured by each other as Sartre imagines, but rather we are actualized by one another in communion with one other. The I/Thou encounter is the only place where each of us can realize our full potential, according to Buber. It's in relationships or communion where your authentic personality is revealed. This is Kierkegaard's concept of the "authentic self." But transcending Kierkegaard, we are not concerned with being morally heroic and obeying God no matter what the consequences. Rather, we are standing in creaturely awestruck wonder at God as individuals without dogma or orthodoxy.

Characteristics of the I/Thou Encounter

The I/Thou encounter is intensely personal. Each participant is absolutely irreplaceable to that relationship. So if two individuals are having an I/Thou encounter, and one leaves the room, the remaining participant cannot pick it up with someone else and continue the same encounter. Following the Israelites' encounter with God at Mount Sinai, God's attention seems to be for the people rather than the individuals who make up that people. The story of Sodom and Gomorrah and Abraham's negotiation with God may well be an attempt to walk that back and correct that impression.

Sodom and Gomorrah is another story we may reflexively assume is about God commanding, rewarding and punishing, but which ultimately stands for something quite different. The erstwhile hero of the story is Abraham's cousin, Lot, who has taken up residence in Sodom with his wife and two daughters. God hears that Sodom is a sinful city and dispatches two angels who appear as men to reconnoiter the situation and destroy the city if God's impression turns out to be accurate. They encounter Lot at the city gates, and Lot insists that they stay with him for the night. All the men of the city surround Lot's house and demand that he send the two men out so that they can sexually assault them. In the first signal that this story is not about morality, Lot offers his two daughters, who he describes as virgins, to the mob instead. No matter how patriarchal the intended audience of this story might have been, it is unbelievable that this would have been recognized as anything but morally abhorrent behavior by Lot. At the end of the story, Lot's daughters get him drunk and have intercourse with him over the course of two nights to perpetuate their family line. Clearly, God was not rescuing the righteous from Sodom. The angels pass judgment and the city, along with nearby Gomorrah, is to be consumed by fire and brimstone. Lot is unable to convince his betrothed sons-in-law to leave, and only he, his wife and daughters escape and are warned to run and not look back. His wife, failing to heed the angels' warning, doesn't quite escape because she looks back at Sodom and is turned into a pillar of salt.[334] Lot gets tired of running and God spares Zoar, a small city nearby, for him to escape to.[335]

The set-up of the story may be an attempt to explain the total destruction of the cities of Sodom and Gomorrah by some natural disaster but the inexplicable 'sparing' of the nearby Zoar, the last of which, at least, was a real place. It may also be an attempt to explain the presence of pillars of salt on the shores of the nearby Dead Sea, or rock formations. But the real importance of the story occurs in the prior chapter, when God alludes to His plan to destroy Sodom to Abraham. Abraham argues with God to spare the city.

God said, "Because the cry against Sodom and Gomorrah is great, and because their sin is very grievous, I will go down now, and see whether their deeds are as bad as the reports which have come to me. If not, I will know."

Abraham came near, and said, "Will you consume the righteous with the wicked? What if there are fifty righteous within the city? Will you consume and not spare the place for the fifty righteous who are in it? May it be far from you to do things like that, to kill the righteous with the wicked, so that the righteous should be like the wicked. May that be far from you. Shouldn't the Judge of all the earth do right?"

God said, "If I find in Sodom fifty righteous within the city, then I will spare the whole place for their sake." Abraham answered, "See now, I have taken it on myself to speak to the Lord, although I am dust and ashes. What if there will lack five of the fifty righteous? Will you destroy all the city for lack of five?"

He said, "I will not destroy it if I find forty-five there."

He spoke to him yet again, and said, "What if there are forty found there?"

He said, "I will not do it for the forty's sake."

He said, "Oh don't let the Lord be angry, and

I will speak. What if there are thirty found there?"

He said, "I will not do it if I find thirty there."

He said, "See now, I have taken it on myself to speak to the Lord. What if there are twenty found there?"

He said, "I will not destroy it for the twenty's sake."

He said, "Oh don't let the Lord be angry, and I will speak just once more. What if ten are found there?"

He said, "I will not destroy it for the ten's sake."

God went his way, as soon as he had finished communing with Abraham, and Abraham returned to his place.[336]

This is Scriptural authorship at its very best and most evocative. One can almost hear Abraham's knees knocking together as he addresses God, acknowledging that he is dust and ashes standing before the Creator of the universe. God relents – although rather than sparing the city, he rescues a group of four inhabitants that aren't all that righteous and loses one in the process. The message is not a moral exhortation against homosexuality or anything else, but rather is a statement about God's morality. God's loving concern is for the individual. God recognizes that individuals, not groups, experience love, happiness, fear and suffering. And it is individuals, not groups, that encounter

God. Much of the narrative that follows the story of Abraham is about the Israelites as a people, and their fate is often decided communally rather than on a case-by-case basis. The story of Sodom and Gomorrah is clearly intended to inoculate us against the impression that God is the God of nations, one side of a war over the other, or any other collective. It stands for the proposition that each of us loved as an individual. "Aren't two sparrows sold for an Assarion coin?" Jesus asks in the Gospel of Mathew. "Not one of them falls on the ground apart from your Father's will, but the very hairs of your head are all numbered. Therefore don't be afraid. You are of more value than many sparrows."[337] This reflects that the I/Thou encounter does not occur between God and group, or through an intermediary, but is a personal encounter. When Moses climbs Mount Sinai to encounter God, the Israelites remain behind. As we shall see shortly, the Israelites never behave as a people who have encountered God for themselves. Their concern is only the law, and ironically or perhaps as a result, they are never capable of following the law. The attempt to meet God through command and through an intermediary may be all that is available to us most of the time, but we must never mistake it for encounter.

According to Buber, the I/Thou encounter changes both participants, which is extraordinary. We readily accept the transformative power of love among human beings, and that God's love has the power to transform us is not a stretch. But it is another matter to assert that we, unfree human beings, have any power to transform God. But the Judeo-Christian God is not the Platonic Unmoved Mover. As we've seen, God may well have tied Himself to the mast and pledged to allow the universe to unfold as it will, with an element of randomness that allows for suffering and, therefore, happiness. The Scriptural passages where human beings appear to convince God not to take certain action, like Abraham outside of Sodom, and Moses at the foot of Mount Sinai, are not meant to indicate that we can change God's mind with a good argument. Rather, in some manner, God can be moved by our attention. Our God is not a god of physics any more than He is a god of command, reward and punishment. Our God is a God of love and warmth – finally and perhaps inexplicably concerned for His creatures, moved by them and changed by them.

Buber says the I/Thou encounter cannot be verbalized. Because the object of the I/Thou encounter is the existence of the other rather than his or her characteristics, putting the encounter into words will never fully capture or convey the encounter to someone who did not themselves participate in it. Trying to communicate the I/Thou encounter will always corrupt the message. Judeo-Christianity is heavily reliant on revelation in Scripture and yet we do not spend much time or energy imagining how that revelation is conveyed to the authors of the words that make up our Scripture. It is too easy to reflexively imagine that God arrives at the prophet's home and begins dictation of the words of Scripture for the prophet to write down verbatim. Scripture does not suggest that it happens this way. God rarely speaks more than a few words. One notable exception (that may indicate God is male after all!) is that He gives excruciatingly detailed unsolicited advice with regards to the construction of things: first the precise dimensions of the Ark of the Covenant,[338] then the Tabernacle Tent,[339] and finally Aaron's priestly garments, each of which consume a chapter or two.[340] This detail is crucial to that narrative, as we'll see in the final chapter of this book. But generally, God is a God of few words. Paul's conversion is accomplished with as few as thirty words.[341] Jesus's baptism takes only eleven words from heaven.[342] The Transfiguration occurs with as few as eight.[343] Pentecost is wordless. The enlightenment of the Buddha is similarly wordless.

Of course one of the most beloved passages of Scripture is the transmission of the Ten Commandments from God to Moses. How can this be said to be non-verbal? We will explore this moment in greater detail shortly, but for now, note that God Himself writes the Ten Commandments with His finger on the first set of stone tablets for Moses. When Moses receives the Ten Commandments a second time, having shattered the first set of stone tablets, the method of transmission has changed. Now it is Moses who writes down the words of God. An extremely interesting and important detail of this event has been lost in almost every version of the Bible. Moses does not write down the Ten Commandments, but rather, he writes down the "Ten Words."[344] God, it appears, merely gives the flavor and essence of His will, and leaves it either to Moses or maybe even for the Israelites huddled at the base of the mountain to discern what He meant. Jewish mysticism has reduced this even further and suggested that God did not convey Ten Words, but rather a single utterance that was not even linguistic, but a sound akin to the sound of the intake of the divine breath.[345] This reflects that God is Wholly Other and is not speaking words to the prophet at all but is conveying inspiration to be ham-handedly reduced to language by the prophet. The Bible is the best effort to record the I/Thou relationship between God and the prophets and other authors of Scripture, but it's always corrupted because they are verbalizing a non-verbal encounter.

The Widow and the Orphan – Non-Verbal Corruption

God delivers a series of additional commands right after the Ten Commandments. Among the most important is His demand that we never abuse widows and orphans:

> No widow nor orphan shall you abuse. If you indeed abuse them, when they cry out to Me, I will surely hear their outcry. And my wrath shall flare up and I will kill you by the sword, and your wives shall be widows and your children orphans.[346]

Our natural impulse is to focus on the moral exhortation that we are to avoid abusing widows and orphans. It appeals to our reflexive desire to equate faith with morality, and it also has colorful, dramatic language, appealing to our retributive side - if we abuse a widow, God will make our wife a widow. It's also a nice, exceptionally easy moral test we can all pass if we're inclined to. You would almost have to be a monster to abuse widows and orphans, so the only people who are likely to get caught out by this command are sociopaths anyway. But what if we are not morally autonomous beings and God is not in the business of command, reward and punishment? If this is not about the moral, what is the transcendent message? What are we to make of this seemingly inescapably retributivist statement?

In recognizing that revelation is not verbal and is not a word for word dictation by God to a prophet, we can recognize that we need to read between the lines and apply science and intuition to revelation to make it whole. Our understanding of our relationship to God must be guided by first principals. That God is just and that He would not punish us for things outside our control is the most fundamental assumption we can and must make about God. Just as I made ever more outrageous mental corrections as I looked for my house in Dollard, we need to be alert to moments when the prophet might have abandoned this principle in favor of an assumption he's made impulsively. We need to tease away what God meant from what the prophet may have inadvertently added as a result of his cultural expectations.

Abraham Heschel writes:

The prophet is not a passive recipient, a recording instrument, affected from without participation of heart and will, nor is he a person who acquires his vision by his own strength and labor. The prophet's personality is rather a unity of inspiration and experience, invasion and response. For every object outside him, there is a feeling inside him; for every event of revelation to him, there is a reaction by him; for every glimpse of truth he is granted, there is a comprehension he must achieve. Even in the moment of the event he is, we are told, an active partner in the event. His response to what is disclosed to him turns revelation into a dialogue. In a sense, prophecy consists of a revelation of God and a *co-revelation of man*. The share of the prophet manifested itself not only in what he was able to give but also in what he was unable to receive. Revelation does not happen when God is alone.[347]

In the ancient world, widows and orphans had no means to provide for themselves and were quintessentially dependent on the unearned accommodation and charity of others for their day-to-day survival. In an overwhelmingly patriarchal society, it could be anticipated that they would never pull their weight, produce anything, or serve any social function. What God was saying here was not a moral exhortation, so much as statement about the nature of His relationship to us – God's morality. In modern faith the idea that God cares for each of us regardless of our social station is universally accepted. But recall that God's constant competition in the Old Testament is Ba'al – a brutal, demanding family of gods with no tradition of love for anyone, let alone social outcasts or the poor. God's loving concern for the widow and orphan would have been an unprecedented message of divine concern for those who could offer nothing in return. This was the message to the prophet. This message of loving the poor and the outcast rather than taking the side of the wealthy and strong, reflects radical grace – unearned love given freely to unfree beings. This is not selective reading, but rather a necessary interpretation if the basic tenets of theistic determinism are true and if we can utilize what science tells us about human nature to discern God's relationship to us.

The Ten Commandments

The intensely personal nature of the I/Thou encounter is even more central to Buber's thought than its non-verbal nature. Buber is led to conclude that the I/Thou encounter can never be legislative – no moral code or command that we are all supposed to follow can be communicated by the I/Thou encounter. Buber would be very suspicious of the story of the Ten Commandments as Judeo-Christianity has interpreted it, and he would say it is a very badly corrupted recordation of an I/Thou encounter between Moses and God. I have a great personal affinity for this aspect of Buber's thought. Buber was an intensely spiritual figure, capable of conveying extraordinary insight into the nature of our relationship to God, and was a committed and devout Jew. And yet Buber, by calling into question the ability of an encounter with God to include moral commands, calls the purpose of the transmittal of Ten

Commandments by God to Moses - arguably the most important moment in Judaism - into question. How can this committed Jew nonetheless reject the idea of Torah? This dichotomy created, for me, the first hint that perhaps faith is not about command, reward and punishment but is about personal encounter. For Buber that which we naturally perceive as commands from God to be obeyed are not commandments at all. They are part of narrative that expresses the covenantal character of God's love for us. The commandments are not what we *must* keep; they are what we *cannot keep* because we are not morally autonomous agents. They are, according to Paul, instituted only to demonstrate to us that we are not made to abide by the law and receive reward and punishment accordingly – that doesn't make any sense if we do not have free will. Rather, we are made with the full knowledge that we are not morally responsible.

The story of the Ten Commandments is undeniably a turning point in the biblical narrative. The story at first appears to be about the moment God imposes His law on the Israelites and they agree to comply and become the Chosen People. But the actual story is more complex and signals to us that perhaps there is more to this story than at first meets the eye.

Having rescued the Israelites from Egypt, God leads them to the base of Mount Sinai. Moses ascends the mountain, and God tells him that God will make the Israelites His own people if they will agree to obey Him. Moses reports the terms of the deal to the Israelites and they immediately agree.

> Moses went up to God, and the Lord called to
> him out of the mountain, saying, "This is what
> you shall tell the house of Jacob, and tell the
> children of Israel: 'You have seen what I did to
> the Egyptians, and how I bore you on eagles'
> wings, and brought you to myself. Now
> therefore, if you will indeed obey my voice,
> and keep my covenant, then you shall be my
> own possession from among all peoples; for
> all the earth is mine; and you shall be to me a
> kingdom of priests, and a holy nation.' These
> are the words which you shall speak to the
> children of Israel."
>
> Moses came and called for the elders of the
> people, and set before them all these words
> which God commanded him. All the people
> answered together, and said, "All that the
> Lord has spoken we will do."[348]

Moses dutifully transmits the people's acceptance to God and
the dramatic prelude to this momentous historical event is set
into motion. God commands the Israelites to sanctify themselves for three days, washing their clothes, abstaining from
sex, and finally marching forward to the very base of Mount
Sinai. On the third day, there is thunder and lightning on the
mountain, thick clouds obscure the peak, and the people hear
a deafening trumpet blast. God Himself descends onto Mount

Sinai wreathed in fire and smoke. The earth quakes, the trumpet blast grows louder. God summons Moses to the mountaintop again and tells him to remind the Israelites that if they see Him, or so much as touch the mountain, they will die. Moses descends and does as he is told. Then God dictates the Ten Commandments from the mountain to Moses and the people below. In terror, the people ask Moses to intervene – to receive the message and transmit it to them. The very first and second commands are not to have others gods and not to make graven images. God interrupts the list of Commandments to emphasize the importance of this one, which the Israelites will almost immediately break:

You shall not bow down to them and you shall not worship them, for I am the Lord your God, a jealous god, reckoning the crime of the fathers with sons, with the third generation and with the fourth, for My foes, and doing kindness to the thousandth generation for my friends and for those who keep my commands.[349]

This is already an expression of mercy for the Israelites before they even break the commandment. Doing the math, being a foe of God must last uninterrupted for 996 generations before God will withhold His kindness. This message is lost in the New American Standard Version and many other popular versions of the Bible because they omit the second reference to "generations" so, instead of God's mercy being virtually assured, it appears God will punish several generations for sin, but His kindness is exhibited to unrelated others. The difference is subtle but the effect is not:

> You shall not worship them or serve them; for I, the Lord your God, am a jealous God, visiting the iniquity of the fathers on the children, on the third and the fourth generations of those who hate Me, but showing lovingkindness to thousands, to those who love Me and keep My commandments.

This is a modern redaction, inadvertently having changed the meaning of the words to make them more severe.

The staccato of the initial Ten Commandments is over, and seeming to re-emphasize and provide even more detail to the first and second commandments, God reminds Moses that the Israelites are to worship only Him and never create idols of silver or gold. The pace of command quickens again and, over the course of the next three chapters, God lays out dozens of more laws and the minimum sentencing requirements for failure to keep them.[350]

Again, the Israelites agree to abide by these laws without hesitation, *"All the words which the Lord has spoken will we do."*[351] Moses writes down the laws, and reads this book of the covenant to the people.[352] A third time the people agree: *"All that the Lord has spoken we will do and we will be obedient!"*[353] God summons Moses to the top of the mountain again, this time to receive the Ten Commandments written by God's finger on tablets of stone. Moses is away for forty days, and the people become worried. While in Egypt, the Israelites, at the behest of God, borrowed silver and gold jewelry from their Egyptian neighbors before the last plague inspired Pharaoh to let them flee.[354] Now the Israelites take their gold earrings out of their ears and give them to Moses's trusted right-hand man, Aaron. Aaron casts the gold into the idolatrous image of a calf.

From the top of Mount Sinai with Moses, God sees that the Israelites have broken the commandment He so recently imposed and they three times agreed to follow. No longer does He refer to them as "the people"; now He refers to them to Moses as, "your people":

Go, get down; for your people, who you brought up out of the land of Egypt, have corrupted themselves! They have turned away quickly out of the way which I commanded them. They have made themselves a molded calf, and have worshiped it, and have sacrificed to it, and said, 'These are your gods, Israel, which brought you up out of the land of Egypt.'"

The Lord said to Moses, "I have seen these people, and behold, they are a stiff-necked people. Now therefore leave me alone, that

> my wrath may burn hot against them, and that
> I may consume them; and I will make of you a
> great nation."[355]

Moses, in a remarkable speech to God, essentially convinces Him not to destroy the Israelites. God relents. When Moses comes down off the mountain, he is furious. No sooner then he reaches the base of Mount Sinai, he throws the stone tablets to the ground and shatters them. Moses demands to know what Aaron was thinking. Like the blame game Adam, Eve and the snake engaged in, Aaron is quick to blame the Israelites and even tries to blame the calf on supernatural forces, telling Moses he simply threw the gold into the fire and out sprang the calf! Moses burns the calf, grinds it into powder and forces the Israelites to drink it.

A critical part of the story that is often overlooked is that God then summons Moses up to the top of the mountain again to receive replacement tablets identical to those Moses broke. Moses obviously sprang for the breakage warranty with Tablet 1.0 and now receives Tablet 2.0 for no additional charge. Upon arrival, before Moses utters a word, God pronounces his forgiveness of the Israelites using the same language He used when He first proclaimed the first and second Commandments:

> The Lord, the Lord! A compassionate and
> gracious God, slow to anger, and abounding
> in kindness and good faith, keeping kindness

for the thousandth generation, bearing crime, trespass and offense, yet He does not wholly acquit, reckoning the crime of fathers with sons and sons of sons to the third generation and the fourth.[356]

Again, an inadvertent redaction appears to have occurred and the first reference to generations in the New American Standard version and this time in even more versions of the Bible, has been dropped and the meaning of the passage changed.[357]

God then repeats some of His earlier commands and re-states His covenant with the people of Israel. This time, God is dictating and Moses is transcribing. For most of my life, I thought this story could have been less awkward with some fairly basic editing. If Moses simply zapped the Israelites with the first set of tablets without destroying them, there would have been no need to have Moses go and fetch a replacement pair. But this is actually at the heart of the story. The Israelites broke the covenant almost as soon as they entered into it. God immediately enters into it again. God knows that we are not morally autonomous beings and our word, even written in stone, is not trustworthy. Moses's very strange punishment; forcing the Israelites to drink the golden calf; is not the sadistic creativity of a man blinded with rage. Instead, it is an acknowledgement, memorialized in the most important moment of the Old Testament narrative, that we are never free of our shortcomings. They are inherent to our nature and we carry them around with us always. We cannot be freed from sin, and we need not bother pledging to do better. God knows of what we are made. In His justice He loves us anyway. Our shortcoming is always with us – we drank the powdered calf and it is part of our nature. God nevertheless engages with us, overlooks this shortcoming that existed from the moment of our Creation and will be with us forever, and loves us nonetheless.

The High Holidays in the Jewish calendar begin with Rosh Hashanah where tradition says God opens the Book of Life and inscribes our names either in the good column or the bad column. For the next ten days we have the opportunity to atone for our sins and change a bad designation before He makes the decision permanent and seals it on Yom Kippur. In the Orthodox tradition, Jews perform a mikveh in those ten days – a full-body immersion in water that is an obvious pre-cursor to baptism. Some perform taschlich and threw pebbles representing their sins into a body of water that is not subject to fluctuations as a result of drought that may re-expose the sins they cast away. This practice receives criticism among some Jews because it makes atonement and divine forgiveness too easy and too automatic. It ought to require, in their view, recompense or at least an expression of sincere regret. On the evening before Yom Kippur, the highest of holidays and the Day of Atonement, Jews celebrate Kol Nidre. They gather in synagogue and declare that any promises made in the coming year are void. The cantor sings three times, with greater volume each time, the words of renunciation:

All vows we are likely to make, all oaths and pledges we are likely to take between this Yom Kippur and the next Yom Kippur, we publicly renounce. Let them all be relinquished and abandoned, null and void, neither firm nor established. Let our vows, pledges and oaths be considered neither vows nor pledges nor oaths.

Then the congregation joins in and thrice repeats a passage from Numbers 15:26:

May all the people of Israel be forgiven, including all the strangers who live in their midst, for all the people are in fault.

This annual disavowal of vows has sometimes been used as a pre-text for anti-Semitism, reasoning that the oath of Jews cannot be trusted because they solemnly disavow them annually. It has even led, historically, to some courts requiring an additional oath of Jews testifying in court. The meaning of *Kol Nidre* is the subject of some mystery even among scholars of Jewish law. Some have surmised that it was a way for Jews who had officially renounced Judaism to avoid persecution, particularly during the Inquisition, to return to God's good graces. Others suggest that disavowal of promises is an imitation of God who broke His own promise to harshly punish the Israelites for breaking His commandment but allowed Himself to be cajoled out of it.

But if we accept that we do not have free will another interpretation reveals itself. If free will does not exist, and if the concept of command includes the possibility of reward and punishment, and if God is just, then God cannot command anything. God's forgiveness is, indeed, totally automatic and unconditional, whether we like it or not. The only obstacle to recognizing God's forgiveness are the false illusions that we have moral autonomy in the first place and that there are commands in the first place. The voiding of all oaths and commands at *Kol Nidre* paves the way for the Day of Atonement because it forces us to recognize this critical Scriptural theme. It tells us that we cannot earn forgiveness with perfect conduct or even by perfect expressions of regret. Our promise to obey isn't worth the tablet it's written on and we need to renounce the promise in order to understand the full breadth and beauty of God's mercy. The story of the Israelites at the base of Mount Sinai is not about people making the free choice to disobey commands and the forgiveness of an angry, petulant God. It is a story about our inevitable inability to make moral choices in the first place, and God's decision to love us anyway. It is an echo of the Garden of Eden. Adam and Eve's inherent shortcoming was a lack of free will. Their mistake was not to disobey a command. Rather, their mistake was that they asserted moral autonomy and the ability to follow commandments, and therefore adopted reasons for all generations to come to judge one another and find each other wanting in direct contradiction of God's advice. They were not ejected from the Garden, but rather made themselves inevitably miserable and condemned their children to murderous hate, by assuming the ability to judge and be judged despite a lack of free will. We cannot walk back into the Garden the way we left – there is a flaming sword in our path. To recognize our true relationship to God, we first have to recognize that we do not have free will, the fact that there are no divine commands, and accept the truly unconditional love of God. The shortcoming God overlooks to love us is far more profound than our last bad behavior – it is the inherent inability to make free moral decisions at all. This is the message of *Kol Nidre*, the message of the Garden, Mount Sinai and, finally as we'll see, Jesus.

We think of the Israelites as being heroes of the story. But when Moses descends the mountain a final time and the Israelites resume their journey, there is no reaffirmation of their acceptance of the covenant or pledge to do better. Moses descends, we are told, with the skin of his face shining with a mysterious light so bright he had to veil himself. This is not a man who is flush with a second chance to follow laws and hopeful that the Israelites will not disappoint again – they do, and we do. This is an exuberant man, radically amazed by the I/Thou encounter with the divine and the radical grace he found there for himself and his people. The Israelites simply fall into line, donate their gold again, but this time to construct the Ark of the Covenant, and head off to the Promised Land.

I/Thou is Not About Moral Heroism

Are they intended to be heroic moral figures having made a free decision to follow God's law? One of the most remarkable things about Scripture is that no one is portrayed as a hero. Noah is at first declared to be righteous "in his age" which may be to say that he was righteous as compared to the others in his cohort, who set the bar pretty low. As we've seen, Noah leaves the ark, cultivates a vineyard and promptly becomes colossally drunk. Abraham passes his wife off as his sister. Lot offers his daughters to a mob in place of the houseguests the mob was after. As his first act upon achieving adulthood, Moses murders someone.[358] The apostles are portrayed as virtually foolish: misinterpreting everything Jesus says, bickering about who is greater and who will get to sit at Jesus's right in heaven. Peter, handpicked to be the leader of the apostles, denies knowing Jesus three times. Moral perfection clearly eludes the protagonists. This ought to be a signal to us that Scripture is not about being moral. Somehow, however, morality seems to creep back into our reading of Scripture, our customs and sacred traditions, and even in Scripture itself. If we are not morally autonomous and if God is fair in His expectations of us, then these constant exhortations to morality must be corruptions of the divine message.

Some will criticize this as the equivalent of "a trophy for every child" in children's athletic programs, and that it is too good to be true that the universe is set up this way. But pessimism is not a philosophy. The more we learn about the universe, the vaster and more abundant its dimensions reveal themselves to be. If we must take a view of the universe as either pessimistic, characterized by scarcity and brutality, or optimistic, characterized by abundance and unity, the latter is more in keeping with our ever-increasing understanding of it. A trophy for every child is a construct of soft-hearted parents who know of what their children are made and who respond to their failure to perform with mercy and acceptance. The God of the Old Testament is the same. He is soft-hearted, knows of what we are made and that His children are by their very nature incapable of performing, and so He always finds an excuse for mercy and acceptance. In fact, if we are not morally autonomous, it would be irrational for Him to respond to us in any other way.

The bitter irony is that when we assume that we will encounter God by following the law, we are in fact placing an obstacle in the path of understanding our relationship to God. The law, in the words of St. Paul, then becomes a stumbling stone to faith[359]. To insist that faith is about law is to assume that we are morally autonomous – it is an imitation of Adam eating from the Tree.

Personal Encounter and Prayer

So the exceptionally personal nature of the I/Thou encounter forecloses the possibility that it can convey commands. It also means that encounter with God cannot occur in a group setting. We cannot engage in a standard operating procedure to encounter God, or set up the perfect retreat and wait for the I/Thou to reliably occur. We cannot line up and receive encounter with God. Whatever may occur in churches, temples and retreats, it is not an I/Thou encounter with God and organized religion makes a mistake when it assumes that attendance at weekly services or Mass or receipt of the Eucharist is synonymous with a personal I/Thou encounter with God and a limit beyond which spirituality cannot grow. We can certainly achieve communion with God and invite and experience His presence in community, but it is not the end of the journey. I will argue later that the sacramental is a critical component of addressing God in community, but it is not personal encounter with God. When Moses encounters God at Mount Sinai, he stands alone. The people of Israel remain below or in the background to later receive Moses's best effort at a description of the non-verbal, personal encounter. This is not to say that personal encounter with God is not possible for everyone - far from it - but it is clearly a solitary endeavor. If we are interested in cultivating the spiritual environment in which the I/Thou encounter is most likely to arise, we will engage in solitary, contemplative prayer.

Rarely did Jesus give a straight answer to a straight question. When the apostles ask Jesus how to pray, he answers them with the Our Father or Lord's Prayer. They take him literally – a decision that religion has largely perpetuated. It may be that while the Temple was available during Jesus's lifetime to serve as a focal point of prayer and ritual, it had been destroyed by the time the Gospels were written, and likely the Jewish methodology of prayer and communion with God was in flux. Jesus is conveying to the apostles that prayer is a deeply personal encounter with God that must come as naturally and as spontaneously as possible. The content of the Our Father is actually a theological disaster. If we fail to pray, God will not lead us into temptation. He will forgive our trespasses even though we may not forgive trespasses against us. One can imagine Jesus rolling his eyes as the apostles commit the words of the Our Father to memory. Once again they play the role of foils who fail to recognize allegory and embrace a task-oriented faith. The Our Father is not extraordinary for its insight, but is beautiful in its simplicity, cadence and its accessibility. Jesus's purpose was not frustrated by the apostles' literalism. Daily prayer is one form of religious observance that is actually on the rise.[360] By making prayer something that we can engage in at a moment's notice, together or in solitude, without books or guides and without buildings or clergy, Jesus placed prayer in a central position in our relationship to God.

Buber's explanation of the nature of the I/Thou encounter between the individual and God suggests a model for prayer. Prayer to seek the I/Thou encounter is distinct, and in fact outright rejects, the idea that prayer accomplishes a purpose. This prayer is not to seek intercession, to express gratitude, to confess bad behavior, worship, or to listen for command, or to be placed on a quest by God. It is not to seek advice or to plumb the mysteries of the universe or to be transformed into a moral hero. It is to encounter God and to be actualized by Him and to actualize Him.

Contemplative prayer is often thought of as the gentle but persistent banishing of all thought from the mind and inviting the voice of God. It seems to me it is closer to the truth to say it is the gentle but persistent banishing from the mind of all the roles and tasks we so naturally and reflexively associate with our relationship to God. We imagine God looking at us without defining our characteristics or whether we're generally good or bad. He is not going to judge us or send us on a mission or demand anything of us. It will not make us a moral hero and it is not moral heroism to be there. For our part, we imagine God not as He who commands, or rewards or punishes. God invites the metaphor of father, but not the commanding judgmental, correcting father, but a father who feels how vulnerable He has become because He's chosen to have a child. This is the most intimate of relationships because God already knows everything about us, He knows of what we are made. We can rest in this relationship. This permits the I/Thou encounter with God to occur, transcending any goals or expectations of one another and revealing our authentic self and God's authentic self. It is deeply personal, non-verbal, and verbally indescribable. Although it is often described as annihilation of the ego, it is more accurately the fulfillment of the self. Like the anemone, it is a positive, joyful, and mysteriously wondrous encounter. This self is what the twentieth century mystic and Cistercian monk, Thomas Merton, called our "true self" - our existential self - as opposed to our "false self" which is made up of our biography and opinions and our place on the moral spectrum. It has seemed to me that some traditional rote, repetitive prayer seeks to distract the false self and by so doing allows the true self to be more fully engaged. Saying the Our Father, reciting a rosary, or reading the Liturgy of the Hours does not completely engage one's mind but seems to distract the part of the mind that is most prone to judgment and evaluation, and is therefore prone to worry, anxiety and repetitive thinking and all the other products of a purposeful, moralistic thoughts. Perhaps that mind is the first of the two Adams described in Rabbi Joseph B. Soloveitchik's famous book, *The Lonely Man of Faith*.[361] Once that mind is otherwise engaged, it seems to allow that part of mind that is quieter but smarter and more creative to begin the process of seeking the existential, the numinous and the Wholly Other. It cultivates the mental hygiene necessary to rest in a relationship that transcends purpose and morality. I think there is a direct relationship between those forms of Christian prayer that seem on their face to be exercises in deliberate purposelessness and Buddhist meditation and its pursuit of mindfulness. The difference is that where Buddhism seeks to subjugate the false self by wrestling with it directly, Christian prayer seeks to subjugate it by distracting it.

We cannot manufacture the conditions that call God down for an I/Thou encounter. Those who are celebrated in revelation as having had encounters with God were almost inevitably not looking for it, not worthy, and often didn't find it welcome. But if we are seeking a God who commands, reward and punishes, then we will be looking in the wrong place and we would be better off not looking at all.

You Cannot Live in the I/Thou – I/Thou Does Not Transform Morally

Judas, the traitor, is dead. According to Matthew, he hanged himself after returning the thirty pieces of silver he was paid by the chief priests to betray Jesus. The chief priests used the silver to buy a burial ground for foreigners called the Field of Blood.[362] According to Acts, Judas purchased the Field of Blood with the silver, tripped in it and, apparently suffering the worst navel hernia in history, "burst open in the middle and all his bowels gushed out.[363] In the meantime, Jesus has risen from the dead, made appearances to the faithful, and ascended into heaven. As promised, the Holy Spirit is about to descend on the apostles in spectacular fashion, appearing as tongues of fire, giving the apostles the miraculous ability to reverse the effects of Babel and to speak and be understood in a multitude of languages. Peter, previously Jesus's foil making blunder after blunder, will now give a rousing speech to the inhabitants of Jerusalem. In contrast to his denial of Jesus a few days prior, he will boldly scold them for the murder of Jesus. The apostles are so transformed so as to be mistaken for being drunk. But even now, when establishing the inerrancy and authority of the new Church might be a priority, Scripture declines to depict the apostles as permanently transformed spiritual heroes. Their first task is to replace Judas. They choose from among the disciples two men; Joseph and Matthias. Sandwiched between Jesus's ascension into heaven and the descent of the Holy Spirit, they engage in what is probably the most pathetic discernment process that could be imagined. They pray for God's guidance and roll dice to choose Matthias.

The failure of encounter with God to permanently transform the moral character of the human participant is a repeated theme. Paul has the most celebrated I/Thou encounter with God in history and it does change him from executioner of Christians to the individual most responsible for the spread of Christianity throughout the world. Nonetheless, his personal shortcomings plague him. His arrogance is immediately evident in his writings two millennia after he wrote them. And so is his inability to live up to his own high estimation of himself. In his letter to the Romans, Paul admits that his conversion didn't seem to have much of an effect on his behavior. He knows what he is supposed to do, but finds himself doing the opposite anyway. His elephant is still in charge and his rider is left to scold it:

> For I don't practice what I desire to do; but what I hate, that I do. But if what I don't desire, that I do, I consent to the law that it is good. So now it is no more I that do it, but sin which dwells in me. For I know that in me, that is, in my flesh, dwells no good thing. For desire is present with me, but I don't find it doing that which is good. For the good which I desire, I don't do; but the evil which I don't desire, that I practice. But if what I don't desire, that I do, it is no more I that do it, but sin which dwells

> in me. I find then the law that, to me, while I
> desire to do good, evil is present. For I delight
> in God's law after the inward man, but I see a
> different law in my members, warring against
> the law of my mind, and bringing me into
> captivity under the law of sin which is in my
> members. What a wretched man I am! Who
> will deliver me out of the body of this death?

It makes one wonder what St. Paul was up to. God does not reject the unworthy – in fact they seem to be His chosen prophets. Nor does He seem to feel any impulse to convert them to moral perfection. It is said of Moses that no prophet has ever arisen in Israel that is like him, and yet at Meribah, Moses pretends to have God-like powers to produce water from a rock and as a result God prohibits him from entering the Promised Land[364]. David is the beloved of God and chosen from youth to be the king of Israel, but years into the divine relationship, David has an adulterous affair with Bathsheba, the wife of Uriah the Hittite, one of his best soldiers. When it turns out David has impregnated Bathsheba, David tried to cover up his paternity by insisting that Uriah take a break from soldiering and spend a night with his wife. Uriah declines to be so comfortable while others are in camps, so David changes tactics and tries to get him drunk so that he would go home and cloud the issue of paternity. Still Uriah resists. Finally, David puts Uriah on the front lines of battle and tells those around him to retreat without him, ensuring his death.[365]

Buber says that you cannot permanently live in the I/Thou encounter. We are creatures of an I/It world and the encounters with each other and the divine that actualize our authentic selves will never completely reform us. We have an image of a saint as someone who has encountered God and is henceforth incapable of behaving badly or for any motivation except the most holy. This concept simply does not exist in Scripture because moral transformation is not the point. The real theme is our lack of any ability to be morally transformed. The pressure is off. God does not expect us to be saintly. He acknowledges that we are what we are and loves us anyway. The whole of Scripture tells that story.

Out beyond the ideas of wrongdoing and
rightdoing,
there is a field. I'll meet you there.
When the soul lies down in that grass,
the world is too full to talk about.
Ideas, language – even the phrase 'each other'
doesn't make any sense.[366]

Chapter Five

Jesus Christ

O come, O come, Emmanuel,
And ransom captive Israel,
That mourns in lonely exile here,
Until the Son of God appear.
Rejoice! Rejoice! Emmanuel
Shall come to thee, O Israel[367]

Introduction; Jesus as Moral Scapegoat

No examination of the Christian faith omitting divine command, reward and punishment can be complete without accounting for Jesus Christ. In orthodoxy, Jesus is our "ransom"; the sacrificial lamb slain to atone for our sins - both that sin which is inherited from Adam and our own sinful behavior. God, enraged by our conduct, must vent His anger somehow. He arrives at the perfect solution – sending His only begotten son to be the object of His divine wrath as His horrified creatures look on. We are spared as a result of this cosmic bait and switch - provided that we believe, undergo baptism, and are sufficiently penitent for our subsequent sins.

To reconcile this understanding of Jesus with the warm, loving God of faith requires that an enormous amount of storyline be added that is not necessarily native to Christianity. C.S. Lewis reimagined the Passion narrative in his book, *The Lion, the Witch and the Wardrobe*. Set in wartime Britain, four siblings are sent to live in a sprawling countryside estate to escape the Blitz. The children find a magical wardrobe that transports them to Narnia, a magical land populated by talking animals, dwarves, giants and Father Christmas. It becomes evident that the children's presence in Narnia fulfils a prophecy that parallels the Christian story. Aslan the lion plays the role of God and the White Witch stands in for Satan. Edmund, the least well-mannered of the four siblings, eats enchanted Turkish Delight offered to him by the White Witch and becomes addicted. His addiction leads him to traitorous behavior in the service of the Witch. Edmund is rescued, but the Witch meets with Aslan and demands Edmund's execution according to the Deep Magic of Narnia – apparently a deal wrought between Aslan and the Witch at the beginning of time that governs how reward and punishment are meted out. Aslan concedes that he is bound by this law, but secretly makes a deal with the Witch that he, Aslan, will be executed in Edmund's place. Aslan is indeed killed but rises from the dead according to a loophole in the law to finally defeat the Witch.

C.S. Lewis' allegiance to Platonism is again clear. Lewis elevates Satan from performing a bit-part in Scripture to the status of a second god, almost God's equal. This allows Lewis to imagine that God, the Form of Good, simply acquiesces in Jesus's death because rules are rules. Jesus's death is necessary because morality, for Lewis, is something that is imposed by a pantheon of divine characters on their morally autonomous subjects to test how they'll respond. Whether the central thesis of Christianity or the storyline of a book, it has the air of the fantastical about it. Why couldn't God simply forgive without a horrific blood sacrifice? Must God share His sovereignty with a nasty rival?

Our lack of free will indicates that Jesus's death for our sins must be understood as something besides an actual human sacrifice to appease an angry God or to comply with cosmic rules of justice. If God sees an individual born into an abusive household, raised to hate, tempted by addictive drugs and wealth always out of reach by legitimate means, condemned to reside in a toxic, violent community with no influences powerful enough to overcome this nurture, and no inborn ability strong enough to escape it - surely God forgives the inexorable result. Surely justice requires mercy. What sense does it make that God cannot forgive this individual without someone standing in as a replacement object of wrath?

We are justifiably perplexed and more than a little discomforted by the idea of God demanding a blood sacrifice in order to withhold His wrath or bargaining with a semi-divine counterpart for our eternal soul. But rather than looking beyond morality, we have remade our understanding of Jesus. He is re-cast again as the moral hero – commanding us to share with others, to be humble, to give charitably, and to develop our talents. We place him on a list of other morally heroic figures such as Martin Luther King, Mother Teresa, and Mahatma Gandhi. Of course, Jesus has the weight of divine authority behind him, so he has a little more oomph than his moral peers. Jesus famously asked Peter, "Who do you say I that I am." – a moment we will examine carefully in the coming pages.[368] Modern Christianity, both liberal and conservative, answers that Jesus's identity is principally moral. But if we are not morally autonomous and if God would not reward or punish behavior over which we do not have control, then what sense can we make of Jesus Christ's moral commands? Indeed, what sense can we make of the concept of sin, which seems to have such a central role in Scripture and Sacred Tradition? What indispensable role does Jesus play if not cosmic sacrifice for immoral conduct or a moral teacher?

Is this chapter, I will argue that we can see Jesus in any of four different ways. We can be fairly certain God is not a moral commander who became incarnate in Jesus to express His commands and threaten reward and punishment, because that implies either that we have free will or we have an unjust God. However, this would not necessarily foreclose the possibility that Jesus intended to provide a moral example for us that we could follow (if our nature and nurture was so inclined) and by providing this example God hoped to make the world a more pleasant place. This is the first way to conceive of Jesus that we will examine. Second, Jesus may be the describer of God's nature – God's authorized moral biographer - which we have already seen is at least partly true. Third, Jesus may be the incarnation of God willing to co-suffer with us which, again, is at least part of the story. Fourth, and finally, Jesus may be the bridge between humanity and God, and that, taken with our lack of free will, may have tremendously more meaning and importance than we have previously imagined.

Each of these views must be tested against the assertion that we do not have free will. Each must also be examined in the context of the Garden story to see if what happened there finds resolution here. Recall the mysterious Tree of Life in the center of the Garden of Eden. As He banishes them from the Garden, God reveals that eating from that tree would have allowed Adam and Eve to live forever. Interesting, there was no initial prohibition against eating from the Tree of Life. Adam and Eve could have presumably achieved immortality if they had eaten from it before they ate from the Tree of the Knowledge of Good and Evil and would not have been disobeying any restriction. But once they asserted their moral autonomy, it was no longer available to them. God placed a flaming sword on the path back not to prevent Adam and Eve from eating from the same tree again, but specifically to block access to the Tree of Life. As I indicated earlier, the idea of an afterlife was well established in Jesus's time. Furthermore, Jesus's resurrection from the dead was not unique in the Bible as Jesus raises his friend Lazarus from the dead, the son of the widow of Nain, and the daughter of Jairus.[369] Both Elijah and Elisha do the same thing.[370] Even Peter and Paul have the ability to raise the dead.[371] So Jesus was likely not resurrected to demonstrate that there is an afterlife or even to be recognized as an event unique in history – the early adherents to Christianity would have thought of it as remarkable but not evidence of any necessarily unique intervention. Rather, Jesus being raised from the dead signals that he has, on some level, eaten from the Tree of Life that was once available but then was not, and some tension that began in the Garden and caused us to be unable to return there has been resolved. How does Jesus's life, death and resurrection resolve the tension of the Garden? Whatever Jesus's role, it must answer this question.

Jesus as Savior and Redeemer, The Incarnation

Finally, each of these four ways of seeing Jesus also should be weighed against Christianity's assertion that Jesus is not merely one good or wise person among many, but is our Savior and Redeemer. In modernity, the idea that Jesus is our Savior and Redeemer is the equivalent of a crazy uncle – we're very fond of him, we feel very sentimentally about him, and we'll invite him over for holidays; but don't really like to trot him out for sophisticated company. Nonetheless, we find ourselves in a faith that places Jesus in a unique familial relationship with God or even a position equal to God – a circumstance made even more remarkable by the fact that ours is a monotheistic faith.

Scripture does not suggest that Jesus's pedigree as Son of God or Incarnation of God conferred unique, special powers on him that he wields to our benefit to save and redeem us. Rather, Scripture indicates that it is Jesus's mere status as Son of God or the Incarnation of God that saves and redeems us. Whatever Jesus may do for us, it is accomplished by his birth and death rather than any action taken on his part.

In Chapter Three, we saw Jesus multiply barley loaves to feed the five thousand in a story that is often used to show Jesus as the cosmic sharer, but in reality is likely meant to show Jesus not just as a peer of the prophet Elisha, but something more. In the Transfiguration,[372] Jesus ascends a mountain with Peter, James and John and is transformed before their eyes. Jesus's garments turn pure white and his face shines like the sun, which is likely supposed to remind us of Moses's face shining when he descends Mount Sinai after his I/Thou encounter with God. Moses and Elijah appear and Jesus converses with them but we are not told what is said. Finally, a cloud comes over the scene and a voice states, "this is my beloved Son with whom I am well pleased; listen to him."[373] Here again is the I/Thou encounter with the God of few words, almost non-verbal but immense in its content - like the Ten Words that became Torah. Again, this story appears to compare Jesus to Moses and Elijah, but then goes further to increase Jesus's standing to something higher. Jesus is not a mere a prophet but is the Son of God.

Throughout the Synoptic Gospels, Jesus refers to himself as "Son of Man." As we've seen, this is what it sounds like: a simple affirmation that Jesus is a human being. But the image of Jesus as mere prophet is inevitably rejected, and He lays claim to something more. When Jesus asks his disciples who they think he is, they indicate that many see him as prophet, but the stakes go higher:

He asked his disciples, saying, "Who do men say that I, the Son of Man, am?"

They said, "Some say John the Baptizer, some, Elijah, and others, Jeremiah, or one of the prophets."

He said to them, "But who do you say that I am?"

Simon Peter answered, "You are the Christ, the Son of the living God."

Jesus answered him, "Blessed are you, Simon Bar Jonah, for flesh and blood has not revealed this to you, but my Father who is in heaven."[374]

Jesus's status as Son of God in the Synoptic Gospels apparently underwent a gradual metamorphosis such that by the time John was written, Jesus is understood to be the incarnation of God. In John, Jesus is the Word made flesh, and John states that he existed in the company of God before the Word was made.[375] Only once does anyone declare Jesus as identical to God in all the Gospels, and it occurs in John and, ironically, it is Thomas after Jesus scolds him for not believing that he was resurrected. Thomas declares Jesus, "my Lord and my God."[376] And it is only in the Gospel of John that Jesus himself hints of his nature as identical to God, stating that anyone who sees him sees the Father, and that he is in the Father and that the Father is in him.[377] But again this confers status as opposed to ability or perspective. As we saw in Chapter Three, when an admirer seeking the keys to eternal life in the Gospel of Mark refers to Jesus as "Good Teacher" Jesus disputes the greeting and says, "why do you call me good? No one is good but God alone."[378] This statement is remarkable on a number of fronts, not least of which is that it is a clear indication that Jesus does not claim to have the same mind or perspective as God. [379] Jesus often speaks to God as though to a third party, such as at the tomb of Lazarus as he prays for his resurrection, and finally when Jesus plaintively calls out to God as he dies on the cross, "why have you forsaken me?"

Son of God

There was evidently a powerful intuition among the Gospel writers that Jesus occupied a unique status with God and that his status, rather than anything he did or taught, changed every-thing for humanity. They had absolutely no interest in *proving* Jesus's pedigree and focused exclusively on finding ways to describe this transcendent reality in a way that conveyed its importance in the language and with the concepts available to them. Certainly, concepts challenging moral autonomy were totally unprecedented.

After Jesus is raised from the dead he appears over the course several days to his followers. Then, according to Mark, Luke and Acts, Jesus is bodily taken up into heaven. In Acts alone are we given detail of this event, and we are told Jesus lifts into the sky and is taken away on a cloud. Elijah, too, was taken into heaven but in his case, he ascended in whirlwind riding a flaming chariot drawn by horses of fire.[380] Matthew and John don't bother to include this event at all in their retellings of the Gospel stories. To them, Jesus's ascension into heaven is dispensable! Clearly, it is not a particular event that is important to these authors but the status of Jesus defined and demonstrated throughout their Gospels.

Similarly, at the other end of Jesus's life, while Matthew and Luke include detailed stories about the circumstances of Jesus's birth, Mark and John omit them entirely. Even between Matthew and Luke, the details are treated as unimportant. Matthew begins his gospel with a genealogy starting with Abraham and Isaac and ending with Jesus and declaring that there were fourteen generations from Abraham to David, fourteen from David to the Diaspora, and fourteen from the Diaspora to Jesus.[381] He must have known full well he had just listed only thirteen generations in two of those periods. In Matthew, the nativity scene is visited by wise men, while in Luke, shepherds make the journey to visit the newborn Messiah.[382]

That a savior would be born to a virgin was foretold in Isaiah, as we are reminded in the opening pages of the Gospel of Matthew, when an unnamed angel, appearing after Mary is found to be pregnant, reminds Joseph of the prophecy: "Behold, the virgin will conceive, and bear a son, and shall call his name Immanuel."[383] The Gospel of Luke includes a variation of this as well, but this time, it is the angel Gabriel who announces an impending pregnancy to Mary and states her son's name will be Jesus. In both cases, it is made clear that Mary is a virgin. However, there is fairly strong evidence this is not a case of Isaiah accurately foretelling the future, but rather a case of Matthew and Luke writing the story of Jesus's birth to fit the prophecy.[384] In the Hebrew, Isaiah prophesied that a *young woman* would give birth to a salvific individual using the Hebrew word "alma." The Septuagint, the Greek translation of the Old Testament that the writers of the Gospel were using, apparently misinterpreted this word as "virgin." This naturally led the authors of Matthew and Luke to believe that Isaiah had prophesied a virginal birth, which was evidently not an accurate expression of the prophecy. Although circumstantial, we certainly have to acknowledge the possibility that Matthew and Luke fashioned the nativity story to fit the prophecy as they knew it. There was no attempt by Matthew and Luke to deceive us, but only to convey the reality that had taken root in their souls and demanded to be shared: that Jesus is the Son of God and that his role was planned by God from the beginning. In any event, a virgin birth has always been a weak argument for the existence of God, but the existence of God is a perfectly good argument for a virgin birth. We don't allow ourselves to believe in God because the virgin birth seems reasonable. We may well allow ourselves to believe in the virgin birth because the existence of God seems reasonable. More importantly, we allow ourselves to believe in Jesus's status as Son of God.

There is no need to untangle this theological bird's nest. If I had an adopted son and a friend of mine asked me if he is my 'real' son, I would of course answer that he is. If my friend pressed me, and demanded to know if my son was my genetic relation, I would answer that my son is my son in every important way.

If my friend was still not satisfied and demanded a straight answer, insisting that I not operate under any false pretenses or delusions, I would extract myself from the discussion. In his zeal for scientific exactitude, my friend is not demanding a more complete answer – he is demanding a narrow-minded parochial one that ignores the very foundation of relationship to characterize it only in such a way that can be scientifically verified. Virtually no one would think he is asking a question of any consequence, even if his question is valid to a point. Virtually no one would suggest my son is anything but my real son, and no more need be said. The precise nature of the relationship is not important; it is in the fact of the relationship that all importance lies. Correspondingly, if another friend insisted that I never discuss the adoptive nature of the relationship with my son, fearing that it will be painful and weaken our familial ties, I would have to decline the advice as wrongheaded albeit well intentioned with confidence that unflinching honesty and forthrightness between us can only enhance the relationship. In Catholicism, we believe that the Eucharist is the true presence of God. Quite obviously, what we mean is that it is God in every important way. If it were actually flesh in every way and we wanted each other to believe that, we would use roast beef instead of bread in the sacrament. We are not interested in illusions or magic; we are interested in transcendent truth. Matthew never bothered to apply the name Immanuel to Jesus ever again in his narratives, which would have been natural if he wanted to deceive us. In fact, Matthew notes that Joseph names his son 'Jesus' exactly one line after reciting Isaiah's prophecy that he would be named 'Immanuel.'

This was not scandalous to them and it should not be scandalous to us either.

Jesus is not intended to serve as a proof of God's existence. The incarnation of God as Jesus Christ, whatever may have happened historically, is not intended to be a statement about genetics or the cataloguing of a magical event, and it is a distraction to define faith in those terms rather than focusing on Jesus's status as Son of God. It would not be difficult for God to have made the circumstances of Jesus's birth occur just the way our traditions say it did, nothing of importance is lost if Jesus is God's adoptive son rather being the product of the union of one human gamete and one divine. I will take the position that the fact that Jesus is the incarnation of God is true in the most important ways, and potentially allegorical only in unimportant ways. Although not particularly important to the Synoptic Gospel writers, the idea of Jesus as both human and divine, despite all the paradoxical baggage associated with such an assertion, has managed to survive, replicate and spread like a virus. The sacred tradition and sacred intuition that has arisen around Jesus since the writing of the Gospels is, in fact, critical to understanding Jesus as our Savior and Redeemer and to our understanding our relationship to God.

Way No. 1 – Moral Example

In his 1963 book, *Honest to God*, John A.T. Robinson, the Anglican Bishop of Woolwich, England, asserted that along with getting rid of the anthropomorphic idea of God tinkering away in a workshop "up there" we should go further and dispense with the idea of a God existing "out there."[385] Instead Robinson conceived of God, citing Paul Tillich, as the "ground of being."[386] "Belief in God is the trust, the well-nigh incredible trust, that to give ourselves to the uttermost in love is not to be confounded but to be accepted, that Love is the ground of our being, to which we ultimately 'come home.'[387] For Robinson therefore, Jesus, now quoting Dietrich Bonhoeffer, is the quintessential "man for others." "Because Christ was utterly and completely 'the man for others', because he was love, he was 'one with the Father' because 'God is love.'[388]

Robinson represents the pendulum swing away from the angry God who demands a blood sacrifice to the opposite extreme - an impersonal Unmoved Mover who represents the Platonic Form of Love. Jesus is literally a personification or incarnation of this principle. To say that Jesus is God incarnate is to say he is simply a really good example of what it would look like if we could emulate the Form of Love.

I obviously don't share Robinson's conception of God as an impersonal force or principle. But here I am primarily using him to stand for those who see the incarnate Jesus as the cosmic nice guy showing us the way to a nicer way of living. Robinson's view is very academic, of course, but a version of his view is very prevalent in modern popular Christianity. Many Christians are all too happy to present Jesus as one among many good moral examples, a moral coach extraordinaire, or a moral super-hero to be emulated. This is attractive to people of faith in a secular culture because it allows us to say, "Look, to be a good Christian just means to be a good person! We don't have to be committed to a supernatural view of things! We're really no different from anyone else!" But Scripture indicates that Jesus is not particularly interested in being cast this way.

Canaanite Woman Revisited

In Chapter Three, we explored the story of Jesus's interaction with the Canaanite woman. There, we saw Jesus being plainly mean-spirited to a woman who'd approached him in desperation seeking a miracle for her sick child. Jesus at first withholds any help, and even withholds his attention, because she is a hated minority. Jesus's nastiness is ancillary to the story and the story was actually intended to show that non-Jews recognized the divinity of Jesus, along with the story of the wise men from the East in the Nativity,[389] the centurion with the sick servant,[390] and the centurion at the foot of the Cross.[391] Jesus's blatantly immoral behavior should not scandalize us because he is not intended to serve as a moral example at all.

This is built into our sacred traditions. The Nicene and Apostles' Creeds entirely omit anything about Jesus being a moral example or teaching us to be well behaved or exhorting us to follow the Ten Commandments. They both begin with the nature of Jesus's birth and end with the nature of Jesus's death, leaving out everything in the middle. Their sole concern is the role of Jesus as Savior and Redeemer, which evidently does not mean provider of a moral map so that we can self-save or self-redeem, but rather means something that transcends morality.

The story of the Canaanite woman is only problematic for those who have abandoned the idea of Jesus as Savior and Redeemer in favor of Jesus as cosmic nice guy or the incarnation of the Form of Love. It indicates a willingness by Jesus, perhaps even a conscious, deliberate decision, to distance himself and God from the role of moral example, moral coach and certainly moral commander.

This is even starker, more unmistakable, in the story of Judas Iscariot.

Judas Iscariot

The Palm Sunday readings are meant to shock us with the sudden change in the way the crowd reacts to Jesus. In the Catholic tradition, before Mass begins, each member of the congregation, holding a palm branch, participates in a procession remembering Jesus's triumphal entry into Jerusalem riding a colt. All four Gospels tell us that as Jesus passes through Bethpage and Bethany on the outskirts of Jerusalem, the inhabitants come out to meet him, throwing palm branches ahead of the feet of the colt he is riding into the city and singing blessings to him.[392] But when Mass begins, the tone changes dramatically and the Gospel readings describe Jesus's last supper, arrest, trial and crucifixion. The adoring, exuberant crowd that greeted Jesus's arrival has been replaced (or have they simply changed their minds?) and now they demand his torturous death. The Catholic lectionary is divided into a three-year cycle – Years A, B, and C – such that every third year the cycle of readings starts over. In Year B, Mark is used and his retelling of the Passion begins with Jesus sharing a meal with his disciples in Bethany when the events leading to Jesus's death begin:

> While he was at Bethany, in the house of Simon the leper, as he sat at the table, a woman came having an alabaster jar of ointment of pure nard—very costly. She broke the jar, and poured it over his head. But there were some who were indignant among themselves, saying, "Why has this ointment been wasted? For this might have been sold for more than three hundred denarii, and given to the poor." So they grumbled against her. [393]

"Good point!" we might think to ourselves. "Think globally and act locally." Jesus as cosmic nice guy would certainly decline an honor that entailed such extravagant waste and insist that it be used to relieve poverty. Surely Jesus, moral super-hero, would use this opportunity to further his divine program of moral teaching. But he does not.

> But Jesus said, "Leave her alone. Why do you trouble her? She has done a good work for me. For you always have the poor with you, and whenever you want to, you can do them good; but you will not always have me. She has done what she could. She has anointed

> my body beforehand for the burying. Most certainly I tell you, wherever this Good News may be preached throughout the whole world, that which this woman has done will also be spoken of for a memorial of her."

What has happened to the humble Jesus who advocates for the poor? We can't help but be sympathetic to the disciples' indignation. Jesus's answer does not satisfy us, and by modern standards, seems almost sardonic - saying that the poor will always be with us, but he won't always be around to receive extravagant honors. Judas Iscariot obviously thinks that Jesus has just revealed himself to be a fraud. The balance of the passage implies that Judas betrays Jesus because Jesus's morality has disappointed and even scandalized him:[394]

> Judas Iscariot, who was one of the twelve, went away to the chief priests, that he might deliver him to them. They, when they heard it, were glad, and promised to give him money. He sought how he might conveniently deliver him.

In this there is caution for us. When we relegate Jesus to the cosmic solicitor of charitable contributions, who rewards altruism and punishes meanness, we not only make faith insipid, we also imitate Judas Iscariot. *Jesus's failure to act in a moral way with the Canaanite woman can be dismissed as not being the important part of the story. But here Jesus's apparent moral failing is precisely the point and we are cautioned not to play the role of the most notorious traitor in history and assume that Jesus is a moral messenger or moral cheerleader.* If we are not morally autonomous and God is just, then God cannot command, reward and punish behavior. It might be reasonable to assume that God would nonetheless make His own contribution to our nature and nurture to encourage better behavior, but even that is not borne out in Scripture and is suspiciously absent from our Creeds. Furthermore, any such mission would have to be considered a partial success at best. Secularists complain that Jesus and indeed all of Scripture serves as a lousy moral guide because he and it can be used to support either side of every moral question. That is because neither Jesus nor Scripture was intended to be a moral guide. If we are to have a meaningful faith and meaningful understanding of Christianity, we have to keep looking deeper to find the transcendent Jesus. Judas wanted Jesus to serve a purpose – a moral purpose - Jesus insisted his message transcended purpose and morality. The point is even more stark when we remember that Satan – a character even more reviled than Judas - in his encounter with Jesus in the desert insisted that if Jesus was the Son of God he would be able to produce bread miraculously and get God's protection from a nasty fall off the pinnacle of the Temple. Jesus refuses to ask God for those things because Jesus understood that God transcends purpose too.

Looking back at the Gospels in light of this theme, we finally must come to the shocking realization that *there is not a single instance in the Gospels in which Jesus advises someone to give away their possessions to the poor in order to improve the condition of the poor.* Rather, Jesus inevitably requires the casting off of wealth and worldly possessions to prepare for discipleship. [395] When Jesus sends his apostles out to spread the message of his ministry, he sends them two by two and directs them to take minimal baggage:

> He called to himself the twelve, and began to send them out two by two; and he gave them authority over the unclean spirits. He commanded them that they should take nothing for their journey, except a staff only: no bread, no wallet, no money in their purse, but to wear sandals, and not put on two tunics. [396]

Once again our instinct to read moralistically suggests Jesus is freeing up some wealth to help the poor. But it is clearly a program to provide his disciples with a spiritual exercise that drives home their dependency and shatters any remaining illusion of autonomy. Jesus is inviting his apostles to live dependently and simply for a while to encourage moral humility – the moral humility Adam and Eve abandoned in the Garden. It was never intended to be produce an economic windfall or to be a permanent embrace of asceticism, but was instead a temporary measure to teach. In fact, Jesus expressly cancels this program at the Last Supper.[397] That the Gospels lack a command to serve the poor is utterly scandalous if we believe that we have free will and God has placed us here to be tested, rewarded and punished according to our autonomous moral choices. But it is perfectly in keeping with an understanding of God free from the Platonic reliance on free will to explain our relationship to God.

Further, the idea that Jesus is a divine moral example does nothing to resolve the tension that arises in the Garden. When Adam and Eve asserted their moral autonomy they set themselves on a bitter course of blame and judgment that almost immediately reached a crescendo in the murder of one of their two sons by the other. The flaming sword east of Eden expresses the fact that you cannot walk back into the Garden by the way you left it. Humanity is not capable of the moral perfection it demands of itself because it is not capable of the moral autonomy it asserted for itself. Jesus as a moral example simply exacerbates the problem that led to Adam and Eve's banishment. It cannot be true.

Way No. 2 - A Describer of God's Morality, but Not Principally

My wife and I exemplify the common wisdom that women mature intellectually earlier than men. When she and I were dating we went to a movie together. As we left she asked me what I thought of it. I remember replying that I didn't like it much because I could not tell what the moral of the story was. She looked at me with a look of kindly patience that has become so familiar to me over the years. She responded that not every story needs to have a moral and that sometimes they are simply character studies. That is Scripture. It is not a story about what we should and shouldn't do, it is a character study of God. In so many places that we think it is describing what our moral code should be, it is actually describing God's moral code.

Jesus sought to describe the nature of God's morality and God's sense of justice. He did not describe divine moral commands or the promise of reward and punishment, but rather he described how God responds to us given our lack of moral autonomy. His answer was mercy. God's justice assumes what we are only now coming to realize; that we are not morally autonomous beings and that justice requires that we escape punishment for our bad behavior altogether, and that those of us inclined by our nature and nurture to be good are not entitled to reward. Jesus's description invited the striking realization that God's justice is totally unlike ours. God's morality is more than merely counter-cultural. God's morality offends our own natural desire to punish the moral freeloader. That desire is the product of our evolution as organisms that developed as a social species in an environment characterized by scarcity. That God, therefore, can disregard freeloading and reward each vineyard worker regardless of their merit is so unnatural to our inborn value system as to be virtually supernatural. The implications of this simple message were profound. The wealthy, the healthy, and the socially connected all had assumed they were that way because they had followed God's commands to be charitable and good citizens and God had blessed them for it and would reward them even more in heaven. Jesus overturned the proverbial tables of the Temple. He said that God does not mete out reward and punishment but suffers with the poor, the sick, the imprisoned and the outcasts and declares them all acceptable in His eyes – all of them are healed of any shortcoming. That Jesus's vision of God's morality would be forcefully and even violently rejected was virtually inevitable. The whole message is summarized at the Cross. The chief priests, elders and scribes - the self-aggrandizing intellectual elite - mock Jesus as he hangs there, insisting that if Jesus's God exists, He would rescue him from the Cross.[398] But they are mocking their own false conception of God – a god who rewards good behavior with protection and rescue and a god who turns stones into bread and demands moral conduct – a conception of God entangled with a Platonic notion of free will rather than grace. Jesus can't answer for that god, because that is not his God. According to Luke, from the Cross Jesus contradicts this conception entirely. Rather than holding his persecutors to account for the free choices that led to his murder, Jesus acknowledges that they are not free creatures that can be commanded, rewarded and punished. Rather, they, and we, are unfree, and a just God knows this. Jesus does not demand contrition. Jesus entreats God, "Father, forgive them for they know not what they do."[399] Jesus's God is the God of the Beatitudes – a God who is not responsible for the misfortunes of the poor or the fortunes of the rich, but can only suffer with His creatures.

This is a powerful message, but is its delivery the principal purpose of the Incarnation? To be so, Jesus's description of God must be unique and original. Jesus needs to be more than just one describer of the nature of God among many. He needs to be a describer *par excellence*. If delivery of a description of God's nature is the role of the Incarnation, at a minimum, the content of Jesus's description of God's nature must be not just uniquely authoritative, but innovative.

But in fact many of the traditions and even sacraments that we reflexively associate with Jesus and assume are innovations of Jesus are actually intended to show that Jesus was a practicing and devout Jew and are not innovative at all. Some of the moral statements of Jesus that we allow ourselves to imagine are critiques of a hidebound Jewish theocracy, actually represent the existing, albeit controversial, Jewish theology of Jesus's time.

When Jesus presented himself for baptism to his cousin, John the Baptist, the idea of being fully immersed in water to ritually purify was not new. Known today among orthodox Jews as *mikveh*, it was required whenever a man ejaculated,[400] after a woman menstruated,[401] after an individual recovered from leprosy[402] and when an individual had touched a corpse.[403] It remains customary in Jewish households that at the Sabbath meal that a blessing is said over wine (*Kiddush*) and over bread (*lechem mishneh* - two loaves to signifying the manna collected by the Israelites in the desert together with the extra loaf that fell to tide them over through the Sabbath) after which it is broken and shared. Jesus's innovation was not the practicing of those traditions, but rather to identify himself with that bread and wine and hint at the incarnation – the identification of himself with God.

What may be more surprising to most Christians is that those values that most embody Jesus, and which we most closely associate with Christianity, are in fact reiterations of values clearly expressed within the Old Testament. In establishing The Golden Rule Jesus is simply reiterating Leviticus 19:18: "You shall not take vengeance, nor bear any grudge against the children of your people; but you shall love your neighbor as yourself. I am God." Jesus is not plagiarizing; he states explicitly that he is not innovating, but is simply restating Torah and what the prophets already said:

> Therefore whatever you desire for men to do to you, you shall also do to them; for this is the law and the prophets.[404]

Even Jesus's statement that, "The Sabbath was made for man, not man for the Sabbath"[405] also was a rabbinic teaching, memorialized in the Mekhilta, circulating about the time the Synoptic Gospels were being written; "The Sabbath is given unto you, not you onto the Sabbath." [406]

What Jesus reveals about God's relationship to us is a continuation of what the Old Testament reveals. Jesus exhorts us not to engage in moral judgment of one another - to forgive under all circumstances - just as the story of Adam and Eve reveals that human unhappiness stems not from sin, but from the illusion and conceit of moral autonomy and the blame, hatred and murderous anger that inevitably springs from it. With his dying breaths Jesus declares forgiveness and continuation of God's covenant even as God's creatures kill His son, not because they are sorry, but for they know not what they do. This hearkens back to the Israelites at the base of Mount Sinai breaking the Covenant before the ink is dry, and God reaffirming the Covenant nonetheless. Jesus tells us that sickness and poverty are not the curse of God, just as Exodus tells us that God's loving concern is at its most urgent and intense for the widow and the orphan.[407] Jesus expects his message of complete, unconditional mercy to be rejected, just as Jonah rejected God's mercy for the Ninevites.

The role of describer of God's nature is not the role of God Incarnate but is rather the role of a prophet. When we want to know the nature of God we look to Scripture and what we find there was written by the prophets. Returning once more to Jesus's question, who the crowd thinks he is; he seems to invite and tease them with the idea that he is nothing special – at best a prophet by using the prophet's moniker, Son of Man:

> [H]e asked his disciples, saying, "Who do men say that I, the Son of Man, am? [408]

While the apostles tell him that some believe he is a reincarnation of one of the ancient prophets of the Old Testament, Peter is uncharacteristically wise and alone is willing to go further.

When Jesus asks Peter, Peter answers Jesus that "you are the Christ, the Son of the living God."[409] For this, Jesus awards Peter with leadership of the Church. Whatever Peter may mean, clearly, being one prophet among many - even being the best prophet among many - is not Jesus's primary role.

After this exchange, Jesus insists that his role be kept a secret: "Then he strictly charged the disciples to tell no one he was the Christ."[410] Jesus makes the same demand in Mark.[411] In fact, in the Gospel of Mark, Jesus insists repeatedly that his status be kept a secret – a tendency that has become known as the "Messianic Secret." In the opening pages of the gospel, an unclean spirit reveals Jesus's status, to his apparent dismay:

> Immediately there was in their synagogue a man with an unclean spirit, and he cried out, saying, "Ha! What do we have to do with you, Jesus, you Nazarene? Have you come to destroy us? I know you who you are: the Holy One of God!" Jesus rebuked him, saying, "Be quiet, and come out of him!" The unclean spirit, convulsing him and crying with a loud voice, came out of him. They were all amazed, so that they questioned among themselves, saying, "What is this? A new teaching? [412]

This is only the first example of several instances where Jesus swears others to secrecy regarding his status.[413] But certainly one of the first priorities of one who is presenting a new teaching (as the members of the synagogue assumed) would be to establish his credentials. But Jesus evidently knows his role is not to teach, but to fulfill something existentially - through his status as the Son of God.

When Adam and Eve ate from the Tree of the Knowledge of Good and Evil they were asserting moral autonomy and implicitly embracing a view of God as moral commander and judge - in contradiction of His advice. Jesus also invited humanity to avoid the idea of God as moral commander and judge, but got an even frostier reception. To understand Jesus as successful Savior and Redeemer and Incarnation of God, we have to keep looking.

Way No. 3 - The God of Compassion

Earlier, I claimed that faith does not necessarily change the circumstances that lead to our suffering, but faith offers the comfort of knowing that God suffers with us. Jesus is the personification and incarnation of that co-suffering. Far from being an Unmoved Mover, this God humbles Himself to share in our every discomfort, disease, and dishonor - even to the point of joining us in our mortality. I attended a retreat several years ago where one of the retreat exercises was to have each participant draw a depiction of suffering. Remarkably, every one of the dozen or so participants drew a representation of an individual isolated from community. This is the heart of suffering – the feeling of isolation and of going through the pain alone and not being understood. For centuries religion compounded rather than alleviated this by assuming that suffering was a curse from God, that therefore God was not with, but rather against the sufferer, and therefore the sufferer was even more, and perhaps more profoundly alone.

How Jesus died is really of no consequence. If he had died of cancer, God nonetheless would have accomplished the goal of demonstrating that He suffers in solidarity with His creatures. Faith's dividend is that we never should feel alone, and the stronger our faith, the more this realization will be of comfort. Elizabeth Kübler Ross, the palliative care pioneer, famously said that a loving caregiver will sometimes just sit with the dying, not necessarily busying themselves with the administration of care, but to be present; in effect, "don't just do something, stand there." Evidently, God cannot take away the cause of our suffering without taking away our capacity for happiness, but He is there with us – regardless of whether we are good or bad, believe or don't believe. Belief simply makes us aware of His presence. Dis-ease, if you can come to be at ease with it, loses its power. There are many desperately afflicted individuals who nonetheless are able to experience ease, and correspondingly, there are many of us who are not afflicted with anything but are nonetheless not at ease. This is the healing that spirituality offers. It is the confidence that we are all in this together and God is there with us too. If God is with us, what can stand against us? Can God intervene to cure our illnesses? Perhaps. But it is unlikely that God would intervene to reward (or fail to intervene as punishment) as a result of anything we unfree creatures might say, do, pray or believe. It is comforting to think we can exert that level of control over God – to act like a pagan shaman, uttering the words that compel God's hand – but if we are unfree creatures and God is just, then He cannot intervene like that. Rather, we can lift up our sick friends, our anxieties, all of our suffering and know that we share them with God and lighten each other's load.

Healthy Christianity includes an inspiration to visit the prisoner. If this is in imitation of God, then we would simply sit there with them, commiserate with them, maybe affirm that judging their past conduct is not God's concern. But it is almost inevitable, with our desire to be purposeful, to reward good behavior and punish bad or freeloading – we wind up seeking the prisoner's repentance in order to restore a relationship to God that was never in jeopardy in the first place, and to do our service hours with them to receive the reward that was always going to be ours anyway. If we believe that God suffers with us, then we won't visit the prisoner to seek reward or avoid punishment, either for them or ourselves. And the thought that if we don't comfort the isolated, God will isolate us is nonsense. Rather, as we'll see in Chapter 6, we will have a natural impulse to share the good news that no matter when we arrived to work in the vineyard – and even if we never managed to work there at all – because we're not free and can't earn redemption, God's redemption is ours. God's mercy is radical mercy.

Compassion is not the Principal Issue

Even if compassion was not exemplified in every word and deed of Jesus, the Christian story - from Christmas through

Easter - is defined by it. Although God's compassion for us is not mentioned in our Creeds, it is implied in every line. The compassion of God expressed through and by Jesus is the extraordinarily beautiful center of many Christians' faith. And it belongs there. So much has been written on this subject that it would be difficult for me to add to it. Mystics seem less anxious than the rest of us in part because they have fully internalized that there is no purpose to fulfill, no test to pass, no task to accomplish. But they also seem less anxious not because they have resigned themselves to their insignificance in a cold, meaningless universe, but because when they gaze into the winter star-studded night sky, they sense the warm, loving compassionate return gaze of God. In that gaze, questions about God's existence seem like foolishness. Although suffering will enter our lives and it may indeed overwhelm us, cause us to despair, and may be more than we can handle, in that gaze nothing can disturb the existential comfort of being a beloved child of God and the object of His loving compassion.

But the message that God suffers with us through Jesus, although extraordinarily comforting, valuable and true, is also not primary. Compassion, although profound and important, doesn't resolve the problem that arose in the Garden in the first pages of the Bible. The wood of the Tree of the Knowledge of Good and Evil is not yet connected to the wood of the Cross. It does not explain Jesus's status as Savior and Redeemer.

Way No. 4 - Dignity

Why does the idea that we don't have free will make us so anxious? Without free will we feel enslaved. We are enslaved to a mechanistic, deterministic universe where everything that happens is either the inevitable reaction to what has happened before according to the laws of classic physics, or is the arbitrary, random effect of quantum physics. It renders us nothing more than complex organic machines responding to stimuli, with no more inherent value or dignity than a toaster or computer. We assume that to have value and dignity means to be able to make the right decision, to choose freely between good and bad and to choose well. To have value and dignity, we assume, we must perform some task that it was possible we wouldn't perform - that we were free to perform or not perform the task - and to choose the good, the socially responsible, and maybe even the selfless. We want to be treated as responsible and competent - capable of self-direction and self-discipline. Our culture in particular values the "self-made man" and the "self-made woman" who pull themselves up by the bootstraps and take adult responsibility and accept blame when it arises. As children we eagerly anticipated the day when we would be considered adults – free, responsible agents and captains of our own destiny. We have a natural and evolved desire to see that the moral freeloader is punished. But our desire for free will goes even deeper. We dread the loss of free will because we feel it deprives us of any reason anyone might have to love us any more than they love someone else, or even something else. Slavery, no matter how benign, always diminishes dignity, and our slavery to the forces of causation feels like the utter destruction of our dignity. To the Christian, determinism deprives us of any reason God might love any human being. It is far more palatable to think that God deprives *some* human beings of love – those who fail to believe, fail to behave, or fail to be contrite – but it's an altogether different order of dread to think that God has no reason to love any of us.

The Incarnation does not cause us to magically have the capacity for free will. The Incarnation is the culmination of a process of adoption that renders whether we have free will or not irrelevant. When the Son of God becomes incarnate as a human being, God adopts humanity as His people. Our acceptance into God's divine family, however we may imagine it, grants us divine dignity and ends our slavery. We are declared loved and accepted. We did not earn this inheritance, but received it in spite of ourselves. God has chosen to overlook something far more serious than our failure to make good moral decisions from time to time. God has chosen to overlook our inability to make moral decisions in the first place. Original Sin is not Adam and Eve's decision to disobey God and eat fruit from a forbidden tree, nor is it the decision to assert their moral autonomy when they had none, but it is rather their utter inability to make moral decisions at all. Original Sin is the causal slavery we dread – the fact that without the intervention of God we are no better, no more significant, no worthier of love than automatons. It is Original Sin because we all share it – no one of us is any more or less free than another – we are all equally enslaved by Original Sin and there is nothing we can do about it ourselves. No one is born without this short-coming or without the impulse to deny it and declare ourselves morally autonomous. Lawrence Kohlberg, one of the most influential psychologists of the twentieth century, theorized that every human person goes through stages of moral development just as certainly as we each go through stages of physical development. The morality of the youngest children in the first two stages are, as we might expect, egocentric and are principally concerned with avoiding punishment and getting self-centered needs met. In adolescence and stage three, the focus becomes what others might be thinking, and the principal concern is being well regarded and to be seen by others as good and acceptable ("Enough about me. What do you think about me?"). The reason the years between elementary school and high school are characterized by so much cliquishness and nasty gossip is that we enter the stage of moral development where we eat from the Tree and after which we want to measure ourselves against others, find our place in the moral and social spectrum, and work out what our biography will be. And although most of us graduate to stage four and beyond, the desire to be well regarded is too inborn and too ingrained in our evolution to shake off entirely. This is what happened in the Garden. Although attaining moral knowledge ought to have been a positive event – as the snake promised it would be - the members of the first family are suddenly gossiping, blaming one another, and even murdering each other. But more than having bad social consequences, moral judgment makes us look at ourselves differently. Suddenly our self-worth and dignity is inextricably intertwined with our moral worth and our social worth. Suddenly we are not valued for our mere existence – we have no intrinsic, ineradicable worth - we are only as valuable as our place on the moral spectrum and our value to society. God begins sewing garments for Adam and Eve but we know and He knows it is not enough. For centuries, religion has largely been an attempt to achieve moral perfection in order to re-enter paradise - to encourage us to increase our moral and social worth - but we run full speed into the flaming sword. Embracing the illusion of moral autonomy and striving for moral perfection is not the road back into the Garden. In fact, that road compounds the problem – it is the problem - and leads in the opposite direction.

Nor is simply embracing our lack of free will the road back. It may seem to the New Atheists that behavioral science is leading us to a utopian society without hate, but raw science cannot account for human dignity. Science can tell us what we are worth as a handful of organic chemicals, and it can measure statistically what we produce and what we consume, and it can place us in innumerable scales of measurement. But it cannot explain our intrinsic value. As we will see, atheistic determinism plunges us into existentialist absurdity and anxiety. Sartre exultantly declared that God does not exist and invested human dignity in our capacity for free will. Behavioral science has bankrupted that investment. Is it philosophically possible that this is the true nature of our situation and as unfree creatures dignity is out of reach for us and life is meaningless and absurd? Yes. If God does not exist, then, it seems to me, that is precisely our situation. Theistic determinism offers a radically different conclusion. God's incarnation is an existential resolution to this problem. By becoming human, God is saying we are more than our biography. We are more than what we can do for God or for one another. We are valuable to God by virtue of our existence alone and His unreasoning decision to value us. We have nothing to offer in return – no amount of good behavior will pay the ransom for God's love,[414] and no amount of bad behavior can diminish it. But, then again, love is not love if it is bargained for. Grace is not grace if it is earned. The Incarnation is the ultimate message of redemption:

> For God so loved the world, that He gave His one and only Son, that whoever believes in him should not perish, but have eternal life. For God didn't send His Son into the world to judge the world, but that the world should be saved through him.[415]

Bridges

This is the culmination and crossroads of many themes of Scripture. The Incarnation is the total destruction of the shame inherent in our unfree nature. God has become one of us and, by so doing, has torn the dividing line between the human and the divine and imbued us with dignity. This bridging of the gap between the divine and the human is a theme repeated throughout Scripture. Jacob, later to be renamed Israel, has a vision of a ladder between heaven and earth where angels freely pass between the two realms and God stands at the top and declares "Behold, I am with you and will keep you wherever you go."[416] After the moral debacle of Mount Sinai, when God should have been at His most distant, instead He demands that the people construct a moveable sanctuary - the Tabernacle Tent - for Him to reside in.[417] God, thereafter, dwells among His people. Isaiah prophesies that a messiah will be born and his name, Immanuel, will mean "God is with us."[418] The Incarnation of God is born, lives and dies as we do. And when Jesus finally breathes his last breath on the Cross, the veil that separates the Holy of Holies in the Temple from the rest of the world, fashioned according to God's instructions in Exodus,[419] is torn in two.[420]

Jesus as the Incarnation of God is also the culmination of the events of Exodus and its theme of Chosen-ness. God notoriously chooses the runt of the litter and the morally imperfect – Noah, Moses, Abraham, and David all manage to be moral disappointments. The Apostles can do virtually nothing right and are treated as almost comedic foils for Jesus. It should come as no surprise that God is seemingly unconcerned with moral perfection, since moral autonomy is beyond us anyway. What is a surprise is God's decision to choose – not to choose one from many – but to choose at all. When Adam and Eve assert their moral autonomy and are ashamed, God did not say "Stop your foolishness! No one cares if you're naked!" Like a parent whose child is afraid of the dark, God doesn't expect us to just get over our shame, He plugs in the nightlight. God's creatures feel the shame inherent in being unfree. God doesn't resolve this for them immediately, but sets about to sew clothing for them to tide them over while He plots His next move. God always plays the long game. The narrative continues and eventually, God finds the descendants of Adam and Eve in slavery in Egypt. The slavery that caused them to assert their moral autonomy in the Garden is now manifested as slavery to Pharaoh. This time, God acts to definitively free them. They are clear of Egypt only three lunar months[421] when they encamp at the base of Mount Sinai and God declares them His people. It is this choice and the covenant between God and the Israelites, rather than the flight from Pharaoh that defines the Israelites from that moment forward. The narrative is clear that God's decision to advocate for this people doesn't make their lives better in the short term and they complain bitterly, as we'll see in a moment. It is God's decision to covenant with them – to choose them and engage with them that will define them for ever after.

When God chose the Israelites at the base of Mount Sinai, He did not choose one people to the derogation of others, He chose to engage with humanity. The tension in God's choice was not whether he would choose the Jews over the Egyptians, Canaanites, Assyrians or others, but whether He would choose at all. God chooses to love humanity instead of disregarding or ignoring it, which might have been the more reasonable choice. In the words of the psalmist:

When I see the heavens, the work of Your fingers,
the moon and the stars You fixed firm.

What is man that You should note him,
And the human creature, that You pay him heed,
And You make him little less than the gods,
With glory and grandeur, You crown him? [422]

The message that we are the Chosen of God is delivered to everyone who hears it. Clearly, one message of Scripture is that we don't deserve God's attention, but it is instantly mitigated by the second message that He chooses to love us anyway. Perhaps nothing that God says in Scripture should surprise us more than the fact that God chose to say anything to us at all. By the act of engaging with humanity and declaring us to be His beloved, He frees us from slavery and grants us a dignity that wasn't otherwise ours. The Incarnation is the culmination of that decision to choose and engage with us and thereby free us from the indignity of being unfree. God is no longer satisfied with sewing clothes to cover our shame. God is no longer satisfied with simply conveying the message of our chosen-ness in a narrative, no matter how powerful. In Jesus, God does something so radical as to be almost offensive to our concept of the sovereign God and becomes one of us.

The Last Supper as Jesus prepares to die, and Passover as God prepares to rescue His people occur simultaneously. For Jews and Christians, this is a moment to reflect on the question, "From what slavery does God free us?" For Christians, the Incarnation of God stooping to wash human feet on this of all nights is intended to arouse a feeling of existential shock.

God not only covers our shame, not only adopts us as His people, not only derogates Himself by becoming one of us, not only suffers with us, but stoops to wash our feet. Peter objects and demands to be useful and serve some purpose. But Jesus rebuffs him.[423] Reminiscent of the alabaster jar, and reminiscent of the passage in which Jesus scolded Martha for busying herself with housework while her sister Mary listened to Jesus, this passage reminds us we don't need to make ourselves useful or reciprocate.[424] In fact, we can't. This is not an opportunity for us to emulate Jesus's fine moral example, but rather to stand in awe of the irrational decision of God to have loving concern for us in the first place. We are an unfree species, driven by our nature and nurture, predictable and a little pathetic, driven by the illusions of moral autonomy in a kind of species-wide conceit that drives us to hate and feel shame. Nonetheless God steps in the breach between divine and human. He chooses us and then He becomes Incarnate among us. The incarnation of God as one of us changes the relationship between the divine and the human much more radically than a message of mere solidarity or proximity. We are invited to familial status. We are given divine dignity.

God's words to a mysterious audience in the Creation story, "let us make man in our image, after our likeliness" is not an invitation to anthropomorphism, but instead, an indication that we were intended from the very beginning to be not just God's creation, but to be a part of His family. Our lack of freedom is not an obstacle to God's loving concern because He would, in the fullness of time, become one of us, share in the shame of not having any capacity to distinguish ourselves morally. The Incarnation of God is not an awkward, antiquated tradition but a critical component in understanding our relationship to God. In the Gospel of John, at the Last Supper, Jesus promises to prepare a place for us in heaven so that we can follow him, but he is characteristically speaking ambiguously and the apostles, characteristically, are missing the point. Thomas asks Jesus, "Lord, we don't know where you are going. How can we know the way?"[425] Jesus replies:

> I am the way, the truth, and the life. No one comes to the Father, except through me. If you had known me, you would have known my Father also. From now on, you know him, and have seen him.[426]

This passage is often taken as a divine command to believe in, and acknowledge Jesus's role – to be Christian rather than anything else. But if our beliefs are a product of our nature and nurture rather than something we can freely decide, then such an interpretation doesn't make sense. Rather, this is all about knowing God and understanding the nature of our relationship to Him. Evidently, no one can come to the Father - no one can understand the nature of that relationship - without understanding Jesus as completing the adoption of humanity by God. Moral lessons are not central to understanding where we stand with God, but this decision to take us as His own holds the one and only key. This is not a path to be chosen to achieve salvation, but the path to understanding that our salvation has already been irreversibly achieved.

Since Adam and Eve, we have resisted the knowledge that we are not free, and imposed on each other murderous moral judgment. Throughout Scripture, God whispers that it need not be this way; that He has the desire and the power to eliminate that shame. As Jesus is being led away from the Garden of Gethsemane, a mysterious naked man literally streaks through the scene.[427] Is this Adam, right after he eats from the Tree, without the clothing God has made for him? This may be the echo of the Garden on Calvary. Adam rejected a fundamental bit of knowledge about human nature – that we are unfree. Since then we have suffered from self-hatred and hatred of each other as we place ourselves on moral scales to see who is better and who is unacceptable. The story of Jesus demands that we figure out what it means to be human and unflinchingly face our lack of free will. Only then does the majesty of God's gift to us become evident. *It reveals that our relationship to God and what it means to be human are inextricably intertwined.* In W. H. Auden's, *For the Time Being, Christmas Oratorio*, as they follow the star to Bethlehem, the Three Wise Men hint that what they are looking for includes a key to understanding who we are as a species:

> At least we know for certain we are three old sinners,

That this journey is much too long, that we
want our dinners,
And miss our wives, or books, our dogs,
But have only the vaguest ideas why we are
what we are.
To discover how to be human now
Is the reason we follow this star.[428]

Earlier, the star is described as an object of dread:

I am the star most dreaded by the wise,
For they are drawn against their will to me,
Yet read in my procession through the skies
The doom of orthodox sophrosyne.[429]

'Sophrosyne' refers to the ancient Greek preoccupation with moral excellence and perfection of character. And, indeed, the person of Jesus as the Incarnation of God is an object of dread for all who insist that our relationship to God must serve some purpose or achieve some moral hurdle, and who define themselves and others in terms of moral achievement.

Shame; Sin as a Human Shortcoming

In *The Idea of the Holy*, Rudolf Otto says that our impulse to think of ourselves as sinful does not come from some specific transgression, as attractive as that may be so that we can draw disparaging comparisons to one another. Rather, it comes from our inevitable sense that, in the face of the numinous majesty of God, we are mere creatures, incapable of encountering

God except with a sense of awesome, incurable inadequacy. We are, by our very nature, profane in the comparison to the Holy. "Mere morality" Otto says, "is not the soil from which … grows the need of redemption." We do not need to atone for our behavior so much as cover the shame of our status as creatures.[430] Otto would not concede that we lack moral freedom, but would acknowledge that morality is not the root of shame, although it may feel like it is.

This idea that 'sin' is not the personal indiscretions of each individual but is somehow a shortcoming common to the entire human species is not a modern invention but was a prominent theme in Paul's theology. In his revolutionary 1963 Harvard Theological Review article entitled, "The Apostle Paul and the Introspective Conscience of the West," Krister Stendahl asserted that we may be making a mistake when we assume Paul's concept of sin matches the modern idea of it as some specific behavior that we feel guilty about. Certainly, Paul engaged in some pretty heavy moral self-criticism, but he also demonstrated that he thought the avoidance of personal sin was possible – and even that he had achieved it. Paul boasts in Philippians, "I was blameless as to righteousness – of the Law that is."[431] But Stendahl contrasts this against Paul's insistence in Romans that no one can keep the Law.

What then? Are we better than they?
No, in no way. For we previously warned
both Jews and Greeks that they are all under

sin. As it is written,

"There is no one righteous;

no, not one.

There is no one who understands.

There is no one who seeks after God.

They have all turned away.

They have together become unprofitable.

There is no one who does good,

no, not so much as one."

"Their throat is an open tomb.

With their tongues they have used deceit."

"The poison of vipers is under their lips."

"Their mouth is full of cursing and

bitterness."

"Their feet are swift to shed blood.

Destruction and misery are in their ways.

The way of peace, they haven't known."

"There is no fear of God before their eyes."[432]

Stendahl suggested that these two concepts - the possibility of individual perfect obedience to the Law and yet nonetheless somehow falling short - should be interpreted as being consistent with one another. The solution is to see Paul's idea of sin as being something shared by Jews, Gentiles and the entirety of the human family rather than something we each do or don't do. This may be why the word "forgiveness" does not appear in any of the epistles attributed to Paul and he instead uses the terms "justification" and "remission."[433] Theologian Joseph Fitzmyer came to a similar conclusion: "The confrontation of the Ego with sin and the law is not considered by Paul on an individual, psychological level, but from a historical and corporate point of view."[434] Fitzmyer equates Paul's concept of sin as shared shortcoming with an Essene text found among the Dead Sea Scrolls:

> As for me, I belong to wicked humanity, to the assembly of perverse flesh; my iniquities, my transgressions, my sins together with the wickedness of my heart belong to the assembly doomed to worms and walking in darkness. No human being sets his own path or directs his own steps, for to God alone belongs the judgment of him ... in His righteousness He cleanses me of human defilement and of human sinfulness ... as for me, I know righteousness belongs not to a human being, nor perfection of way to a son of man.[435]

Our fundamental human shortcoming is not the accumulation of less-than-perfect behaviors, but our lack of dignity as slaves of causality; unable to make moral decisions for ourselves at all. So our profanity cannot be cured by the promise of good conduct or a blood sacrifice. But God becoming one of us, taking the form of a slave[436] as Paul puts it, becomes our atonement and covers our profanity, because we are forever after identified with the divine. This is a story of immense power and beauty. When God becomes human, the soul feels its worth and a weary world, beaten down by millennia of moral judgment, the vain seeking of reward and the imposition of arbitrary punishment, rejoices.

Shame is a virtually universal experience. Everyone, except the pathologically arrogant, feels shame, though we experience it as something personal to each of us. As a result of that experience, we generally try to relieve our shame on a personal and individual basis. We try to overcome our individual shortcomings, we try to be properly contrite of our bad behavior, and we try to overcome the weight of our bad behavior with good behavior on imaginary scales of justice. But our shame is not related to our bad behavior – it is related to our inability to freely choose good or bad behavior because of our inherently unfree nature. Since the Garden, we have whitewashed this shame by denying it - claiming we have moral autonomy. The result is moral judgment and human conflict. This represents a fundamental problem for the faithful and non-believer alike, but is particularly painful to the faithful because it is an insurmountable obstacle to understanding the nature of our relationship to God, which is the basis of faith and places faith in direct conflict with science. It places faith on a foundation of sand, susceptible to heaving and shifting with every new philosophical, moral and scientific innovation. Faith is not belief in free will. Faith is embracing our lack of autonomy and responding to the divine's acceptance of us not after having resolved our lack of freedom but despite our lack of freedom. What God forgives is not something as pithy and insipid as whether we have shared, developed our talents, and acted with humility. Rather, God forgives a profoundly more fundamental and intractable shortcoming that makes even the most egregious crime pale in comparison. God's acceptance truly cannot be earned – we don't even have the causal ability to do so. This is how we should see sin and forgiveness – our 'sin' is inherited, but God's mercy is radical and overwhelming. He grants us divine dignity for nothing. We are all freeloaders. Spending any time placing each other on a moral spectrum is an irrational, foolish game. We are not called to forgive each other's' bad behavior. Rather, we are called to understand our nature as unfree and the nature of our dignity as being divinely granted - not earned – in other words: grace.   Jesus's incarnation and death were not a cosmic skeet shoot or the satisfaction of a divine bloodlust. Rather, it was God once again fashioning garments to mitigate our shame as a species. It was a drawing of an undeserving creature into the loving embrace of its Creator.

With a few exceptions, every Catholic Mass begins with the recitation of the Penitential Act. Frankly, I have spent most of my life hating it:

I confess to almighty God
and to you my brothers and sisters,
that I have greatly sinned,
in my thoughts and in my words,
in what I have done and in what I have failed
to do …

And at this point, the members of the congregation ritualistically beat their chests in sorrow as they proceed:

> through my fault, through my fault,
> through my most grievous fault.
> Therefore I ask blessed Mary ever-virgin,
> all the Angels and Saints,
> and you my brothers and sisters,
> to pray for me to the Lord our God.[437]

This has always struck me as a terrible way to begin Mass. It seems to be a virtually medieval groveling for sinful behavior. It even includes some stylized self-flagellation!

But the Penitential Act is always immediately followed by the Kyrie in which the congregation asks for mercy with a three-word entreaty, repeated three times: "Lord have mercy. Christ have mercy. Lord have Mercy." No sooner has this been recited that the virtually exultant Gloria is sung: "Glory to God in the highest, and on earth peace to people of good will!"

I have come to believe this is a most extraordinary and appropriate way to begin Mass. If sin is our inherent inability to choose, the Penitential Act is our communal acknowledgement of that condition. We follow it without interruption with a call for divine acceptance not because we've earned it, but because God unilaterally covenanted that it is ours. God does not wait for an apology – He knows it is not forthcoming because He knows of what we are made. And with the certainty that He has once again overlooked our shortcoming, we sing. As the beginning of our communal addressing of God, in rapid fire succession, we say we're terrible, we ask for divine love anyway, and we celebrate its arrival. Our universal shame is relieved, and we need only believe it.

The Desire for Re-Enslavement

Not only do the Israelites fail to earn God's loving concern for them, breaking the covenant instantly only to have God re-covenant with them – but they also always seem to seek the opportunity to be re-enslaved and grouse about how much better it was for them in Egypt. Fortunately, God imbues us with divine dignity whether we like it or not – and for the most part, we don't like it. As we've seen, we are pre-disposed to reject the idea that we lack free will and are happy to embrace moral judgment, even if that means inviting Plato into Christianity. That God expects us to react that way is reflected throughout Scripture. Throughout Scripture the theme of rejection of God's prophets reverberates culminating in the Cross. We are a stiff-necked people and God always remains patient. He understands our desire for moral autonomy is deeply ingrained, and He forgives even our desire not to be forgiven. When Pharaoh's heart is hardened the last time and he sends his chariots out to recapture the Israelites at the Red Sea, the Israelites tell Moses "Is not this what we said to you in Egypt, 'Let us alone and let us serve the Egyptians'? For it would have been better for us to serve the Egyptians than to die in the wilderness."[438] God closes the Red Sea on Pharaoh's forces and the Israelites continue their journey. In the very next chapter, as they arrive at Marah, they discover the water is undrinkable.[439] The Israelites complain to

Moses. God shows them an antidote and then leads them to Elim, where there are twelve springs of water and seventy palm trees; an abundance of what they wanted. No sooner have they left Elim that they are complaining about Moses again because they are hungry and miss the food in Egypt. "Would that we had died by the hand of the Lord in the land of Egypt, when we sat by the fleshpots and ate bread to the full; for you have brought us out into this wilderness to kill this whole assembly with hunger." God responds with manna, bread from heaven to feed them.[440] And sure enough, the next day bread and meat, in the form of quail, rain from heaven in abundance. No sooner do they travel into the next wilderness that they are thirsty again and complaining again. "Why did you bring us out of Egypt, to kill us and our children and our cattle with thirst?"[441] Moses strikes a rock with his staff and water gushes out. Only after this series of epic failures of faith do the Israelites arrive at Mount Sinai to screw up again. We think of the Israelites as a changed people after Sinai, but they are not. As they leave the wilderness and approach the Promised Land, they send spies to reconnoiter. The spies bring back grapes so large that one bunch has to be carried on a pole by two men. But they claim they saw giants, the mythological Nephilim from the story of Noah, and that they have no hope of conquering the land. Again, the people complain, "Would that we had died in the land of Egypt! Or would that we had died in the wilderness! Would it not be better for us to go back to Egypt?"[442] God has had enough and curses the Israelites to wander the wilderness for forty years. Like children demanding, "are we there yet?!" from the back of a car, the din continues. All the while - though God sometimes can't figure out why and we certainly never get the impression it is earned - He sticks with the people. He knows their nature and that they cannot obey commands even for the most abundant rewards or the most heinous punishment. He won't take it back. We are family.

Conclusion

If we acknowledge that we don't have free will, the tension between Christianity's two competing conceptions of God as being both harsh judge and unconditionally loving evaporates. It turns out we are our own harsh judges, seeking to find dignity by falsely asserting that we have moral autonomy. Perhaps against any expectation, behavioral science reveals a cadence in Sacred Scripture and Sacred Tradition that affirms that God is extraordinarily loving – more unreasonably loving than we previously had imagined   and that human dignity is not so much inherent but inherited. The language of faith that we have intuitively adopted and preserved for many centuries makes perfect sense. Jesus died for our sinfulness, but perhaps a more profound sinfulness than we might otherwise have imagined. We rely on unearnable grace, and may be surprised at just how unearnable it really is. We are the recipients of radical forgiveness because God has chosen to overlook something far more severe than anything we can do - our inability to make moral choices at all. Rather than requiring that each of our lives serves a purpose, God ensures they are saturated with meaning. Jesus stands for the audacious assertion that we are all children of God and that He has inculcated each of us with dignity that would otherwise have been out of our reach - we who should have lived our lives beneath God's notice. Jesus represents hope in what otherwise would have been an impossible darkness. At the star-lit moment of the incarnation, we were freed of that which drove us from the Garden and enslaved us. Jesus is not a cosmic nice guy or moral example but Savior and Redeemer; an irreducible, critical element in any calculation of human worth.

Christendom, under the influence of Platonism, has defined the Incarnate God as a moral commander and moral example. This seemed like a noble enterprise. Who can argue with the need to be a good person, develop our talents, serve one another, and give to the poor? Why not yoke the influence of faith in front of such laudable goals? What's wrong with selling the alabaster jar? As an added benefit, this project made Christianity largely indistinguishable from the secular world, which shared the vast majority of its values, and allowed Christians to erase anything that distinguished their faith lives and the rest of their lives. But faith's message, it turns out, transcends questions of right or wrong and establishes a far more fundamental moral issue without which we quickly lose our bearings. Faith alone asserts that each of us is a child of God and bearer of divine dignity. The moral consequences of that assertion is our next concern.

O holy night! The stars are brightly shining.
It is the night of our dear Savior's birth.
Long lay the world in sin and error pining,
'Til he appeared and the soul felt its worth.
A thrill of hope, the weary world rejoices,
For yonder breaks a new and glorious morn.[443]

Chapter Six

A Letter from a Faithful Nation

But let's lie in wait for the righteous man,
because he annoys us,
is contrary to our works.
He professes to have knowledge of God,
and calls himself a child of the Lord.
He became to us a reproof of our thoughts.
He is grievous to us even to look at,
because his life is unlike other men's,
and his paths are strange.
He boasts that God is his father.
Let's see if his words are true.
Let's test what will happen at the end of his life.
For if the righteous man is God's son, he will
uphold him,
and he will deliver him out of the hand of his
adversaries.
Let's test him with outrage and torture,
that we may find out how gentle he is,
and test his patience.

Let's condemn him to a shameful death,
for he will be overseen according to his words.
Thus they reasoned, and they were led astray[444]

Faith is finally not about accomplishing anything. Faith does not demand self-improvement, or developing our talents to return them at the end of our lives with a profit. Nor does faith demand social progress either in a liberal or a conservative way. Faith is the affirmation that we have inherited dignity as a result of our status as the adopted children of God. Stretching all the way back to the Garden, through Moriah, and Mount Sinai and culminating at the Cross, faith is about acknowledging that we are not free, but that God has scattered that impenetrable darkness by choosing to love us anyway. This is an extraordinary gift, but it is a transcendent one. It does not change our physical circumstances, does not promise that those of us who believe it will be rewarded with good fortune, wealth, health, social acceptance or a divine rescue when times are tough. As the beloved of God, we will still suffer bad luck, poverty and illness. Further, our status as children of God will not necessarily distinguish us morally. God will not protect us from our nature and nurture and we may well find ourselves lower on the moral spectrum than some of our secular peers. The advantage of faith, if there is one, is simply the comfort derived from knowing that we are the beloved of God, to the extent we allow ourselves to believe it. It is what Paul called, "the peace of God that surpasses all understanding." [445]

Faith is also not an inoculation against unbelief or against adopting incorrect ideas about God. When God promised Abraham and Sarah that they would have child in their old age, Sarah laughed pessimistically.[446] Genesis records that God seemed actually hurt. He asks Abraham why she would laugh, and Sarah denies that she did. Of course, Sarah does give birth just as God promised, and lest we believe that Sarah's laugh is an inconsequential sideline, their son is named Isaac, which means "he who laughs"[447] and Sarah states that the tables have clearly turned and she expects everyone to laugh at her pessimism now.[448] Isaac's son, Jacob, is renamed Israel after he struggles with God. Here, in the first family of faith, their persistent pessimism, doubt and struggles with God are memorialized in their very names. Faith is ultimately not about belief but about trust. It is trust that God has, in fact, made the choice to love us, though we can't imagine why. Because we are not free to choose in any autonomous way, we cannot serve any practical purpose for God. Faith is the ultimate existentialism: our biographies and lists of accomplishments or failures is of no consequence; only God's choice matters. Transcendence is not just one characteristic of faith; it is central to it. To have faith means to transcend the idea that we are what we can do for God, and God is what He can do for us and accept that we live purposeless lives, and can do so joyfully, because our lives are saturated with meaning. Faith is not about the magical or the moral. Faith is story of the acquisition of dignity by the sons and daughters of God.

Dignity, of course, is not measurable. Though the story recorded in Scripture with crescendos at Mount Sinai and Bethlehem represented a cataclysmic moment in history rivaling the blast of Creation itself, no scientific instrument could pick up the reverberations resonating throughout the universe. No one weighed more or less, acted better or worse, or worked any harder or less hard for self-improvement or social progress. It was merely a message, divinely revealed and deeply inspirational, that took centuries to travel the globe in fits and starts and continues to ebb and flow to this day. Dignity can be dismissed by those who commit to believing only what can be measured, and by those who lose faith in it.

Sophie's Choice

In William Styron's classic 1976 book, *Sophie's Choice*,[449] the main character, Sophie Zawistowska, is a beautiful young Polish woman living in Brooklyn after having barely survived Auschwitz. Only in the last pages of the book does the full horror of Sophie's experience there emerge. She is not Jewish, but rather begins life as a devout[450] Roman Catholic and the daughter of an anti-Semitic professor in Cracow. When the Nazis invade, despite being sympathetic to their goals, her father is swept up in the execution of intellectuals. Sophie's husband becomes part of the Polish resistance and is also killed. Sophie herself remains fastidiously neutral during the occupation despite the murder of her father and husband and refuses to participate in the resistance movement. Nonetheless, she is arrested by the Nazis for bringing a ham to her very ill mother in violation of the law that ensures all meat goes to the German military. Her arrest coincides with a sweep of the resistance movement from which she tried so hard to distance herself. She is dealt with harshly, and sent with her seven-year-old daughter, Eva, and young son, Jan, to Auschwitz. Upon her arrival, a sadistic Nazi doctor forces her to choose which of her children will be immediately gassed and which will be permitted to survive the day and join the other prisoners in the camp. The moment is, of course, excruciating. Sophie at first refuses to make such a choice, but faced with the death of both of them, she chooses her son, and her daughter is torn from her arms and killed. She is devastated by grief and guilt that never ends.

Shortly thereafter, Sophie loses her faith. Being fluent in both Polish and German and an accomplished stenographer, she is enlisted to serve as a secretary for the Nazi officer in charge of the camp. While fulfilling this role, Sophie lives in the cold, dank basement of the otherwise well-appointed home the officer occupies with his family. One day, while Sophie is in the officer's office in the upper part of the home, his spoiled daughter plays records on a phonograph downstairs. The song is Joseph Haydn's *Creation* oratorio:

> The heavens are telling the glory of God. The wonder of His works displays the firmament. To day, that is coming, speaks it the day; the night, that is gone, to following night. The heavens are telling the glory of God. The

wonder of works displays the firmament. In all
the land resounds the Word …

Sophie begins to pray. But at that moment, the music abruptly
stops and the record is replaced by the child downstairs with, of
all things, *The Beer Barrel Polka*. It is the perfect metaphor for
Sophie's situation, and the events of her life from that moment
forward are a banal circus, characterized by the classic atheistic
existential elements of absurdity, anxiety and hopelessness.

There is a bitter irony that her father encouraged the Final
Solution, but himself became a victim of it together with his
daughter and grandchildren. Sophie too, is buffeted along in
a world that is harsh, cold, and unpredictable. She attempts to
seduce the Nazi officer in an attempt to get her son released from
the camp, but she fails and she never does see her son again.
When the camp is finally liberated she is almost left for dead.
She finds herself several months later in New York, still bearing
the camp tattoo and still terribly scarred and unhealthy. Her
life remains a study in absurdity. She falls in love with Nathan, a
brilliant man who, it is revealed, is schizophrenic and a cocaine
addict. Nathan alternates mercurially from ecstatic highs to
grinding lows. He is nurturing and caring some of the time, but
within moments can become explosively violent, and physically and verbally abusive. Sophie is utterly unable to assert her
own dignity because she has come to see life as meaningless
and grim, and, more importantly, is herself unanchored from
any sense of her own dignity. This was the profane specialty

of the Nazis – to overcome the optimistic nature of their victims and nurture a sense of hopelessness.[451] Sophie becomes a sexual plaything for everyone she encounters, and obediently and quietly tolerates every injury and insult. She is treated as someone who has no inherent worth – an assessment in which she apparently concurs. She is raped by a fellow prisoner in the camp and she is violently groped on a crowded subway in New York and cannot find her voice to fight back or even object. In a drug fueled high, Nathan insists on urinating on her, and she complies. When Nathan leaves her in a rage, she takes up with the narrator of the story, Stingo, and becomes his afternoon's entertainment, casually smearing his semen on her face while engaging in chirpy dialogue, but then immediately attempting to drown herself. While the Nazis failed to incinerate her body, Sophie willingly incinerates her own God-given dignity for nothing. In modernity, Sophie might have broken unsavory records on Tinder. Like the occupants of hell in *No Exit*, she seeks redemption from people as broken and as incognizant of their God-given dignity as she is.

Sophie's loss of faith and loss of a sense of inherent dignity coincide. In a camp for displaced persons in Sweden after being rescued from Auschwitz, Sophie meets a deeply religious Jewish woman who also emerged from the death camps. Sophie marvels that this woman survived. She marvels even more at the faith that likely preserved her soul.[452] Sophie explains that she knew that God had forgotten her: "I just knew, I just knew that only a God, only a Jesus who had no pity and who no longer care for me could permit the people I loved to be killed and let me live with such guilt."[453] Her rejection of faith expresses itself most vehemently later in an unreasoning anger for two elderly nuns that approach her and Stingo in a bar in Brooklyn. The nuns are looking for charitable contributions but Sophie angrily drives them away. She tells us the nuns make her feel rotten, "groveling in front of a God who must be a monster, Stingo, if He exist. A monster!"[454]. Sophie has lost faith not in the transcendent Christian God, but in a hybrid god, the Platonic Form of Good, that does not exist. In contradiction of the message of the Beatitudes, Sophie's religion taught her that faith is about magic and morality: be a good, moral person and you will be magically rewarded with protection, wealth and happiness. If you are a bad person, you are cursed with sickness, poverty and social rejection. The sacramental music has ended and *The Beer Barrel Polka* has begun for Sophie. When the storm came; when Chaos flooded her world, her faith could not heal her, bring her comfort or assert her dignity. Though faith could have placed her on the Ark and God could have closed and locked the door behind her to preserve her identity, her uniqueness, and her status as a child of God despite the rest of her identity and her reality being swept away, she had not heard that Good News. Her religion did not give her the capacity to turn around her understanding of God from the Platonic hybrid that commands, rewards and punishes, to the Christian transcendent God Who suffers with us and declares us beloved. Just as she was caught up by Nazi bureaucracy and tormented to near extinguishment, so she sees herself as caught up in the absurd bureaucracy of life, buffeted along to an inevitable death.[455]

God on Trial

Also set in Auschwitz is the 2008 public television play, *God on Trial*. A group of Jewish prisoners establish a court among themselves to prosecute God for violating His Covenant with His Chosen People and allowing the Holocaust to occur. They thoroughly explore all the classic expressions of the Problem of Evil. Lest the audience forget the gravity of their situation as they debate good and evil with judicial detachment, the eerie barking of a German Shepherd guard dog outside the barracks periodically reminds us. They are ultimately flummoxed. Like Sophie, they find God guilty and decide that God has sided with the Germans in blatant violation of the Covenant. As the trial concludes, the verdict is spoken and they are led to the gas chamber and their death, one prisoner plaintively asks what they are to do now. The rabbi among them answers simply, "Now we pray." Being deprived of yarmulkes, each prisoner places a hand on top of his head and prays the haunting Psalm 90 as they enter the gas chamber.

Their outcome was no better than Sophie's as a result of their faith. I am certain they (or the people they represent) were just as anxious and frightened on many levels. But they had, by luck, the nature and nurture to reach out to God and to perhaps feel the warmth of the gaze of God at a critical moment. It is what Judaism calls the *Shefa* - an abundant and constant flow of grace from the divine that cannot be diverted, obstructed or destroyed by the meddling of a bunch of beings without the moral autonomy to do otherwise. The prisoners in the play reached out to God hoping for the Passover God who rescues with a strong hand, but were satisfied with the God can only suffer with us and whose relationship to us may not serve any practical purpose but nonetheless imbues life cruelly shortened with immense meaning. I read of a study several years ago that concluded that people without children are happier than people with children. I suspect people with children are, in fact, subject to more anxieties, have more numerous concerns, and are just generally more exposed to hurt in the world than our childless counterparts. We certainly have less personal freedom (shockingly less). On a scientific, measurable level, the childless may be happier. But there is an existential, transcendent connection between parent and child that perhaps does not translate into anything purposeful but that nonetheless generates meaning and makes everything worth it. Perhaps neither is 'happier' than the other, but that they merely define it differently.

Unlike Sophie, because of the advantage of nature and nurture, the men of *God on Trial* are able to understand God not as serving a practical purpose, but rather as a transcendent concern. We are not what we can do for God, and God is not what He can do for us. Kierkegaard suggested that Abraham was a knight of faith because he obeyed God despite the absurdity of God's command. In fact, in that story it was God who was the knight of faith; loving us despite the fact that we are unfree creatures that can do nothing to earn that love. Abraham assumed that God was like Ba'al and all other gods before Him, and would demand a sacrifice, performance, the development of talents. Instead, God forbad any sacrifice. The characters of

God on Trial are human knights of faith. Having determined that, for whatever reason, God was incapable of changing their circumstances, they would nonetheless seek to encounter Him.

What ultimately separates a person of faith from a secular person who might nonetheless believe in a divine being is whether we can accept a transcendent God: one who promises nothing, threatens nothing, commands nothing, and provides nothing but the dignity that comes from the status of being His beloved. To the question, "What is God for?" the person of faith has no answer because the question itself reveals a fundamental failure to understand the nature of God's relationship to us. Our God is not a small god. He is not a good luck charm, or a moralistic prude. Our God is not a peevish god of liberals or conservatives, annoyed by establishment or anti-establishment sentiments. Our God is the God of colliding galaxies; the God of salvation, redemption, and grace. Our God is the irreplaceable, transcendent root of human dignity.

New Atheists Just Don't Get It; Hitchens and Mother Teresa

It is this transcendent nature of faith that wholly escapes the New Atheists. Several times in the Gospels, Jesus heals someone of blindness, leprosy or even pulls them back from the brink of death and doesn't take credit himself but rather states emphatically that it is faith of the petitioner who made the miracle happen.[456] As if to make the point even more emphatically, all three Synoptic Gospels tell the story of a hemorrhaging woman who surreptitiously reaches to touch Jesus's clothing and is healed as a result.[457] In Luke, Jesus turns around at this moment, having felt the power leave him, and demands to know who has touched him. Clearly, the author intends to convey that the healing Jesus brings to us comes about as a result of his status, not because of any action on his part. To receive the benefit of God's love, one need only to believe that it is their birthright. In one poignant miracle story in the Gospel of Mark, a father asks Jesus to intervene on behalf of his epileptic son.[458] He tells Jesus that he asked the disciples to help but they were unable. Jesus, apparently exasperated with his disciples' failure, exclaims, "O faithless generation, how long am I to bear with you?" The father asked Jesus again to help, 'if he can.' Jesus is exasperated again and repeats, "If you can! All things are possible to him who believes." Immediately, we are told, the father cries out "I believe, help my unbelief." Apparently even the mere desire to believe brings about the comfort of faith. This should come as some comfort to Peter, always the foil, who briefly can walk on water but almost immediately finds himself sinking. Jesus saves him and demands, "O man of little faith, why did you doubt?"[459] No one has managed to repeat the miraculous elements of these stories again in two millennia of extraordinary expansion of faith. The Gospel writers' clear intent was not to have people drown themselves in acts of faith but rather to indicate that faith is not about intervention by Jesus or God to change the circumstances in which we find ourselves, but rather to indicate that faith has a transcendent outcome rooted in trust rather than magic.

Horseman of the New Atheism, the late Christopher Hitchens, savaged Mother Teresa in his crassly entitled book, *The Missionary Position, Mother Teresa in Theory and Practice*.[460] He has two principal criticisms. The first is that Mother Teresa was insufficiently critical of those from whom she received donations or with whom she allowed herself to be photographed, such as Jean-Claude Duvalier of Haiti, Hillary Rodham Clinton (reviled by Hitchens for her failure to enact universal health care while serving as First Lady[461]), disgraced former mayor of Washington D.C., Marion Barry, and the face of the saving and loan scandal of the 1990s, Charles Keating. Hitchens believes that he has caught Mother Teresa in the most degenerate hypocrisy. But most Christians instantly recognize this is Mother Teresa's imitation of Jesus, seeking out the tax collectors and the prostitutes (even allowing one to anoint him with expensive oil), and forgiving sins 'while we are yet sinners.'[462] But the heart of Hitchens' criticism appears to be that Mother Teresa did not dedicate herself exclusively to changing the economic condition of the poor and medical condition of the suffering and maximizing wealth, but included in her ministry an attempt to connect those who suffered with the comfort provided by God. Obviously, as a self-described anti-theist, Hitchens dismissed the existence of God. He nonetheless is ready to pass judgment on whether God is as useful as he imagines faith requires. Hitchens sneeringly related a story of an interview given by Mother Teresa, in which she described a terminally ill patient in her care suffering tremendous pain:

With a smile, Mother Teresa told the camera
what she told this terminal patient: "You are
suffering like Christ on the cross. So Jesus
must be kissing you." Unconscious of the
account to which this irony might be charged,
she then told of the sufferer's reply: "Then
please tell him to stop kissing me." There are
many people in the direst need and pain who
have had cause to wish, in their own extremity,
that Mother Teresa was less free with her
own metaphysical caresses and a little more
attentive to actual suffering.[463]

What Hitchens fails to see is that there is more to the human
person than can be reduced to a sterile medical diagnosis and there is more to suffering than the underlying disease. We should generously allow ourselves to imagine that
Hitchens would insist on the best medical care for everyone
for whom he could afford to provide it. It is more difficult to
imagine what comfort Hitchens would seek to provide a dying
person in pain beyond what medicine can offer to resolve.
Perhaps her efforts were frustrated in this particular case, but
Mother Teresa encouraged belief to encourage comfort; belief
is needed if faith is to provide comfort. Faith has no power
be of comfort to the non-believer. This is not because belief
is some kind of price of entry for magical intervention, but
because you simply cannot be comforted by something that

you don't believe exists. There are several places in the New Testament where Jesus discordantly asserts that the rich will become richer and the poor will become poorer; including in both Matthew and Mark when he is asked about the parable of the sower who sows seed randomly in different kinds of soil with varying degrees of success.[464] Jesus may be making a fairly simple observation: if you are inclined toward seeking faith by your nature and nurture, it is more likely to cultivate itself in you and enrich you. If you are not, then it will not. This is not an exhortation to believe, but a reflection of the mechanics of belief. The sower is not a personification of God so much as a personification of luck. It is a variation on the theme of "ask and you shall receive." Faith is also no lasting comfort unless the true nature of our relationship to God is accepted. No one comes to the Father but through the realization of our unfree nature and God's unreasoning decision to love us anyway.[465] When tempted by Satan at the beginning of his ministry with the power to dominate and enslave humanity, Jesus refuses and pursues instead the extraordinary mission of giving us dignity instead. Mara tempted the Buddha with the same power as he leaves his palace for the first time, and is rebuffed. At the Last Supper, Jesus washed his apostles' feet as a powerful message that God frees us from slavery to give us dignity, not to impose a new slavery.[466] He said that he did not consider us servants but friends.[467] Peter did not want it. He insisted he was too small, too insignificant, too unfree to receive this honor. Jesus's response is harsh. He warns Peter that the gift is compulsory. He must accept having his feet washed by God incarnate.[468] The message is clear: To encounter God and be comforted by

Him, we have to accept that we stand before Him with empty hands and are declared beloved anyway.

Hitchens's mistake is that he assumes changes in economic or medical circumstances are the measure of the worth of faith. If there is no magical or moral intervention, faith has nothing to offer to Hitchens. Hitchens's unreasoning anger toward Mother Teresa has an extraordinary literary parallel in the unreasoning anger Sophie expresses towards the two nuns she encounters. For Sophie, if God does not intervene, faith has no value. Hitchens makes the same calculation. Elsewhere in his book, Hitchens criticizes Mother Teresa's decision to use a generous donation to buy a chalice to be used in one of her facilities' liturgies. He admits being confused by the story of Judas insisting that the alabaster jar could have been sold to provide food for the poor and Jesus's enigmatic response that the poor will always be with us. Hitchens states bluntly: "Either one eschews luxury and serves the poor or one does not."[469] Hitchens is making the same mistake as Judas - insisting that faith's only aim should be assisting the poor and any transcendent concern has no social utility. He is succumbing to Satan's temptation to believe that we live by bread alone and if God doesn't provide it then faith is nonsensical. An atheistic determinist can make no sense of inherent or inherited dignity. The New Atheists want God to answer physics riddles, intervene to change circumstances, or command good, social behavior – the magical and the moral. Their view ultimately reveals a grossly unsophisticated understanding of faith and ignores, whether deliberately or not, the transcendent Christian God in favor of the Platonic hybrid. That people of faith can be interested in understanding and encountering the transcendent is not even thinkable. That we can be comforted without a change in circumstances is incomprehensible. It is seeing only the duck head and never seeing the rabbit head in the optical illusion in Chapter Two and angrily insisting it is not there. As he is delivering his farewell address in the Gospel of John, Jesus's apostles ask him how he will manifest himself in the future. Jesus answers, "Peace I leave with you. My peace I give you. Not as the world gives do I give you. Let not your hearts be troubled, neither let them be afraid."[470] If the Christmas story is not a scientifically verifiable story about divine gametes entering a human woman, it can have no value for Hitchens and his colleagues in the New Atheism. If fault or inconsistency can be found in the moral narrative of Scripture, it can have nothing of value to say to us and is 'dangerous.' The New Atheists must wonder with frustration how faith can survive universal education and instant fact-checking on the internet. But what they see as a lack of sophistication, an untoward clinging to superstition, and a deliberate gulling of vast swaths of helpless human beings, actually reveals the fundamental shortcoming of the New Atheists themselves – the inability to account for the power of the transcendent.

When atheists are in a conciliatory mood they may seek common ground by noting with approval all the good work people of faith perform in the name of their God. "If only we could drop this superstitious God stuff" they might reason, "we'd all really be in the same place." Many people of faith are all too eager to collaborate in this and re-cast God to be more useful. And so the parable of the sheep and the goats, with its implicit command, reward and punishment structure is "beloved" and our most common expression of what God "wants." But for the person of faith, the nature of God is never the answer to the question, "what is God for?" Faith is the wordless, inexpressible, deeply personal and individual response to awe. All of our gratitude, love and charity, and all of our worship and praise are all simply weak attempts to express this awe and are never substitutes for it. We cannot drop the transcendent God because He is the center of our universe and although He does not command us, His existence informs our every act. God is not a social utility. God is not what He can do for us and we are not what we can do for Him. God is Who is.

The New Atheists' critique of faith is so over the top and strident because they don't understand its foundation. They measure faith by social utility. Faith is good if it encourages advantageous social behavior and bad if it does not. We fear what we don't understand and the New Atheists fear faith because it does not ascribe to the orthodoxy of social utility and is therefore incomprehensible. The New Atheists are standing at the edge of the Grand Canyon wondering what all the fuss is about because they are turned the wrong way and are facing the parking lot. People of faith can try to describe it to them, to insist that they trust them and their intuition, and encourage them to open your eyes wider, but none of it will help. What is needed is *metanoia* – a word usually translated as 'repentance' in Scripture but also means a complete turning around or change of perspective – in this case from utility to transcendence. Faith is not about good behavior, bad behavior, guilt, innocence, or repentance. It is about, by virtue only of our nature and nurture, being lucky enough to see - and to sense the loving gaze of God.

Responding to the Gift: Love One Another

How should the faithful respond to this immense divine gift? Does the reality of God translate into any sort of moral duty? To put it in terms of classic philosophy: can we turn 'is' into 'ought'? Does being a person of faith leave us free to choose any course of conduct that might appeal to us, or should we have allegiance to a specific way of being in the world? Is the moral narrative that seems to be so prominent in Scripture just an illusion or something that we need to reject in favor of moral relativism?

In the Gospel of Matthew, while the Pharisees try to trip up Jesus with questions about paying tax to Caesar, the Sadducees join in and try to make an afterlife (clearly something Jesus spoke of and supported) seem implausible by asking to whom a woman who remarries several times following the death of successive husbands would be married in heaven. Jesus stumps them all with his wise answers. Finally, a lawyer emerges from among them and asks Jesus which of the commandments is the greatest. His intention is likely hostile: to get Jesus to say something contrary to the orthodoxy of the day.[471] Jesus replies by saying all of the law is summarized by two commandments:

'You shall love the Lord your God with all your heart, with all your soul, and with all your mind.' This is the first and great commandment. A second likewise is this, 'You shall love your neighbor as yourself.' The whole law and the prophets depend on these two commandments.[472]

Jesus has stumped these theologians again because he is simply quoting Deuteronomy and Leviticus.[473] The second 'commandment' is, of course, the Golden Rule and is expressed by Jesus in each of the three Synoptic Gospels.[474] In Matthew, the rule is stated twice, having been a part of a laundry list of proverbs Jesus offers to his apostles along with 'judge not lest you be judged,' and 'don't throw pearls before swine.'[475] The Golden Rule is good, solid, practical moral advice. If you want to know how to treat someone under most circumstances, you can just ask yourself how you would want to be treated. It is to be found not only in the Old Testament but also, in one form or another, in almost every wisdom tradition, whether deist or non-deist, including ancient Greek philosophy. Its practical effect is immediately obvious. If you do something nice for someone, they are more likely to be well disposed towards you and return the favor. If you are a freeloader, you can expect others to rejoice in your failures. It is in perfect harmony with our human nature. It is run-of-the-mill reciprocity. It does not represent challenge, but is a statement of moral economy – of cause and effect, reward and punishment.

But in contrast with the Synoptic Gospels, in the Gospel of John, Jesus expresses the foundation of faith not in response to peevish challenges from the Pharisees and Sadducees, but as the crescendo of his speech to the apostles at the Last Supper as he prepares himself and them for his death. Instead of the practical tit-for-tat moral advice of the Golden Rule, here Jesus reveals the Golden Thread of the Old and New Testaments that ties the Garden, Moriah, Sinai, and Calvary together:

> This is my commandment, that you love one another as I have loved you.[476]

In fact, he expresses it twice in the same speech. This is dramatically different from the Golden Rule. We are no longer invited to view each other on a human scale, but rather we are invited to view each other as objects of divine love and receivers of divine dignity. We are asked to acknowledge that the touchstone of our worth is not in our biography, but in God. We are not measured by worldly considerations,[477] but are measured on a cosmic scale.

But there is a deliberate irony in this statement that Christianity has historically overlooked. Love cannot be commanded. Love can be nurtured, cultivated, and encouraged, but it cannot be a requirement or obligatory and still be recognizable as love.

We know this. But our desire to be commanded, measured by our performance, rewarded for our compliance and punished for freeloading encourages us to reinterpret Jesus's statement into something less. Jesus did not command us to love, we might reason; rather, he commanded us to imitate love and act in ways that imitate what we might do if we felt love. By this rationale, faith doesn't require us to feel differently about each other, but just requires a lukewarm moral response practically indistinguishable from secular morality: meet unmet needs, cultivate our talents for the common good, act charitably and speak kindly. But it is more likely that Jesus really meant *love* - and that faith is not about *acting* like we're in love, but is about actually *falling in love*. In Chapter Two I explored the neuro-mechanics of faith and asserted that prayer and meditation allow us to temporarily suppress the functioning of our parietal lobe and causes our sense of self to diminish and our sense of the unity and 'oneness' of all things to flourish. Perhaps this is the difference between love that we think is commanded and requires us to be fair, moral and socially responsible, and love that is felt in our bones with a spiritual urgency and is experienced much more like a profound truth than a command. Perhaps the kind of love arrived at rationally with our parietal lobes fully engaged is what the Greeks called '*philos*,' and love that is non-parietal and super-rational is the divine '*agape*.' Faith is not about performing tasks for each other or meeting each other's needs and earning God's reward or avoiding God's punishment. Rather, it is about seeing each other in a radically different way. God is not saying, "Love one another or I won't love you." If we are unfree, then that is nonsensical. Rather, God is saying, *"If you saw each other as I see you, you would love one another as I love you."* God loves us unconditionally, irrevocably, and regardless of our usefulness. God doesn't love us more when we are good, and our successes are not a sign of God's approval. If God plays favorites at all, it is with those of us and those parts of us that are poor, outcast and even badly behaved as a result of our fear and brokenness. If we see each other as essentially the products of our nature and nurture but as the adoptive, chosen children of God then we acknowledge that there is no reason to be angry with one another, but every reason to feel brotherhood and sisterhood with one another. We might abandon hate altogether. In the paradoxical parable of the sheep and the goats, Jesus declares, "when you serve the least among you, you serve me."[478] This is not a threat or warning that he is walking the Earth in disguise looking for good and bad behavior, but is rather a profound statement of adoption and the unity of all human beings with each other and with the divine. If we strive to see each other as God does, we inevitably see objects of divine love and members of a divine family.

The Incarnation is a message of total equality. We are forgiven far more egregious a shortcoming than our last episode of bad behavior. This is the message of radical forgiveness and radical grace. God forgives - totally overlooks – our lack of free will and our inability to be responsible for anything or earn anything in the first place. Without God we are animated clods of earth. It should give us immense confidence as we live our lives not denying our nature, but embracing it as something that

God has overcome. Implicit is a message of total, radical equality among us. Since no human being has more free will than any other, then those of us who act well and believe appropriately have no advantage over those who are unrepentant or deny that any of this exists in the first place. Each of us is totally and equally dependent on God's decision to love us and grant us divine dignity. As St. Paul said to the Galatians:

> There is neither Jew nor Greek, there is neither slave nor free man, there is neither male nor female; for you are all one in Christ Jesus. If you are Christ's, then you are Abraham's offspring and heirs according to promise.[479]

This should be and must be grounds for the greatest humility when we interact with each other. Although, on a practical, social level, we must judge each other to determine who can do a job better, who serves as a better example, who can be trusted and who must be incarcerated, on a more fundamental faith-based level, we have no grounds to judge one another as being a better or worse person or the object of hatred or outrage.

It is said that every Iranian household contains a copy of the Koran and a copy of the poetry of Hafez, a fourteenth century Sufi poet and mystic. Hafez beautifully expresses the hold equality has on us given our divinely imbued dignity:

If God invited you to a party
and said,
"Everyone in the ballroom tonight
Will be my Special Guest"
How would you then treat them
When you arrived?
Indeed, indeed!
And Hafez knows
There is no one in this world
Who
is not upon
His Jeweled Floor

Our dignity is God's gift to us. Each of His children inevitably is born and dies with the same amount as each of His other children, although we may dismiss it. We are all equally blessed by it, and none of us is cursed by being left out. When we are tempted to announce ourselves "blessed" because we have food on the table or money in the bank or got the job we were praying for, in so doing we're implying that those without food, money and jobs are less than blessed. We can know instead that we have all received a much greater blessing in equal abundance – the loving concern of our God despite our existential inability to earn it. If we have food to eat in abundance, let it be a symbol of this divine gift, knowing that no matter how much we have, it is a poor surrogate for God's abundant grace. And that we are being thankful not for a few mouthfuls of food - certainly not for a few more mouthfuls than our poorer neighbors - but rather we are thankful for the irrational regard God has for His unfree creatures. This is a beatitude.

God's justice is mercy, and so it must be with us. We are naturally, as a result of our evolution, willing to love the person who hurt us if they apologize and if they compensate us. If they are unapologetic and we have to suffer permanent loss, what love we can muster usually is just forbearance of retaliation. We translate the 'command' to love as the 'command' not to take revenge, which is an impoverished definition of love. That is not Christian love. That is the worldly economy. Jesus said that that if you love only those who love you, you are no more advanced than secular society,[480] and we should strive to imitate God, "For He makes His sun to rise on the evil and the good, and sends rain on the just and the unjust."[481] We Christians claim to be eager to love one another. But unless we can shed our natural impulse and desire for retribution, that love will always erode to something much less than actual love. We need to be able to robustly forgive, and to love in a manner that is more than the absence of hate, but is active compassion and empathy and identifying with one another. Christianity is more than forgiveness; it is the dedication to enhancing the God-given dignity each of us possesses. Where we find dignity-robbing poverty, whether it is economic, spiritual, social or otherwise, the Christian response has been and should always be to do our best to alleviate it. This is not the response to a command to receive reward or avoid punishment, but is rather simply the acknowledgment of divine truth that calls for our allegiance. We should be gentle with one another, love one another, and finally protect and promote each other's dignity not because we're commanded to do so, but because it is a reasonable reaction to our lack of moral autonomy and God's choice, revealed in Scripture, to overlook that fact.

Existential v. Utilitarian Human Value

The New Atheists might complain that divine enforcement - the idea that God commands moral behavior and rewards and punishes us according to our actions - was the one thing faith offered to morality that science could not. If God is not the enforcer, then faith has nothing unique to tell us about how we should treat one another. After all, as I asserted in Chapter Two, the existence of a more-or-less universal moral code is better explained by evolution than C.S. Lewis's claim that morality comes from God. We are all naturally inclined to empathy as a result of the circumstances in which we evolved as a social animal. And although it has always been a theme of Scripture that we should forgive one another, the message was always hedged a little in favor of judgment and it was science that that finally made the compelling argument that we are not morally free and so hatred is outright irrational. If science can conclusively make the case for love, empathy and forgiveness, they may argue, we need not trouble ourselves with our divine inherence or immeasurable, unverifiable notions of dignity. Ironically, Christianity has often strived to do what the New Atheists are now doing: accentuating how Christian ethics are just secular ethics expressed with the language of the divine. But faith and secular ethics do not necessarily complement each other. In fact, they conflict.

The key distinction is that while theistic determinism and faith express human value in existential terms – human dignity as a free gift – atheistic determinism inevitably expresses human value in utilitarian terms – human worth dependent on productivity and morality. Allegiance to the idea that our value is inherent and has nothing to do with our usefulness has a profound impact on how we define morality.

For centuries, both Christianity and the secular world assumed that we have inherent value and dignity as a product of our free will. Whether our free will was the gift of God or simply a mysterious capacity of our brains was not important. As we saw in Chapter Four, even avowed atheists like Jean-Paul Sartre could find human dignity in our capacity for radical freedom. However, behavioral science and philosophy have now conclusively determined that we don't have free will and the moral consequences are beginning to reverberate. Faith can acknowledge that we are not free but recognize that each of us nonetheless has inherent, irrevocable dignity as the beloved of God. Our value does not come from our usefulness - we are more than our biographies. However, if atheism acknowledges that we are not free, it does not have recourse to anything divine, transcendent or inherent to anchor human dignity. From an atheistic perspective, we are merely complex organic machines toiling unknown and unloved in the Void. While atheistic existentialism could find nobility in how we freely decide to face the absurdity and anxiety of this existence, atheistic determinism concludes that we cannot achieve any nobility on our own. Pulling oneself up into the air by the bootstraps is as impossible as it sounds. From that perspective, if human beings are to have any worth, it must be something measurable, quantifiable and scientifically provable. Inevitably, atheistic determinists measure us by our social usefulness and utility. To them, we can be nothing more than our biography because nothing more exists.

As Abraham stood between God and Sodom, God expressed a remarkable moral principal that was almost without precedent at the time. Abraham asked God, "what if there are fifty righteous within the city? Will you consume and not spare the place for the fifty righteous who are in it? May it be far from you to do things like that, to kill the righteous with the wicked, so that the righteous should be like the wicked. May that be far from you. Shouldn't the Judge of all the earth do right?" God would not impose collective punishment.[482] God would not sacrifice one individual to accomplish a broader social goal (albeit a destructive one). The theme recurred in Moriah, when God declined the sacrifice of Isaac to seal the covenant with the billions of members of the Abrahamic faiths to come. If Jesus is thought of as a sacrifice, it is only because the concept of sacrifice is turned on its head – the Incarnation of God will allow only Himself to be the sacrificial lamb in the ultimate self-sacrifice. God does not see us as indistinguishable from one another. He does not consider us as parts of a collective, but sees each of us as a complex, unique universe unto ourselves with an inimitable perspective and a never-to-be-repeated beauty. God does not count up how many of His children might be benefitted if one can be killed. Our worth is not cumulative such that two of us are more valuable than one. Sophie's choice is as impossible for God as it was for Sophie. In the eyes of God each of us is a beloved child, without needing to serve any purpose. In the Gospel of John, after Jesus raises Lazarus from the dead, the chief priests and Pharisees gather to decide what to do about him. They claim to be concerned that Jesus's continued performance of miracles will cause everyone to believe in him and cause the Romans to destroy the Temple and the nation. Caiaphas, the high priest for the year, decides Jesus must be executed to avoid this. To highlight his villainy, the Gospel notes that Caiaphas says, "you do not understand that it is expedient for you that one man should die for the people, and that the whole nation should not perish."[483] This drives Jesus underground but at his arrest, John's Gospel notes that he is brought first to Caiaphas's father-in-law's house and we are reminded of Caiaphas's utilitarian decree.[484]

Every wisdom tradition includes some manner of advice to diminish the self and control the ego, but to my knowledge not one them suggests that the self must be subjugated to the collective. Rather, the False Self, defined by biography and valued by utility, must recede so the True Self, defined and valued existentially, can flourish. God acknowledges that each of us is an irreplaceable part of the I/Thou encounter between ourselves and God. If we see each other as God sees us, then everyone of us has equal dignity and is equally sacred and precious regardless of our social utility. Divine dignity is not and cannot be diminished. It is the *Shefa*.

The atheistic determinist perspective is very different. Inherent dignity finds no support in science, cannot be empirically tested or measured, and is therefore irrelevant. Jeremy Bentham, the father of utilitarianism, called the idea that we have intrinsic worth or rights, "nonsense on stilts." Instead, Bentham and his colleagues noted that it is inviolable human nature that we desire pleasure and avoid pain. As such, he reasoned, whatever action promotes the greatest pleasure for the greatest number of people is the moral one. Bentham does not see individuals as ends onto themselves. Rather, for Bentham, individuals are irrelevant and it is the collective happiness that is the most important. This is a direct contradiction of God's moral economy as expressed at Sodom. A utilitarian god, having counted the good and the bad and decided it was bad on balance, would have destroyed the good and the bad together at Sodom without hesitation.

Jeremy Bentham's utilitarianism was developed further by John Stuart Mill, the son of John Mill, a friend and philosophical sympathizer of Bentham's. While Bentham used the word "utilitarianism" perhaps as little as once, it was John Stuart Mill who was responsible for appropriating it as a name for this philosophy.[485] Raw utilitarianism, as we saw in Chapter Three, can offend our intuitive grasp of morality. Raw or "act utilitarianism" would say that we should turn over an innocent individual to a violent mob to prevent the death of a larger number. Mill softened that result and asserted that the greatest happiness is achieved when we respect individual rights and promote fairness, which led him to a value system that can, under some circumstances, value individual happiness above the group's. Mill's 1859 essay, On Liberty, is a clear expression of those principals:

> The object of this Essay is to assert one very simple principal, as entitled to govern absolutely the dealings of society with the individual in the way of compulsion and control, whether the means used be physical force in the form of legal penalties, or the moral coercion of public opinion. That principal is that the sole end for which mankind are warranted, individually or collectively, in interfering with the liberty of action of any of their number, is self-protection.[486]

Mill is by no means abandoning utilitarianism, but he is proposing a longer view of happiness. Instead of looking at each action as a discrete instance generating either pleasure or suffering for the greatest number, he wants us to consider what values and policies lead to the greatest pleasure or suffering for the greatest number.

> I regard utility as the ultimate appeal on all ethical questions; but it must be utility in the

largest sense, grounded on the permanent interests of man as a progressive being.[487]

Mill went further and ranked different kinds of happiness as either lower or higher, and declared that intellectual pleasures have an intrinsically higher value than bodily pleasures.[488] Although Mill did not label it, this sort of refinement to utility became known as "rule utilitarianism." So, when faced with the angry mob demanding the innocent victim, the rule utilitarian could argue that the greatest happiness will result in respecting basic principles of fairness and protecting the innocent victim. Mill goes on to defend in terms of utility many classic civil liberties including the freedom of expression, assembly and religion.

But the question remains: what is it about our birth that enslaves us to the will of the collective? Why should an individual be valuable only if it pleases a larger number to treat him that way? By what authority, other than the threat of force, can two people insist that one person serve them or be useful to them or maximize their pleasure? Neither Bentham nor Mill express a clear answer.[489] There are many problems with utilitarianism, but the most fatal is that it values human beings according to their usefulness to one another. Utilitarianism's moral economy relies on simple math: two is always greater than one, and so the needs of the many must outweigh the needs of the few. God's moral economy is different. Sometimes one plus one does not equal two. If you light a candle with two matches, the flame does not double in size or heat. The dignity of the individual, as a child of God ransomed at a high price from causal irrelevancy, is the irreducible unit of measurement and cannot be aggregated. Dignity is not cumulative. God does not see us as having collective worth. God does not favor one nation over another, one side of a military conflict over another, one political impulse over another or (for crying out loud) one sports team over another. He does not weigh us against each other or place our happiness in a scale. He is with each individual person and suffers with them in their pain and rejoices in their happiness, and adopts them into divine grace and dignity.

Mill's respect for the individual is built on shifting sand; the collective's interests are more valuable and compelling than the individual's and if the individual's interests have any value, it is because of the community's interest in permitting them. Such a theory will always be subject to erosion. In the opening pages of *On Liberty*, Mill states that "it is hardly necessary to say" that his principle of individual liberty does not apply to children who need to be protected from themselves because they have not yet "attained the capacity of being guided to their own improvement by conviction or persuasion."[490] But as confidence in determinism and its influence in public policy grows, one must ask if this legitimate authority to compel children won't be extended to adults. Mill already includes for treatment as children, "those backward states of society in which the race itself may be considered as in its nonage." "Despotism" Mill writes, "is a legitimate mode of government in dealing with barbarians, provided the end be their improvement, and the means justified by actually effecting that end."[491] This is abhorrent racism, but also highlights the fact that utility makes the community the ultimate unit of moral concern, but that community is imaginary. Like two rivers coming together, where one ends and the other begins is only an arbitrary construct. A community is whatever we define the collective to be: a town, a state, a nation, a race – and excludes anyone we want. In utility, there is no imperative to love the stranger. It excludes anyone for whom it makes us collectively happier that he or she is excluded.

In *The Moral Landscape*, Sam Harris comes to precisely the same utilitarian conclusion. Reluctant to use collective happiness or pleasure as the cornerstone of his moral theory he nuances it and relies instead on collective well-being. Harris announces, "While I agree ... that it is reasonable to wonder whether maximizing pleasure in any given instance is 'good', it makes no sense at all to ask whether maximizing well-being is 'good'."[492] Harris's focus on whether it is pleasure or well-being that ought to be maximized distracts him from wondering whether maximizing either one is the proper aim of morality or public policy. He simply accepts without criticism that the worth of human beings is cumulative – that the well-being of two necessarily outweighs the well-being of one. And indeed, if you insist on dismissing as superstition anything that is not measurable with scientific instruments, you are inevitably led to that conclusion. However, far from 'making no sense at all', most Western political systems are founded on principals of limited government which identify individual rights as preeminent and affirm that we are each naturally or divinely endowed with certain inalienable rights that are not ignored at the pleasure of the majority. Central to Western jurisprudence is the affirmation that we are not tools of the collective but have an inherent "right to be let alone."[493] This undergirds the right to privacy held so dear by both sides of the political spectrum. It means we are free to make our own decisions because they are what we want, even when they do not maximize our own or others' well-being.

Cain is Utilitarian

After they are expelled from the Garden, Adam and Eve have two children, Cain and Abel. The story follows the Biblical convention of casting the eldest son and natural heir, Cain, as the foil and as the example of what *not* to do. Cain is a tiller of soil and as such, his sacrifice to God is fruit of the earth. Abel was a shepherd and sacrificed the best of his flock to God. The story follows another biblical convention in that Abel's animal sacrifice was favored.[494] Cain is crestfallen that God doesn't have the same regard for his sacrifice as Abel's. God tries to buck him up and warns him that whether his sacrifice is favored or disfavored the danger of sin is always present.

> For whether you offer well,
> or whether you do not,
> at the tent flap sin crouches[495]

If Cain's parents ever realized that their fundamental short-coming was their lack of freedom and their 'sin' was to assume they were morally autonomous and could assert moral judgment, Cain has forgotten the lesson. Cain lures Abel into a field - his territory - and kills him there. Why was Cain so angry that he would kill his own brother? The story doesn't offer any overt reason. Abel didn't abuse Cain or sabotage his sacrifice. Abel wasn't even a freeloader – he worked as hard as Cain to prepare his sacrifice. Cain is jealous. He is his father's son and has inherited Adam's sin. He asserts his moral autonomy and exercises moral judgment, compares himself to his brother and finds himself lacking. In a manner of speaking, Cain eats from the fruit of the Tree of the Knowledge of Good and Evil and sees that he is naked. Cain has determined that he is nothing more than is biography. This is the inevitable result of Cain's nature and nurture. When Cain is born, Eve exults in a very odd way, and speaks of Cain as a possession. She says, "I have got me a man with the Lord." In fact, Cain's name is a play on the Hebrew verb *qanah*, which means "to acquire."[496] No individuals in the Bible are described more exclusively in terms of their biography than are Cain and Abel. We are told simply, "Abel was a keeper of sheep while Cain was a tiller of soil."[497] There is no other character development and little plot development before Cain kills his brother. For Cain, his worth is calculated by the worth of sacrifice and what he brings to the table. He concludes that his younger brother is better than him. In a world where worth is determined by conduct and utility, Cain believes he is worth less. In the face of this existential threat, Cain reasons that by killing his brother he removes the competition and makes himself the most valuable.

When God confronts Cain and asks him where Abel is, Cain's reply is chilling: he asks, "am I my brother's keeper?"[498] Cain's question is shocking in its lack of any empathy, but it is a valid one if you ascribe to his world view. His question demands a reason for him to love Abel. It is fundamentally utilitarian. "What's in it for me? What purpose does Abel serve? Give me a reason to love my brother. Tell me something about Abel's biography that makes me his keeper." If dignity is not inherent, then neither Cain nor his brother has any inherent value. Under those circumstances, why can't Cain make the decision to shake off the impulse of empathy for something that works better for him? In a precursor of the worst despots in history, Cain rationalizes away the dignity of his fellow creature, kills him without empathy, and does so with the righteous confidence that Abel either deserved what he got or at least that Cain had no obligation to recognize his dignity.

God's love is existential. He does not place us in the scales and deem us useful or deserving. He loves His unfree creatures even though they are unfree. The fact that we screw up from time to time isn't even relevant. Even in the face of Cain's total failure to love for love's sake, God does not punish him, but rather reminds him that his decision to judge others and place them in the scales of utility will lead to Cain's unhappiness. Like his parents, he will be a restless, anxious wanderer. Ironically fearing that someone else will do to him what he just did to Abel, Cain bemoans his fate. And just as God busily knit clothing for Adam and Eve to mitigate their self-imposed shame, God puts a mark on Cain to warn others not to morally judge Cain. This is the leitmotif of Scripture: despite God's warnings, we assert our freedom and find only shame. God does what He can to cover our shame. In the fullness of time, the appearance of Jesus will complete the process an imbue us with dignity. The question is whether we will accept it and whether we will recognize and respect it in others.

Faith is not a mechanism for moral enforcement. Nor is faith an explanation for our inclination to love and feel empathy. Finally, faith is not the exclusive voice for universal forgiveness and abandonment of hate, as the atheistic determinists have made the same argument. However, while the New Atheists have argued forcefully against hate in the absence of free will, with a smirk they replace hate with a cold calculation of the needs of the collective. Faith alone challenges us to see ourselves and each other existentially; having inherited, inherent value.

Neither Liberal nor Conservative

Something like the liberal/conservative culture war going on today was underway in Jesus's time as well. The Pharisees were the equivalent of modern-day liberals; they were willing to more loosely interpret Scripture to include (as we've seen) an after-life. The Pharisees also evidently valued out-reach to non-Jews and had an active program of conversion. They were willing to break with tradition and buck the system and likely had an anti-establishment bias that would appeal to liberals.

The Sadducees, on the other hand, had a much more static view of Scripture and were clearly more closely associated with the Temple – so much so that they seem to disappear when the Temple was destroyed. They, evidently, had a pro-establishment bias that would appeal to modern conservatives. Both groups are cast as the villains of the Gospels and it is tempting to envision them as having callous disregard for the poor, outcast and sick in contrast to Jesus. But as we've seen, the poor were not always Jesus's first priority either. What united the Pharisees and the Sadducees against Jesus was the idea that God commanded, rewarded and punished while Jesus cast God as transcending purpose and morality. Although in our era the liberal and conservative sides of the political spectrum each call Jesus their own, Jesus seems to ascribe to both and neither; sometimes demonstrating a clear pro-establishment bias but just as often stridently criticizing the establishment.

In the Gospel of Matthew, during the Sermon on the Mount, Jesus declares an anthem to the establishment and traditional rules:

> Don't think that I came to destroy the law or the prophets. I didn't come to destroy, but to fulfill. For most certainly, I tell you, until heaven and earth pass away, not even one smallest letter or one tiny pen stroke shall in any way pass away from the law, until all things are accomplished.[499]

In the three Synoptic gospels, Jesus makes a show of being utterly unconcerned with overturning the establishment – even the establishment of the military occupiers of Israel. The Pharisees try to catch Jesus in hypocrisy by asking if people of faith should pay taxes to the Romans. They clearly expected Jesus to be politically partisan and to call for civil disobedience to the Roman occupiers; something they could have used to justify his arrest. Instead, Jesus indicates that his concerns transcend politics and invites his followers to "give back to Caesar what is Caesar's."[500] Earlier in the Gospel of Matthew, Jesus performs the miracle of producing money from a fish's mouth to pay his and Peter's Temple tax so as to avoid giving offense.[501] He even goes so far as to encourage his followers to obey the Pharisees' commands: "The scribes and the Pharisees sit on Moses's seat, so practice and observe whatever they tell you…." But, in contrast to his pro-establishment proclivities, he qualifies this in the same breath: "… but do not do what they do; they preach but they don't practice."[502] In the Gospel of Luke, Jesus personifies anti-establishment sentiments: "I came to throw fire on the earth. I wish it were already kindled. Do you think that I have come to give peace in the earth? I tell you, no, but rather division."[503]

In all four gospels, Jesus overturns the money changers' tables in a zealous rage. This story is well loved by both sides of the political spectrum. On the one hand, Jesus is defending the sanctity of the Temple and upholding a sense of the sacred and traditional. On the other hand, he is exposing and criticizing the establishment, shaming even the priests for making the

Temple a consumerist enterprise.[504] Jesus espoused a vision of God that transcended and even contradicted liberal and conservative assumptions of the time, and continues to be counter-cultural today. We assume the great moral and political controversy of our day is whether we should be pro-establishment conservatives or anti-establishment liberals. The issue that Jesus, and indeed all of Scripture addresses is much more important than political considerations. In fact, the enduring question is whether we will continue to see individuals as inherently valuable or whether we will see each other as only as valuable as our contribution to society. Will we value each other existentially as a community of the children of God, or as a utilitarian means to a collective end?   Ironically, both conservatives and liberals perceive God through a moral lens. Both are ultimately Platonically dualistic; equating God with the command to engage in good, socially useful behavior in exchange for reward or love or the avoidance of punishment. Liberals like to read the Beatitudes and the story of Lazarus as the divine celebration of poverty and the dire critique of the establishment and the wealthy. Conservatives admire the Beatitudes for the imperatives that they see there – the traditional commands to be addressed and fulfilled. The Beatitudes and the story of Lazarus are meant as a rejection of the idea that wealth is a blessing from God and poverty is a curse, to affirm that God is not the dispenser of good and bad fortune, karma, or reward and punishment. Liberalism and conservativism tend to conspire to actually reverse the meaning and re-assert God's role as commander, rewarder and punisher - God as the Form of Good – and place all of faith in direct conflict with behavioral science. Making faith about God's moral commands is a comfortable place; our natural desire to hate the freeloader is satisfied and confirmed. On the other hand, we are left to wonder what is so counter-cultural about Jesus's message if it is all about being a good person. How are Christians distinguished from our secular brothers and sisters of both sides of the political spectrum who most often act just as morally, charitably, and kindly as we do? It renders our faith lukewarm and insipid. By adopting this Manichean view of God, we use God's name to command moral behavior, which seems laudable, but it inevitably leads us to condemn and divide in God's name. Faith is counter-cultural not because it is ultra-conservative or ultra-liberal, and is not counter-cultural because it imposes the harshest rules or the harshest social criticism or the harshest punishment. It is counter-cultural because it is an affirmation of God's adoption of us as His children and all practical, utilitarian concerns take a back seat.

Religion is not Dangerous

The arguments advanced by the New Atheists against the existence of God are not new. What is new is the vehemence of their rhetoric. In his vitriolic book, *The End of Faith: Religion, Terror and the Future of Reason*, Sam Harris insists that "a glance at history, or at the pages of any newspaper, reveals that ideas that divide one group of human beings from another, only to unite them in slaughter, generally have their roots in religion."[505] Harris does not distinguish between violent extremists and moderates. He believes that religious moderation comes from our failure to read Scripture in its entirety. If we only knew what the Bible said, Harris argues, we would be obligated to punish children who fail to worship God by stoning them to death.[506] The development of chemical, biological and nuclear weapons of mass destruction has made continued tolerance of faith untenable. Harris seeks to prevent the destruction of the world, literally, by igniting a conceptual revolution to finally end faith.[507]

Harris examines the historical record and finds that religion is at the explicit root of many of the world's most recent conflicts, including the conflicts between Israelis and Palestinians, the Yugoslav Wars, the Troubles in Northern Ireland, and the Sudanese Civil Wars. This is, at best, a selective reading of history as each of these conflicts had multiple roots including ethnic, political and colonial ones that by most accounts were more responsible for the underlying conflict than the religious one. Of the conflicts that harnessed the power and authority of nations to kill millions, one needs to go back over three hundred fifty years to the Thirty Years War to find one that was triggered by overtly religious strife. The American Civil War, World War I, World War II, Korea, Vietnam, which are together responsible for many tens of millions of deaths, were not religious conflicts. The Cold War – the only instance outside of World War II where the use of weapons of mass destruction was actually threated, was a secular war. Countless violent deaths occur each year between individuals across the United States and the globe which are not religious fights but occur despite faith and because faith and the message of faith were not strong enough. Harris asserts in the alternative that some of the bloodiest regimes of the modern era - those led by Mao, Stalin and Hitler - deserve to be considered 'religious.' Harris argues that Stalin and Mao's policies amounted to a "political religion" because they were "cultic and irrational."[508] His placement of the Third Reich in the religious column is just as ephemeral. According to Harris, the Holocaust resulted from a *religious* loyalty to Hitler together with an orthodoxy of racial purity that was a "direct inheritance from medieval Christianity." This is, of course, a stretch of ludicrous proportions as each of these regimes was, in fact, either officially atheist or openly hostile to faith.

To say that religion is dangerous is hyperbole at best. It is certainly not scientific objectivity. Atheism, in its short time on the global stage and with its relatively minuscule following, has a vastly disproportionate amount of blood on its hands. But in fairness, what motivated the worst of the modern totalitarian regimes to mass murder was not atheism on its own but a tendency, inspired by atheistic determinism, to see human dignity as something granted by society and therefore renegotiable if it is not socially expedient rather than something endowed by the divine and indelible. Being an atheistic determinist regime doesn't make you bad, but it does change your concept of rights from something inherent and inalienable in the individual person to something utilitarian and very much less than inherent. This is why both religious and non-religious people are wary of determinism and the utilitarianism that inevitably follows from it. It is associated with the worst human impulses to social design including the Darwin-inspired eugenics programs of the 1930s in the United States and Nazi Germany which saw humanity as a mere raw material for social improvement.

The totalitarian regimes of the last century did not act with zealous religious hate but something much creepier: dispassionate confidence that they had shaken off the sentimental dogma of faith and were doing the hard, dirty work of pursuing a modern, scientific, or political ethic. They were doing what they had to do for social expediency. All of these regimes would point directly to the influence of social science and political science as the inspiration for their most murderous policies. Heinrich Himmler publicly acknowledged the Nazi policy of the extermination of the Jewish people in a speech to the SS in October of 1943. He conceded that perhaps their actions ran against their own empathetic instincts, but social expediency demanded them. This is not hate. It is cold, calculating and - although twisted - reasoned argument for genocide. He marveled that they had remained "decent" through it all:

I am now referring to the evacuation of the Jews, the extermination of the Jewish people. It's one of those things that is easily said: 'The Jewish people are being exterminated', says every party member, 'this is very obvious, it's in our program, elimination of the Jews, extermination, we're doing it, hah, a small matter.' And then they turn up, the upstanding 80 million Germans, and each one has his decent Jew. They say the others are all swines, but this particular one is a splendid Jew. But none has observed it, endured it. Most of you here know what it means when 100 corpses lie next to each other, when there are 500 or when there are 1,000. To have endured this and at the same time to have remained a decent person — with exceptions due to human weaknesses — has made us tough, and is a glorious chapter that has not and will not be spoken of. Because we know how difficult it would be for us if we still had Jews as secret saboteurs, agitators and rabble-rousers in every city, what with the bombings, with the burden and with the hardships of the war. If the Jews were still part of the German nation, we would most likely arrive now at the state we were at in 1916 and 17.[509]

Note the total discordance with the dialogue between Abraham and God at Sodom. If Himmler was asked if he would spare, for the sake of a few, a people who he imagined in his venomous mind had committed crimes, the answer would clearly have been a cold "no." Faith done wrong is scary. But atheistic determinism done right and followed to its logical conclusion is even scarier. The atheistic Khmer Rouge, in its desire to create a utopian agrarian communist society, famously adopted as its creed, "To keep you is no benefit. To destroy you is no loss." It is the ultimate utilitarian conception of human dignity.

Contrasted to the creed of the Khmer Rouge, God's creed is "Behold, I have engraved you on the palms of my hands."[510]

It is practically cliché to say science cannot account for human meaning. But any value system that says it dismisses the divine because it is invisible and unmeasurable can, and perhaps must, eventually dismiss human dignity as well. Without some sort of spirituality, science will have no way of establishing human dignity. It has innumerable ways of measuring us and telling us how we are different, but cannot distinguish whether those differences are relevant or not. A scientific utopia is a moral hell.

Animal Farm

The action in George Orwell's 1946 book, *Animal Farm,*[511] occurs on a farm in the English countryside owned by human beings and populated by talking pigs, horses, goats, dogs and other animals. Mr. Jones, the owner of the farm, has fallen on hard times, drowns his worries in alcohol, and habitually neglects the animals. Old Major, an old boar looked up to by the other animals, has a strange dream one night and calls a meeting of the farm animals to describe it. In a rousing speech, Old Major rallies the animals to throw off the tyranny of the human beings who enslave them and operate the farm as a socialist utopia, in which the product of the animals' labor is their own. He then teaches the animals a song, the lyrics of which came to him in his dream. *The Beasts of England* is a patriotic call to arms against tyranny, and all the animals, carried away in excitement, belt it out with gusto. Old Major dies a few days later, but as he intended, his dream lives on. It is generally accepted among the animals that the pigs are the smartest animal among them. Two pigs, Napoleon and Snowball, elaborate on the basic principles of Animalism imparted by the late Old Major. Shortly thereafter, after a particularly bad bender, Mr. Jones fails to feed the animals for several days. In desperation, one of the cows breaks open a storage shed and the animals help themselves to the feed. Jones and his human henchmen try to restore order and whip the animals out. The animals, as much to their own surprise as the humans', reflexively fight back and successfully drive the human beings out of the farm. The farm theirs, the animals set out the inalterable laws that will govern their community. The Seven Commandments are written on the side of a barn.[512] They are:

---

1. Whatever goes upon two legs is an enemy.
2. Whatever goes upon four legs, or has wings, is a friend.
3. No animal shall wear clothes.
4. No animal shall sleep in a bed.
5. No animal shall drink alcohol.
6. No animal shall kill another animal.
7. All animals are equal.

The animals, other than the pigs, had difficulty mastering reading and so Snowball further reduced the seven commandments to one manifesto which subsumed all the other commandments within it: "Four legs good, two legs bad." This was easily memorized and the sheep grew fond of bleating this commandment over and over again.

But things start going awry pretty fast. When two of the dogs have puppies, Napoleon whisks them away from their mothers so that he can educate them in a secluded place in the barn. Milk from the cows and apples from the field are soon distributed exclusively to the pigs putatively so that they can be healthy and energetic in their leadership of the other animals. A dispute arises between Snowball and Napoleon and Napoleon's plans with regard to the puppies becomes clear when they, now full grown dogs, attack and expel Snowball from the farm, leaving Napoleon in exclusive control. Napoleon consolidates his authority and outlaws the weekly communal discussion of policy. Even some of the pigs are dismayed but they are cowed by the growling dogs and the incessant bleating of the Animalist manifesto by the sheep essentially ends discussion. Suddenly the pigs move into Mr. Jones's abandoned house and, the other animals learn, sleep in the beds. The animals look back at the seven unalterable commandments, but discover they were not that unalterable. Someone has revised the language to say that, "No animal shall sleep in a bed *with sheets.*" One by one, the pigs violate and revise the commandments until they are wearing clothes, drinking alcohol, and arrange for one of the horses to be sold for glue. The farm animals work hard for the improvement of the farm and to bring in harvests, but their lifestyles never improve and the unspoken suspicion is that the pigs are syphoning off all the profits. Finally, one day the pigs emerge from Mr. Jones's house walking awkwardly on two legs.

The sheep, having been re-educated, bleat a new manifesto to drown out any protest: "four legs good, two legs better!" And the final commandment on the barn has been re-written to say that all animals are equal but some animals are more equal than others."

Animal Farm and the Slow Erosion of Human Dignity

A spat arose between Horsemen of the New Atheism, Daniel C. Dennett and Sam Harris revolving around whether the fact that we have purely material bodies subject to causal, deterministic forces leaves any room to believe that we nonetheless have something close enough to free will to be worth wanting. Harris felt that any backsliding on this issue ("compatibilism") was a distraction not worth discussing and ultimately damaging to the cause. Dennett disagreed, and asserted that what we think of, and value as freedom is really the ability to reflect on, represent, and defend our reasons for believing things or acting in a certain way.[513] To be "free" in this manner of speaking means to be persuadable by reasons, well informed of the nature of reality, and capable of realizing when we are being manipulated.[514] As an example of the last, Dennett recalls an episode of the television show, Candid Camera, in which the host, Allen Funt, placed an umbrella stand with useless pieces of steel tubing in a department store with the sign "50% off. Today only!"[515] Several people bought them and Funt entertained his television audience by asking the purchasers why they would do such an irrational thing. For Dennett, these customers were displaying a lack of freedom that would have been avoidable if they had been nurtured in a different way. This is not freedom from causality *per se* because, for Dennett, "A proper human self is the largely unwitting creation of an interpersonal design process in which we encourage young children to become communicators and in particular, to join our practice of asking for and giving reasons, and then reasoning about what to do and why."[516] In other words, whether we are ultimately "free" by Dennett's definition, is nonetheless a product of our nature and nurture. So far, I can't disagree with Dennett. But Dennett does not attribute any sort of inherent dignity to this exercise of "freedom" which is lucky because many of us would not achieve it, whether as a result of mental handicap or educational insufficiencies.[517] Such a theory would put Dennett in some very ugly philosophical company as we have already explored. Indeed, Dennett seems outright allergic to notions of dignity, and sees them as nefarious. Dennett presumes that any concept of dignity cannot be inherent but must rely on a capacity for moral responsibility. He sees our desire for inherent dignity as founded on "darker reasons" and "bloodthirsty elements" – the evolved desire to see the freeloader punished and ourselves vindicated.[518]

One can be fairly certain that as one of the Horsemen of the New Atheism, Dennett confidently sees faith as misinformation and a failure of freedom rather than a sensitivity to a transcendent reality. Does this make faith one of "those backward states of society" that for Mill justified a despotic intervention? Probably nothing so heavy-handed. Dennett would likely like to see memetic engineering used to remove faith from human culture.[519] Fellow Horseman of the New Atheism, Richard Dawkins, first used the word "meme" in *The Selfish Gene*[520] to mean the packets of cultural information that self-replicate and are passed among human beings almost like genes, such as a tune, fashions fads, and ideas. Some memes are naturally predisposed to survival and some more inclined to die out quickly; sometimes they change in the course of transmission. The meme for faith, naturally, is held up for particularly harsh criticism by Dawkins.[521] Dennett envisions society "no longer bound by the inefficient, wasteful, mindless trial and error of natural selection" of memes, but one of "intelligent (re)-design."[522] Dennett finds the utopian possibilities intriguing, but is at least momentarily circumspect about the Orwellian nature of the enterprise:

> One wouldn't want to tamper carelessly with that set of practices, the fruits of thousands of years of genetic and cultural evolution. It could undo a lot of valuable R&D … On the other hand, if done with discernment and understanding, some tampering could strengthen and enhance those designed, making up for missed opportunities or blurred perceptions. Moreover, some deliberate intervention might help extinguish any unfortunate variants of our practices that can be seen to be self-defeating.

His circumspection seems to abandon him, however, a few pages later when he ambiguously declares that "The field of public health expanded to include cultural health will be the greatest challenge of this century."[523]

If our opinions and desires are the product of nature and nurture and we have no inherent dignity, then perhaps it makes sense to allow a collective to re-engineer our opinions and desires to maximize well-being. If we have inherent dignity, however, then the fact that two people might prefer that our opinions and desires be re-engineered does not give them the authority to do so. Just as the science of genetics led to eugenics until its association with Nazi Germany extinguished interest, so it appears the science of memetics will lead to what I will call "eumemetics." Certainly, human beings have long made decisions about with whom to have children based on some broad brushstrokes understanding that their chosen mate's genetic lineage will be tied up with their own in their children. There is something far creepier when those choices are made politically with the authority and enforcement of the state. So also, we have long understood that we influence each other for better or for worse in our every interaction. Certainly a scientific approach to that process might be more efficient, but it ought to give us even greater pause.

Whatever hint of hesitancy Dennett may feel about engineering faith and other impulses deemed dangerous or wasteful out of society is not shared by Harris, who is much blunter. Harris sees no moral difference between violent extremist faith and faith that is moderate and non-violent. Religious tolerance represents the fundamental danger. He writes:

> One of the central themes of this book, however, is that religious moderates are themselves bearers of a terrible dogma: they imagine the path to peace will be paved once each of us has learned to respect the unjustified beliefs of others. I hope to show that the very ideal of religious tolerance – born of the notion that every human being should be free to believe whatever he wants about God – is one of the principal forces driving us to the abyss.[524]

Much attention has been lavished on the ambiguous (but in almost every case, deist) religious beliefs of the Founding Fathers. But it bears recognition that although some of the authors of the Bill of Rights may have been non-Christian, it was a nation that was and remains overwhelming Christian that adopted as law, protected and cherished notions of religious freedom for hundreds of years. Their faith not only included room to tolerate other beliefs, but demanded it. There are always exceptions and places where clearly we could have done better, but the overwhelming tone has been one of religious tolerance and inclusion. In pursuing this principal of justice, even the most insignificant expressions of faith have often been expunged from public spaces to avoid giving the slightest of offense. But the rules written on the side of the barn are changing already. Harris hopes to enforce freedom *from* religion, and mocks the idea that every human being should be free to believe whatever he wants about God (except him, presumably). To the extent such a project is successful, it may protect us from terrorism and that may well be a measurable good. But we will have allowed something immeasurable but potentially of immeasurable value to be engineered out of us.

As *Animal Farm* closes, the other animals sneak up to Mr. Jones's house, where the pigs and some humans from neighboring farms are drinking and toasting their newfound common interests over an evening game of cards. The animals find it difficult to distinguish the faces of the pigs from the faces of the human beings and they realize they have traded one slavery for another. The New Atheists believe that faith enslaves us to a commanding God who metes out reward and punishment through allegiance to foolish superstition. In fact, faith is the story of how God frees us finally and completely with the language of Incarnation, Redemption and Salvation not to command as slaves, but to wash *our* feet and welcome us as His Chosen People. This is freedom worth wanting. We are valued existentiality, not for what we can do for God, but simply by virtue of our status as members of His family. We are made in His image and He chose to be made in ours. We could have expected that God would free us from slavery and place us under His own power, but He clearly doesn't – He calls us "friends."[525] He relinquishes and destroys the master/slave relationship. The New Atheists demand that we declare faith dangerous and abandon what cannot be proven by science.

They offer, in return, a world safe from terrorism and other religiously inspired evils. No person of faith in a transcendent God can accept such a bargain regardless of its implications. But even the practical price of such a bargain is high because it exchanges inherent dignity for enslavement to utility.

Esau and Jacob: Selling Our Birthright

Jacob, soon to be renamed Israel, is the second born son of Isaac. In fact, the story tells us he is named "Jacob" or "Ya'aqob" because he was holding onto his twin brother Esau's heel or "aqeb" as they were born.[526] Because he is second in line, Jacob would not ordinarily receive the benefit of the covenant promised to his father Isaac by God. When they are young adults Esau has taken his birthright for granted and Jacob exploits him:

Jacob boiled stew. Esau came in from the field, and he was famished. Esau said to Jacob, "Please feed me with some of that red stew, for I am famished." Therefore his name was called Edom.

Jacob said, "First, sell me your birthright."

Esau said, "Behold, I am about to die. What good is the birthright to me?"

Jacob said, "Swear to me first."

He swore to him. He sold his birthright to Jacob. Jacob gave Esau bread and lentil stew. He ate and drank, rose up, and went his way.

So Esau despised his birthright.[527]

We have it within our power, and we have the natural inclination, to re-enslave ourselves and each other for virtually nothing and yoke ourselves to usefulness and utility. We lose our birthright not by a violent confrontation, but with our insipid consent. We can commit ourselves to a purely reasonable view of humanity, and discover that it is as plastic and changeable as every other human impulse. We can define ourselves by our position on a moral spectrum, or by what we do rather than who we are. We can erode our dignity and our freedom with even thinner pretexts and find ourselves in another generation or two with no awareness whatsoever of our divine inherence and divine dignity. Paul, again writing to the Galatians, seemed to urge them not to re-enslave themselves after being freed from "elemental principles" which, I allow myself to imagine, is the lack of dignity that arises from a lack of free will without intervention by God:

But I say that so long as the heir is a child, he is no different from a bondservant, though he is lord of all, but is under guardians and stewards until the day appointed by the father. So we also, when we were children, were held in bondage under the elemental principles of the world. But when the fullness of the time came, God sent out his Son, born to a woman, born under the law, that he might redeem those who were under the law, that we might receive the adoption of children. And because you are children, God sent out the Spirit of his Son into your hearts, crying, "Abba, Father!" So you are no longer a bondservant, but a son; and if a son, then an heir of God through Christ. However, at that time, not knowing God, you were in bondage to those who by nature are not gods. But now that you have come to know God, or rather to be known by God, why do you turn back again to the weak and miserable elemental principles, to which you desire to be in bondage all over again?[528]

Conclusion

Faith's decision to cast the God of Jacob as a synonym for Plato's Form of the Good led to our re-enslavement. While Scripture is consistent with the idea that we don't have free will, but that we have dignity anyway as God's adopted children, Plato's philosophy was absolutely dependent on the idea that we have free will, and any dignity and worth we achieve is through good behavior. This hybridization of faith required that we abandon the idea that God is sympathetic and moved to love for us, in favor of a god who is unmovable by definition. It also led to the idea that God is responsible for suffering and maybe even imposes suffering in response to our moral failings. Worse, it led us right back to what the Garden story warned us against:

placing each other on a moral spectrum that inevitably leads to division and hate. It caused us to understand God in terms of command, reward and punishment and to abandon the idea that God is unconditionally loving and transcends purpose and morality. It even caused us to believe in two gods of almost equal power in eternal conflict over our souls. It deprived faith of its power to comfort and to defend the dignity of individuals.

Something is changing, however. Our willingness as a people of faith to abide by this hybridization of Christianity and Platonism seems to be waning. The New Atheists are insistent that faith itself be stamped out. However, few are heeding that call. Instead, people of faith in vast numbers are making the decision not to participate in public expressions of faith and faith traditions. So far, this book has focused almost exclusively on faith and said almost nothing about religion. That will be the subject of the next and last chapter.

Chapter Seven

The Case for Organized Religion

Thus says the Lord of hosts: "Old men and women, each with staff in hand, shall again sit in the streets of Jerusalem. The city shall be filled with children playing in her streets." Thus says the Lord of hosts: "Even if this should seem impossible in the eyes of the remnant of this people, shall it in those days be impossible in my eyes also?" says the Lord of hosts. "I will not deal with the remnant of this people as in formers days, says the Lord of hosts, for it is the seedtime of peace: the vine shall yield its fruit, the land shall bear its crops, and the heavens shall give their dew; all these things I will have the remnant of the people possess."[529]

Religion, Not Faith, Is Diminishing

It is widely assumed that faith is collapsing. In fact, although the trend against faith is negative, atheists still represent an extremely small percentage of the population. According to the Pew Research Center's 2014 U.S. Religious Landscape Study,[530] which surveyed more than 35,000 Americans about their religious affiliations, the percentage of adults who identified itself as Christian decreased between 2007 and 2014 by almost 8% from 78.4% to 70.6%. In the same period, atheism went from just 1.6% to a still small 3.1% (and within the study's margin for error).[531] One can fairly assume that the New Atheists' brand of atheism, characterized by outright hostility to faith, is a small fraction of even this small number. Agnosticism rose from 2.4% to four percent in the same seven years. The big news in the study was in those who identified as "nothing in particular" – the "nones" - which rose from 12.1% to an even more sizable 15.8%. This represents by far the largest net gain among all affiliations. It is a consolation to note, however, that many of these individuals are neither atheists nor agnostics and that in an interim 2012 study over thirty percent of this group said that religion was still either "very" or "somewhat" important to them. Over half described themselves as "religious" or "spiritual but not religious" and sixty-eight percent of this group responded that they either absolutely believed in God or a universal spirit or believed but were less certain. Twenty-one percent reported they prayed daily.[532] Even among those who affiliate with a particular denomination, however, participation in weekly religious services is fairly weak. Among those who identify with the Protestant community, attendance has remained steady but at rate of less than fifty percent.[533] In Catholicism, however, where rates of Mass attendance exceeded sixty percent in the 1970s, rates of attendance are now at less than forty percent.[534] Even still, Catholics are praying at least weekly at a rate of eighty-six percent, and Protestants exceed even this extraordinary number, topping out at ninety percent.[535] This represents a small *increase* from seven years ago for both denominations. So, while faith is holding its own, those who have decided to practice their faith alone - the "spiritual but not religious" - is growing steadily. Clearly, faith - belief in God and the desire to personally engage with God - is not deteriorating. Rather, it is religion – the desire to engage with God as part of a community - that is in bad shape.

Why is Affiliation Ending?

From its earliest days, thanks at least in part to the influence of Platonism, Christianity has held two competing concepts of God. On the one hand, God forgave everything and required nothing. His love was unconditional, unbounded, unearned and freely given. Jesus was our Redeemer and Savior. God created humanity not to serve any purpose except to be the objects of divine love. On the other hand, God was just. God would accept repentance late in the day, but repentance had to come before the final accounting to avoid retribution. God was loving, but He was a harsh master and demanded a return on His investment. God invited all to the banquet, but would deal harshly with those refused to wear their wedding garment. Jesus was not so much a Redeemer and Savior by his status as the Incarnation of God, but rather a divine moral teacher and provider of a roadmap to self-redemption and self-rescue with good behavior, charitable giving and development of talents for the common good. God created humanity to be tested, commanded, measured and appropriately rewarded or punished. These two concepts of God contradicted one another. As a result, Christianity made acceptance of paradox a virtue. This book's central theme is that science and philosophy's conclusion that we don't have free will reveals that this second concept of God must be a fraud – a hybrid of the God of Abraham and the god of Plato. Of course, the first concept of God – the transcendent, mystical, existentialist God - is hard to talk about. By its nature, transcendence is difficult, mysterious, and other-worldly. By its nature, transcendence doesn't lend itself to everyday language. The second concept of God is much easier to talk about. Our evolved brains, particularly the male brain that almost exclusively defined religion for centuries, and our Western culture and mentality, naturally crave clearly defined goals, metrics for success, and reward and punishment. Furthermore, Plato's theory of the Form of Good did double-duty: in addition to allowing us to embrace our desire to be commanded, rewarded and punished it suggested a proof of God's existence using the physics of the day. There was no need to challenge ourselves to turn around our natural way of thinking – it was all very easy. It was seductive to believe that we were the objects of God's love because we earned it – we obeyed His commands and, when we fell short, knew the formula of repentance to get back in His favor. Contrary to the protestations of the New Atheism, organized religion rarely demanded hate or harsh punishment - at least not beyond anything secular society was calling for. It was not the motivating idea behind the Holocaust, the Great Leap Forward, the Killing

Fields or the Stalinist Purges. But with its focus on morality, faith rendered itself insipid. Rather than exploring faith as a transcendent concern, religion became an exploration of, and exhortation to moral duties. Whether or not Christianity consistently met its own high moral standards is not the point. In those places and times where prosperity and political stability led to circumstances where moral challenges were small and suburban, religion simply adjusted itself to command small, suburban morality: charity, the development of talents, humility and modesty. For centuries, organized religion set itself apart as being the only institution that spoke with moral authority and that had as its principal aim the moral development of its members. There was no pressure to challenge this status quo. People of faith were happy to attend weekly religious services. Here, their children would hear regular moral lessons which, if they were taught elsewhere, were often taught in a context of religion. At weekly services, people of faith might hear something that inspired them to great moral heights or at least invigorated their ongoing efforts at self-improvement. Maybe more cynically, they might imagine their neighbors being morally shaped by what they heard and themselves as morally justified.

It is that exclusive nature of religion's hold on morality that has changed in recent decades and especially in the last two decades in which organized religion has suffered so many losses. Our moral narrative in most faith communities is that the moral climate is deteriorating and greater and greater immorality is tolerated. In fact, it seems to me the opposite is the case. We live in a recently inaugurated hyper-moral age.

In 1980, CNN first went on air. It heralded an age of twenty-four-hour news. Prior to that, the network anchors generally had half an hour a night in which to summarize the events of the day. Obviously with such a short timeframe, and the expectation of objectivity and the deliberate avoidance of sensationalism, the news was largely delivered without moral commentary. With twenty-four-hour news, and with competition as cable news programs proliferated, those self-imposed restrictions disappeared. For the past three decades, moral failings (and to a lesser extent, moral successes), are studied in excruciating detail with multiple commentators rewinding the tape indefinitely all day and all night. In 1988, the Writers Guild of America, the union responsible for generating scripts for network television, went on a lengthy five-month strike. Necessity breeds invention and, deprived of dramatic scripts, the networks embraced a new genre – reality television. Shows featuring people in real-life stressful or competitive conditions proved to be endlessly entertaining. Shows like MTV's *The Real World*, and later, *Survivor*, allowed a national audience to sit in collective moral judgment of the often outrageous conduct of these newly minted reality television stars. In 1990, perhaps capitalizing on the public's clear fascination with morality, reward and punishment as demonstrated by the cable news and reality television, the *Law and Order* television show first aired (a series, in which, incidentally, my aunt-in-law, Carol, appeared several times). This one show was wildly successful and had real staying power. It became a franchise and spawned a new genre of crime fiction and non-fiction on cable television that persists and continues to flourish to this day. At about the same time *Law and Order* first aired, the internet became widely available. About a decade later, in 2002, Friendster, the archetype for social media, went online and Facebook arose as its competition by 2004. Before this moment, if one wanted to express one's moral position to a large group of people and did not have access to a pulpit, the next best thing was a bumper sticker. If one had many strongly held moral views, one could have many bumper stickers. The natural limitations of this form of expression are obvious. But while a bumper sticker had to be smaller than a Tweet, a social media post (other than a Tweet) could be pages long, include professionally edited video, and could be directed to everyone's social circle immediately. It could even duplicate itself, go viral and reach millions within a few days. While eventually the back of even a large (usually late model) car can run out of room for additional bumper stickers, a social media page has unlimited capacity for moral opinions. And the expression of opinion is so easy! We can "like" something or scroll past it without a moment's reflection. In 2007, less than a decade ago and about the time Pew did its benchmark study of religious affiliation, Apple released the first iPhone. Although there were many precursors, the technological advance the iPhone represented, and its success and market penetration, were unsurpassed. Here was a device that moved internet connectivity from the desktop to our pockets and allowed near constant access to internet news and social media and the moral judgment that goes on there. Most of us now get alerted by our phones when something newsworthy happens, including from time to time, some moral failing by some individual half-way across the globe. It also put a video camera in every pocket connected to an eternal memory so any example of bad conduct can be recorded, shared and reviewed forever whether the subject is a misguided politician or a misguided teenager.

Moral disapproval and enforcement have been crowdsourced. Where once moral goading was confined to the pulpit, now it bombards us constantly. The vast majority of us willingly chooses every day to receive this bombardment. It demonstrates an almost unlimited appetite for moral judgment. The Tree of the Fruit of the Knowledge of Good and Evil can't pump out the fruit fast enough. But the standards for moral behavior are not becoming more relaxed with the proliferation of moral analysis and enforcement. If anything, they are becoming harsher and more unforgiving; the calls for blood and vengeance and justice on social media and cable news would be the envy of the most venomous fire and brimstone preacher. These new cultural forces certainly hold crime up for opprobrium but also punish all the traditional 'seven deadly sins' as avidly as any religious impulse ever did. God help he or she who is found guilty of lust, gluttony, greed, sloth, wrath, envy or pride. Those who fail to meet the accepted norm – either by liberal or conservative standards or both - are hounded to the ends of the earth. Moral sensitivities are on a hair trigger. Social media moves from moral outrage to moral outrage with regularity. And it's no wonder – to our primordial brains which don't distinguish between digital and reality, the moral outrage on our screens is happening in our presence. It calls to our evolved need to punish those who threaten our clan. Worse, it foments the powerful moral illusion that we must have an opinion ready for every controversy and that the collection of our opinions is our identity.

We tend to think about the decline in affiliation as being a problem confined to faith and arising from issues unique to faith - belief in the unprovable, and hope in the seemingly impossible. But the same fracturing that is occurring in religious affiliation is also occurring in political affiliation. In 2014, thirty-nine percent of Americans identified themselves as independents, which is the highest proportion in the seventy-five years of polling on the issue.[536] The same phenomenon is occurring in both politics and religion because both have positioned themselves principally as moral commentators. Both now find themselves outclassed in that category by technology.

In the last few decades as religion suffered massive losses there have been no new arguments against the existence of God. There has been no new general spiritual deterioration that causes people to fall away from religion. The New Atheists and their angry rejection of religion has remained a tiny movement. But in that time there has been a quiet, dispassionate but massive departure from religion. Organized religion is not suffering these losses because it is being too conservative or too liberal, or because science has disproven the reasons for faith. But for centuries organized religion has virtually ignored the transcendent God in favor of the commanding god and teaching that to be a good person is God's primary command. The problem is that the lesson was wholeheartedly accepted. For a generation we taught our children that all God wants is that they be good people. They are good people. And they see people around them with no faith who are just as good and charitable and kind as they are. And so the only reason we gave them to pay any attention to the divine has become irrelevant. Religion now finds itself in a position where it is competing in a vast moral marketplace and its product is almost indistinguishable from the products being offered by virtually everyone else.

As I argued in the previous chapter, genuine faith has a firm allegiance to certain moral positions, some of which are inconsistent with a purely secular morality. Faith in a transcendent God inevitably leads to the desire – not the command – to preserve and enhance the dignity of each of God's children and not treat them as tools of the collective. People of faith can't simply hand off the moral conversation to the secular world. But we cannot mistake faith's transcendent message for a moral one and expect to survive. Having told its members that faith is about being exhorted to be good, religion now sees its members leaving in droves now that they are being exhorted to be good throughout the day in far more compelling fashion. That God became incarnate to tell us to be good, use our talents, share and be humble makes faith a children's story. It should not surprise us that if we make faith a children's story, they will abandon it when they grow up. In fact, it may also be that more and more are leaving organized religion because the idea that it is about morality is so prevalent and unchallenged and they see that the morality encouraged by secular culture is less ambiguous and more consistent than the morality encouraged by their churches.

But faith was never about morality. Faith was about encountering the transcendent, mystical God Who knew that we were not morally autonomous but chose to love us anyway in an existential way – not because of what we can do for Him. Faith had warned us in the Garden not to presume moral autonomy, and in Moriah faith sought to eliminate once and for all the idea that we must please God with sacrifice and performance and burnish our biographies. And at the base of Sinai and again at the Cross, faith declared us the chosen, and finally the adopted sons and daughters of God and imbued us with divine dignity. But we didn't hear it. Our desire to judge the freeloader seduced us into accepting a concept of God alien to Scripture and more at home in ancient Athens. Science and philosophy, by asserting that we are not moral creatures, revealed that this hybrid god was a false god – an idol. It calls for us to return to relationship with the God of Abraham and illuminated the transcendent, mystical, existential, purposeless nature of that relationship – perhaps just in time. Karl Rahner, perhaps the most famous Catholic theologian of the last century, once said that, "the Christian of the future will be a mystic or will not exist at all."[537] People of faith have reflexively resisted the idea that we do not have free will because it seemed to explode a critical component of our understanding of God and a central message of Scripture. But I have argued that a lack of free will is not only compatible but in perfect harmony with faith and Scripture. Accepting this is nonetheless hard because it is hard to imagine that our personal relationship with God is purposeless and that we do not need to achieve any goal or serve any purpose. Jesus was not killed because he said we must be kind and loving to one another. He was killed because he said nothing we do or don't do will change our status as children of God, and no misfortune or good fortune is proof of the opposite. That is the challenge of faith – to accept the view that God commands nothing at all. The challenge of religion is even greater. When we gather together in groups in God's name, the temptation is practically overwhelming to assume that we must be there to accomplish some measurable benefit and achieve some practical goal. To be fair, religion has expressed God as a transcendent concern, but under the slightest pressure it allows itself to be beguiled into the language of command, reward and punishment and to become virtually synonymous with it. The advent of the hyper-moral age was inevitably going to devastate organized religion.

Liturgy

Abiding in God in solitude makes some sense to us. Sitting prayerfully with God for no particular reason and with no expectation of supernatural reward does not conflict with our expectations.   But where does organized religion fit in?   Didn't I say earlier that an I/Thou encounter with God is not possible for a group?   How can organized religion, which is by its nature so institutional, actively promote transcendence and mysticism, which are by their nature so non-institutional?   This is the question of the spiritual but not religious. Is anything lost by seeking God by one's self instead of in community?

Liturgy is public religious worship. The word "liturgy" comes from the Greek, "*leitos*" meaning "public" and "*ergos*", meaning performance, work or energy.[538] Liturgy, therefore, is fundamentally something performed not by oneself but by and in a community. Liturgy, not doctrine or a set of beliefs, is what fundamentally separates the religious from the 'spiritual but not religious.' If the expression of an individual's spirituality is limited to prayer, meditation, reflection or ritualism, without the participation of anyone else, they clearly have adopted a doctrine of some sort, but what they have rejected is liturgy. Christians often believe that to win back the 'spiritual but not religious', they must introduce them to spirituality, or make a good argument for the existence of God, or orchestrate their encounter with God. But this overlooks the fact that their audience already claims to be spiritual, and we have no reason to doubt them. What we need to do is not nearly as overwhelming or mystical a task as introducing the human to the divine. Rather, it is to simply make a good argument for liturgy and approaching God together.

Liturgy takes innumerable forms and I will define it very broadly to include anything done in the context of the sacred according to a shared ritual. Catholicism's strength is liturgy and it, along with Anglicanism and Lutheranism are sometimes considered 'liturgical' while others are considered 'non-liturgical.' I am making no such distinction here. Communal hymns, prayer, and sitting in silence in the context of the sacred all qualify as liturgical for my purposes. For Catholicism, the Mass includes two major liturgies: The Liturgy of the Word, in which the first and second readings are read, followed by the Gospel and the homily, and the Liturgy of the Eucharist, in which the gifts of bread and wine are presented and consecrated and communion is received. These are liturgies because they must be performed in community. Liturgies don't have to happen in the same geographic location to be considered public. The Liturgy of the Hours - the seven daily prayers of the Church - is considered a liturgy because members of the Church across the globe say the same prayers during the course of the day. Of course, there are less ancient expressions of faith shared with far smaller groups which are liturgies too, such as saying grace at meals, familial prayer, the innumerable household traditions that have gathered around the celebration of Christmas, and anything else that is the expression of faith that is shared among two or more people in deliberate community in the context of the sacred.

For generations, people of faith assumed that they were commanded by God to participate in their denomination's liturgies and that those who did would be rewarded, and those who did not would be punished or had to rely on God's mercy to overlook the failure. This perspective always had a fundamental problem in that it was clear that millions of God's children who never heard of the command would be consigned to, at best, a second rate relationship with God. The mercilessness of such a god contradicts what our deepest intuition of God tells us, and organized religion's failure to consistently contradict it because of its allegiance to Platonic free will is undoubtedly responsible for much of the flight from church pews. Theistic determinism makes this an even more stark issue. Even among those who had the opportunity to hear God's command to worship, how zealously they obeyed that command would depend not on free will but on the circumstances of their birth, upbringing and the experiences they may or may not have had in adulthood. A just God cannot reward or punish that behavior which could not be freely chosen. What we know about human behavior and the most basic concepts of fairness, definitively demonstrate that to participate in liturgy cannot be a command of God. God cannot reward or punish our impulse to worship, and God cannot be shamanistically compelled to do what we desire as a result our performing the right ritual. Religious institutions - by which I mean all of us and not just the clergy - have failed to answer the question, "why do liturgy?" Liturgy has become simply the framework from which we hang our good deeds rather than a transcendent concern.

Exodus

Before the escape from Egypt, biblical characters regularly built altars and engaged in ritualistic sacrifice, the most prominent being the near sacrifice of Isaac by Abraham in Moriah,[539] but there was no indication that they were conscious of binding themselves to a larger community through shared tradition or liturgy.[540] The first hint of communal observance of religious ritual is the artifice God instructs Moses to use to get the Israelites out of Egypt. Following God's instructions,

Moses tells Pharaoh the Israelites, as a group, must journey three days into the wilderness to make a sacrifice to God. Their intention is to abscond once they are far enough away to make their escape. Pharaoh doesn't buy it and makes the Israelites produce the same number of bricks but now, as punishment for Moses's impertinence, they must gather their own straw. Frustrated, Moses and God begin a program of essentially terrorizing the Egyptians with ever more annoying and finally deadly plagues. Of course, it is the death of the firstborn of Egypt that finally does the trick. Cleverly integrated into the instructions the Israelites receive to avoid being caught up in the divine carnage is the first detailed liturgy in the Bible. God gives Moses and Aaron detailed guidelines for that night and for the remembrance of Passover each year. Every household is to purchase a lamb and roast it (not boil it) and eat it with unleavened bread and staff in hand to recall their haste in leaving Egypt. The lamb's blood is smeared on the doorpost and lintels of the Israelites' homes to indicate which house God is to pass over in executing the plague. Exodus records simply that the people did as they were instructed.[541] Pharaoh succumbs and the Israelites make their escape.

Remember!

As the Israelites are fleeing, God keeps up the demand that they remember Passover, as if He is anxious that they not forget to do it. "This day shall be to you for a memorial, and you shall keep it a feast to God: throughout your generations you shall keep it a feast by an ordinance forever."[542] Three times,

Moses or God anticipates that the children of the Israelites in future generations will ask what the purpose of this liturgy is.[543] Moses will do it again as he prepares the Israelites for his death and their passage into the Promised Land.[544] In each instance, the answer is remembrance of God's rescue of His people. This is one of extremely infrequent moments where God connects a verbal transcript to liturgy.[545] In almost every other case, Biblical liturgy is non-verbal and expressed solely through physical acts. Another example is the *Shema* – the first words every member of the Jewish community is supposed to say at the beginning of the day, and the last words they are to say at the end of their day and end of their lives. As we saw in Chapter One, it begins "Hear, O Israel, the Lord is our God, the Lord is one."[546] Remarkably, even when there is an obligation to speak, it is an exhortation to listen to a reminder about our relationship to God! The message is the same: "Remember where you come from! Remember you are mine!" God is like a parent seeing his children leave home, knowing that by their nature they will inevitably define themselves by their standing in others' eyes and could wind up selling their birthright for nothing. "Remember who you are!" God cries insistently, "You are small, but you have incalculable dignity just by your status as a child of God!" "I don't know what life will bring you, but there is virtually no moral quandary you can't navigate and virtually nothing you can't endure if you only remember who you really are!"

This same plea that we remember our inherence is reflected as the tension mounts to a crescendo in the New Testament.

In the Gospels of Mark and Matthew, the dialogue at the Last Supper is remarkably brief: Jesus predicts his betrayal by Judas and then immediately institutes the central Christian liturgy: identifying himself with bread and wine to be consumed by his faithful.[547] It is the ultimate statement of irrevocable unity with the divine, but is virtually non-verbal. In Mark, Jesus consecrates the bread by saying simply, "Take, this is my body."[548] With the exception of Luke, in which Jesus deals with a spat among the apostles about which of them is greatest and predicts Peter's denial of him, there are no teachings or exhortations. As with the Creed, there is no moral dogma, but only a simple statement of our status as the vessels of divine dignity. Nothing is required of us. We are simply exhorted to remind ourselves who we are to God.

Scripture is replete with reminders and exhortations to be reminded of the indissoluble bond between God and humanity. God institutes the tradition of circumcision to remind Abraham's descendants of His covenant.[549] God places the rainbow in the clouds to remind Himself and as a sign to Noah's descendants of His covenant.[550] If the groundwork for encountering God can be laid in any organized fashion, it is to do the hard, counter-cultural work of reminding us, and helping our community remember, that we are not what we can do for God, and God is not what He can do for us. Liturgy reminds us of who we are.

Transcendence and Sacrament

When the Israelites reach Sinai for the climax of the Old Testament story, the action is interrupted by immensely detailed and complex instructions for liturgy. This lesson in transcendence occupies so much of, and such a prominent position in arguably the most important book of the Old Testament, that its importance cannot be doubted. It is wedged right in the middle of the story of the Ten Commandments and right in the middle of the action. When the Israelites reach Mount Sinai, Moses goes up the mountain to receive God's commands. He returns and relates them to the Israelites verbally, and they enthusiastically agree to follow them. He writes them down in a book, offers animal sacrifices on an altar, and reads them to the people from the book. Again, the Israelites enthusiastically agree. God then invites Moses up the mountain again to receive the commandments on stone tablets that God had apparently already prepared. It is during this absence that the Israelites grow impatient, fashion the idolatrous golden calf and violate the commandment of God. Moses goes up, but instead of simply receiving the tablets and coming back down, God engages in an extraordinarily lengthy forty-day instruction on how to build the Ark of the Covenant, a table for the Ark to sit upon, dishes for incense and food, a six-branch menorah, the Tabernacle Tent, a veil to separate the merely holy parts of the Tent and ultimately the Temple from the holiest (behind which John the Baptists father would encounter the angel and which will be torn in two at the moment of Jesus's death), a mobile altar, and a mobile court in which the Tabernacle Tent is to be placed. He also gives Moses instructions for the construction of the Mercy Seat – a lid for the Ark of the Covenant made of pure gold and featuring a pair of cherubim facing one another with wings outstretched. This was to be God's seat when He spoke to Moses in the Tent.   Outside the Tent, the Israelites were to place an enormous bronze bowl or lavar so that the priests could purify themselves before entering the Tent[551] All are to be fashioned of the finest and most expensive materials. This fully occupies Chapters 25, 26, and 27 of Exodus. The next chapter is a detailed instruction on how to fashion the vestments Aaron, who is to be consecrated as the high priest, is to wear and pass down to his successors. The level of detail of this wardrobe would bore even Tim Gunn and, again, the materials are of the highest caliber. Chapter 29 describes how exactly Aaron and his sons are to be consecrated for service as priests and how the Tabernacle is to be consecrated for God's presence. The materials for Aaron's consecration include a young bull and two rams, unleavened bread, unleavened cakes, unleavened wafers - all, of course, made from the finest ingredients. Most of these are incinerated in front of the tent or outside of the camp. Aaron and his sons receive what remains to eat, but whatever they don't finish in a single day is also incinerated.[552] The Tabernacle itself is consecrated daily with a lamb in the morning and another in the afternoon so something is always burning in front of the Tabernacle. At the end of this chapter, God reveals what is received in exchange for all of this effort. Stone will not be turned into bread and misfortune will not be avoided, and God will not guarantee our right conduct or right belief. He will simply be present to them:

It shall be a continual burnt offering throughout your generations at the door of the Tent of Meeting before the Lord, where I will meet with you, to speak there to you. There I will meet with the children of Israel; and the place shall be sanctified by my glory. I will sanctify the Tent of Meeting and the altar. I will also sanctify Aaron and his sons to minister to me in the priest's office. I will dwell among the children of Israel, and will be their God. They shall know that I am the Lord their God, who brought them out of the land of Egypt, that I might dwell among them: I am the Lord their God[553]

The story of Judas's reaction to the woman who pours an expensive alabaster jar of oil over Jesus instead of selling it and giving the proceeds to the poor is almost certainly intended to trigger a memory of this part of Exodus with its extravagant waste. Rather than providing a moral lesson, Exodus deliberately ignores questions of morality and provides a lesson in transcendence. The extravagance of the Exodus rituals is not an expression of a primordial belief that the best crops and animals have to be fed to God. Rather, like the alabaster jar, it is a statement that encounter with God, although it provides no measurable profit, is nonetheless of extraordinary value. As Jesus asserted to Satan: man does not live by bread alone.

When we re-cast organized religion as a mechanism for social improvement and the vehicle for charitable works, we miss the point entirely. When we decry the ornate churches and seemingly purposeless ritual of organized religion, and when we wonder whether we could be doing more social good in that hour of time, we do what Judas and Satan did; when we demand that faith produce bread we reject the transcendent value of faith. *Ironically, to make organized religion more meaningful, we have to make it less purposeful.*

The theme persists into Leviticus where the punishment for fraud or robbery is established:

> He [the robber or fraudster] shall restore it in full, and shall add a fifth part more to it. He shall return it to him to whom it belongs in the day of his being found guilty. He shall bring his trespass offering to God: a ram without defect from the flock, according to your estimation, for a trespass offering, to the priest. The priest shall make atonement for him before God, and he will be forgiven concerning whatever he does to become guilty.[554]

This is not the brutal justice we are used to seeing in Biblical narratives. A twenty percent penalty if you manage to get caught and prosecuted in the era before fingerprinting would hardly provide a disincentive to engage in this serious, violent crime. But the goal of the law is not to eliminate robbery, but rather is to eliminate the guilt of the person who engaged in it and short-circuit the moral narrative of blame and hate that we are inclined to attach to robbery. Here again is the acknowledgement that we are not morally autonomous and that our worth is unaffected by our behavior. We are not our last bad act. Faith is not about morality.

The leitmotif of transcendence is shot through all of Exodus in the *ever-present dual themes of Asymmetry and Proximity*. That our relationship with God is asymmetrical is an inescapable fact. Our most basic intuition of God is, as Rudolf Otto noted, a realization of our creatureliness in the face of His vertigo-inducing absolute and overwhelming power. This is the source of Buber's feeling of dangling over the abysmal depths of God. God is a fearsome God not because He threatens us, but because He is the Wholly Other, numinous Creator who placed the world on its foundations and Who's presence inspires fear and trembling. Any liturgy that hopes to represent our relationship to God cannot imagine God in domesticated terms as though we are free creatures and can offer Him our good behavior. The asymmetry of our relationship also highlights that while disliking the freeloader and craving judgment, reward and punishment is human, God's world view is very different and other-worldly. While the vast asymmetry in our relationship to God can inspire agoraphobic fear, it should also inspire comfort knowing that God does more than forgive – He totally disregards behavior. Exodus expresses this through the incorporation of every extravagance imaginable. Whether the Israelites ever in history achieved or even attempted to achieve this grandeur is far from the point. The narrative is what matters and the message that our relationship to God is more than the insipid command to be patient and kind and humble, give to charity and develop our talents. Something far more cosmic is at work. God, who was justified in ignoring His insignificant, unfree creatures – the creatures who allowed themselves the pretention of significance and moral autonomy in the Garden - nonetheless adopted us as His own. God chooses Proximity. Interred in the Ark within the Holy of Holies is the Covenant: the bargain humanity could not keep, the moral accomplishment it stridently insisted it could reach but by its very nature never will, the Covenant that had to be unilateral because we had nothing to offer in return. Placed above it is the Mercy Seat. The God Who no one can see and live and Who naturally inspires dread, will now sit with His creatures and be reliably present. This is the concept of Sacrament. Our Platonic-infused concept of God as Unmoved Mover implied a distance between ourselves and God or at least a diffusion of God so that He existed equally at all times and in all things. This is foreign to Judeo-Christianity, but in our embarrassment over thinking of God as 'out there' we allowed ourselves to think of God as nowhere. God invites us to create holy time and sacred spaces in which to perform our liturgies and guarantees He will be present. God does not guarantee the Israelites happiness or that their circumstances will not change. The catastrophe of the Diaspora to Babylon would not have been a future, unanticipated embarrassment to the authors of the Old Testament as they were well aware of it.

In Deuteronomy, Moses predicts the Diaspora and the helpless grief of the Israelites.[555] In fact, the first five books of the Old Testament were likely compiled from various sources after the Israelites return from the Babylonian Diaspora.[556] God merely guarantees His presence, His eternal loving concern, which is the root of our dignity. If we do not have free will and God is just, then the Sacrament of Baptism or any sacrament cannot be the granting of some wish that without the proper liturgy would not have granted. Rather it is the assurance of the presence of God as we celebrate what He has already done for us. The themes of Asymmetry and Proximity express that we are small but loved anyway. One without the other fails to meet our intuitive sense of God and threatens to render faith insipid.

This dual theme of asymmetry and proximity represented in the Tabernacle Tent has been well translated, in my opinion, to the sacred traditions surrounding the tabernacle in my native Catholic faith. In the Catholic tradition, the consecrated bread is kept in a tabernacle in a prominent place in the Church, generally no higher or lower than the place from which the Word is read. We genuflect every time we pass in front of the tabernacle and accord it much respect in recognition of the presence of God within it and the asymmetry of our relationship to God. But then, in the course of the Mass, we consume the consecrated bread in a confident expression of our God's choice of proximity. We both bow before it, and eat it. Liturgy done well is a collection of the physical expressions of these themes.

Non-Verbal and Non-Dogmatic

Faith is like driving; everyone going slower than us is stupid, and everyone going faster than us is crazy. We modern Christians are apt to judge a congregation by the quality of the homiletics or sermons and by its place on the political spectrum. We decide whether it's worth our time to go based on the worth of what we expect to hear from the pulpit. I am not suggesting that this doesn't matter, but it is instructive that Exodus doesn't even mention it. While organized religion is self-destructing largely over moral differences with members of its congregations as each congregation occupies a narrower and narrower portion of the political spectrum, Exodus isn't even playing that game. In Exodus, the dogma of Asymmetry and Proximity is implied by the physical manifestations of faith and conveys the fundamental creed of faith – that we are not what we can do for God, and God is not what He can do for us and all that follows from that simple concept. The instructions for liturgy in Exodus are an acting out of the Scriptural story that culminates with our adoption as sons and daughters of God rather than a theological or moral analysis of it. This is not a compromise of faith but is rather its highest expression. In fact, we are warned off dedicating our churches and temples as places for moral education. In the Book of Numbers[557], the Israelites once again complain about their living conditions in the wilderness compared to Egypt. They are receiving manna each day but yearn for the meat they received in slavery. Both God and Moses are angry, but Moses is clearly feeling the strain and nearly broken with the task of leading the ungrateful

Israelites through the wilderness. God solves the immediate problem by causing flocks of quail to fall from the sky around the camp in such great numbers that, God says, the Israelites will eat them until quail is coming out of their noses and they will never want meat again. God then turns to help the over-burdened Moses. God tells Moses to muster a group of seventy elders to receive some of the spirit previously entrusted only to Moses so that they can help him. In stark contrast to the elaborate consecration of Aaron and his assistants as priests, there is no consecration ritual for what passes from Moses to the seventy elders. They simply stand around the Tabernacle Tent and are infused with the spirit. *It is critical to notice that Aaron and Moses have entirely distinct roles.* While Aaron fulfills the role of priest and liturgist, Moses is a prophet charged with relating what he hears from God to the people. While liturgy is entrusted only to a few with defined credentials, the role of prophet is much more open. In fact, as the seventy are exhibiting their new powers of prophecy, Moses's attendant sees two men who were not chosen prophecy in the camp as well. The attendant is outraged and runs to tell Moses to restrain them. Moses declines. "Are you jealous for my sake? I wish that all God's people were prophets, that God would put His spirit on them!"[558] Refusal to limit prophecy to a consecrated few is a value shared by the Christian story as well. In the Gospel of Mark, the apostle, John, sees someone casting out demons in Jesus's name and tells him to stop. [559] Jesus contradicts him and tells him to allow anyone to act in his name. This is a faith committed even when its success was not at all certain, to a dynamic, organic understanding of God that reaches deep into the congregation to ensure an ever-evolving understanding. The Ten Commandments and the Beatitudes initially read like detailed moral manifestos, but as we've seen, they are the opposite. They are props in a story about humanity's natural and insurmountable inability to act in a morally autonomous way and the assurance that good and bad fortune cannot be the reward and punishment of God. The Scriptural model requires that prophecy remain open to new ideas. In this way science and faith are parallel. A scientist is not someone committed to a set of facts and who is pledged to defend them against all threats. That is closer to the definition of a politician. Rather a scientist is committed to a methodology of inquiry - questioning, hypothesizing and analyzing - rejecting what doesn't work and building on what does. It implies humility rather than authority. The Scriptural model demands that faith be treated the same way. It is consistently those without credentials who are held up as models of prophecy: children, centurions, Samaritans. Even the prophet Amos was nothing more than a dresser of sycamores – someone who pierced the husk of sycamore fruit to help it ripen. Perhaps revelation places prophecy so firmly outside of organized religion because it realized that the I/Thou encounter with God is totally personal and will never occur as a group or to an elect chosen by us. Although religion can invite God to bend a little closer to the earth in sacrament, religion cannot curate the I/Thou encounter between God and the individual. God's message to each of us of radical mercy and grace and dignity is not legislative and cannot be conveyed by an institution. Organized religion has tried to combine the roles of Aaron and Moses. We expect our clergy to be liturgists and prophets at the same time – and often moral philosophers and moral examples too. We expect the clergy to say something prophetic from the pulpit regularly and on cue. Many who have left the practice of faith in community have done so because the clergy has disappointed their expectation that they will act like prophets. I am reminded of a story Abraham Heschel tells of a rookie reporter who is asked to cover a socialite wedding. He returns dejected and tells his editor that there was no story because the groom didn't show up.[560] This is precisely what is happening to organized religion today. Many of us are showing up at church expecting to hear a moral lesson and see a moral example. We leave dejected when our expectations are disappointed. But morality is not the sensational story we're there to cover. It is precisely the lack of a moral lesson and the brokenness of everyone regardless of their involvement in religion that is the real news – the Good News. Aaron represents the priesthood and his role included shockingly little analysis or theology and focused instead on manifesting through liturgy - physical acts - the asymmetry and proximity of God to His people. Organized religion has often done too much talking and not enough doing. It has dabbled in eumemetics rather than respecting the ability of each individual to find God. As Jesus is scolding John for prohibiting uncredentialed prophets, his reasoning is interesting. He says "Don't forbid him, for there is no one who will do a mighty work in my name, and be able quickly to speak evil of me.[561] Jesus has confidence that God is a reality, not just an idea, and that anyone seeking God in good faith will find Him eventually. Organized religion often has not had that level of confidence in its followers and has sought to provide explanation and purpose where its charge is to provide meaning.

Goal-Oriented Purposelessness - Heroics

For liturgy to be effective, it must reflect the transcendence and purposelessness of our relationship to God. From the lengthy instruction on Aaron's consecration and a shorter section on the construction of a secondary altar, Exodus returns to the story of Moses coming down the mountain to discover the golden calf and to confront Aaron and the Israelites for their total failure to follow the commandments. God overlooks the Israelites' moral shortcomings and affirms His covenant with them. Then, right when we think we've left the boring part behind and left biblical fly-over territory, Exodus describes in exacting detail how the Israelites comply with God's instructions to construct the Tabernacle Tent and the accoutrement that go with it. Vast swaths of the language we just read is repeated word for word to demonstrate how what God said should be done is in fact done by the Israelites.[562] They give up the gold they pilfered from the Egyptians until Moses and Aaron have vastly more than they need to complete the work. In sharp contrast to their total failure to obey the moral commandments of God, the Israelites literally have to be held back in their enthusiasm in following the liturgical commandments.[563] The irony is exquisite. The Israelites are playing the foil again. Even as they engage in an exercise in transcendence, acknowledging that as creatures who lack free will they are not going to achieve anything that is relevant to their worth, they are trying to overachieve and establish benchmarks for success. I am reminded of a story a monk once told me about a novitiate who, when Lent arrived and it was time to fast, ate less and went longer without food than anyone else in the monastery. Before joining the monastery, it turns out, this novitiate had been an attorney and put in longer hours and worked more weekends and holidays than anyone else in his firm. Heroics in liturgy are misplaced. Liturgy is fundamentally an acknowledgment that we are small – and the realization that we don't have free will makes us smaller still – and we are utterly helpless in any project to earn the gift of God's attention and the divine dignity that our faith tells us we have. We have no ability to reciprocate and give a gift in return, but it is far too great a gift to ignore. Certainly, part of our response is to protect and enhance the God-given dignity of others, but if we define our response that way we risk forgetting who we are and neglecting the very foundation on which we wish to build. Purposelessness on purpose, that does not allow itself to be hijacked into achievement or social purpose, is a critical element of religious life.

10,000 Hours

Faith is also like driving in that everyone thinks they are an expert. The New Atheists invariably characterize faith in the most simplistic, cynical manner possible. Are they deliberately setting up a straw man so that they can triumphantly reveal the inadequacies of their own making? Or are they actually just profoundly unsophisticated about faith? Faith is perhaps the only human endeavor where people who have taken no interest in it since childhood nonetheless believe themselves to be masters of it.

In his book, *The Outliers: The Story of Success*, Malcolm Gladwell described the 10,000-hour rule. Social science, according to Gladwell, has revealed that the idea that some people are just "naturals" at certain tasks is a myth. Similarly, the idea that people simply work very hard and intensely – the "grinds" – to become top performers is also a myth. Mastering a discipline simply takes a certain amount of practice; usually around 10,000 hours.[564] This may simply be the time it takes for our material brains to physically wire new connections associated with a new skill. In fact, it has been demonstrated that practice causes physical changes and growth in our brains. [565] Researchers at Oxford's Department of Clinical Neurology recently reported that MRIs of the brains of research subjects who practiced juggling thirty minutes a day for six weeks showed a five percent expansion of white matter over a control group that did not practice.

The idea that we can enhance our faith with lengthy practice is not something we readily accept. We reflexively prefer the lightning bolt download of wisdom and revelation. Certainly, when the Holy Spirit descends on the apostles at Pentecost, they appear to be instantly converted from bumbling foils to august and competent leaders of the Church (unless throwing dice for Judas's replacement was intended to show some need for more practice). But the examples of the prophet being identified and still having a great deal of work to do, is by far the more prevalent storyline. Perhaps the most famous instant conversion story is that of Paul, who credited his complete turnaround to his vision of Jesus on his way to execute warrants on Christians in Damascus. I have suggested that this was an I/Thou encounter between God and Paul and that it did indeed happen in a discrete moment in time. But it is interesting that, in Galatians, Paul tells us he left his I/Thou encounter with God and dropped out of sight for three years to process the event in Arabia.[566] He returned with an entirely new theology. He went from persecutor of the nascent Church to the author of letters that are read as part of the Liturgy of the Word almost every Sunday of the year. Did Paul spend his 10,000 hours in Arabia to work out the implications of what he had experienced in that moment on the road to Damascus? Did he build new brain tissue to accommodate his revelation? Did Julian of Norwich use her time in the anchorhold to unpackage the message of transcendence she received during her fever? In any event, the instructions for the liturgy in the Old Testament indicate an awareness that we must remain constantly engaged in order to master what faith offers us. Aaron is to burn sacrifices all day and all night, but the layperson had liturgies to observe as well. The cornerstone of lay liturgy was undoubtedly the observance of the Sabbath which, by enforcing rest, again invited the narrative of purposelessness.[567] The rest of the *Shema*, recited twice daily, demands that we constantly practice the remembrance of our relationship to God:

> You shall love the Lord your God with all your heart, with all your soul, and with all your might. These words, which I command you today, shall be on your heart; and you shall teach them diligently to your children, and shall talk of them when you sit in your house, and when you walk by the way, and when you lie down, and when you rise up. You shall bind them for a sign on your hand, and they shall be for frontlets between your eyes. You shall write them on the door posts of your house and on your gates.[568]

And then, of course, there are the feast and fast days,[569] dietary restrictions,[570] and the ritual purifications for various sins and bodily impurities which, in prudish ancient Israel, probably entailed constant interaction with the Temple. In modernity, we have dispensed with most of that for good reason, but have not replaced it with anything that required comparable attention. Nearly two hundred years of weekly attendance at religious services would be required for someone to invest 10,000 hours in mastering faith. Clearly, organized religion, to fulfill its Scriptural mandate, must prepare us to continue to engage in liturgy – not just good behavior – outside of the church or temple. Instead, while everyone is intimately aware of the Church's teachings on contraception and has a fully formed argument whether for or against, how to pray or how to observe the Sabbath in a way that is true to our relationship to God is a muddle.

In the New Testament too, God seems well aware of our fickle nature and the need for reminders of His relationship to us. In the Gospel of Luke, Jesus exhorts his follows to pray often. Strangely, the figure we might be tempted to see as representing God in this story is an atheist and a self-interested jerk:

> He also spoke a parable to them that they must always pray, and not give up, saying, "There was a judge in a certain city who didn't fear God, and didn't respect man. A widow was in that city, and she often came to him, saying, 'Defend me from my adversary!' He wouldn't for a while, but afterward he said to himself, 'Though I neither fear God, nor respect man, yet because this widow bothers me, I will defend her, or else she will wear me out by her continual coming.'" The Lord said, "Listen to what the unrighteous judge says. Won't God avenge his chosen ones who are crying out to him day and night, and yet he exercises patience with them? [571]

Jesus makes the human being the protagonist and the judge in this parable an unsavory character because this is one of the rare instances in Scripture where we are not being told about the nature of God or His morality, but are rather being told what is healthy for us to do and what will strengthen faith and maximize faith's ability to comfort us. It is a parable not about how to get God to do something for us, but an illustration of persistence; continual and engaged remembrances of our heritage to overcome our natural propensity to forget and seek re-enslavement.

Details Convey Transcendence Rather than Morality

What the Garden story, the Moriah story, the Sinai story and the story of the Incarnation reveal is not a God who imposes an innovative moral code with new commands, and new promises of reward and punishment. The moral code of ancient Israel was very similar to the moral codes of the cultures around them. Greek culture valued humility, development of talents, and leading a morally perfect life at least as much as the Israelites did and its mythology promised reward and punishment in the afterlife long before that concept developed in Judaism. C.S. Lewis was correct to acknowledge that with some insignificant exceptions, morality is the same across cultures and religions. What set Israel apart was that it claimed an existential relationship to God that transcended good and bad behavior. God was not what He could do for Israel, and Israel was not what it could do for God. This was revolutionary and, three thousand years later, remains revolutionary. When Israel addressed itself to this existential God it did not do so to encourage rain to fall, or crops to grow, or make women fertile, to bring good fortune or serve any practical purpose. The Exodus liturgy did not seek to prevent crime but sought only to remove any reason to remember or avenge a crime. Its liturgies are notable in their total lack of any goal aside from inviting the presence of the divine. Its liturgies are also notable in their overwhelming attention to truly inconsequential detail. There seems to be a detailed instruction for accoutrement beyond number, right down to the snuffers and trays and utensils for the Tabernacle menorah and the belt for Aaron's vestments.

Scripture does not offer a reason for the details of liturgy. Reasons are the death of liturgy. Rather, it is the inconsequential, arbitrary nature of the details that conveys the message of transcendence. In this, Exodus is demonstrating an extraordinarily clear-eyed understanding of human nature. Liturgy does not speak to the rider, which comes up with reasons to justify where the elephant has already decided to go. Liturgy speaks only to the elephant, and does so by having us physically and mentally engaged in plainly inconsequential things. It acts out the transcendent nature of our relationship to God rather than arguing for it. When Moses first encountered God at the burning bush, God demanded that Moses remove his sandals because he was walking on holy ground.[572] God was not appealing to Moses's reason, He was engaging Moses in something far more compelling – Moses's inborn intuition of the asymmetry of their relationship at the same time God was declaring His proximity.

The Details Convey Transcendence – Creating A Transcendent Environment

In *The Tipping Point,* Malcolm Gladwell explores those socio-biological dynamics that cause an idea to suddenly reach a tipping point and become viral or epidemic. He recalls New York City in the 1980s where the crime rate had exploded to over 2,000 murders each year and 600,000 serious felonies.[573] Crime reached a high in 1990 and then dropped in a few short years such that there were suddenly two-thirds fewer murders and half the serious felonies.[574] New York City wasn't the only beneficiary of this tipping point, as crime dropped dramatically throughout the nation in the same period. Gladwell notes that the reduction in crime is clearly related to the decline in the use of crack cocaine, the recovery of the economy, and the aging of the American population. However, these conditions were slow to take root in New York City, but crime dropped anything but slowly there. Gladwell suspects the implementation of the "Broken Window" theory of crime, first by the New York City Transit Authority which operates the subway system, and then by the city itself, was a primary factor in the reduction in crime. The Broken Window theory holds that if a window is broken and not repaired, passersby will get the impression that "no one cares and no one is in charge."[575] As the feeling of disorder gets a foothold, more windows are broken and the feeling of disorder spreads and gets more intense and finally more serious crime becomes inevitable. A tipping point is reached. The Transit Authority used this dynamic to its advantage and tipped the behavior in a more positive direction. While the instinctual response to an epidemic of crime might be to spend every resource on the most serious crimes, the Transit Authority focused also on the more minor crimes that set the tone for the others. The Transit Authority created a program to clean off the ubiquitous subway car graffiti that had almost become synonymous with New York City, and kept it off. Meanwhile, the Transit Authority police, led by the dynamic William Bratton, cracked down on turnstile jumping. When he was appointed to head the City's police force, he ordered his officers to crack down on the squeegee men who would clean your windshield and rip off your windshield wiper if you failed to pay them, and public urination, littering and other quality-of-life crimes. The success of these programs in reducing serious crime indicated an astonishing conclusion: *criminal behavior doesn't create the criminal environment, but rather it is the criminal environment that creates the criminal behavior by permitting or even inviting it.* By allowing the deterioration of the surroundings of people who, by nature and nurture, might be casually inclined to crime, a message is received that crime is permissible and, on some level, expected.

Exodus appears to have come to the same conclusion almost three millennia earlier. It seemed to intuit that *transcendent behavior doesn't create a transcendent environment. Rather, a transcendent environment creates transcendent behavior by permitting it and inviting it.* The text of Exodus sought to ensure the physical surroundings of the Israelites at worship would engender a sense of the transcendent. But even more importantly, Exodus sought to build an architecture of liturgy that could be practiced anywhere and under any circumstance and which would invite the participant into sacred, transcendent space and time.

Children will not understand the language of transcendence until they are in their mid-teens at the earliest. There is little point in speaking to young children who are still developing their moral sense and moral identities about existentialism, purposelessness and the ineffable. But if as children they are never in a purposeless environment that transcends the moral spectrum, the intuition naturally within them to understand God fails to get the permission it needs and withers. Every generation has to answer anew for itself whether it will bring their children to church and why. Is it to learn morality? Is it to fulfil a divine command to earn reward or avoid punishment? Is it to convince them that the magic that occurs in the stories is historical? Is it to sit in tidy rows and line up in a tidy line to encounter God? Or is it to practice and develop their inherent capacity for transcendence so that they can encounter the living God in the I/ Thou? If organized religion has a goal, it is to assist us in raising our children with the sense of the transcendent they are born to experience and nourish the sense of their divine dignity that is their birthright. The Scriptural model suggests this is best done with attention to detail, to ensure our liturgies convey transcendence. Organized religion has often thought of itself as the vehicle to pass down an authoritative and fully processed code of conduct and belief – a spiritual and moral eumemetic. Instead, it should seek to prepare the groundwork for them to explore on their own terms the transcendent nature of their relationship to God and encounter Him there in a non-legislative, radically personal way. This is purposelessness on purpose.

The Details of Liturgy Are Subject to Change – As Long as They Convey Asymmetry & Proximity

Although the inclusion of details was critical, the specific details of the liturgy described in Exodus were not important and were open to change from the beginning. Liturgy is a dance choreographed by us (not God) but in which God always reliably participates. For all the detail Exodus committed to the proper program of animal sacrifice, Jeremiah denied God ever required it, and Amos asserted God would not accept it[576]. Modern Scripture scholarship theorizes that the book of Exodus we have today was compiled from existing sources and edited at least four hundred years after Solomon's Temple was completed and the Tabernacle Tent was rendered obsolete as the central site of worship. In fact, the compilation of Exodus occurred after the Babylonians had destroyed the Ark, which was never replaced even though the Temple was rebuilt almost immediately upon the Israelites return to Jerusalem. Nonetheless Exodus contains an excruciatingly detailed account of elements of a practice surrounding the long-gone Tabernacle Tent and that no one expected to engage in. Clearly, perfect adherence to the details of the liturgy was not the point of the revelation that formed Exodus. Everything was subject to change and reformation in reaction to changing circumstances, but the themes of Asymmetry and Proximity always were carried forward.

Of course, it is possible to have all the accoutrement of a liturgy and follow all the steps of a liturgy and still fail to find meaning in them. Psalm 50 is a sustained diatribe against those who offered animal sacrifice shamanistically, expecting to have fulfilled some divine requirement, rather than allowing the transcendent meaning to change their lives. The Psalmist was quite blunt in stating that the sacrifices did not accomplish anything for God, but needed to be meaningful:

If I were hungry, I would not tell you,
for the world is mine, and all that is in it.
Will I eat the meat of bulls,
or drink the blood of goats?
Offer to God the sacrifice of thanksgiving.
Pay your vows to the Most High.
Call on me in the day of trouble.
I will deliver you, and you will honor me.[577]

Liturgy brings us into the presence of God but is not intended to imitate an I/Thou encounter. It is not a success when it engenders feelings of awe or wonder and a failure when it does not. Liturgy done with care and mindfulness reminds us that God is both Wholly Other and has chosen to be Incarnate, which in turn reminds us that we are both small and imbued with divine dignity. The Catholic tradition to dip a hand into a basin of holy water at the entrance to the church, although executed in a moment and usually reflexively, is a liturgy of extraordinary beauty. But we can lose sight of its meaning and render it shamanistic, which is a short step away from insipid. It recollects the Israelites at the base of Mount Sinai constructing the bronze laver according to God's instructions to purify themselves before entering the presence of God. Our hands will not be cleaner as a result. Nor will we be any spiritually or morally purer. We should not emulate Peter at the Last Supper and demand that we be allowed to wash our head and feet in it too. It is an affirmation that the story of Exodus - and the Garden, Moriah, Bethlehem and Calvary - is the story of God's pursuit of His insignificant, misguided creatures to make them His sons and daughters. We have nothing to offer in return for the extraordinary grace, and the acknowledgement of that fact is liturgy. We ritualistically purify ourselves to remind ourselves that we are small, but invited into proximity with the Holy. There is no transcript for these themes, except to be ready when our children ask us what the purpose of liturgy is, and to answer by starting a conversation of the transcendent: that it is in remembrance of God's rescue of His people.

Casting Off Detail

To the extent organized religion has successfully preserved the purposelessness in liturgy, it has often been subject to incremental erosion. In the Bavarian parable of Hans im Glück (Hans in Luck), Hans gradually bargains away a fortune to relieve himself of inconveniences:

Hans worked hard for seven years but wishes to return to see his poor mother. His master pays him his wages which amounts to a lump of gold the size of his head. Hans puts the gold in a handkerchief and starts out on his journey jogging but soon becomes tired. He spots a rider on horseback and seeing the ease at which the horse travels he offers to exchange his lump of gold for the horse. Happy with the exchange, the man gives him the horse and Hans rides off.

The horse bolts and Hans gets bucked off, whereupon he meets a shepherd who convinces Hans to trade his horse for a cow, telling Hans that a cow can provide milk, cheese and butter and is of more leisurely company. Hans takes him up on the offer and continues his journey only to find that the cow is dry and not producing any milk as he had been told.

Disgruntled with the cow, Hans meets a butcher who gives him a pig for the cow. Thanking the butcher for the pig Hans sets off jogging again, hopeful he has now found an ideal travel companion. Alas, Hans meets a countryman who informs him that the pig's owner is the squire and he is in danger of being arrested for taking the squire's pig. Hans takes the countryman's goose in exchange for his pig, happy that it will provide a good roast and a supply of goose fat.

At his next stop in a village Hans meets a scissor-grinder and explains his story to him. The scissor-grinder offers him a grindstone for his goose arguing that a grindstone will provide a source of income. Hans happily exchanges the goose for the grindstone. He continues on his way, but is tired carrying the grindstone and is short of money for food.

Hans stops for a drink on the banks of a river, the grindstone falls into the deep water and is lost. Hans is happy to be rid of the heavy grindstone and being free of all troubles. He walks on to his mother's house and recounts his lucky tale.[578]

Affiliation in religious institutions seems to be reaching a terrible tipping point. To try to tip affiliation in the opposite direction it is tempting to focus solely on solving the most obvious and serious failings of our religious institutions: the moral failures, the failure to say something that is worth the time we've invested and say it in an engaging style, the failure to create a welcoming environment, and the failure to commit sufficient resources to social causes. These are all important but do not speak to our intuitive sense of God and the deepest roots of our relationship to Him. They speak instead to our natural desire to measure, judge, reward and punish which true faith seeks to challenge. The decks of religious observance are dangerously awash and there are very many well-meaning individuals who are insistent that the answer is to pump evermore programs and policies for progress on board. Meanwhile, it is the seemingly inconsequential elements of religious observance that may be the most critical but which receive only embarrassed attention and are jettisoned as just not useful enough and too burdensome at the first sign of trouble. Lost details are broken windows in the architecture of liturgy. It may well be that it is the details of liturgy that, taken together, create an environment of transcendence that prepares the ground to understand God.

Why Does Revelation Want Us to Do This Together?

If we recast our understanding of our relationship to God as transcending purpose and morality, then it is inevitable that we must also recast our understanding of our relationship to each other as transcending purpose and morality. There are many practical reasons for participating in liturgy, whether it is the observance of a tradition with many but in solitude, or observance as part of a congregation gathered together physically. Certainly, we are a social animal and we do most things best when we do them together. We instinctively share the sacred. Perhaps our primordial minds still feel a certain level of security by approaching the fearsome God of our asymmetric relationship as a group. Participating in liturgy creates a climate of transcendence that allows us to develop an instinct for and understand the transcendent and potentially for it to go viral. Participating in liturgy helps us remember the story of God's rescue of His people from causal ignominy and His adoption of us as His sons and daughters. It allows us to challenge the notion of the Platonic-hybrid god that plays to our worst impulses, and gives voice to our intuitive knowledge of God as only radically loving, and not commanding, rewarding and punishing. It helps us counteract our desire for re-enslavement. It helps us maintain the richness and meaningfulness of our liturgies that seep into our lives and invite us to proximity to a God rather than slowly sloughing off what might not speak to us on a given day until it is all gone. Finally, liturgy helps us to be guided by mercy.

But the highest reason for participating in liturgy is not practical but spiritual. If we are not morally autonomous and our dignity is our inheritance from God, then we are more than our biographies or our place on the moral spectrum in the eyes of God. *And we should be more than our biographies or our place on the moral spectrum in each other's eyes too.* If we are asked to explain out loud what "being in community" means, within a few words we will find ourselves talking about mutual obligations and responsibilities and roles. It is virtually inevitable. We are accustomed to gathering together to accomplish goals. We gather together in what passes for community to pursue occupations, hobbies, charity, and exercise. When we gather together in what appears to be purposelessness, we most often distract ourselves with competition (our own, or watching someone else compete) or entertainment. In modernity, we are certainly far more isolated than evolution ever prepared us for. And what passes for community now is so overheated and purpose-driven that it will never satisfy our inborn need for real, transcendent connection. Faith declares that community can be, and should be existential. Faith declares that we come together simply to affirm that we each transcend purpose and morality and have worth, dignity and sanctity inherent in our status as children of God. The revelation that authored Exodus clearly intended that we come together in sacred space and time regularly for the purposeful expression of that purposelessness and sought to give expression to our deepest, truest selves. Liturgy is the practice of simply being with one another in the context of the sacred. We certainly have obligations to one another, but that is not what binds us together. We are bound to one another in our common relationship to God. We can't live in an I/Thou relationship, and can't curate an I/Thou relationship in liturgy, but we can live mindfully in sacred relationship with one another. In that kind of relationship, we can reveal where we are weak or broken, and expect radical forgiveness and mercy that comes with an understanding of the nature of our common relationship to God that transcends every weakness and brokenness.

A Vision of the Future

Copernicus's claim that the Earth rotated around the Sun instead of the other way around, and Darwin's claim that life evolved over time, each in apparent contradiction of Scripture, were paradigm shifts that were initially assumed to threaten the very foundations of faith. Over time, with gradual acceptance, they strengthened faith. Rather than understanding God as the solution to physics and biology riddles, faith, so informed by science, came to understand God's role as transcending such practical concerns. It helped us move past an anthropomorphic vision of God to seeing Him as the numinous Wholly Other. Eventually, the fact that we are not morally autonomous will become as almost-universally accepted as Copernicanism and Darwinism. This is not a call to accept it – *it is a prediction of its inevitability*. It may feel like a lack of free will directly contradicts Scripture and threatens the foundations of faith. It was the aim in this book to convince you, the reader, that the opposite is the case. The idea that we do not have free will is not only consistent with Scripture but forms the heart of a major theme of Scripture and runs throughout the storyline from the Garden to the Cross. The conclusion that we don't have free will doesn't weaken faith, but strengthens it and prepares it to realize its full power in our lives.

The theme was hidden in Scripture. In the earliest days of Christianity, we were tempted away from a Scriptural understanding of the God of Abraham by a hybrid Platonic god that made philosophical sense for a time and appealed to our natural desire for moral autonomy that our Scriptural heritage was trying to warn us about. It was an awkward marriage and forced us into an impossible contradiction: a God Who loves unconditionally and saved and redeemed us once and for all, and a god who judges, rewards and punishes in a suspiciously human way. So powerful and ingrained are the forces that tempt us to claim moral autonomy, that nothing else seemed more plausible and we accepted the paradox. Rather than embrace its intuitive grounding, it sought to justify itself with Platonic physics. Although they shared a common Platonic ancestry with faith, while science and philosophy advanced steadily, faith remained mired in ancient notions of moral autonomy. Faith was forced into ever more fanciful explanations and ever more mean-spirited moralities to defend the positions it felt it now depended on for its existence. Finding transcendence hard to incorporate, organized religion defined itself more and more by morality. Overtaken by secular morality, it found itself rendered nearly irrelevant. Remaining committed to faith was itself an act of faith.

Science will once again wake us up from our dogmatic slumber and reveal that God is more transcendent then we ever gave Him credit for. This is not a death but a resurrection. Faith will trade a foundation built on sand for a stone foundation.

As faith and religion come to accept that we don't have free will, those elements of faith that insulted our intelligence and were mean-spirited will fall away effortlessly. Faith that chooses not to eat any further from the Tree of the Knowledge of Good and Evil is perfectly compatible with science and philosophy and inevitably stands for unconditional love and mercy. Such a faith will champion inherent human dignity with a strong, confident voice against those who would value each of us only for our social utility. If members of such a faith ignore the poor, are inhospitable to the poor in spirit, or belittle their own dignity or the dignity of others, such a faith will not condemn or claim their separation from God but will work even harder to imbue them with a sense of their divine inheritance. Such a faith will treat good behavior as a symptom of faith rather than the goal of faith. It will break the alabaster jar and attend to transcendence before practicality.

The Old Testament parallel of the alabaster jar story appears in the First Book of Kings. The Israelites have settled in the Promised Land and Solomon has built the first Temple. However, the kings that rule the people gradually descend into Ba'al worship and built altars on which to sacrifice children to win the favor of this god of storms and fertility.[579] We are introduced to the powerful prophet, Elijah[580] as he announces that God will challenge Ba'al's ability to bring rain by imposing a harsh drought. Elijah is miraculously fed twice a day by ravens but even he has to move on when the creek he is drinking from dries up. Elijah encounters a widow and her son who are much worse off than he and on the edge of death as a result of the drought. With a shocking lack of humanity, Elijah asks the widow for some bread. The widow resists and tells him that she has only enough flour and oil to make a last meal for herself and her son before they die. Elijah, however, persists and demands that she make him the bread, but promises that her provisions will not give out until the drought subsides, and miraculously, he is proven right. This is the same story whose retelling inspired Jesus's childhood neighbors in Nazareth to try to kill him. The message is the same as the alabaster jar and the temptation of Jesus by Satan: in relationship to God, attend to transcendent first even though it seems like an extravagance when faced with issues of dire moral consequence. Only then will we act out of true love instead of a pale imitation of it.

Although they try, different religious traditions have interacted with each other about as smoothly as tweens at a middle school dance. By identifying themselves by their moral differences, each religious tradition has caused every interaction to be fraught with moral insecurities. If being the top of the moral spectrum is part of your group's religious identity, it is hard to justify interacting with anyone else without condescension. As transcendence becomes religion's primary concern, religious traditions will distinguish themselves with liturgy rather than dogma. Our justification for being one denomination rather than another will be based on how we prefer to address God in community – the choreography that speaks to us most richly - rather than any claim to moral superiority. The faith of the future, I suspect, will include more interest in others' sacred narratives and wisdom traditions. The acknowledgement that each of our liturgies is choreographed by us, but equally acceptable to God as any other, will allow faith to become a dynamic, scintillating tapestry of liturgies - not an amorphous combination of all that is both inoffensive and inconsequential to all, but a collection of individual traditions in all their glorious diversity.

The narrative that is sometimes built around the departure of so many from affiliation is that they lack an intuition of God. The opposite may be the case. The Platonic-hybrid god that reliably intervenes on behalf of well-behaved people, who is a divine good luck charm, who is the solution for every gap in scientific knowledge, and for whom justice means retribution, was inevitably going to violate our intuitive understanding of God. Organized religion – by which I again mean the rest of us as much as the clergy – did little to address this obvious contradiction. Perhaps some of the "nones" simply lost patience with the widespread slandering of the God of their intuition. As faith broadly adjusts to the idea that we do not have free will, becomes more transcendent, and speaks of a God who suffers with us and for whom justice is universal mercy, I suspect some of the nones will see their intuitive sense of God reflected in religion and will find their way back. Finally, maybe the tide of nones leaving affiliation with any tradition will turn into a tide of "alls" who fully engage with their native tradition and participate in true long-term community there in the context of the sacred, but also feel free to tap the liturgical beauty and wisdom of every other faith.

There is no reason for pessimism among people of faith. Faith's inevitable embrace of science will lead it back to the God of Abraham and the God of our deepest intuition. That is the faith that ignited the stars over Moriah, inspired the prophets and the mystics, culminated with the Incarnation of God as one of us, and swept through the world. As religion embraces its role as cultivating an understanding of our relationship to God that transcends purpose and morality, it will be preparing the ground for generations of emerging mystics and prophets. Who knows what encounters with God await humanity. We can have confidence in the power of the revelation that brought us this far and its inherent promise that the next three thousand years will better than the first.

> Let all mortal flesh keep silence,
> and with fear and trembling stand.
> Ponder nothing earthly-minded,
> For with blessings in his hand,
> Christ our God to earth decendeth,
> our full homage to demand.[581]

I would be very happy to know your impressions of this book. Please email me at:

stephan@stephangrozinger.com

Bibliography

Auden, W.H., *For the Time Being, a Christmas Oratorio*. Princeton: Princeton University Press, 2013

Alter, Robert, *The Five Books of Moses: A Translation with Commentary*. New York: W.W. Norton & Company, 2004

Alter, Robert, *The Book of Psalms*. New York: W.W. Norton & Company, 2007

Barks, Coleman, *The Essential Rumi*. New York: Harper One, 2004

Beilby, James K., and Eddy, Paul R., eds., *Justification: Five Views*. Downers Green, Illinois: Intervarsity Press 2011

The Treatise of St. Bernard, Abbat of Claivaux, Concerning Grace and Free Will Addressed to William, Abbat of St. Theiry. London: Society for Promoting Christian Knowledge, 1920

Bornkamm, Günther, *Paul*. Minneapolis: Fortress Press, 1995

Brown, Raymond E., Fitzmyer, Joseph A., and Murphy Roland E., eds., *The New Jerome Biblical Commentary*. Saddle River, New Jersey: Prentice Hall, 1990

Brown, Raymond E., *An Introduction to the New Testament.* New York: Doubleday, 1997

Brown, Raymond E., *The Birth of the Messiah: A Commentary on the Infancy Narratives in the Gospels of Matthew and Luke.* New York: Random House, 1993

Buber, Martin (Walter Kaufmann, ed.), *I and Thou: A New Translation.* New York: Simon & Schuster, 1970

Bultmann, Rudolf (G.R. Beasley-Murray, R.W.N. Hoare & J.K. Riches, trans.), *The Gospel of John: A Commentary*, Philadelphia: The Westminster Press, 1971

Dawkins, Richard, *The Selfish Gene.* Oxford: Oxford University Press, 2006

Dawkins, Richard, *The God Delusion.* London: Bantam Press, 2006

Dennett, Daniel C., *Freedom Evolves.* New York: Penguin Books, 2004

Dennett, Daniel C., *Elbow Room: The Varieties of Free Will Worth Wanting.* Cambridge, Massachusetts: Bradford Books, 1984

Edwards, Paul, ed. *The Encyclopedia of Philosophy.* New York: Collier MacMillan Publishers, 1967

Ernst, Carl W., *Sufism: An Introduction to the Mystical Tradition of Islam.* London: Shambhala, 2011

Fadiman, James & Frager, Robert, eds., *Essential Sufism*, New York: Harper One, 1997

Fitzmyer, Joseph A.. *Romans, A New Translation with Introduction and Commentary by Joseph A. Fitzmyer* , The Anchor Bible Series. New York: Doubleday (1993) 465

Gillman, Neil, *Sacred Fragments: Recovering Theology for the Modern Jew*. Philadelphia: The Jewish Publication Society, 1990

Gillman, Neil, *The Death of Death: Resurrection and Immortality in Jewish Thought*. Woodstock, Vermont: Jewish Lights Publishing, 2000, 2002, 2006

Gladwell, Malcolm, *Outliers: The Story of Success*. New York: Back Bay Books, 2008

Gladwell, Malcolm, *The Tipping Point: How Little Things Can Make a Big Difference*. New York: Back Bay Books, 2002

Grahame, Kenneth (Seth Lerer ed.), *The Wind in the Willows*. Cambridge: The Belknap Press of Harvard University Press, 2009

Gulley, Philip & Mulholland, James, *If God is Love: Rediscovering Grace in an Ungracious World*. New York: Harper Collins, 2005

Jonathan Haidt, *The Happiness Hypothesis: Finding Modern Truth in Ancient Wisdom*. New York: Basic Books, 2006

Haidt, Jonathan, *The Righteous Mind: Why Good People Are Divided by Politics and Religion*. New York: Vintage Books, 2012

Harris, Sam, *The End of Faith: Religion, Terror, and the Future of Reason*. New York: W.W. Norton & Company, 2004

Harris, Sam, *The Moral Landscape: How Science Can Determine Human Values*. New York: Free Press, 2010

Harris, Sam, *Free Will*. New York: Free Press, 2012

Heschel, Abraham Joshua, *The Sabbath*. New York: Farrar, Straus and Giroux, 2005

Heschel, Abraham Joshua, *Man is Not Alone*. New York: Farrar, Straus and Giroux, 1979

Heschel, Abraham Joshua, *God in Search of Man*. New York: Farrar, Straus and Giroux, 1983

Heschel, Abraham Joshua, *The Prophets*. Peabody, Massachusetts: Hendrickson Publishers, 2009

Hitchens, Christopher, *The Missionary Position: Mother Teresa in Theory and Practice*. New York: Twelve Edition, 1995

John-Julian, *The Complete Julian of Norwich*. Brewster, Massachusetts: Paraclete

Press, 2009

Jowett, Benjamin, trans., Pine, Joslyn T., ed., *Plato's The Republic*. Mineola, New York, Dover Publications: 2000

Kierkegaard, Søren (C. Stephen Evans, ed. And Sylvia Walsh ed. and trans.), *Fear and Trembling*. Cambridge: Cambridge University Press, 2009

Kuhn, Thomas S., *The Structure of Scientific Revolutions 2nd ed.* Chicago: University of Chicago Press, 1962. 1970.

Lewis, C.S. *Letters to Malcolm: Chiefly on Prayer.* New York: Harcourt, 1992.

Lewis, C.S., *Mere Christianity.* New York: Harper One, 1952

Lionni, Leo, *Fish is Fish.* New York: Dragonfly Books, 1970

Mays, James L., ed., *Harpers Bible Commentary.* New York: Harper Collins, 1988

Merton, Thomas, *New Seeds of Contemplation.* New York: New Directions Publishing, 2007

Mill, John-Stuart (John Gray, ed.), *On Liberty and Other Essays.* Oxford: Oxford University Press, 1991

Mill, John Stuart (George Sher ed.), *Utilitarianism.* New York: Hackett Publishing Company, 1979

Newberg, Andrew B., *Principles of Neurotheology.* Burlington, VT: Ashgate Publishing Company, 2010

Nietzsche, Friedrich (H.L. Mencken, H.L., trans.), *The Antichrist.*

Oliver, Mary, *New and Selected Poems, Vol. 1.* Boston: Beacon Press, 1992

Orwell, George, *Animal Farm.* New York: Harcourt Brace Jovanovich, 1946

Otto, Rudolf (John Harvey, trans.), *The Idea of the Holy.* Oxford: Oxford University Press, 1958

Priestley, Joseph, *Free Discussion of Doctrines of Materialism and Philosophical Necessity*. 1778

Rae, Alastair I.M., *Quantum Physics*. London: Oneworld Publications, 2014

Robinson, John A.T., *Honest to God*. Louisville, Kentucky: Westminster John Knox Press, 2002

Sartre, Jean-Paul (S. Gilbert, trans.), *No Exit and Three Other Plays*. New York: Vintage Books, 1989

Schwarz-Bart, André (Stephen Becker, trans.), *The Last of the Just*. New York: The Overlook Press, 2000

Smith, Christian, Longest, Kyle, Hill, Jonathan, Christoffersen, Kari, *Young Catholic America: Emerging Adults In, Out of, and Gone from the Church*. Oxford: Oxford University Press, 2014.

Soloveitchik, Joseph B., *The Lonely Man of Faith*. New York: Three Leaves Press, 1965

Stendahl, Krister, "The Apostle Paul and the Introspective Conscience of the West" Harvard Theological Review Vol. 56, No. 3 (July 1963). 201

Styron, William, *Sophie's Choice*. New York: Vintage Books, 1979

Tillich, Paul, *The Shaking of the Foundations*. Eugene, Oregon: Wipf & Stock, 1948

Tippett, Krista, *On Being. Janna Levin, Mathematics, Purpose and Truth*. (April 3, 2014) [audio podcast]

Tippett, Krista, *On Being. Jonathan Haidt – The Psychology Behind Morality.* (June 12, 2014) [audio podcast]

Tippett, Krista, *On Being. John O'Donohue, The Inner Landscape of Beauty.* (January 26, 2012) [audio podcast]

Tippett, Krista, *On Being. Lawrence Kushner, Kabbalah and the Inner Life of God.* (May 15, 2014) [audio podcast]

United States Conference of Catholic Bishops, *Compendium Catechism of the Catholic Church.* Washington, D.C.: Libreria Editrice Vaticana, 2006

Wright, Robert, *The Moral Animal: Why We Are the Way We Are: The New Science of Evolutionary Psychology.* New York: Vintage Books, 1994

Endnotes

1   U.S. Religious Landscape Survey, February 2008

2   Abraham offers water to the three angelic strangers to wash their feet (Genesis 18:4), Lot offers them the same courtesy as they arrive in Sodom (Genesis 19:2). See also Genesis 24:32, 43:24; 2 Samuel 11:8

3   Rudolf Bultmann, *The Gospel of John: a Commentary* (Philadelphia: The Westminster Press, 1971) 466; See also 1 Samuel 25:41; Luke 7:44

4   John 1:1-5

5   John 20:28

6   John 13:6-7

7   John 16:29

8   John 13:8

9   John 13:9-10

10   John 13:12-16

11   John 15:18, 20

12   John 16:1-3

13   John 13:34

14   John 14:15, 14:21, 15:10; 15:12, 15:17

15   Psalm 103: 10-14

16   *The Treatise of St. Bernard, Abbat of Claivaux, Concerning Grace and Free Will Addressed to William, Abbat of St. Theiry* (London: Society for Promoting Christian Knowledge. 1920) 5.; St. Bernard was channeling St. Augustine who said "If there is no grace of God, how does he save the world? And if there is no free will, how does he judge the world." Epistle 214.

17   Isaac Bashevis Singer as quoted in Stefan Kanfer, *Isaac Singer's Promised City*, City Journal (Summer, 1997)

18   http://www.cnn.com/2006/WORLD/europe/11/08/atheism.feature/index.html

19   http://www.cbsnews.com/news/outspoken-and-outrageous-christopher-hitchens/

20   Sam Harris, *The End of Faith: Religion, Terror, and the Future of Reason* (New York: W.W. Norton & Company, Inc. 2004) 14-15.

21   Ibid., 15.

22   Ibid., 13-14.

23   Sam Harris, *Free Will* (New York: Free Press. 2012) 12.; Daniel C. Dennett. *Freedom Evolves* (New York: Penguin Books. 2003) 1.

24   Sam Harris, *Free Will and "Free Will": How My View Differs from Daniel Dennett's*. (blog) http://www.samharris.org/blog/item/free-will-and-free-will

25   Matthew 18:21

26   Thomas S. Kuhn, *The Structure of Scientific Revolutions 2nd ed.*) Chicago: University of Chicago Press, 1962. 1970) 53-54

27   Psalms 103:12

28   Abraham Joshua Heschel, *God in Search of Man* (New York: Farrar, Straus and Giroux, 1955) 1.

29   Exodus 33:19

30   Exodus 3:14; Robert Alter, *The Five Books of Moses: A Translation with Commentary* (New York: W.W. Norton & Company, Inc. 2004) 321.

31   Deuteronomy 11:13

32   1 Thessalonians 5:16 et seq.

33   Invitatory of The Liturgy of the Hours (New York: Catholic Book Publishing Corp., 1975)

34   Genesis 2:4-9, 15-25, Genesis 3:1-23

35   Genesis 4:12

36   Genesis 4:13

37   Baruch Spjnoza, for instance, not only denied human free will but also conceived of God in this linear way. Paul Edwards, ed., *The Encyclopedia of Philosophy*, vol. 7 & 8 (New York: Macmillan Publishing Co., Inc. & The Free Press) 540.

38   Exodus 33:18-23

39   Exodus 33:11

40   Genesis 16:13

41   Genesis 32:28

42   Robert Alter. *The Five Books of Moses: A Translation with Commentary.* (New York: W.W. Norton & Company, 2004) 181.

43   Genesis 32:30

44   Paul Rincon, *Neutrinos – 'Superheroes of the Particle World.* (October 6, 2015) BBC News website. http://www.bbc.com/news/science-environment-34454831

45   Abraham Heschel, *God in Search of Man* (New York: Farrar, Straus and Giroux. 1955) 187; see also Neil Gillman, *Sacred Fragments: Recovering Theology for the Modern Jew* (Philadelphia: The Jewish Publication Society. 1990) 79-80.

46   See, e.g.: Krista Tippett, *On Being. Janna Levin, Mathematics, Purpose and Truth.* (April 3, 2014) [audio podcast]

47   "There are more things in heaven and earth, Horatio, than are dreamt of in your philosophy." Hamlet, Scene V.

48   Geoff Brumfiel, *Charles Towns, Laser Pioneer, Black Hole Discoverer, Dies at 99.* NPR – All Things Considered (January 28, 2015)   http://www.npr.org/blogs/thetwo-way/2015/01/28/382178361/charles-townes-laser-inventor-black-hole-discoverer-dies-at-99

49   Matthew 25:31-45

50   Raymond S. Brown, Joseph A. Fitzmyer, Roland E. Murphy, *The New Jerome Biblical Commentary* (Upper Saddle River, New Jersey: Prentice Hall, 1990) 669.

51   W.H. Auden, *For the Time Being, a Christmas Oratorio* (Princeton: Princeton University Press, 2013) 16.

52   *Pax.* D. H. Lawrence. From THE COMPLETE POEMS OF D.H. LAWRENCE by D.H. Lawrence, edited by Vivian de Sola Pinto & F. Warren Roberts, copyright © 1964, 1971 by Angelo Ravagli and C.M. Weekley, Executors of the Estate of Frieda Lawrence Ravagli. Used with permission of Viking Books, an imprint of Penguin Publishing Group, a division of Penguin Random House LLC.

53   Matthew 2:16

54   Raymond Brown, et al., *The New Jerome Biblical Commentary*, 1248

55   Matthew 2:22

56   Matthew 8:8

57   Mark 15:39, Matthew 27:54. Interestingly, although Matthew and Luke probably both used Mark's Gospel as a starting point, and while Mark and Matthew have the centurion declare Jesus the Son of God Luke, only has him declare him innocent (Luke 23:47).

58   Acts 17:22

59   *The Republic*, Book 6, Section 509b

60   Paul Edwards, ed., *The Encyclopedia of Philosophy*, Vol. 6, pg. 354

61   No relation to the individual to whom the Gospel of Luke and Acts are addressed (Luke 1:3 and Acts 1:1)

62   A point made in the eighteenth century by Immanuel Kant

63   Paul Edwards, ed., *The Encyclopedia of Philosophy* Vol 6 p. 454

64   Joseph Priestley, *Free Discussion of Doctrines of Materialism and Philosophical Necessity* (1778) 164

65   The Odyssey. Book XII, lines 46-70, 190-250

66   Fr. John-Julian, *The Complete Julian of Norwich*. (Brewster, Massachusetts, Paraclete Press, 2009) 159.

67   Psalm 103:14

68   Daniel C. Dennett, *Freedom Evolves* (New York: Penguin Books 2003) 1.

69   See 2 Peter 2:4 and the non-biblical Book of Enoch 20:2

70   No relation to the Archelaus of the Gospel of Matthew.

71   Benjamin Jowett, trans., Joslyn T. Pine, ed., Plato's *The Republic* (Mineola, New York, Dover Publications: 2000) 274

72   Genesis 6:3; Interestingly, several generations after Noah continued to live several hundred years and Sarah and Abraham both exceeded the one hundred twenty-year deadline (so to speak).

73   Genesis 9:29

74   Genesis 5:22-24

75   2 Kings 2:11

76   Psalm 6:5-6 (Robert Alter, *The Book of Psalms*. (New York: W.W. Norton & Company, 2007) 15-16

77   Psalm 115:16-17 (Robert Alter, *The Book of Psalms*. 410)

78   Psalm 30:3 (Robert Alter, *The Book of Psalms*. 102)

79   Psalm 49:15:16. (Robert Alter, *The Book of Psalms*. 714)

80   Psalm 139:7-8 (Robert Alter, *The Book of Psalms*. 480).

81   Isaiah 38:17-18

82   Neil Gillman, *The Death of Death, Resurrection and Immorality in Jewish Thought* (Woodstock, VT: Jewish Lights Publishing, 2000, 2002, 2006) 115-116

83   Mark 12:18, 26-27; Sadducees apparently died out following the destruction of the Temple in the year 70 as they are not mentioned as a living sect again (see Raymond Brown, et al, *New Jerome Biblical Commentary* 1244.)

84   Acts 23:1-10

85   2 Maccabees 7 includes a story in which seven brothers and their mother are tortured in an extremely grisly fashion while they affirm their confidence in an afterlife and, very clearly, expect to be reunited with the body parts which are being taken away from them by their torturers (See, for instance, 7:10-11). 1 and 2 Maccabees are, however, apocryphal and no longer part of the Jewish canon.

86   Luke 24:38-43

87   Acts 1:9

88   Luke 16:19-26

89   Wisdom of Solomon 3:7

90   Wisdom of Solomon 2:2-3

91   Wisdom of Solomon 7:24-29

92   Raymond Brown, et al. The New Jerome Biblical Commentary. 510

93   Although Catholic doctrine is not at all consistent on this subject, it is nonetheless interesting to note that at least some papal encyclicals seem to suggest that the body and soul are one: "Man, though made of body and soul, is a unity. Through his very bodily condition he sums up in himself the elements of the material world." Pope Paul VI. (December 7, 1965). 233 *Gaudium et spes*. 14 § 1 quoted in *The Catechism of the Catholic Church* §364

94   C.S. Lewis, Letters to Malcolm. (New York: Harcourt, 1992) 17.

95   Interestingly, our friend Joseph Priestley was well ahead of his time in saying that we do not have immaterial souls, but rather our thoughts are the product of processes that occur within our material brains.

96   1 Corinthians 2:9, quoting Isiah 64:4

97   James Gorman, *Ancient Bones That Tell a Story of Compassion*, The New York Times (December 17, 2012)

98   Seeker.com, *Earliest Traces of a Disables, Aged Human Found: Discovery News* (February 11, 2013)

99   C.S. Lewis, *Mere Christianity*. (New York: Harper One, 1952) 25.

100   Lewis's Platonism goes so far as to also insists that there must be a "Bad Power" with nearly the same powers as the "Good Power" which has made the free choice to rebel against God and to sabotage us (pp.45-46)

101   Isaac Bashevis Singer as quoted in Stefan Kanfer, *Isaac Singer's Promised City*, City Journal (Summer, 1997)

102   Matt 7:12, Luke 6:31; Mark 12:31. A variation reappears at Matt 19:19 and 22:39: "You shall love your neighbor as yourself." In both cases, Jesus is referencing Leviticus 19:18

103   John 13:34.

104   Genesis 18:25

105   Wright, Robert. *The Moral Animal*. (New York: Vintage Books, 1994) 3.

106   *See, for example*, Jonathan Haidt, *The Happiness Hypothesis: Finding Modern Truth in Ancient Wisdom*. (New York: Basic Books, 2006) 236-239.

107   Nell Greenfield Boyce, *Dogs Understand Fairness, Get Jealousy, Study Finds*. NPR (December 9, 2008)

108   Alix Spiegel, *When the Trust Hormone is Out of Balance*, NPR – All Things Considered (April 22, 2010) http://www.npr.org/templates/story/story.php?storyId=126141922

109   Matthew 26:21-35; Mark 14:18-31; Luke 22:2-40; John 13:21,37, 16:31

110   John 21:15-17

111   John 13:23-26

112   John 21: 22

113   Genesis 1:1-3 as quoted in Robert Alter, *The Five Books of Moses,* 17

114   Genesis 1:3-26

115   Exodus 3:14-15

116   Gunther Bornkamm, *Paul.* (Minneapolis: Fortress Press, 1995) 4-5

117   Bornkamm, *Paul,* 6

118   Matthew 23:15 quoted in Bornkamm 10.

119   Heschel, *God in Search of Man.* 120.

120   John 20:29

121   *See, for example,* Andrew B. Newberg, Principles of Neurotheology (Burlington, VT: Ashgate Publishing Company, 2010).

122   (Unattributed) Kaninchen und Ente, Fliegende Blätter (October 23, 1892)

123   There is some question whether Julian was her given name or one that she adopted when she became an anchorite. Fr. John-Julian, *The Complete Julian of Norwich* (Brewster, Massachusetts, Paraclete Press, 2009) 21.

124   Fr. John-Julian 17

125   Fr. John-Julian 109, 211-213

126   Fr. John-Julian 147

127   Fr. John-Julian 211-213.

128   Jonathan Haidt, *The Righteous Mind: Why Good People Are Divided by Politics and Religion* (New York: Vintage Books, 2012)

129   Krista Tippett, *On Being. Jonathan Haidt – The Psychology Behind Morality.* (June 12, 2014) [audio podcast]. The study to which Dr. Haidt refers was not published at the time of this writing.

130   Jonathan Haidt, *The Righteous Mind: Why Good People Are Divided by Politics and Religion,*152

131   Michael Bloomberg, *Mike Bloomberg Delivers Remarks at Harvard University's 363rd Commencement Ceremony* http://www.mikebloomberg. com/news/mike-bloomberg-delivers-remarks-at-harvard-universitys-363rd-commencement-ceremony/ (May 29, 2014) MikeBloomberg. com

132   Richard Dawkins, *Why There Almost Certainly Is No God.* The Huffington Post. October 23, 2006. http://www.huffingtonpost.com/richard-dawkins/why-there-almost-certainl_b_32164.html

133   Psalm 139:13-16

134   The authors of Scripture referred to the earth with a lowercase "e" because they would have had no idea that they resided on a planet.

135   Genesis 7:11, 18. Alter, Robert, *The Five Books of Moses.* (New York: WW Norton & Company, 2004) 44-45.

136   Genesis 9:20-27

137   Genesis 8:22.

138   Matthew 15:21-28

139   Leviticus 19:33-34; See also Leviticus 19:18, Exodus 12:48-49; Exodus 22:21; Deuteronomy 10:19; Deuteronomy 23:7, Psalms 146:9; But in contrast, see Exodus 34:11-16

140   Deuteronomy 2:1

141   Deuteronomy 3:18

142   Deuteronomy 7:16-20

143   Deuteronomy 20:15

144   Deuteronomy 12:29

145   Deuteronomy 13:15

146   Numbers 31:7,14

147   1 Samuel 15:3

148   Exodus 7:9

149   Exodus 7:22

150   Exodus 22:17,18; See also Leviticus 19:26; 19:31; 20:27

151   1 Samuel 28

152   Mark 6:1-6; Luke 4:16-30; Matthew 13:53-58

153   Genesis 3:14-19

154   Matthew 26:55-61, 27:4-; See also Mark 14:57-59 and 15:29

155   John 2:19

156   John 6:48-69

157   John 2:6

158   Ephesians 1:1; 2Corinthinans 1:1

159   Andre Schwartz-Bart, *The Last of the Just* (New York: The Overlook Press, 1959) 4-5

160   See, for instance, James Fadiman & Robert Frager Eds., *Essential Sufism*, (New York: Harper One 1997) 4-5; and Carl W. Ernst, Sufism (Boston & London: Shambhala 2011). 58 et seq

161   *See*, Raymond Brown et al, *The New Jerome Biblical Commentary*. pp. 4.

162   Genesis 6:1-4 as translated in Robert Alter, *The Five Books of Moses*. 38-39.

163   Genesis 6:5-13

164   Genesis 6:19

165   Genesis 7:2

166   Genesis 8:20

167   2 Thessalonians 3:17. See *also* 1 Galatians 6:11.

168   Scholars generally agree that 1 Thessalonians, Galatians, Philippians, Philemon, 1 and 2 Corinthians and Romans were genuinely written or dictated by Paul, while there is reason to doubt 2 Thessalonians, Colossians, Ephesians, Titus, and 1 and 2 Timothy are authentic. See Raymond Brown, *An Introduction to the New Testament*. (New York: Doubleday, 1997) 407

169   Revelation 22:18-19

170   1 Thessalonians is probably the first book of the New Testament to be written; probably in the year 50 or 51 and less than twenty years after the death of Jesus. Raymond Brown. *An Introduction to the New Testament*. pp.457

171   Raymond Brown. *An Introduction to the New Testament*. pp.127

172   Luke 6:20

173   Matthew 5:3

174   Matthew 22:1-14, *See also*, Luke 14:15 et seq

175   James L. Mays, Gen. Ed., *Harpers Bible Commentary*, (San Francisco: HarperSanFrancisco, 1988) 975; See also R. Brown, *An Introduction to the New Testament*, 196.

176   Matthew 22:13; Only the first (generous) part of this parable of the wedding feast exists in the apocryphal Gospel of Thomas (Saying 64).

177   The king's decision to kill those who declined the invitation was probably intended to indicate that refusing the invitation has worse consequences than just missing a good time. The invitation to the wedding is a call to wholeness, like the prohibition against eating from the Tree of the Knowledge of Good and Evil. Declining the invitation feels like a death.

178   Mark 4:26-29

179   Mark 4:31

180   Matthew 13:24

181   Matthew 13:31

182   Matthew 13:36-43

183   Mark 4:1-9; Matthew 13:18-23

184   Mark 4:10-20

185   Mark 4:15; Matthew 13:19

186   Genesis 1:1-2

187   Genesis 50-2-4, 26

188   Exodus 1:1-11

189   Exodus 2:1:10

190   Exodus 14:13-14

191   2 Kings 6-14

192   Exodus 7:3.

193   Exodus 7:13 – 9:35, 10:1, 11-10, 14:4, 14:8

194   Deuteronomy 23:7

195   Exodus 3:1-15

196   Exodus 3: 16-17

197   Exodus 4:1-9 – yes, here is an example where the magic really is meant to convince of divine authority.

198   Exodus 4:10-16

199   Exodus 13:21-22; 14:24

200   Luke 1:13; 1:30

201   John 20:27 and Luke 24:36

202   Exodus 14:13-14

203   John 9:1-34

204   Job 1:3

205   Job 2:9

206   *See, for instance,* Job 21:7-16

207   Job 38:4-7

208   Raymond Brown, *The New Jerome Biblical Commentary.* 4834.

209   Job 32:1 – 37:24

210   Raymond Brown, *The New Jerome Biblical Commentary.* 484.

211   Raymond Brown, *The New Jerome Biblical Commentary.* 12; Robert Alter, *The Five Books of Moses.* 26

212   Genesis 3:14-15

213   Job 1:7

214   Deuteronomy 8:3

215   Psalm 91[90]:11-12

216 Deuteronomy 6:16

217 Deuteronomy 6:13

218 Matthew 4:1-11: *See also*, Luke 4:1-13; Mark 1:12-13

219 Luke 4:2 and Matthew 4:2

220 Matthew 4:11, Mark 1:11-13

221 Matthew 27:39-44; Mark 15:29-32; Luke 23:35-37

222 Luke 13:1-5

223 Luke 13:1-5

224 Matthew 14:13-21; Mark 6:31-44; Luke 9:10-17; John 6:5-15.

225 See, for instance, Philip Gulley & James Mulholland, *If God is Love* (New York: Harper Collins Publishers, 2005) 224

226 2 Kings 4:42-44

227 Raymond Brown, *Introduction to the New Testament*. 178.

228 Matthew 5:3-12

229 Luke 6:20-22

230 Luke 6:24

231 Isaiah 7:14 and Matthew 1:23. *See also*, Joshua 1:9, Isaiah 41:10, Deuteronomy 31:6, Matthew 28:20; Hebrews 13:5, Romans 8:38-39; Matthew 6:25-34, Revelation 3:20, John 14:16-17, Psalm 139:7-10, Psalm 23:4; Zephaniah 3:17

232 Luke 16:19-31

233 The author of Luke may himself believed this story was a critique of wealth rather than a critique of the theology that wealth is a sign of God's favor. The Parable of Lazarus is preceded by the Parable of the Dishonest

Steward (Luke 16:1-9). A steward of a rich man is told he will be fired. He immediately partially forgives the debts other servants owe to his master. Rather than feeling cheated, the rich master praises the steward! The story is expressed as, "make friends for yourself with dishonest wealth so that when it fails you will be welcomed into eternal dwellings." Luke appended two proverbs critical of wealth to this parable, culminating with the memorable, "You cannot serve God and mammon." (Luke 16:13), so he may have been accumulating all the remembrances he thought dealt with the theme of wealth. But another possibility is that this is a warning to the Pharisees and other religious authorities of the time who wielded their authority harshly – assuming the poor, the sick and the outcast were cursed or forgotten by God. Jesus acknowledged that their authority was legitimate (Matt 23:3) but was very critical of how they used it. Their power was temporal and their stewardship would end - it would not be recognized in 'eternal dwellings'. Jesus is warning them to ingratiate themselves with those they think are forgotten by God so that the tables aren't unexpectedly turned.

234   Luke 16:24-25

235   Raymond Brown, *An Introduction to the New Testament* 179

236   Matthew 19:24; *See also*, Mark 10:25

237   Mark 1:16-20, Matthew 4:18-22

238   Mark 1:6; Matthew 3:4

239   Matthew 11:19; Luke 7:34

240   Interestingly, it was only when he rejected asceticism that the Buddha achieved enlightenment.

241   See, *for instance*, Luke 7:36-50; 14:1; Matthew 9:10; Mark 2:13

242   Of course this is to say nothing of the kingly gifts of gold, frankincense and myrrh, which were likely mere symbols. One tantalizing clue into the holy family's finances and that may indicate their resources were limited appears in Luke 2:22-24. After birth, women were considered unclean until they offered a sacrifice at the Temple. According to Leviticus 12:6-8, a lamb (as a "burnt offering") and one turtledove or pigeon (as a "sin offering") are to be sacrificed unless the petitioner cannot afford a lamb in which case she may offer two turtledoves or pigeons (one as a burnt offering and the other as a sin offering). In Luke, we are told Mary scarified two turtledoves for this purpose "according to the law of Moses." (Luke 2:22-24). So, while Mary and Joseph could afford to make the long trip to Jerusalem, they may not have been able to afford the premium sacrifice. Note, however, that in Leviticus 5:7, if one has become unclean even accidently, he or she must offer a lamb as a sin offering but may offer two turtledoves or pigeons if the lamb is beyond their means, or, if that too is too expensive, may offer a measure of flour. Perhaps Jesus's parents were middle class: not wealthy enough for the lamb, but capable of affording the turtledoves.

243   Luke 2:41

244   Luke 2:7

245   Isaiah 1:3 as quoted in Raymond Brown, *An Introduction to the New Testament*, 419

246   Luke 2:12

247   See also, for example, Galatians 3:7-14

248   Song of Songs 5:2 as quoted in Heschel, *God in Search of Man*, 146

249   Heschel, *God in Search of Man*, quoting *Midrash Rabba,* The Song of Songs 5:2 and *Zohar*, vol. III, p.95a,

250   Maimonides, Guide for the Perplexed, Part III, Chapter 27.

251   http://en.wikipedia.org/wiki/Dollard-des-Ormeaux

252   Jerome S. Bruner and Leo Postman, *On the Perception of Incongruity: A Paradigm* (1949). Journal of Personality, 18, 206-223.

253   Luke 15:29

254   Paul Tillich, *The Shaking of the Foundations*. (Eugene, Oregon: Wipf & Stock, 1948) 161

255   Matthew 20:13-15

256   Matthew 20:16

257   Luke 4:16-30

258   Isaiah 61:1-2

259   1 Kings 17

260   2 Kings 5

261   Zachariah 8:23

262   Isaiah 60:4-6

263   Luke 17:11-19

264   Luke 17:18

265   Luke 13:22-30

266   Luke 4:16-30

267   Matthew 20:13-16

268   Sam Harris, *The End of Faith: Religion, Terror and the Future of Reason* (New York: W. W. Norton & Company, 2004) 15.

269   Luke 12:49-53 quoting Micah 7 in which the prophet predicts that the divine message and the messenger will be rejected.

270   Jonah 3:4-5

271 Interesting, no dialogue is attributed to Jonah while he was in his home country. Is this a continuity error as the redactor splices together two or more stories? Or is Jonah misremembering?

272 Jonah 4:2-3

273 Jonah 4:4

274 In an obvious continuity error, we had been told one line prior that Jonah built a booth for himself to provide shade and now a plant is appointed by God to provide shade. Was this the result of a redactor's desire to preserve Jonah's use of a booth, which probably reminded him of Sukkot, or the festival of booths – a recollection of the Israelites time in the desert and an allegory for the transitory nature of human life?.

275 Jonah 4:9-11

276 Jeremiah 7:9-11

277 Mark 11:15-19; Matthew 21:12-17; Luke 19:45-48 and 20:1-8; John 2:13-16

278 Psalm 69:21; John 19:29 See also Matthew 27:48 and Mark 15:36.

279 http://en.wikipedia.org/wiki/Lucius_Tarquinius_Superbus; See also Livius, Titus. *The History of Rome, Vol. 1.* Electronic Text Center, University of Virginia Library.http://etext.virginia.edu/etcbin/toc-cer-new2?id=Liv1His.sgm&images=images/modeng&data=/texts/english/modeng/parsed&tag=public&part=54&division=div2

280 Matthew 25:14-30

281 Luke 19:12-27

282 C.T. Onions, ed. *The Oxford Dictionary of English Etymology.* (Oxford: The Claredon Press, 1966) 900.

283 Matthew 20:16

284   Compare Matthew 25:29 to Luke 19:26. This passage exists independent of any narrative in the apocryphal Gospel of Thomas (Saying 41) It also appears again in Matthew 13:12, where it seems to serve another purpose.

285   Matthew 24

286   Matthew 24:29

287   Matthew 26

288   Luke 17:22-23, 26-37; Luke repeats the warning while Jesus is in Jerusalem – Luke 21:8-9

289   Luke 18:31-34, 35

290   Luke 19:43-44; 20:6-7; 21:20-37

291   Luke 20:9-14,

292   I am indebted to a brilliant monk of the same order as St. Bernard for this concept. Fr. Robert Morhous, O.C.S.O. of St. Joseph's Abbey in Spencer, Massachusetts provided the broad brushstrokes of this interpretation in a private conversation.

293   1 Samuel 9:21

294   1 Samuel 16:11

295   Matthew 25:30;

296   Luke 13:27

297   Matthew 13:42, 50

298   Matthew 24:51

299   Matthew 25:31

300   Daniel 7:13; 8:17

301   Kenneth Grahame, *The Wind in the Willows* (1908).

302   Sartre, Jean-Paul (S. Gilbert, trans.), *No Exit and Three Other Plays.* (New York: Vintage Books, 1989) 45.

303   Krista Tippett, *On Being.* John O'Donohue, The Inner Landscape of Beauty. (January 26, 2012) [Audio podcast]

304   Abraham Heschel, *Man is Not Alone* (New York: Farrar, Straus and Giroux, 1951) 265

305   In the Gospels of Mark and Luke, John is with them as well

306   Matthew 17:5

307   Mark 8:6; Luke 9:33

308   Luke 10:38-42

309   See Chapter 5.

310   John 12:3-6. Although John indicates that Judas' real disappointment was that he would not be able to steal the proceeds of the sale, his motivation is clearer in Mark and Matthew - but the woman who anoints Jesus is not specifically identified as Mary. The differences between the sisters' temperaments persists when their brother, Lazarus, dies. Martha rushes to meet Jesus at the tomb, while Mary remains at home until Jesus summons her. It is busybody Martha who is concerned that Jesus will be offended by the smell of the long-dead Lazarus (John11:20, 29, 39).

311   Rudolf Otto, *The Idea of the Holy.* p. xii

312   Rudolf Otto, *Naturalism and Religion* (The Project Gutenberg EBook) 245 [319]

313   Rudolf Otto, *Naturalism and Religion* 249 [324]

314   Rudolf Otto, *The Idea of the Holy.* 5-7

315   Rudolf Otto, *The Idea of the Holy.* 10, 22.

316   Rudolf Otto, *The Idea of the Holy*. 13

317   Rudolf Otto, *The Idea of the Holy*.25.

318   Rudolf Otto, *The Idea of the Holy*.31

319   Rudolf Otto, *The Idea of the Holy*.32

320   Rudolf Otto, *The Idea of the Holy*.33.

321   Acts 22:20; See also Galatians 1:11-20

322   Acts 15:19-20, 29; See also Galatians 2:11-21. We are given the full text of their edict: "The apostles, the elders, and the brothers, to the brothers who are of the Gentiles in Antioch, Syria, and Cilicia: greetings. Because we have heard that some who went out from us have troubled you with words, unsettling your souls, saying, 'You must be circumcised and keep the law,' to whom we gave no commandment; it seemed good to us, having come to one accord, to choose out men and send them to you with our beloved Barnabas and Paul, men who have risked their lives for the name of our Lord Jesus Christ. We have sent therefore Judas and Silas, who themselves will also tell you the same things by word of mouth. For it seemed good to the Holy Spirit, and to us, to lay no greater burden on you than these necessary things: that you abstain from things sacrificed to idols, from blood, from things strangled, and from sexual immorality, from which if you keep yourselves, it will be well with you. Farewell."

323   Genesis 12:1-3.

324   Genesis 12:10-20; 13:1-2

325   Genesis 20

326   Genesis 12:2

327   Genesis 13:16

328   Genesis 15:5

329 Genesis 22:1-3

330 Genesis 22:15-18

331 1 Kings 18:20-40

332 In fact, Leviticus specifically prohibits sacrificing children to Molech: Leviticus 18:2; 20:1

333 Neil Gillman. *Sacred Fragments; Recovering Theology for the Modern Jew* (Philadelphia: The Jewish Publication Society,1990) 130-131

334 Genesis 19:1-26

335 Genesis 19:18-23

336 Genesis 18:20,21,23-33

337 Matthew 10:29-30, *See also*, Luke 12:6-7

338 Exodus 25

339 Exodus 26-27

340 Exodus 28

341 Acts 9:4-6, *Compare*, Acts 26:14

342 Matthew 5:17; Mark 1:11; Luke 3:22

343 Mark 9:7; Matthew 17:5 (fourteen words); Luke 9:35 (nine words)

344 Exodus 34:27-29 as translated by Robert Alter, *The Five Books of Moses*. 512.

345 Tippett, Krista, *On Being. Lawrence Kushner, Kabbalah and the Inner Life of God*. (May 15, 2014) [audio podcast]

346 Exodus 22:21, Robert Alter, *The Five Books of Moses*, 445-446.

347 Abraham Heschel, *God in Search of Man* (New York: Faraar, Straus and Giroux 1955) 259-260

348   Exodus 19:3-8

349   Exodus 20:5-6; Robert Alter, *The Five Books of Moses.* 430

350   Exodus 21-23

351   Exodus 24:3

352   Exodus 24:4

353   Exodus 24:7

354   Exodus 11:2, 12:35

355   Exodus 32:7-10.

356   Exodus 34:7

357   Compare: The LORD, the LORD God, compassionate and gracious, slow to anger, and abounding in lovingkindness and truth; who keeps lovingkindness for thousands, who forgives iniquity, transgression and sin; yet He will by no means leave the guilty unpunished, visiting the iniquity of fathers on the children and on the grandchildren to the third and fourth generations.

358   Exodus 2:11-15

359   Romans 9:30

360   General Social Survey as quoted in *Young Catholic America, Emerging Adults In, Out of, and Gone from the Church*, Christian Smith et al (Oxford: Oxford University Press 2004) 35

361   Joseph B. Soloveitchik, *The Lonely Man of Faith.* (New York: Three Leaves Press, 1965)

362   Matthew 27:1-8

363   Acts 1:18-19

364   Numbers 20-13

365   2 Samuel 11

366   Coleman Barks, *The Essential Rumi*. (New York: Harper One, 2004) 36.

367   *O Come, O Come, Emmanuel*, Hymn

368   Mark 8:29, Matthew 16:15, Luke 9:20.

369   (Lazarus) John 11:1-44 (son of the widow of Nain) Luke 7:11-15; (daughter of Jairus) Luke 8:41,42,49-55)

370   1 Kings 17:17-22; 2 Kings 4:32-35; 2 Kings 13:20,21

371   Acts 9:36-41; Acts 20:9,10

372   Matthew 17:1-9; Mark 9:2-8; Luke 9:28-36

373   Matthew 17:5

374   Matthew 16:13-18 *See also*, Mark 8:29, Luke 9:20

375   John 1:1, 17:5

376   John 20:28

377   John 14:8-11

378   Mark 10:18; *See also*, Luke 18:18.

379   Matthew 2:1-12

380   2 Kings 2:11

381   Matthew 1:1-17

382   Luke 2:8-20

383   Matthew 1:23 *quoting* Isaiah 7:14

384   Raymond E. Brown, *The Birth of the Messiah: A Commentary on the Infancy Narratives in the Gospels of Matthew and Luke* (New York: Doubleday, 1993) 145.

385   John A.T. Robinson, *Honest to God 40th Anniversary Edition* (Westminster John Knox Press, Louisville 2002) 13

386   John A.T. Robinson. 22 *quoting* Paul Tillich *The Shaking of the Foundations* Pelican (1962) p.63.

387   John A.T. Robinson 49

388   John A.T. Robinson 76

389   Matthew 2:1-2

390   Luke 7:1-7

391   Matthew 27:54

392   In the thee year cycle of readings according to the Catholic lectionary, Matthew 12:1-11 is read in Year A; Mark 11:1-10 or John 12:12-16 is read in Year B; and Luke 19:28-40 is read in Year C.

393   Mark 14:1-11. This occurrence happens at the same time in the Gospel of Matthew 26:3-16; See also John12:1-8, 13:2 and Luke 22:2-6, 7:36-50

394   At least in the Gospels of Mark and Matthew. It is interesting that in the Gospel of John, John is careful to note that Judas' outrage was rooted in the fact that Judas was the treasurer of Jesus's group and wanted to have the oil sold so that he could steal the proceeds. Luke evidently did not think the chronology was important, and the anointing becomes a story of forgiveness of a sinful woman. Both Luke and John blame Judas's betrayal on the influence of Satan.

395   Other than Judas's advocacy for using the expensive oil for the benefit of the poor, there is only one overt instance where someone advocates for charity to the poor for the sake of the poor and that is John the Baptist addressing the crowd as he baptizes them: "And the multitude asked [John], 'what then shall we do?' And he answered them, 'He who has two coats,

let him share with him who has none; and he who has food, let him do likewise.' (Luke 3:10-11). The closest Jesus gets to such a statement may be Matthew 19:21, when he advises a supplicant, "If you want to be perfect, go, sell what you have, and give to the poor, and you will have treasure in heaven; and come, follow me." But this is the casting off of possessions to prepare for discipleship rather than a policy to reduce poverty and, as we saw in Chapter Three, it is the opening to a story of the impossibility of earning grace. Similarly, in Luke 12:16-34, Jesus tells the story of the rich farmer who builds additional barns to house his bumper crop. As the parable winds down, he says "Sell that which you have, and give gifts to the needy. Make for yourselves purses which don't grow old, a treasure in the heavens that doesn't fail, where no thief approaches, neither moth destroys. For where your treasure is, there will your heart be also." But clearly this is not an imperative to improve the lives of the poor – interjected in the same parable is Jesus's Buddhist exhortation not to worry about tomorrow (*See also,* Matthew 6:24-33). Jesus urges us to focus on eternal things rather than those things you leave behind at death.

396   Mark 6:7-9; Luke 10:1-4

397   Luke 22:35-26

398   Matthew 27:43; *See also,* Mark 15:30-32; Luke 23:35-37

399   Luke 23:34

400   Ejaculation occasioned by sexual intercourse (Leviticus 15:16-18) is treated with less alarm than when it is occasioned otherwise (Leviticus 15:1-15).

401   Regular menstruation (Leviticus 15:19-14) is treated with less alarm than menstruation that is not within cycle (Leviticus 15:25-30)

402   Leviticus 14:1-9

403   Numbers 19:19

404   Matthew 7:12; *See also,* Luke 6:31 "And as you wish that men would do for you, do so to them."

405   Mark 2:27

406   Mekilta 31:13, *cited in* Abraham Joshua Heschel, *The Sabbath.* 17

407   Exodus 22:22

408   Matthew 16:12; *See also,* Luke 9:7-8, 19; Mark 8:27-30

409   Matthew 16:15, *See also,* Luke 9:20; John 6:69

410   Matthew 16:20

411   Mark 8:30

412   Mark 1:23-27

413   Mark 1:44;

414   Isaiah 44:21-23; Psalm 49:6-9

415   John 3:16-17.

416   Genesis 28:12-15

417   Exodus 25:8-9

418   Isaiah 7:14 and Matthew 1:23

419   Exodus 26:31. *See also,* Numbers 4:5

420   Mark 15:38, Matthew 27:51; Luke 23:45

421   Exodus 19:1

422   Psalms 8 quoted in Robert Alter, *The Book of Psalms.* (New York: W.W. Norton & Company, 2007) 23-24)

423   John 13:8

424   Luke 10:38-42; *See also,* Exodus 14:14; Psalm 46:10;

425   John 14:5

426   John 14:6-7

427   Mark 14:51; This part of the story was not transcribed by either Matthew or Luke. Did it fail to make sense to them?

428   W.H. Auden, *For the Time Being, a Christmas Oratorio.* (Pronceton, NJ: Princeton University Press, 2013) 28

429   Auden, *For the Time Being.* 26

430   Rudolf Otto, *The Idea of the Holy.* 50-55

431   Philippians 3:6, *quoted in* Krister Stendahl, "The Apostle Paul and the Introspective Conscience of the West" *Harvard Theological Review Vo. 56, No. 3 (July 1963).* 201

432   Romans 3:9-18

433   Stendahl, 202

434   Joseph A. Fitzmyer, *Romans, A New Translation with Introduction and Commentary by Joseph A. Fitzmyer,* The Anchor Bible Series. New York: Doubleday (1993) 465 See also, Gunther Bornkamm, Paul. Minneapolis: Fortress Press (1995) 123; and Raymond E. Brown, et al *The New Jerome Biblical Commentary.* p 1408 and Raymond Brown, *An Introduction to the New Testament.* 568

435   Fitzmyer, *Romans.* 465, quoting Hôdāyôt (Thanksgiving Psalms) from Cave 1

436   Philippians 2:7.

437   English Translation of the Roman Missal, International Committee on English in the Liturgy, Inc. (2010)

438   Exodus 14:12

439   Exodus 15:23

440   Exodus 16:4

441   Exodus 17:3

442   Numbers 13:2-3

443   *O Holy Night*, Hymn

444   Wisdom 2:12-21

445   Philippians 4:4-7

446   Genesis 18:11-15

447   Robert Alter, *The Five Books of Moses*. 102

448   Interestingly, within a few lines it is the sight of a laughing Ishmael, Abraham's first son by Hagar and the predecessor of The Prophet Muhammed, that appears to inspire Sarah to demand that he be exiled. Robert Alter, *The Five Books of Moses*. 103 fn 9.

449   William Styron, *Sophie's Choice* (New York: Vintage International, 1976).

450   William Styron, 87

451   William Styron 256

452   William Styron 92

453   William Styron 93, See also 214

454   William Styron 213.

455   William Styron 215.

456   Matthew 9:29 (blindness); Mark 10:52 (blindness); Luke 17:19 (leprosy), 7:9 (the centurion's servant), 8:48 (Jairus' daughter)

457   Mark 5:24-34; Matthew 9:20-23; Luke 8:43-48

458   Mark 9:24

459   This motif and language is mirrored in the stories of Jesus calming the storm in all three Gospels (Matthew 8:25, Mark 4:40 and Luke 8:25.

460   Christopher Hitchens, *The Missionary Position, Mother Teresa in Theory and Practice* (Twelve Edition., New York 1995)

461   Christopher Hitchens 9

462   Romans 5:8; See also Matthew 9:10

463   Christopher Hitchens 44

464   Matthew 13:12; Mark 4:25; The remark is also made in connection with the Parable of the Talents (Matthew 25:29; Luke 19:26) and the Parable of the Watchful Servant (Luke 12:48) but I have argued they likely serve an entirely different purpose there.

465   John 14:6

466   John 15:15

467   John 15:15

468   John 13:3-11

469   Christopher Hitchens 30

470   John 4:27

471   Although in Mark's version (Mark 12:28-34), Jesus and the lawyer end the encounter by expressing mutual respect.

472   Matthew 22:37-40;

473   Deuteronomy 6:5 and Leviticus 19:18

474   Mark 12:31; Matthew 22:39; Luke 6:31; Galatians 5:14;

475   Matthew 7:12

476   John 15:12; 13:34

477   John 14:17; 15-19

478   Matthew 25:31-46

479   Galatians 3:28

480   Matthew 5:46

481   Matthew 5:45

482   In Exodus, as Moses is pleading that God not destroy all of Israel for the sin of constructing the idolatrous golden calf, God indicates he would not punish the Israelites collectively but rather only those individuals who were guilty: "But the Lord said to Moses, 'Whoever has sinned against me, him will I blot out of my book.'" (Exodus 32:33) RSV.

483   John 11:50

484   John 18:14

485   Paul Edwards, ed. *Encyclopedia of Philosophy* Vol 8, 208; See also fn 1 Utilitarianism 7.

486   John Gray ed. *On Liberty and Other Essays* (Oxford: Oxford University Press 1991)14-15

487   John Gray ed. *On Liberty and Other Essays* 15

488   George Sher ed. *Utilitarianism.* (New York: Hackett Publishing Company, 1979) 8-9

489   Paul Edwards, ed. *Encyclopedia of Philosophy* Vol. 1 282, 283

490   John Gray ed. *On Liberty and Other Essays.*14

491   John Gray ed. *On Liberty and Other Essays.* 14-15.

492   Sam Harris, *The Moral Landscape*, 12

493   4 Harvard Law Review 193 (December 15, 1890)

494   See the story of Jacob and Esau: Genesis 25:27-29

495   Genesis 4:6-7 as translated by Robert Alter, *The Five Books of Moses*, 30. Interestingly, most common interpretations of the Bible translate this to say the precise opposite: "You will be accepted if you do what is right. But if you refuse to do what is right, then watch out! Sin is crouching at the door, eager to control you." (New Living Translation).

496   Robert Alter, *The Five Books of Moses*, 29

497   Genesis 4:2

498   Genesis 4:10

499   Matthew 5:17-18. In Luke, this statement precedes the Parable of Lazarus (Luke 16:17).

500   Mark 12:16; Matthew 22:21; Luke 20:25.

501   Matthew 17:24-27

502   Matthew 23:1-3

503   Luke 12:49, 51

504   Mark 11:15-19; Matthew 21:12-17; Luke 19:45-48; John 2:13-16

505   Sam Harris, *The End of Faith: Religion, Terror, and the Future of Reason*. (New York: W.W. Norton & Company, 2004) 12

506   Sam Harris, *The End of Faith: Religion, Terror, and the Future of Reason*. 18

507   Sam Harris, *The End of Faith: Religion, Terror, and the Future of Reason*. 14, 224

508 Sam Harris, *The End of Faith: Religion, Terror, and the Future of Reason*. 79

509 The Posen Speech (October 6, 1943) http://en.wikipedia.org/wiki/Posen_speeches

510 Isaiah 49:16

511 George Orwell, *Animal Farm* (New York: Signet Classics,1946)

512 George Orwell, 33

513 Sam Harris, *Free Will and "Free Will", How my View Differs from Daniel Dennett's*, (April 5, 2012) (blog) http://www.samharris.org/blog/item/free-will-and-free-will

514 Daniel C. Dennett, *Freedom Evolves*, 284; See also http://philosophy-bites.com/2012/08/daniel-dennett-on-free-will-worth-wanting.html

515 Daniel C. Dennett, *Freedom Evolves*,269

516 Daniel C. Dennett, *Freedom Evolves*,273

517 Daniel C. Dennett, *Elbow Room*, 154

518 Daniel C. Dennett, *Elbow Room*. 154

519 Daniel C. Dennett, *Elbow Room*. 266

520 Richard Dawkins, *The Selfish Gene*. (Oxford: Oxford University Press, 2006) 192

521 Richard Dawkins, *The Selfish Gene*, 194.

522 Daniel C. Dennett, *Freedom Evolves*,266-67

523 Daniel C. Dennett, *Freedom Evolves*, 304

524 Sam Harris, *The End of Faith: Religion, Terror, and the Future of Reason*. 14-15

525   John 15:12-17

526   Robert Alter, *The Five Books of Moses*, 130

527   Genesis 25:29-34

528   Galatians 4:1-9

529   Zechariah 8:4-6, 11-12.

530   Pew Research Center Religion and Public Life: *America's Changing Religious Landscape* (May 12, 2015) http://www.pewforum.org/2015/05/12/americas-changing-religious-landscape/

531   Pew reporting a margin for error for atheists of 3.7% and for agnostics of 3.1%. http://www.pewforum.org/2015/05/12/appendix-a-methodology-3/

532   Pew Research Center Religion and Public Life: *"Nones" on the Rise* (October 9, 2012) http://www.pewforum.org/2012/10/09/nones-on-the-rise/

533   Pew Research Center Religion and Public Life: *U.S. Public Becoming Less Religious* (November 3, 2015) http://www.pewforum.org/2015/11/03/u-s-public-becoming-less-religious/

534   Ibid. See also Christian Smith et al, *Young Catholic America Emerging Adults in, out of, and Gone from the Church.* (Oxford: Oxford University Press, 2014) 53

535   Pew Research Center Religion and Public Life: *U.S. Public Becoming Less Religious* (November 3, 2015) http://www.pewforum.org/2015/11/03/u-s-public-becoming-less-religious/

536   Pew Research Center U.S. Politics & Policy: A Deep Dive Into Party Affiliation (April 7, 2015) http://www.people-press.org/2015/04/07/a-deep-dive-into-party-affiliation/

537   Karl Rahner, *Theological Investigations*, Vol. XX, p. 149

538   These are the roots of "*leitourgia*", a derivative of "*leitourgos*", meaning "public servant"

539   Genesis 22

540   Cain, Abel, Noah and Jacob all offer sacrifices to God on altars (Genesis 4:3, 8:20; 35:14; 46:1); Abraham builds altars in Canaan, Bethel and Hebron (Genesis 12:7, 8; Genesis 13:18) and on one altar, offers animal sacrifices that Abraham does not burn – rather, Abraham dreams that a fire pot and flaming torch pass between the pieces of the butchered animals (Genesis 15:9-18). Other primitive elements of ritual occur as well: Noah is given the dietary restriction not to eat meat with blood still in it (Genesis 9:4), the custom of circumcision is instituted with Abraham, starting with Ishmael and repeated with Isaac (Genesis 17:9-27, 21:4), after he rescues Lot and his other relatives from capture, Abraham is blessed by Melchizedek, who we are told is the king of Salem and a priest of El Elyon, a Canaanite sky god (Genesis 14:18-20; Alter p. 72), Jacob commands his household to purify themselves and change their garments before they journey to Bethel to build an altar (Genesis 35:1-2) - perhaps the same altar built by Abraham?).

541   Exodus 12:28

542   Exodus 12:14

543   Exodus 12:26; Exodus 13:8, 14

544   Deuteronomy 6:20-21

545   Another one is Deuteronomy 26:4-10 which requires the congregant, in precise ritualized words, to retell of the rescue story.

546   Deuteronomy 6:4

547 In Luke, there is a spat among the apostles about who is greatest and Jesus instructs them to serve.

548 Mark 14:22.

549 Genesis 17:9-14

550 Genesis 9:14-17

551 Exodus 30:17-21

552 Exodus 29:34

553 Exodus 29:42-46

554 Leviticus 6:5-7

555 Deuteronomy 28:32

556 Raymond Brown, et al. *The New Jerome's Biblical Commentary.* 4

557 Numbers 11:25-29

558 Numbers 11:29

559 Mark 9:38-43

560 Abraham Heschel, *God in Search of Man.* 25

561 Mark 9:39

562 Exodus 36:8-38 repeats Exodus 26:1-32, Exodus 37:1-28 repeats Exodus 25:10-21, 25:23-40 and 30:1-10, and Exodus 39:1-31 repeats Exodus 28:5-42. Robert Alter, *The Five Books of Moses.* 520, 522 and 528

563 Exodus 36:5.

564 Malcolm Gladwell, *Outliers: The Story of Success.* (New York: Back Bay Books, 2008) 41

565 http://news.bbc.co.uk/2/hi/health/8297764.stm

566 Galatians 1:16-18

567 Exodus 23:12. *See also* Genesis 2:1-3; Exodus 16:26; Exodus 20:8-11; Exodus 31:12-17

568 Deuteronomy 6:4-9

569 *E.g.*: Exodus 23:14

570 *E.g.*: Exodus 23:19

571 Luke 18:1-8; See also the Parable of the Friend in the Night, Luke 11:5-8, another instance where the protagonist is the human being rather than God.

572 Exodus 3:5

573 Malcolm Gladwell, *The Tipping Point: How Little Things Can Make a Big Difference.* (New York: Back Bay Books, 2002) 135

574 Malcolm Gladwell, *The Tipping Point.* 137

575 Malcolm Gladwell, The Tipping Point. 141

576 Jeremiah 7:21-22; Amos 5:22-27

577 Psalm 50:12-15

578 https://en.wikipedia.org/wiki/Hans_in_Luck

579 1Kings 16:32-34; See also, Raymond Brown, et al., *The New Jerome Biblical Commentary.* 71

580 1 Kings 17:7-15

581 *Let All Mortal Flesh Keep Silence,* Hymn

STEPHAN GROZINGER

Stephan Grozinger graduated from the University of St. Michael's College at the University of Toronto (9T2) with a concentration in moral philosophy. He obtained his law degree from The University of Connecticut School of Law (1995) and practices commercial real estate law.

A native of Dollard-des-Ormeaux, Quebec and Ridgefield, Connecticut, Stephan lives with his wife, Claire, and daughter, Zoë, in Weston, Connecticut and Wellfleet, Massachusetts.

You can visit Stephan's blog on the subject matter of this book at www.faithonastonefoundation.com.